D0643326

WINNER TAKE ALL

The Trans-Canada
Canoe Trail

English R.

York Factory

Nelson R.

Burntwood R.

Rock Depot

Sturgeon-Weir R.

Grass R.

Chatham House

Fox R.

Hayes R.

BEAVER L.

KNEE LAKE

CROSS L.

OXFORD LAKE

Cumberland House

MOOSE L.

Echimamish R.

PLAYGREEN L.

Carrot R.

The Pas

Fort Bourbon

Norway House

CEDAR LAKE

Red Deer R.

LAKE WINNIPEG

SWAN L.

LAKE WINNIPEGOSIS

Fort Bourbon

L. DAUPHIN

Bas de la Riviere

LAKE MANITOBA

Hudson Bay

Churchill

Fort Maurepas

Winnipeg R.

York Factory

Hayes R.

Major fur trade routes

JAMES BAY

0   500

miles

Fort Albany

Rupert R.

LAKE MISTASSINI

Rupert House

LAKE ST. JOSEPH

Albany R.

Moose R.

Moose Factory

THE WOODS

LAKE NIPIGON

Missinaibi R.

Abitibi R.

LAKE ABITIBI

RAINY LAKE

Kaministikwia R.

TROUT LAKE

LAC DES QUINZE

St. Lawrence R.

Fort William

Michipicoten R.

Ottawa R.

Troi Rivieres

Quebec

ny R.

Grand Portage

LAKE SUPERIOR

Sault Ste.Marie

North Channel

French R.

Mattawa R.

LAKE NIPISSING

Montreal

Lachine

Richelieu R.

Criquamegon

Georgian Bay

Nottawasaga Bay

LAKE CHAMPLAIN

Wisconsin R.

Green Bay

Michilimackinac

L. HURON

SIMCOE L.

Bay of Quinte

Mississippi R.

LAKE MICHIGAN

Manitoulin I.

Barrie

Toronto (York)

L. ONTARIO

Albany

Boston

Niagara Falls

Detroit

LAKE ERIE

New York

WINNER TAKE ALL

The Trans-Canada Canoe Trail

DAVID LAVENDER

McGraw-Hill Book Company
NEW YORK / TORONTO / ST. LOUIS
DÜSSELDORF / MEXICO / PANAMA

Part-title illustrations courtesy of
New York Public Library Picture Collection.

Book design by Stanley Drate.

1 2 3 4 5 6 7 8 9 0 B P B P 7 8 3 2 1 0 9 8 7

Library of Congress Cataloging in Publication Data

Lavender, David Sievert, 1910–
Winner take all.
(The American Trails Series)
Bibliography: p.
Includes index.
1. New France—Discovery and exploration.   2. Northwest, Canadian—Discovery and exploration.   3. Fur trade—Canada—History.   I. Title.
II. Series.
F1030.L44   971.01′1   77-4864
ISBN 0-07-036678-0

The painting reproduced on the jacket—"The Old Pacific Express," by Arthur Heming—is from the collection of Mr. and Mrs. Fenner F. Dalley.

The map of Canadian fur-trade routes on pages ii and iii is by David Lindroth.

This, too, is Mildred's

CONTENTS

PART THREE

Pedlars Extraordinary

PART FOUR

Beyond the Mountains

PART FIVE

The Great Struggle

Prologue: The Long Trail Awinding

In London one autumn day in 1801 Alexander Mackenzie began writing a preface to a book he had just composed about his adventures in North America. The deeds were notable. During the late spring and early summer of 1789 he and a small party of French-Canadian voyageurs, fortified by Indian interpreters and hunters, had followed the breaking of the ice in the far Northwest down a giant river (later it was given his name, the Mackenzie) as far as tidewater on the Arctic Ocean. Four years later, in 1793, he had taken another small party through the mountainous central regions of today's British Columbia to the Pacific. Probably they were the first men of any race to cross the continent north of Mexico. Certainly they were the first whites.

In spite of those accomplishments, Mackenzie felt obliged to use part of his preface for explaining his failures as an explorer. He had had no training as an anthropologist or naturalist, he confessed. Besides, the demands of each day's journey had prevented dallying.

"I had to encounter perils by land [he wrote] and perils by water; to watch the savage who was our guide, or to guard against those of his tribe who might meditate our destruction. I had, also, the passion and fears of others to control and subdue. To day I had to assuage the rising discontents, and on the morrow to cheer the fainting spirits of the people who accompanied me. The toil of our navigation was incessant, and oftentimes extreme;—and in our progress over land we had no protection from the severity of the elements, and possessed no accommodations but such as could be contained in the burden on our shoulders, which aggravated the toils of our march, and added to the weariness of our way."

No time for curiosity: Mackenzie had not taken that weary road for national or personal glory, or for adding items of pure knowledge to the world's store of geographical information, or even for love of adventure, although such elements were involved. Rather, the effort had been devoted to quickening commerce in a single commodity. The long title of his book reveals it: *Voyages from Montreal, on the River St. Laurence, Through the Continent of North America, to the Frozen and Pacific Oceans: in the Years 1789 and 1793. With a Preliminary Account of the Rise, Progress, and Present State of the Fur Trade in That Country.*

Voyages and fur: to Mackenzie, to the company directors who commanded his loyalty, and to the country that became Canada, the linkage was fundamental.

Spain monopolized the precious minerals of Mexico and Peru. The young United States looked westward to what seemed inexhaustible acres of prime agricultural land. As her counterpart to those resources, French and then English Canada possessed a stupendous fur reserve made possible by the fact that the vast northland contained one-half of all the fresh water on the globe. Or, to borrow the words of historian-geographer-canoeist Eric W. Morse, ". . . there are as many miles of inland waterways in Canada as in all the other nations of the world combined."

More than half of the streams, rivers, marshes, and lakes that provide that amazing statistic either touch the edges of or flow through the northland's huge forest belt. Mingled with the evergreens of the interminable woods are stands of deciduous willows, poplars, aspen, and birch. Those soft, graceful trees provide the material from which beaver make their dams and lodges, and on whose bark they feed. Disturbed only occasionally by early hunters, beaver were once one of the most numerous animals in northern North America.

Their availability nearly doomed them. For almost three centuries, roughly from 1550 to 1835, beaver fur was in high demand in Europe as a source of felt; from this felt stylish hats for men could be pressed. Nor was it a one-way trade. The Indians, who in the northern forests were the primary hunters of beaver, were equally voracious in their demands for hatchets, knives, kettles, awls, guns, woollen clothing, liquor, and, as items of personal vanity, mirrors, beads, and packets of vermilion for reddening the parts in their glossy black hair. The business generated by the trade —literally a trade, goods swapped for pelts—was of some consequence to the emerging factories of France and England.

Neither distance nor the water in which the beaver built their domed homes of sticks and mud protected them. Long before the coming of the whites, the Algonquian peoples of the northern part of the St. Lawrence drainage had learned to strip the pale rind off birch trees, fit it over a frame of cedar slats, and thus make a canoe light enough so that one or two men could portage it around rapids or between watersheds, yet strong enough so that it could transport from two to ten persons and their equipment on journeys of scores of miles or more. In those canoes the Indians carried back to their villages the iron tools they obtained at the annual trading fairs in the St. Lawrence Valley. During winter, when fur was prime, they used the implements for tearing down the lodges of their prey. When spring came they loaded the fruits of their toil into their canoes and returned to the St. Lawrence in search of new manufactured items.

If the commerce had stayed local, serious problems might have been avoided. Heavy hunting exterminated nearby beaver, however, and fresh pelts could be obtained only by contacting distant tribes. At first Indian middlemen performed this function, buying merchandise on credit from the French and carrying it in their canoes far and wide through the streams and lakes that feed into the St. Lawrence. Unhappily competition between tribes for the profits that resulted led to explosive wars, and as a result French *coureurs* entered the fray, using native canoes and fighting beside their Indian allies as they moved deep into the forests in quest of new sources of fur.

Indian rivalries were only part of the French-Canadians' problem. North of the St. Lawrence–Great Lakes waterway a huge inland sea—Hudson Bay—spills over from the Atlantic into the heart of the continent. The bay's southwestern shore is nearly 1500 miles closer to the Saskatchewan River, gateway to the Far West, than were the docks at Montreal, and when a London-based firm, the Hudson's Bay Company, gained control of the inland sea, a fierce new element was introduced into the race for the beaver of the interior.

This complex commercial warfare between invading whites and their Indian supporters did not end when England ousted France from North America in 1763. Rather, it intensified. New traders, many of them Scots, swarmed into Montreal, wrested control of the commerce from the defeated French-Canadians, developed huge new freight canoes as much as thirty-six feet long, and by sheer muscle, bold planning, and unabashed chicanery sought to overcome the advantage in distance possessed by their rivals in the great bay.

Before the struggle was over, the men from Montreal, banded together as the famed North West Company, were exporting each year more than three-quarters of the beaver offered for sale by the Indians of Canada and a large part of the northwestern United States as well. And yet that wasn't enough. Reaching recklessly for still more, the Nor'Westers tumbled into ruin.

The pages that follow tell the story of the principal figures in this wilderness warfare and of the watery trails they used in reaching for their hearts' desires. Eventually the main stem of the interlocking waterways spanned the entire continent, a 4000-mile stretch without a duplicate in North America. It was singular in yet another way, too. Except for a few Catholic missionaries, occasional scientists, and an artist or two, travel over those thousands of difficult but often breathtakingly beautiful miles was limited to company officers and employees. Neither soldiers, settlers, nor vacationists used more than short segments of it. First and last it was a commercial highway and in that respect unique in the English-speaking world.

Commerce was not the whole of the story, however. Adventure, challenge, spaciousness, contact with the Indians among whom many of the men found enduring loves, the white immensity of winter, the flash of sunlit water across granite boulders—those things, too, were part of the lure.

Innocent in their greed, the trail's creators were the first despoilers of native life, both animal and Indian. But they were not aware of what they were doing—a doing that many of them cherished intensely. "They pulled the wilderness round them like a cloak," wrote historian Bernard De Voto; "they wore its beauty like a crest." Such are the men, lapped in wonder and bound toward futures they could not predict, that we will follow toward the setting of their sun.

PART ONE

Fleur-de-Lis

I

The Wings of Hope

$\mathcal{B}$y chance Jacques Cartier's two sixty-ton ships from St. Malo dropped anchor in what is now Gaspé Harbor, Province of Quebec, just as 200 canoe-borne Indians—men, women, and children— came swarming around the headland, bound on a fishing expedition. At first the sixty-odd whites kept cautiously to their vessels, but the voluble amiability of the newcomers soon reassured them. Besides, circumstances were conducive to friendliness. The weather was balmy—it was mid-July, 1534—and the harbor, encircled by hills clad with evergreens, was beautiful. After seven weeks spent crossing the Atlantic and then nosing in and out of a multitude of rocky harbors in the still unnamed Gulf of St. Lawrence, the sailors were ready to relax.

On July 22 casual contacts developed into a party. Whites and Indians mingled where grassy openings in the forest ran down to the sand. Each group sang its country's songs to the other, with much merriment as one side tried to pick up and imitate the other's tunes. The Indians were entranced by the glass beads, combs, knives, and little hawks' bells that the whites distributed among them. The young women expressed their gratitude by the native custom of running their hands up and down the donors' arms. The French found this pleasing, and, although their captain does not record the fact in his journal, they no doubt found ways of carrying the intimacies farther.

All in all a successful day. Still, Cartier could not help being condescending about his new friends. They were savages, he wrote. (The French, it is interesting to note, seldom followed the habit started by Columbus of referring to the aboriginal inhabitants of North America as Indians. To Gallic writers they were *sauvages, peaux-rouges* (redskins) or *indigènes*.) Cartier said savages, or wild men, not because the people were ferocious but because they were poor and uncivilized. "They go altogether naked saving their privities, which are covered with a little skin," and furs that some of them draped on their shoulders. They ate their meat and fish after barely warming it. They slept without bedding on the ground beneath their overturned canoes. Except for the canoes and their fishing nets, the sum of their possessions "was not worth five sous" —and yet for what they were doing they needed nothing more, a point that seems not to have occurred to Cartier.

And then there was their hair. The *sauvages* somehow plucked or shaved their heads smooth except for a scalp-lock atop the crown, which they let grow "as long as a horsetail, and then with leather strings bind it in a knot upon their heads." In time similar scalp-locks, coupled to the wearers' uncleanly personal habits, led the French to apply the name Huron to a prominent tribe that lived near the eastern shore of one of the upper Great Lakes. The term derived from *huré,* meaning "bristly." In France *huron* was a derogatory word that signified "lout" or "ruffian."

The scalp-lock on the people Cartier met in Gaspé Bay does not mean that they, too, were Hurons. The hair style was common to one of the major groups of natives inhabiting North America, the Iroquoian people. Their homeland extended from the St. Lawrence Valley inland to the eastern shores of Lake Huron and south around Lake Ontario in what is now upper New York state. Although some of the bands within that broad area were hostile to each other, they were considered related because they spoke dialects belonging to the same basic language stock.

To what branch of the Iroquois the canoe-travelers in Gaspé Bay belonged is uncertain, even though Jacques Cartier, a methodical man, did write down phonetically, for future reference, some of the recurring words he heard. More than three and a half centuries later, scholars of the Smithsonian Institution's Bureau of American Ethnology compared Cartier's fragments with known Iroquoian dialects. The speakers, they concluded, had indeed been Hurons. Examination of various artifacts, however, has made more recent investigators less certain. They will concede only that Cartier came into contact with a people who spoke an Iroquoian tongue.

Academic fussiness? Not entirely. From a historical standpoint alone one would like to be more positive. For one thing, Cartier's meeting with those dusky-skinned, exotically coiffured people marked the beginning of a relationship that for another 166 years would dominate Canadian affairs, including the unremitting push to find a usable route, by water, across a hostile continent to the long-sought Sea of the West, the Pacific.

Be all that as it may, Cartier's French enjoyed their stay with those wandering people from—well, sign language did not reveal exactly where, except that the fishermen's permanent home was evidently inland from the tip of Gaspé Peninsula. They may have tried to describe the great river that borders the peninsula on the north, but if so Cartier failed to grasp their meaning. Besides, time was running short. On July 24, the captain began preparations to continue his journey.

His first step was to show what his presence in the area meant. He ordered his sailors to cut down two trees from the edge of the forest near the shore. From these the ships' carpenters fashioned a cross that, when raised, would stand thirty feet tall. They inscribed on one of the timbers *Vive le Roy de France,*" and just beneath the point where the beams crossed they placed a wooden plaque on which were carved three fleurs-de-lis. They dug a hole into which the base of the cross could be thrust and with ropes and straining muscles heaved the timber upright. The French then knelt around the base of the cross, raised their hands toward heaven, and with a prayer concluded their symbolic act of taking possession of the land. That done, they returned in their longboats to their ships.

They were immediately followed by a single birchbark canoe containing five people. One, clad in a shaggy bearskin, Cartier recognized as the leader of the Indian fishermen, a chief called Donnacona. With Donnacona were his brother and three sons. Obviously they had grasped the point of the cross-raising and were angry. Standing in the canoe, Donnacona pointed to the cross, scowled, and with sweeping gestures indicated that the country belonged to his people.

Hoping to remedy his blunder, Cartier prevailed on the quintet to board his ship. Somehow he made Donnacona believe that he had erected the cross only as a means of finding the harbor when he returned another year. Then, acting apparently on the spur of the moment, he asked permission to take Donnacona's two oldest sons, teen-agers named Domagaya and Taignoagny, to France with him. He explained, or thought he did, that he wanted to facilitate future communication by training the boys as interpreters. He may also have remembered that other explorers, beginning with Columbus, had taken native Americans back to Europe as proof that they had reached unknown lands—lands that merited further attention. If the court was sufficiently impressed, one could count on continued employment.

Donnacona agreed to as much of the proposal as he understood. Perhaps he hoped that Cartier's sense of responsibility to the boys would guarantee another visit from these strange, bearded people with their marvelous ironware and cloth. Possibly, so speculates Samuel Eliot Morison in *The European Discovery of America*, he also wanted to lure the French into an alliance against his enemies —a not unfamiliar instance of Indians trying to exploit whites instead of the other way around.

The next morning the French sailed out of the harbor. Historically speaking, they were on a belated journey. Although France was bounded on two sides by saltwater and although her fishermen were among the world's best sailors, constant foreign wars and internal religious strife had kept the country from plunging into the Age of Discovery with the same verve that her maritime neighbors had shown. Jacques Cartier, born in 1491 in the rugged seacoast village of St. Malo, was a generation behind Columbus. He had scarcely entered school in 1497 when John Cabot, reasoning correctly that the short way from Europe to Asia lay in higher latitudes than those being followed by the Spanish, had sailed west from Bristol, England, to a landfall near the northern tip of Newfoundland.

Portuguese and Spaniards quickly followed Cabot to see what he had discovered—after all, the Pope had divided the New World between *their* nations—and one of the former, João Fernandez, a part-time *lavrador* (farmer) of the Azores, had by an odd quirk of nomenclature attached the name of his trade to that most non-agricultural of lands, Labrador. But neither Fernandez nor his fellow spies had detected signs of mineral, silk, spice, or even a possible passageway to the spots where those treasures existed. Just fish. Millions upon millions of codfish. They sailed home and reported, shrugging.

Fish were important to Catholic Europe, nevertheless. Fast days abounded, and during the warm summers untainted meat for non-fast days was hard to come by. (The ready sale of spices from the Orient resulted from their ability to mask out the taste of spoiling meat.) During the early 1500s, accordingly, fishermen from Spain, Portugal, France, and England began resorting to the great banks (shallows) off Newfoundland. Several never returned. Those who did left few records. Yet we do know that by the time Jacques Cartier had reached manhood and had attained his rating as a master pilot, scores of ships were making the crossing each year. Cartier completed at least one such round trip and possibly more, as well as other ventures to Brazil. He was a good mariner, well trained, careful, and diligent.

During those same years, Portuguese ships circling Africa were bringing home exotic wares from the Orient. Cortez plundered Mexico while Magellan was proving how big the earth really was and how much water it contained by circumnavigating South America on his way around the world.

These and other restless journeys stimulated Europe's learned cartographers to endless speculation about the geography of lands yet undiscovered. One ingenious theory went as follows. The amazing amount of water in the Southern Hemisphere was surely balanced by an equal mass of land in the North. Portuguese navigators had noticed, meanwhile, that as they coasted north along Asia the land trended eastward. Simultaneously, Spanish navigators working from Panama north past Mexico noticed that North America's far coast pushed steadily westward. Did the leaning continents join in the north? (They almost do at Bering Strait.) If such a junction existed, then the upper part of North America might amount to nothing more than a big peninsula jutting out from Asia. From that followed the exciting thought that some great river like the Rhine or some land-girt sea like the Baltic might afford ingress to Asia or at least to a spot from which the kingdoms of Cathay could be reached by a short caravan trip overland.

Nor need Cathay be the only goal. The northern reaches of the

New World might contain as much mineral wealth as did the southern. Finally, there was this obvious gap: no one had explored the North American coast between Florida, with which the Spaniards were familiar, and the banks of Newfoundland, where the fishermen went every year. In those seven hundred miles of unknown land some kind of passageway to the east might very well exist.

Stirred by such hopes, a colony of Italian silk makers located in Lyons, France, began urging the country's energetic, innovative monarch, Francis I, to join the thrust into the New World. The upshot was the dispatching in 1523 of a Florentine navigator, Giovanni da Verrazano, to find, for France, a way to Cathay. Verrazano not only failed but jumped to an extraordinary conclusion. While cruising off Cape Hatteras, he encountered the sand spits that for many miles border Pamlico Sound. Westward beyond the low, flat spits lay water unbounded by any land discernible from lookouts on the masterhead—a circumstance familiar to Carolina yachtsmen even today.

Was the water the western ocean? Curiously, Verrazano ignored the small inlets through which he could have sent an exploring longboat. Instead, standing well out to sea to avoid reefs, he pressed northward looking for a strait big enough to admit his ship. He never found anything that appealed to him, and after reaching the east coast of Newfoundland he returned to France. On resuming the search in 1528, he bent southward into the Caribbean. There he was captured and eaten by Carib Indians.

He left a troublesome heritage. Unable to dismiss Verrazano's western ocean as the mere sound it was, armchair cartographers kept shifting it around throughout the interior of North America as best suited their fancies. For more than a century the vision of some huge inland lake or salt sea that could be reached by strait or river and that would open a shortcut to Cathay bedeviled the explorers of North America. Every Indian tale of shining waters beyond the horizon brought the hope alive again. Cartier was but one among many who felt the tug of the dazzling idea.

His desire to reach into the unknown set him apart from most of his fellows. The St. Malo fishermen he accompanied at least once to Newfoundland were explorers only by need. Not curiosity but their pursuit of codfish showed them, for instance, that Newfoundland's rugged east coast was scalloped by almost innumerable deep bays and fjordlike openings. This knowledge led them to assume for years that the ten-mile-wide span of sea between the island's northern cape and the shores of Labrador was a fjord like the others. The assumption showed in the name they gave the narrow inlet—Baie des Chasteaulx, from the castlelike rocks bordering it. But the span wasn't a bay with a closed end, as one ship pushing out in front of the others eventually discovered. It was a strait, today's Belle Isle Strait, and it opened into what promised to be an enormous gulf. Jacques Cartier, some historians surmise, was with the sailors to whom this accidental revelation came.

A huge, presumably unexplored gulf! The odds in favor of grand discoveries were high. Supported by the Admiral of France and by the abbot of sea-girt Mont-Saint-Michel near St. Malo, Cartier gained the attention of Francis I. Francis appointed him "Captaine et Pilot pour le Roy," granted him 6,000 gold livres for outfitting two small ships, and directed him to sail on beyond the Baie des Chasteaulx in search of, first, a passage to China and, second, of "certain isles and countries where there is said to be found a vast quantity of gold and other rich things."

The ships left St. Malo on April 20, 1534. Aided by favorable winds, they made so swift a crossing that they reached Newfoundland while icebergs were still thick along the rough east coast. May was waning before they were finally able to creep around the north cape and swing southwest through Belle Isle Strait, past a repellant countryside "composed of stones and frightful rocks and uneven places"—the south coast of Labrador.

The strait behind him, Cartier began his circle of the new gulf by striking south along Newfoundland's west coast and then southwest to the central part of what eventually was named Prince Edward Island. To his joy the nature of the country changed radically. The shores along which he coasted were "full of beautiful trees, meadows, fields of wild wheat and pease in flower as fair and abundant as I ever saw in Brittany. There are plenty of gooseberries, strawberries, and roses of Provins." The advancing summer was hot—so hot that he gave the name "Chaleur" to the magnificent inlet that he located early in July well north of Prince Edward Island.

In Chaleur occurred one of those incidents that, in the words of Bernard De Voto, cause "the twitch of a nerve that comes from certain inexplicable data." For three days the French were beset by Micmac Indians clamoring to swap furs for whatever hatchets, knives, cutlery, beads, and the like that the French were willing to part with. Recall that this supposedly was unknown country. Yet those Micmac Indians knew that the whites who appeared from across the sea would buy peltries. On his part Cartier was well stocked with the sort of articles the Indians wanted. The syllogism has an unavoidable end: both races must have been prowling the vast gulf to their mutual advantage much earlier than records indicate.

The prowling had been random, however. No one had codified results and put down data in such a way that monarchs and their merchant princes would be willing to pay for it. Aware of this, Jacques Cartier, an eminently practical man, was careful to describe everything he saw in a journal that could be submitted for examination whenever circumstances warranted.

At first his findings were not heartening. Chaleur turned out to be a bay and hence opened no passageway across North America. But the circle of the gulf had not been completed yet. Stubbornly optimistic, Cartier sailed on north, found Gaspé, and experienced his chance meeting with Donnacona's fishermen.

A very different people from the Micmacs, the new Indians were unsophisticated about furs. This suggested that they had come from a place too distant to have been penetrated as yet by European trade influences—but a place that was nevertheless approachable by water, as their birchbark canoes indicated. The supposition could be important. Hence Cartier did with Donnacona what he seems to have made no effort to do with the Micmacs: he asked for and gained permission to take two impressionable Indian lads with him to France.

And so, with Domagaya and Taignoagny dressed now as sailors and making pests of themselves as they ran about the decks, Cartier continued his northward probe. He finished rounding the snout of Gaspé Peninsula and ran into a dense bank of fog. Retreating from it, he encountered the island of Anticosti, which lies like a great tongue in the mouth of the St. Lawrence River. After curving around Anticosti's tip, he went back almost to the island's far end. Actually, he did not know it was an island, but supposed it was a cape jutting out from Gaspé. At the time the point was irrelevant,

for as he inched westward against adverse winds he realized that
Labrador was no great distance away. From the strong ebb currents
that gripped his ships—and perhaps from crumbs of information
gleaned from the Indian boys—he deduced that the inlet was not
another bay like Chaleur. It was either a river mouth or, better
yet, a strait, and might lead . . . who dared say where?

On August 1 he called his officers to his cabin for a conference.
He pointed out that further penetration of the unknown waters in
the face of contrary winds would be slow work and that the ships
were running short of supplies. Moreover, too long a stay might ex-
pose their return journey to the fierce storms that wracked the
North Atlantic each autumn. Might it not be wise to delay further
exploration until the following year?

His listeners agreed, which would help him disarm future criticism about the inconclusiveness of his voyage, and on August 2,
1534, the two ships turned homeward, riding fast on the wings of a
singing gale.

II

The Great River

*T*he next year the king sent Jacques Cartier back to the New World with three ships—*La Grande Hermine, La Petite Hermine,* both larger than the vessels he had commanded in 1534, and *L'Émerillon,* a small pinnace that would be useful for finding safe routes through narrow passageways.

Narrow ways there would be. From halting conversations with Donnacona's two sons, whom he was taking back to the New World with him, Cartier had learned that the opening he had discovered the year before was a river mouth, not an easily navigated strait. The information did not dismay him. According to the Indians the river was so large that none of their countrymen had reached its sources. Perhaps not, in birchbark canoes. But a pinnace like *L'Émerillon* could thrust to the very edges of Asia, if the stream extended that far, as Cartier had convinced himself it did. He was sanguine enough that he was prepared to winter somewhere along the riverbanks and then continue his search through another season, if that proved necessary.

On August 10, 1535, he sought shelter for the night in a small harbor on the north bank of the river's broad mouth. The date marked the feast day of an early Christian martyr, St. Lawrence, and so, as Catholic explorers often did, Cartier attached the name of the day, Saint Laurins, to the place. Later writers, misinterpreting the locale he meant, extended the casually given appellation not only to the huge gulf he had circumnavigated the previous summer, but also to the river and even to the Laurentide Highlands in the north.

As for the stream, Cartier himself sometimes called it *la grande rivière de Hochelaga* and on other occasions *le chemin de Canada.* He had those names from Domagaya and Taignoagny, and they reflected a good deal of confusion.

The Indian lads had not proved to be apt students in France, and the stumbling talks Cartier had held with them had been further clouded by his own ignorance, his own assumptions. He had no way of knowing, for instance, that Iroquoian people did not name regions but only villages and prominent natural features. On the other hand, he did know that Europeans had applied the term "kingdom" to the Aztec and Inca empires that the Spanish had occupied. Thus wishful thinking led him to attach the European concept, "kingdom," to the places the boys told him about. He understood that Hochelaga was a city, but in his writings he also referred to it as a realm. The strongest power along the river, it lay somewhere upstream from what he gathered was the subordinate kingdom of Canada. Canada was where the boys lived, in a village called Stadacona. Or so Cartier wrote, giving currency to a name that eventually would experience even greater expansion than "St. Lawrence."

Somewhere to the north or west of Hochelaga and Canada was another "kingdom" the boys called Saguenay. Saguenay, Cartier gathered, was enormously rich in ways that sounded to him like Asia. As a result he was anxious to reach Stadacona and learn from the boys' father more about the best approaches to Saguenay than the lads could tell him.

But one cannot hurry nature. The current of the St. Lawrence proved to be so strong that frequently the ships had to heave to and wait for flood tide to lift them a few miles farther along their way. At times the sailors aided wind and tide by laboring over the great sweep oars with which the vessels were provided. Islands made navigation intricate, and the Indian brothers were inadequate pilots. This meant frequent backbreaking work over the heavy hemp lines with which soundings were taken.

It was a beautiful trip, nevertheless. Spare though Cartier's account is, it reflects some of the excitement he felt as the river, ninety miles wide at its mouth, slowly narrowed, bordered on the north by striking cliffs and on the south by luxuriantly forested hills. The wayfarers saw right whales and white whales, seals and walrus. Many deer were visible ashore. Grape vines hung heavy with fruit, and Cartier marveled at spruce trees apparently growing out of solid rock. The weather was surprisingly hot, even on the water.

On September 1 at a place the Indians called Tadoussac, he worked the ships into a protected harbor at the mouth of a gloomy chasm. Here a big river from the west broke into the main stream. It was the Saguenay, the road to the kingdom of the same name, "as our men from Canada have told us." Or so he thought.

Unwilling to risk that ominous-looking stream so late in the year and understanding from the boys that their home village was close now, he spent only a single night at Tadoussac and then pressed on up the St. Lawrence. Word of the ships' slow approach flashed ahead. Soon Donnacona appeared with an escort of twelve birch-bark canoes to greet his sons. After the joyous family reunion, Cartier, together with some of the gentlemen volunteers who had joined the expedition in the hope of obtaining land grants in America, left the big ships at anchor, climbed into longboats, and were rowed upstream behind the excited Indians. As they progressed, the river narrowed; cliffs soared. Presently, where the stream was only half a mile wide, the travelers were awed by one of the grand sights of the eastern part of the New World, a huge rock promontory formed by the junction of the St. Charles River with the St. Lawrence. Quebec stands there today.

Huddled at the base of the cliffs was the unprepossessing village of Stadacona. It consisted of a handful of unkempt, Iroquois-style longhouses—pole frameworks covered with slabs of bark. Beyond the dwellings were gardens. As the boats approached, the residents flocked to the shore, the women wading out knee-deep to sing songs of welcome. The faces and bodies of both males and females were garishly painted.

Cartier cut the ceremonies as short as he could and returned to the ships. The narrowing of the river had stirred his apprehensions, and he had decided to go into winter quarters near Stadacona rather than press his luck any further that year. Because St. Malo, France, and Stadacona, Canada, were on approximately the same latitude he anticipated a short confinement.

And so, on September 14, he warped the three ships into a quiet anchorage formed by a backwater near the mouth of the St. Charles, a few hundred yards from the village. Reaching the spot nearly 800 miles inland had been a more remarkable feat of navigation than he realized. Upwards of another century would pass before other pilots would risk the island-studded waters above Tadoussac in anything larger than pinnaces.

He was not content, however. Before ice closed in, he wanted to see the bigger town of Hochelaga and a nearby tributary which, so he divined from the halting talk of his Indian boys, furnished an alternative route to the Kingdom of Saguenay. Accordingly, while men of the two larger ships started work on a fort for protection during the winter, Cartier readied little *Émerillon* for a flying trip upstream. The evening before his departure, he told Domagaya and Taignoagny, who had agreed to go along as interpreters, to be ready to leave in the morning.

To his astonishment they refused. Their father supported them. The resistance was climaxed by medicine men dressed in horns, their faces blackened with soot, who danced, pranced, and predicted in dire tones that the French would die amid ice and snow if they dared venture any farther upstream.

Cartier sensed that for some reason of their own the people of Stadacona wished to keep him away from Hochelaga. What he did not—could not—appreciate was the way in which this small episode epitomized the upheaval that white contacts were already bringing to Indian social and cultural patterns. When the natives along the coasts of Labrador and Newfoundland had first obtained from overseas fishermen manufactured cloth, iron pots, needles, steel-bladed hatchets, knives, little mirrors, and ornamental trinkets, they had touched what to them was unbelievable magic.

For thousands of years they had cooked food by dropping hot stones into water contained in tightly woven baskets or in fragile clay pots. By way of comparison, consider what it meant to own a kettle that could be placed directly on the fire and moved from camp to camp without injury. Compare hacking down a tree with a stone ax and fires built at its base to felling one with a steel-bladed hatchet; perforating bark for a canoe with an awl instead of with a piece of bone; wearing a woollen or calico shirt rather than one of buckskin that turned shapeless, cold, and heavy under rain or snow.

Nor was convenience the whole of the story. Whoever possessed even meager stores of manufactured goods could wield power over tribes that had none—both commercial power built on the control of trade and political power for dictating terms of confederation. Donnacona and his followers had grasped these potentials almost at once. Here at their fingertips lay the means of ending the dominance of Hochelaga. Accordingly, they used every device they could think of, short of physical force, which they dared not risk, to keep the French in the harbor at the foot of the great rock.

Cartier declined to be swayed. He placated Donnacona by giving him two swords—priceless!—and two brass bowls. His artillerymen fired the cannon of *La Grande Hermine,* a demonstration that set the Indians howling "so that you could have thought hell had broken loose." But he could not pry an interpreter from them. Stubbornly he determined to go ahead in spite of the handicap. He chose four of his more dependable gentlemen as companions, and on September 19, 1535, boarded the pinnace. Twenty-eight sailors turned the ship upstream, towing two longboats behind.

They spent ten days traveling eighty miles to Lac Saint-Pierre, a wide, shallow bulge in the river. There the water was completely fresh, and the tide ceased to be an influence. Using oars, the sailors cautiously crossed the shoals to a maze of islands at the lake's upper end. Although Indians on the bank pointed out the proper channel, the water level at that season was so low that Cartier decided not to risk it. Accordingly he transferred himself, the gentlemen, and part of the crew to the longboats. Three days of rowing against the current, interrupted by occasional stops to converse by signs to Indians along the way, brought them to the vicinity of Hochelaga. It was late Saturday afternoon, October 2, 1535.

Arguments about the exact landing place still gust through Canadian historical circles.* One school holds that, in spite of an increasingly stiff current, the newcomers persisted until the deep rumble of rapids ahead warned they could go no farther. Other historians place the landing farther downstream near the point where the Jacques Cartier bridge now spans the St. Lawrence. Wherever it was, the adventurers were greeted by hundreds of In-

* An excellent summary is in James F. Pendergast and Bruce G. Trigger, *Cartier's Hochelaga and the Dawson Site* (McGill-Queen's University Press, London, 1972).

dians whose scouts had been following their approach for some time. The women sang a welcome much as those at Stadacona had done, and as the Europeans disembarked, they were showered with handfuls of crumbled cornbread, symbol of hospitality for weary travelers.

Earlier, in France, Cartier had picked up a few Iroquoian phrases from Domagaya and Taignoagny. He had added a few more words at Stadacona. Thus, though he soon realized that the people pressing about him spoke a somewhat different dialect from the one used downstream, he was able to make himself understood after a fashion.

Gaining quiet finally, he directed the women to sit in rows in front of him while he passed out "tin beads and other trifles." The amenities observed, he and his heavily outnumbered men retired prudently through the dusk to their longboats, where they sat hunched with their weapons throughout an uncomfortable night. Until dawn the Indians on the shore kept dancing and singing around their fires.

At sunrise the captain and his gentlemen donned armor and plumed helmets. They transformed twenty soldiers into an honor guard by arming them with pikes. (A few of the seamen remained behind to watch the longboats.) Surrounded by ecstatic Indians, they marched through an oak grove toward a tall hill that Cartier named Mount Royal, the source later of the name Montreal. At that point he was more than 900 miles from the open ocean at Newfoundland. New York City is separated from the Mississippi River by approximately the same distance.

The oak forest gave way to cultivated fields of corn, squash, beans, and melons. After a three-mile walk the adventurers reached a palisade "two lances" in height. Composed of ragged walls of logs and poles leaning triangularly together for solidity, the barricade was roughly circular and pierced by a single gate. Near the top of the inside wall was a gallery reached by notched poles from which defenders could shoot arrows and hurl rocks at attackers. Obviously peace was not taken for granted at Hochelaga.

The town inside the palisade consisted of fifty or so rectangular houses covered with bark like those at Stadacona. Each was about seventy-five feet long and perhaps thirty feet wide. A dark, smoke-filled corridor entered by a single door ran the length of each structure. At intervals along this corridor fires smoldered for cooking and for warmth. On either side of the fires were tiers of bunks, the domiciles of perhaps as many as ten different families. The lower bunks, equipped with furs often crawling with lice, were used for sleeping; the upper for storing clothing, household utensils, tools, weapons, and the like. In spite of vents in the barrel-shaped roofs, the interiors of the longhouses were hot and fetid. But the inhabitants did not seem to mind any more than European peasants and laborers of the same era minded their unsavory, unsanitary quarters.

The haphazardly placed longhouses surrounded a kind of plaza into which the Europeans were led. The throngs of Indians parted, and nine or ten men entered carrying a chief on a big piece of deerskin. The conveyance was not ceremonial as with some tribes, but the result of the chief's being partly paralyzed.

Somehow the Indians gained a notion that the whites possessed healing powers. Cartier was persuaded to rub the chief's leaden limbs. Afterward dozens of lame or blind adults and mothers with babies in their arms crowded around the newcomers for a portion of the magic. As the excitement subsided, Cartier read in Latin from the New Testament, distributed gifts, and closed the meeting by having his trumpeters sound a fanfare. The Indians were enthralled.

All this was hastily done. Cartier was anxious to see from the neighboring hilltop as much of the country beyond the rapids as was possible. He managed to convey the wish to the chief, who ordered three Indians to serve as guides.

The sight was spectacular. Northward the Laurentian Mountains formed an undulant horizon. Southward the explorers could make out spurs of the Adirondacks in New York. Between the mountain ranges spread forests of evergreen mixed with deciduous trees whose leaves were beginning to blaze with the reds and yellows of autumn. Drawing a silver line through that Persian carpet was the St. Lawrence River, surging out of the southwest for as far as Cartier could see.

A mile or so southwest of the foot of Mount Royal the stream broadened into a large lake, today's Lake St. Louis. Its outlet, due south of the mountain, was blocked by the tumultuous rapids the French had heard the night before. The three guides indicated that farther upstream were more rapids, but after a traveler had passed them he could sail uninterrupted for three moons, into huge lakes whose far borders touched . . . what? The question was a mockery. Cartier's ships could not possibly surmount that rage of white water south of Mount Royal.

There was much he missed. The forests rolling north from the foot of the mountain hid from him the river arms that make Montreal an island. In addition, Lake St. Louis and the Lake of Two Mountains immediately west of it were so big that apparently the French did not even detect the broad Ottawa, flowing between conical hills to mingle in the lakes with the St. Lawrence. But the Indians told him about the river, and he was dismayed afresh. The Ottawa (not yet named that) must be the other stream that, according to Donnacona's sons furnished an alternate approach to the kingdom of Saguenay. But water approaches to the Ottawa apparently were blocked by the same set of howling rapids that closed off the St. Lawrence.

Trying to assuage his frustration, Cartier sought to learn by talk what he could not see. Having noticed a few copper ornaments among the residents of both Stadacona and Hochelaga, he showed his guides a piece of the same metal "and pointing toward the said region [the Ottawa], asked by signs if it came from thence? They shook their heads to say no, showing us that it came from the Saguenay, which lies in the opposite direction." They also laid hold of Cartier's silver whistle, hanging on a chain around his neck, and of the gilt handle of a dagger worn by one of the sailors. "Saguenay! Saguenay!"—but this time they pointed up the Ottawa River toward a place where they said bad people lived. Those Indians had similar metal but it came from still farther away, from "Gitchee Gumee."

Stitching all this together as best he could without an interpreter, Cartier decided that the kingdom of Saguenay occupied a huge parallelogram lying between two rivers that rose far to the west, the Saguenay, which joined the St. Lawrence at Tadoussac, and the Ottawa. He concluded further that the kingdom of Saguenay, in addition to being rich in mines of its own, was allied with other mining nations farther west.

Later explorers learned better. There was no kingdom of Saguenay. What Cartier had been hearing about was a complex trade route that began at the far end of Lake Superior ("Gitchee

Gumee") another 900 miles west of where he stood. The Indians
in that vicinity had long since found the deposits of native copper
that occur there. Because the crude tools and polished ornaments
they made from the metal were highly prized, aborigine traders had
spread it over much of North America. Even before Cartier's time,
Verrazano had noticed that the Wampanoags of Rhode Island
esteemed beyond all else the few pieces of wrought copper they
owned.

The metal Cartier saw had not been carried through the five
Great Lakes on its way to the St. Lawrence. That route was too
roundabout. Instead, the traders who handled it had taken it in
their canoes along the sinuous rivers and twining lakes that crease
the granite of the Canadian Shield, that amazing sheathe of ice-
scoured rock which covers most of the land north of the St. Lawrence, the Ottawa, and the upper Great Lakes. At different trading
fairs in the remote wilderness the bits of copper had fallen into the
hands of some of the nomadic Algonquian tribes, principally Montagnai hunters, who roamed the headwaters of the Ottawa, the
Saguenay, and a river later called the St. Maurice. These people
added the metal to the furs they prepared for clothing and bedding
and carried the goods down the tributary streams to the Iroquoian
villages along the St. Lawrence. There they fished, fattened up
from the hard winter, and also obtained, through barter, the corn
that they would use during the next cold season as a supplement
for their undependable supplies of wild meat.

Not unreasonably, Cartier grasped none of this. Wearied from
his long journey—except possibly for Cabeza de Vaca of Spain,
roaming during those same years through Texas and southern New
Mexico, no other European had yet penetrated so far inland in
North America—he sensed only that his dreams of Asia and even
of Saguenay had come to a blank end here at the foot of "a *sault*
of water, the most impetuous that one could possibly see." Too discouraged by the sight to explore right then for a possible way
around the barrier, he led his men down the mountainside to their
longboats. After scarcely twenty-four hours in the vicinity of Hochelaga, obviously the key town of the river, they started back through
falling golden leaves to Stadacona.

The winter that ensued dismayed them still more. By mid-Novem-
ber ice had locked the ships into their harbor. By January snow

was four feet deep. Even inside the holds of the vessels and in those sections of the fort beyond the heat of the roaring fireplaces, frost coated the walls to a depth of three fingers or more. Yet the Indians, to Cartier's continuing amazement, regularly wandered out of their bark houses almost naked.

They were not supermen, however. Lack of fresh food in their diets brought on violent attacks of scurvy. Dozens of Stadaconans died; more were miserably ill. Thinking that some mysterious epidemic was to blame, Cartier ordered the Indians to stay away from the whites and his men to avoid the village, especially those houses where unwed girls in search of husbands gathered for experimental sexual runs with whoever chose to try them out. The precautions were unavailing. Soon the French too were felled by the ailment. The gums of the sufferers rotted; their teeth fell out. Arms and legs, freckled with spots like flea bites, grew swollen and sore. Digestive tracts ached; breathing was difficult.

When men began to die, Cartier ordered one of the corpses dissected. The desperate search revealed nothing useful to the amateur physicians. Help came finally from Domagaya. He, too, had had a touch of the disease but was recovering, as were most of the people in the village who had not already succumbed. The cure, he said, was a broth made by boiling the bark and needles of a certain evergreen tree in water.

Indian women helped Cartier gather a supply of branches. No one today is certain what the tree was—white spruce perhaps, or, more probably, the variety of northern white cedar sometimes called arborvitae. Evidently the tenuous approach of spring had started the sap rising, for it seems improbable that dormant inner bark and needles could be effective. And why had the Indians waited so long before utilizing the remedy?

Wasting no time on such speculations, the French stripped bark from the branches, ground it as fine as they could, and plunged it along with handfuls of needles (or feathery little leaves if the parent tree was a cedar) into boiling water. Results were miraculous. Some of the sailors even supposed that the brew cured their syphilis. All the doctors in Europe, Cartier declared, could not have done in a year what that primitive remedy accomplished in a week. It was high time. Before the cure took effect, twenty-five men had died.

Throughout this miserable period, its tensions increased by the
Indians' pilfering of French artifacts, for which they had an insatiable desire, Cartier kept brooding about the future. Asia obviously was beyond reach, and to that extent the king would regard
the expedition as a failure. But Saguenay! Proposals to conquer the
kingdom as Cortez had conquered Mexico might still command
Francis's interest and, as a corollary, keep Cartier himself gainfully
employed.

He pumped Donnacona for information. Like most Indians, the
chief sought to please the questioner by telling him what he wanted
to hear. Donnacona also enjoyed being the center of rapt attention
as he spun his tales of gold and rubies, of exotic fruits and spices,
of white-skinned people who dressed as the French were dressed.
Yes, Saguenay would do very well as a surrogate Asia. And the
way to prepare for the conquest, Cartier decided, was to plant a
colony of Frenchmen somewhere along the St. Lawrence between
the Saguenay and Ottawa rivers. The settlement need not be an
undue drain on the royal treasury, for, as the corn and melon fields
of the Indians demonstrated, the land was fertile enough so that
families could soon support themselves. As the colony took root, it
could be used as a base for further explorations—surely there were
alternate routes around those rapids—and, eventually, as a staging
point for whatever military moves seemed advisable.

Hearing what the Indians had to say of Saguenay would help
convince Francis of the worth of the plan. Unfortunately, some of
the whites had harassed the villagers for their thieving, and the
two camps were now very close to a serious breach. Since none of
the leading men would agree to cross the ocean voluntarily, a kidnapping became necessary.

Cartier began his preparations early in May while the river was
still in flood; less than two weeks earlier great cakes of ice had
been bobbing down the current. He shook out the sails on *La
Grande Hermine* and *L'Émerillon,* but abandoned *La Petite Hermine* because scurvy had not left him enough able-bodied men for
manning her. He then erected a wooden cross beside the empty fort
and invited a few of the leading villagers to a ceremony of farewell.
While they were off guard armed sailors seized the chief, his sons
Domagaya and Taignoagny, and two headmen and rushed them

aboard *La Grande Hermine*. While his crew held off the distraught villagers with leveled cannon and readied lances, Cartier promised to bring the victims home the next year. Hastily then he set sail down the flooded stream before it was really safe to do so.

Alas for plans. When he reached home, France was again at war with Spain. Francis I, who had personally led his army into some of the battles, was captured and ransomed and an unstable peace treaty had been signed (1538) before Cartier could command his monarch's attention. But when that attention came at last it was unstinted.

France's war-drained treasury needed the bullion that Saguenay, as painted by Donnacona, could provide. (Realizing he could not get home unless an expedition were authorized, the ailing, grieving chief heaped marvel on marvel.) Beyond that, a French colony in North America offered means of challenging the presumptions of Spain and Portugal that they owned the whole new world and most of unknown Asia, too, on the strength of a papal bull. Actual possession, Francis snapped to the ambassadors of those nations, was what counted. To give substance to the contention, he set about launching the colony Cartier had recommended.

In one sense Cartier had worked too well. The king demoted him to vice-commander and placed the expedition in charge of a court favorite, Jean-François de la Roche, Sieur de Roberval. No sense of pressure hurried Roberval along his way. Working pretty much on his own during the spring of 1541, Cartier assembled five ships at St. Malo but then ran into trouble recruiting personnel. By nature most French people were disinclined to plunge into the unknown, and the stories Cartier's seamen had told about Canada's terrible winters did nothing to overcome the reluctance. In the end the captain had to use the king's authority to seize and impress part of the crewmen he needed. Roberval helped him fill his quota of settlers by delivering in chains at St. Malo a number of convicts of both sexes.

Not all the supplies Roberval wanted for his part of the fleet had yet been delivered at St. Malo. Moreover, he was short of funds. The latter deficiency he proposed to remedy by quick raids on merchant shipping in the English channel—sheer piracy, since France was temporarily at peace with everyone. He therefore told

Cartier to precede him to America and select a site for the new settlement. Roberval would follow as soon as possible, perhaps within weeks.

How many sailors, convicts, and gentlemen adventurers were aboard France's first five colonizing vessels is unknown. Whatever the number, they had to share the space below decks with cows, horses, pigs, goats, poultry, and stacks of equipment. There were no Indians. The adult kidnap victims from Stadacona, along with four small children Cartier had picked up somewhere along the St. Lawrence in 1535–36 had all succumbed to the ills of civilization.

Storms scattered the fleet. One ship almost ran out of fresh water and had to substitute cider to keep the animals it carried alive. Eventually the five vessels all met at rendezvous off Newfoundland and after passing through the gulf crept in a cautious line up the St. Lawrence. On August 23, 1541, exactly three months out of St. Malo, they dropped anchor off Stadacona.

Landing with a strong guard, Cartier admitted to the Indians that Donnacona had died—this pleased the chief who had taken his place—but lied about the others. They were all married, he said, and were being treated as such fine lords in France that they had not wished to return home quite yet.

He did not linger to see how the excuses went down. The tensions that had threatened to disrupt his stay at the village five years before had convinced him that the two races should not live close together. Accordingly he continued another nine miles upriver to a promontory on the north shore. He named it Cap Rouge because of the reddish tinge in the soil. There he put part of his colonists, flabby from long confinement on shipboard, to work planting gardens. The rest began hewing wood and laying foundations for a walled town named Charlesbourg-Royal after one of the king's sons.

On September 2 Cartier reduced the number of persons who would have to be fed through the winter by sending two ships home to report on accomplishments so far. He then led two longboats filled with his stoutest sailors upstream for another reconnaisance of the rapids beyond Hochelaga.

Again he missed the river arm, Rivière des Prairies, that after leaving the Lake of Two Mountains flows along the back (west) side of Montreal Island. By following that shortcut he could have by-passed the rapids above Hochelaga and have crossed the Lake of Two Mountains to what he understood was the route to Saguenay, the Ottawa. But perhaps the Indians of Hochelaga, like those of Stadacona, did not want him to reach the tribes of the interior and so stayed silent about the by-pass. Not that it mattered in the long run. The Ottawa, too, boiled with rapids which the French, as their actions on the St. Lawrence showed, were not adaptable enough to surmount.

Cartier made no attempt to obtain birchbark canoes from the Indians, although he knew by then that the small craft, unlike wooden longboats, were light enough to be portaged around unnavigable water by one or two men. Stubbornly he double-manned one of his heavy craft and tried to thrust it up the rapids south of Mount Royal by brute strength. The effort failed almost as soon as it began. He compromised then. He and his men crossed below the rapids to the north shore of the St. Lawrence and on foot skirted the white water and part of Lake St. Louis until they were able to regain the river. They followed the St. Lawrence upward to another formidable *sault*. By then they were out of food, and when Indians assured them that still more rapids lay ahead, they turned back to Charlesbourg-Royal. Cartier was thoroughly dejected. He had found no practical way of reaching the interior, and there was no sign of Roberval, whose support was badly needed.

In its own way the winter of 1541–42 was as taxing as that of 1535–36. Although the colonists managed to blunt the onslaught of scurvy, Indians in ambush picked off numerous woodcutters from parties that ventured into the forest for the fuel they must have or perish. Cartier gave the number of those slain as thirty-five, though possibly he exaggerated in order to impress the king with the hopelessness of the situation, for by then the survivors were demanding that they leave this dreadful land and return to France.

Cartier stalled them for six or seven weeks after the breakup of the ice, hoping that Roberval had perhaps wintered farther down the stream and would soon appear with reinforcements. His colonists spent the time energetically digging up eleven barrels of selected rock veined with a showy yellow metal that they were sure was gold. They also found silver, so they thought, plus a basketful of shiny crystals that might be diamonds. According to French law, one-third of that treasure belonged to the finders, but of what use were gold and diamonds in the wilderness? They must go to France.

June came, but no Roberval. Yielding at last, Cartier ordered the cheering settlers aboard the ships. To replenish their food and water for the long leap across the Atlantic, they put into St. John's harbor on the east coast of Newfoundland. To their chagrin they saw, riding at anchor amid several fishing vessels, three big ships flying the colors of the king of France. It was Roberval's fleet, only weeks out of St. Malo.

Roberval ordered the newcomers back to Charlesbourg-Royal. Cartier protested: his men would mutiny first.

Roberval was adamant. They were under royal orders to found a permanent colony and must do so. Cartier bowed in apparent acquiescence, but late that night raised sail and under cover of darkness slipped quietly out of the harbor.

Roberval continued up the St. Lawrence to the abandoned town. There he learned at first hand the reason for Cartier's defection. During the months of bitter cold scurvy killed fifty of approximately 150 people. When morale sagged the commander fought it with floggings, chains, and even one hanging for petty theft. In the spring he pushed upstream with seventy living skeletons in eight longboats. Like Cartier he tried to use raw strength for forcing a way up the rapids at the foot of Mount Royal. One of the boats overturned and eight men died, some drowned and some battered to death on the rocks. Utterly discouraged in his turn, Roberval turned back then and sailed to France. There he found people holding their sides with laughter over the riches of Canada. Gold? Cartier's metal had turned out to be iron pyrite. The diamonds? They were crystals of mica and quartz. *C'est un diamant du Canada* became a folk saying for whatever was showy but worthless.

The king lost interest in Canada, and yet Cartier seems not to have been disgraced and in fact spent the rest of his life in comfort ashore at St. Malo. Indeed, in opening one of the great river gateways into North America, he had accomplished much. Granted that cold, scurvy, Indians, rough water, and, most crippling of all, his own misconceptions had halted him short of the goal he had set, still his instincts had been partly right. There was wealth in that iron country, but finding it would demand a less stereotyped kind of vision than Cartier had brought to his task from years of seafaring. There were usable highways, but first adventurers would have to swallow their European pride and imitate *les sauvages* in adapting to the demands of geography. Only then would they be able to break out of the St. Lawrence into Canada's vast, fur-rich shield of Pre-Cambrian granite and there, with infinite difficulty, make a fresh start toward the distant Pacific and the shores of Asia.

III

Enter the Beaver

*W*hen Jacques Cartier died, aged sixty-six, of a plague that swept through St. Malo in 1557, he still had not collected all the money he felt Francis I owed him for his American adventures. The family took up the dunning. Wearied of the importunities, another king, Henry III, settled the account in 1587 by means of a grant that cost him nothing. He declared that for the next twelve years the only persons entitled to trade for furs or mine copper in New France were Cartier's grandnephews, Étienne Chaton and Jacques Noël.

The recipients of the privilege were not young men. Forty-six years earlier, in 1541, Jacques Noël, barely in his teens, and possibly Chaton as well had accompanied their great-uncle as far up the St. Lawrence as Charlesbourg-Royal. Ever since, it is fair to assume, the two men had followed with interest the rising popularity of a pursuit that Cartier had not deemed worthy of mention in his reports to Francis I—namely, the fur trade.

The change had been brought about quite haphazardly by fishermen searching the Gulf of St. Lawrence and the river mouth for cod. During the middle years of the sixteenth century the number of vessels had increased steadily from the twenty-seven Cartier had seen on encountering Roberval at St. John's, Newfoundland, in 1542 to an estimated three hundred from all the countries of western Europe in 1578.

The fishermen used one of two methods in curing their catches, most of which were taken by hand lines rather than in nets. One was to gut each cod as it was lifted on the deck, toss it into a barrel of brine, and, after all the barrels were full, to sail home to dry the fish on arrival. The other method was to cure the catch in some likely cove near the fishing areas. This involved the building of a wharf, of wooden frames on which the slabs of fish could be dried after cleaning and splitting, and of huts in which the shore crews could live during the weeks the process required. The shipowners who built these camps generally returned to them year after year, until shortages of wood and crowding by other vessels forced them to seek new locations.

These semi-permanent camps facilitated contact with the Indians. Soon the white workers were exchanging fish hooks, fishing lines, knives, pots, and other small articles with their visitors for miscellaneous furs. On reaching their home ports, the Europeans sold their acquisitions for whatever price they could get—a welcome addition to the meager returns from the fishing voyages. (The sailors worked on shares, and small they were.)

When the fur trade began, the market in Europe was limited, by and large, to marten, mink, otter, and sable that judges and prelates used for adorning their robes. The Indians, however, preferred to hunt beaver. The animals were relatively large—adults weighed from forty to sixty pounds each—and they were numerous. One estimate—by Professor Harold A. Innis in his book *The Fur Trade in Canada*—says that at the time of the coming of the Europeans there were ten million beaver in Canada.

The most obvious signs of their presence in a forest were clusters of short stumps, their upper ends shaped like crudely sharpened pencils. If fresh, these stumps meant that beaver were at work each night felling poplar, birch, and occasional evergreen trees to obtain the bark they used for food and the wood they needed for building materials. Nearby there was certain to be a pond whose level was maintained by a dam ingeniously constructed of interlaced logs and twigs plastered over with mud. Somewhere behind the dam was a house, or "lodge," built of the same materials and shaped like a large, inverted bowl some twenty feet in diameter at the base and three to five feet high. The floor of the chamber in which the animals lived was about six feet across but only inches above water level.

The Indians used a variety of methods for capturing beaver. One was to arrange heavy pieces of wood to fall on them when the animals tripped a release mechanism. Another, which depended on encountering the animals on land, was to run them down with dogs. During winter they could often be snared under the ice in nets baited with their favorite food, pieces of poplar wood.

Patterns changed after whites had introduced hatchets and light crowbars called ice chisels. (Steel traps did not appear until well into the eighteenth century.) Hunters used these new tools during winter for breaking through the roofs of the beaver lodges. As the house disintegrated, the quarry—there might be as many as eight or ten in a single dwelling—naturally fled outside, seeking refuge where there was an air space for breathing between water and ice. The Indians found these spots by tapping on the ice with a club. If the surface sounded hollow, they moved off a step or two and chopped open a hole. They caught the beaver by reaching through with a curved stick, or so says missionary Father Paul Le Jeune in *The Jesuit Relation* of 1634. This was an uncertain method, however, and if conditions allowed before the freeze-up, the Indians avoided it by breaching the dam impounding the beaver pond and then breaking into the lodge after the falling water level had left the animals no place to turn.

Beaver were a popular quarry because they yielded high returns for effort expended. The meat was good to eat, the broad, flat tail in particular being considered a delicacy. Pelts were large. Five or six stitched loosely together were enough to make a robe for wearing or sleeping on. Whites called fur done up in such fashion "coat" beaver and prized it for its versatility. During the Indians' wearing of the robe, the coarsest guard hairs fell out, leaving pelts that could be worked in France into especially lustrous displays. Moreover, the sweat and body grease of the Indian wearer made the skin softer and more pliable than that of any other pelt. Apparently the same impregnations also imparted desirable qualities to the dense, soft underfur. This underfur, often called beaver "wool," could be even more valuable than the main pelt. Each of the small hairs bristled with microscopic barbs that under pressure helped bind the wool into a handsome and durable felt.

When beaver had still lived in Western Europe—this was before Cartier's time—felt made from beaver wool had been extensively used in the manufacture of hats. But that practice had died out

with the beaver and was not revived until beaver pelts began showing up during the middle part of the sixteenth century as part of
the miscellaneous bundles of fur brought back from northern edges
of North America by the cod fishers. Seafaring merchants from the
Netherlands noted the pelts and recalled that the Russians had invented a secret process for "combing" fur in such a way that underfur could be removed without injury to the skin or the guard hairs.

Capitalizing on the knowledge, the Dutch bought up all the
beaver pelts that appeared in the French seaports and carried them
through the Baltic sea to Archangel. Eventually they returned with
two salable items, a fur for adornment and wool for felt. Felters'
guilds sprang alive again, first in Paris and a little later in London.
By about 1580 beaver hats, which wore well and could be shaped
into almost any desired model, had become a new rage for both
civilians and military men. More than ever then, sailors took to
cramming their sea chests full of the kind of merchandise the Indians liked best, and, instead of deprecating the time the savages
spent hunting beaver rather than mink, they now encouraged it.

Although beaver were widely distributed throughout North
America, the best pelts came from Canada's huge Pre-Cambrian
Shield. This enormous armadillo shell of granite spreads from the
Gulf of St. Lawrence north through Labrador and Ungava, encases
all but the southern part of Hudson Bay, reaches west from the St.
Lawrence River to lakes Huron and Superior, and then veers northwest around the Great Plains almost to the Arctic-bound Mackenzie
River. Ancient glaciers have scoured the primal rock into a wrinkled
plain that contains few prominent peaks but is filled with a multitude of ponds, lakes, and streams. Though the soil is shallow, forests grow thick. Along the more sluggish streams and beside the
ponds and marshes grow profuse stands of poplars, birch, and willow that provide limitless food for beaver. The animals become big
and fat, and because of winter's intense cold develop fur that is
thick, glossy, and almost black.

Three big rivers, the Ottawa, the St. Maurice, and the Saguenay,
drain into the St. Lawrence from that part of the shield lying southeast of the height of land enclosing Hudson Bay. In that tumbled
area of dark forests, glinting lakes, and roaring waterfalls roamed
Indians speaking the Algonquian tongue. Notable among them were
the Montagnais, so named by the French for the rough country the

tribe inhabited. Long before the appearance of Cartier, the Montagnais had developed a brisk trade—furs and hides for corn—with the agricultural Indians who lived in towns scattered along the St. Lawrence Valley from Stadacona to Hochelaga and beyond. Switching their trade to whites, who offered more enticing articles than just corn, came as naturally to them as had the hunting of the beaver in the first place.

The annual summer meeting place of Europeans and native Americans became Tadoussac, where the Saguenay flows into the St. Lawrence. Tough Basque whalers were probably the first whites to build crude summer facilities there, but, as competition for curing grounds increased and the possibilities of the fur trade grew apparent, other ships from other nations began venturing into the vicinity. Soon merchants were dispatching vessels to the trading fairs for pelts alone, never mind the fish.

The Indians demand for trade goods was insatiable. First was the problem of replacement. Awls, chisels, and kettles were lost; hatchets were blunted on rocks; knife blades and mirrors were broken; cloth and fishing lines wore out. Goods of all sorts were interred with their owner at elaborate burial rites, and new items were needed in their place. On top of this was the eagerness of families who had never owned manufactured goods to obtain them.

Coat beaver brought in more of these wonderful items than did anything else, but coat beaver took time to produce. The Montagnai bands soon stripped the areas where they hunted. Searching for new supplies, they turned toward more distant tribes, working along the established trade routes by which copper from Lake Superior still moved east. As they knew from their dealings in corn, there was profit to be made from controlling the flow of commodities. Hence they were very jealous of efforts by other tribes, particularly the corn-growing Iroquoian groups south of the St. Lawrence, to cut in on the new commerce. Skirmishes unrecorded by history broke out between the rivals, and as animosities increased so did the likelihood that the whites would sooner or later be called on to choose sides in the contests.

Nor were rivalries limited to the Indians. As felters called for more and more beaver wool, the merchants who handled cargoes bound to and from the St. Lawrence began speculating on how best to rationalize the still chaotic trade and thus increase the profits they derived from it.

One problem was the increasing sophistication of the Indians. In the early days of the trade they had offered almost incredible amounts of fur for the simplest tools. Then, as whites began thronging about them, they took to demanding more for their goods. Shoestring speculators went along rather than lose their investments, and the result was a ferocious competition that hurt everyone except the Indians.

Hoping to restore order to the trade, the more influential of the Europeans set about trying to eliminate their rivals. The most useful tool for doing this was deemed to be a royal edict that would grant to the favored company so sweeping a trade monopoly that outsiders could find no opening through which to crawl.

It was against this background that Cartier's grand-nephews, Étienne Chaton and Jacques Noël, in 1587 approached Henry III with an offer to settle their claims against the court in return for an exclusive right to trade for furs and mine copper within the huge area drained by the St. Lawrence. Relieved to be rid of such pests, Henry assented, whereupon the recipients of the grant went energetically to work. In 1588 Noël pushed longboats as far up the river as the rapids that had thwarted his great-uncle. His primary intent in going so far probably was not beaver pelts—let the *sauvages* bring those to the Tadoussac rendezvous—so much as it was the finding of a route to the mines from which Indian traders regularly carried artifacts of pure copper. Unfortunately for that dream, the tumult of white water at the foot of Mount Royal baffled him as completely as it had Cartier.

The European merchants at the mouth of the Saguenay were meanwhile hooting scorn at the new firm's pretensions of monopoly. They had been trading freely in the New World for years, and they declined, royal parchment or not, to be displaced by upstarts. The next winter some of them managed to gain the king's ear and persuade him to revoke the fur-trading clause, at least so far as Frenchmen were concerned. This action left Chaton and Noël with only one exclusive right, to mine copper. Since they saw no feasible way of reaching the mines, wherever they were, they gave up the business and disappeared from the records.

In spite of the example of their defeat, other wilderness entre-
preneurs kept striving for special privilege. They found a lever in
the increasing activities of the English. The power of that island
nation was rising as rapidly as Spain's was declining. This presented
France with a strong new enemy off her northern flank. Nervously,
Henry's court watched for every sign of potentially dangerous
activity on the far side of the channel, including exploratory trips
aimed toward the New World.

One tarnished pursuit to which English navigators gave new
sheen was that of finding a direct sea route to Asia. Because fishermen by then had pretty well covered the upper parts of the North
American coast as far as Labrador, Albion's search for the Northwest Passage, as it became known, swung toward the Arctic. Between 1576 and 1578 dour Martin Frobisher made three fruitless
casts among the dead-end inlets and ice-choked passages north of
Hudson Strait, which he somehow missed. John Davis followed in
1585–87 with no better success.

Simultaneously, in several separate excursions between 1585
and 1587, two redheaded half-brothers, Sir Humphrey Gilbert and
Sir Walter Raleigh, endeavored to plant colonies south of the St.
Lawrence, on the coasts of what are now Maine and North Carolina. Their efforts also failed—Gilbert died during a shipwreck—
but the French took no comfort from that. If the English persisted,
as well they might, the St. Lawrence, its furs, its still undiscovered
copper mines, and the hoped-for route to Cathay by river and lake
connections would be bracketed between the arms of an unfriendly
power.

It behooved France, therefore, to strengthen her claims to the
land by establishing viable colonies of her own. Unhappily for the
project, the new king, Henry IV, was so entangled in civil and
foreign strife that he could not finance that effort from the national
treasury. Accordingly he assigned it to private enterprise. In return
for transporting settlers to the New World and sustaining them during the early years when they could not support themselves, the
cooperating entrepreneur would be given letters of patent conveying extensive powers, including a monopoly of the fur trade of all
New France.

Working hastily, the early fur companies bungled things and lost
money. The first colonists they took across the Atlantic fared even

worse: the majority of them lost their lives. In 1598 agents of the Marquis de la Roche simply dumped sixty convict-settlers onto an island south of Nova Scotia and let them survive as best they could with the meager help of one annual supply ship. Only eleven survived to be evacuated five years later.

La Roche in the meantime sold his grant to a merchant of Dieppe named Pierre Chauvin. In 1600 Chauvin, assisted by François Gravé, Sieur du Pont, commonly called Pontgravé, set down fifty colonists beside his gloomy fur-trading post at Tadoussac. Cold and scurvy killed all but sixteen. Trading in beaver, however, was tempting enough that after Chauvin died in 1602 Pontgravé made arrangements to continue the work in association with a financier named Amyar de Chastes.

The two men decided to approach the colonizing requirements in their charter more cautiously than their predecessors had and at least locate a habitable site before importing settlers. To aid in the exploratory work, Pontgravé enlisted an amateur geographer known to both him and the king—a one-time soldier and wanderer named Samuel de Champlain.

The decision proved crucial. Champlain at that time had no commitments to the fur trade. He went along simply to discover facts about climate, soil fertility, harbors, latitudes and longitudes, and navigational hazards that no one before him had bothered to note scientifically. That was his passion: to see and, having seen, to understand. To that extent he was unique in the northern part of North America. For a full century men with only a tunnel vision of the future had been exploiting the cod banks around Newfoundland and the beaver ponds north of the St. Lawrence, yet during that time not a single settlement had taken root to strengthen French claims to suzerainty over the potentially valuable region. During two-thirds of a century no one had gone farther inland than Cartier had in 1536. No one, in short, really knew what the land offered. From that standpoint, the coming of a visionary, even one whose administrative talents were as limited as Champlain's, was long overdue.

IV

The Visionary

$\mathcal{S}$amuel de Champlain was born into a sea-faring family in the coastal town of Brouage, France, sometime between 1567 and 1570. As a young man he fought in the internecine wars by which Henry IV established the legitimacy of his reign. When peace came his uncle, a shipper of means, found him a job as captain of one of several vessels carrying Spanish veterans of the European wars to new lives in the West Indies. For two years Champlain roamed Spanish America with more freedom than most non-Spaniards were allowed. He visited Havana and Mexico City and crossed the Isthmus of Panama to its southern side, where he was deeply stirred by the sight of the South Sea, as the Pacific was then called. As others had done before him, he mused on the possibility of cutting a canal through the narrow strip of jungle.

On returning from America he wrote an account of his travels. The textual portions of the book had little to recommend them. Some parts were plagiarized; others were filled with unverified tall tales. But the rough, vigorous drawings and navigational charts he prepared as illustrations impressed his acquaintance, François Gravé, Sieur du Pont, and were partly instrumental in Champlain's being invited to accompany, as an observer, the small fleet that the reorganized monopoly sent across the ocean to New France in the spring of 1603.

Just short of Newfoundland one of the ships, commanded by a Captain Prévert, swung south to trade, explore, and expel intruders from the coasts of Acadia, as Nova Scotia was then called. Pont-gravé and Champlain continued with the other vessels to the deep, hill-girt harbor at Tadoussac, where they landed on May 27.

Indians were assembling for the trading fair. All were members of the Algonquian language group—Etchemins from the northern part of today's Maine, Montagnais from the upper Saguenay, and Algonkins from the higher reaches of the majestic river later called Ottawa. They were pleased with themselves. Their war parties had surprised a band of Iroquois somewhere up the St. Lawrence and had killed, they boasted with exaggeration, no fewer than a hundred of the enemy.

Pontgravé had with him two Montagnais whom he had taken to Paris for a visit. One of these returning travelers made a long speech to the gathering at Tadoussac. He lauded the might of France and stated that the king wanted to help the Algonquians make peace with the Iroquois, or, that failing, to crush the enemy in a great campaign. Delighted by the prospects, the principal sagamore (chief) among the listeners recommended, in a stately speech, that his fellows enter into an alliance with the French. The audience agreed with three explosive sounds that Champlain rendered in writing as "Ho! Ho! Ho!"—a cry no stranger to Indian ears than "Hear! Hear!" to an audience of English or "Right on!" to students in American universities.

Cementing this alliance gave still more justification to the feast called *tabagie* that was being prepared to signalize the victory over the Iroquois. Already eight or ten large kettles filled with chunks of meat from moose, bear, seal, beaver, and wild fowl were simmering over fires on the beach. When everything was ready, the Algonquians and their visitors dipped into the pots with bowls made of birchbark. Champlain did not relish the saltless stew, and he was repelled to see the Indians wind up the feast by wiping their greasy hands on their own hair or on the shaggy coats of their dogs.

Dancing followed. To the Europeans the gyrations seemed odd. The participants, Champlain wrote, stayed in one spot while they made "certain gestures and movements of the body, first lifting up one foot and then the other, and stamping upon the ground." At intervals they slapped their knees with their hands and shouted in chorus the standard cry of approval, "Ho! Ho! Ho!"

The whites waited patiently, hoping that as soon as the ceremony was over trading could begin. But no. A fleet of two hundred canoes filled with Algonkins put into the harbor under the beetling rocks. They too had killed Iroquois, and so there had to be another *tabagie.*

This one was more ceremonious. The sagamore of the new-comers was seated on the ground between two poles bedecked with the scalps of the vanquished. The females of the group already on the beach then formed a line in front of the chief. What followed popped the eyes of the whites. "Suddenly all the women and girls proceeded to cast off their mantles of skins, and stripped themselves naked, showing their privities [the French never failed to mention the casual displays of genitalia among the Indians] but retained their ornaments of *matacheas,* which are beads and braided cords of porcupine quills, dyed of various colors."

The naked chorus sang to the visitors, concluded with a soprano "Ho! Ho! Ho!" and decorously reclothed themselves. Gift giving, foot racing among the men, and more feasting followed. After that the traders, colorfully bedecked to impress their colorful customers, were at last able to break out their goods both on shipboard and in little booths on the beach and begin their bargaining.

Champlain, who had studied Cartier's accounts closely and had talked at length with traders about the St. Lawrence, perhaps sensed even then that the celebrations he had witnessed could be harbingers of trouble for the monopoly. Balances of power among the tribes were shifting. Since Cartier's time the Iroquoian villages of Stadacona on the site of Quebec and the much larger settlement of Hochelaga on Montreal Island had disappeared. Why? No one knows. Early historians believed that the inhabitants of the towns tried to set themselves up as middlemen controlling the trade with the lower St. Lawrence and that the Algonquians responded by sweeping them out of the way. Modern students lean toward more prosaic reasons—crop failure, epidemics introduced by the whites, or perhaps predictions by Indian shamans that the time had come to abandon the towns.

Where the exiles went is another mystery. If they were true Hurons, as was once believed, they may have drifted west to join their fellow tribesmen along the eastern shores of Lake Huron. If they were more closely related to one of the five tribes known as Iroquois—the Mohawks, Oneidas, Onondagas, Cayugas, and Senecas—they perhaps moved south to live in one of the wooded valleys of upper New York state. In any event, they left a vacuum behind them. By Champlain's time the valley of the St. Lawrence was, like bloody Kentucky, a no-man's land, crisscrossed at frequent intervals but not occupied for long by war parties of contending Algonquian and Iroquoian tribes.

To a man charged, as Champlain was, with examining the forces that might affect the location of the monopoly's proposed colony, the situation was critical, and he asked the chiefs at Tadoussac for more information. They told him, perhaps slyly, that they needed help. Although they had achieved victories that spring, the Iroquois were a more numerous and stronger people than they. The enemy would strike back ferociously, and the St. Lawrence, highway to the fur-rich interior, could not be kept safe for travel and settlement unless the French assisted.

Although Champlain never realized the truth, the analysis was not wholly accurate. The sedentary Iroquois were numerous only in respect to the Algonkins and Montagnais. But more enemies than those roving tribes ringed the series of parallel valleys that the Iroquois clung to between the upper reaches of the Hudson River and the southeastern shores of Lake Erie. Most implacable of the foes was another nation that spoke an Iroquoian dialect and followed timeless Iroquoian customs. These were the Hurons. In spite of similar life-styles, however, the two groups had no more use for each other than did sixteenth-century speakers of related Romance languages, the French and the Spanish.

In searching for an internal strength that would help them ward off external dangers, the Iroquoians of present-day New York had evolved a political organization unique among American Indians. This was the Great Council of the five tribes. Each fall forty-nine representatives met at the principal town of the Onondagas to discuss major affairs that affected or might affect the well-being of all Iroquois. Emergency meetings could be summoned by any of the tribes whenever conditions seemed to warrant.

Originally the Council had been formed to control disruptions caused by blood feuds. These were occasioned when a member of one clan was killed or injured by someone outside his family. Villages handled such breaches of the peace by requiring the guilty person to give rich gifts to the bereaved. But when the breach was occasioned by an outsider, matters grew more complex. Among most Indians no intertribal courts existed to help the family of an injured person obtain redress. Accordingly the male members of the family, egged on by the women, undertook to settle scores by slaying a member of the offending tribe—or even by bringing home captives that were forcibly adopted as substitutes for the dead warrior.

Disruptive feuds between related tribes weakened all of them. Accordingly the Council was created about 1450 to maintain harmony among the five associated groups in upper New York. As anthropologist Anthony F. C. Wallace has pointed out in *The Death and Rebirth of the Seneca,* there was nothing new about such ethnic confederations among the many peoples inhabiting the Northeastern woodlands. "But the Iroquois League was to them as ice is to water: a rigid crystalline form of a normally shapeless substance. . . . 'We bind ourselves together,' said the mythological founder, Dekanawidah, 'by taking hold of each other's hands so firmly and forming a circle so strong that if a tree should fall upon it, it could not shake or break it, so that our people and grandchildren shall remain in the circle in security, peace, and happiness.'"

Extending peace to surrounding nations, so it was said, was among the Council's long-range objectives, and the chiefs often insisted that at times they did rein in on the ambitions of village hotheads. In so doing, however, they ran counter to Indian psychology. A male passing from puberty into maturity proved his manhood by joining a war party. Since his emotions could not be released through ritual battle against any of the five Iroquois tribes, he and his fellows turned on outsiders. Atwood speculates that this shifting of drives for revenge onto outside tribes, and eventually onto Europeans, helps account for the ferocity with which those Iroquois war parties that were unrestrained by the Council attacked and tortured their foes. Inevitably the sufferers retaliated in kind.

By Champlain's time the blood feuds had been given new impetus by the fur trade. The Iroquois wanted a share of the marvelous goods that white traders for many years had been bringing to the lower St. Lawrence. The Algonquians, who could not get enough merchandise for their own needs and for trade with beaver-producing tribes farther inland, were determined to keep all other Indians away from the whites. They struck at Iroquois war parties venturing onto the St. Lawrence, and were ruthlessly attacked in return as vengeance and trade rivalries became inextricably mixed.

By the Algonquians' own admission, they often got the worst of the exchanges. Why then did the French ally themselves with the weaker party?

Greed and complacency provide the answers. The best furs came from areas in which the Montagnais, Algonkins, and Hurons were entrenched. Hence friendship with those tribes had to come first. The French, moreover, were confident that they could end what seemed to them picayune wilderness wars either through diplomacy well larded with presents or by giving the Iroquois an example of what European military technology could do to them if they persisted in their pugnacity. The Algonquians, grasping the feeling very quickly, made the most of it by pleading piteously for assistance, and so the drift toward trouble and suffering slipped steadily on.

Indian affairs were only one of Champlain's responsibilities. He had also been directed to explore as much of the surrounding country as he could during the summer. This accorded with his own desires, and on June 11 he turned one of the ships' longboats up the gorge of the Saguenay. Today's tourists find the cliffs and forests beautiful. Champlain, who was looking for farmland, thought them ugly. Yet he would have gone farther if he could have. The Montagnais who were with him told him that they traded in the northwest with a people who often visited the shores of a vast saltwater sea. Excited, Champlain, talking through interpreters, pumped his new friends for details. At the conclusion of the session, he wrote, "It is some gulf of this, our sea [the Atlantic] which overflows in the north into the midst of the continent."

What he had "discovered" was, of course, Hudson Bay. As yet no white man, excepting possibly some Viking, had beheld it. How big was it? How far west did it lead? Was there a connection with another gulf overflowing from the Pacific? Could he, Samuel de Champlain of France, succeed where Martin Frobisher and John Davis of England had failed and find a passageway around the top of North America?

The answers would have to wait. Dead ahead loomed a waterfall around which his sailors probably could not carry the longboat.

Even if they should succeed, they would encounter more rapids, a big lake, long portages, and unfriendly Indians before reaching the gulf. Or so said the Montagnais, who, like all native middlemen, did not want the whites to trade directly with the distant tribes.

Besides, the St. Lawrence still awaited exploration. Returning to Tadoussac, Champlain picked up Pontgravé, who had stayed behind trading. With a small crew they headed southwest up the main river in a twelve-ton pinnace they had brought across the ocean on the deck of one of their larger ships. Behind them they towed a longboat.

Champlain saw several spots that impressed him. One was the deserted site of Stadacona, where the river was compressed between the cliffs of Quebec. A strong colony there, supported by a fortress atop the precipices, could keep the Indians of the interior from taking their furs to outlaw traders down the river—and check the outlaws from moving up to the Indians.

Another strategic site—the French reached it after transferring to the longboat—was the junction of the St. Maurice with the St. Lawrence. Here the main river narrowed abruptly after flowing through a wide stretch called Lac St. Pierre. Although the St. Maurice was difficult to navigate as it wound southward through the granite of the Shield, many Indians used it in order to avoid the Iroquois who often lurked along the lower reaches of the Ottawa farther west. Sometimes they were hit anyway, here at the narrows. Champlain advised Pontgravé to build a fort at the river junction for the protection of the monopoly's customers. As soon as the Iroquois realized that ambushes were no longer productive, perhaps they would sue for peace. Then the monopoly could have their trade, too.

Near the island-choked upper end of Lac St. Pierre, where the city of Sorel now stands, the explorers encountered yet another big river, this one entering the St. Lawrence from the south. Today it is known as the Richelieu. Champlain called it "The River of the Iroquois" because it led straight to the land of the Mohawks.

A large group of Algonkins were camped at the river mouth, working up courage for another raid on the enemy. The sight of the whites made them want to show their bravery, and off they went. As they moved south Champlain's party accompanied them for several miles. En route the geographer learned that travelers could easily pass from the lake at the head of the Richelieu into another river that flowed south to what he presumed was Spanish Florida. This was the yet-unnamed Hudson, and again he had anticipated one of Henry Hudson's "discoveries"—in quotation marks because the Indians had known all these things for generations.

So much to see and no time in which to see it! Returning to the St. Lawrence, the explorers continued upstream to the thunderous rapids at the southern base of Mount Royal. Champlain reacted much as Cartier had. "I assure you I never saw any torrent of water pour over with such force as this does." He walked to the head of the white water, and from Algonkins he met learned data similar to that which Cartier had picked up—except that no Indian tried to tell him of the marvels of the Kingdom of Saguenay, perhaps because he knew better than to ask naïve questions.

Several leagues up the St. Lawrence, the Algonkins said, was a huge fresh water sea (our Lake Ontario). A monstrous waterfall (Niagara) separated that lake from another (Erie). From there on geography grew misty. But somewhere, so Champlain understood his interpreter to say (he himself never learned to handle any Indian tongue with dexterity), was a lake whose waters were salty. Remembering his own short crossing of Panama and the ocean that Verrazano said he had glimpsed across the sandspits off North Carolina, Champlain jumped to a conclusion built mostly on hope: "Without doubt, from their account, this can be nothing else than the South Sea." From Hudson Bay to the Pacific—surely there was a passageway somewhere out there!

Years before, Jacques Cartier had heard of the same lakes, but after failing to surmount the rapids with his double-manned longboat, he had let himself be distracted by mythical Saguenay. Champlain was more persistent and more adaptable. If longboats could not be used, why not try Indian canoes?

Was the thought original? Many Europeans had seen Indian canoes since Cartier's time, and it would be strange if no one before Champlain had recognized their worth. Yet there are no reports that anyone did recommend them for inland travel. Preconception wears blinders. The *sauvages* were uncivilized. It followed that the

boats they built were flimsy, primitive, and undependable. European pinnaces, longboats, or wooden bateaux were the only proper
vehicles for moving merchandise along the waterways.

By that time Champlain had seen enough of the native craft to
know better. Hundreds of them loaded with furs, men, women, and
children had filled the harbor at Tadoussac. They were not flimsy;
they were simply light of weight. One or two men could turn them
upside down on their shoulders and carry them past rapids or over
heights of land to different drainage systems. By such means furs—
and iron kettles—were transported across the hundreds of miles
between the St. Lawrence and Hudson Bay.

Nor were the canoes primitive. Shortly after the French had
transferred to their longboat near Quebec, a pair of bark canoes
more than twenty feet long, each capable of carrying half a ton of
merchandise, had skimmed by them with mocking grace. European
technology! Six or more sailors strained with all their might at the
longboat's oars, yet the two paddlers in each Indian canoe had
made them look as clumsy as if they had been anchored. Rowers,
moreover, could not see where they were going. Paddlers faced
ahead, an item of no small import to war parties moving into unfriendly territory.

The craft, moreover, were fully dependable. Life depended on
them. They were marvels of environmental adaptation, constructed
with meticulous care from natural materials available near most of
the villages of the wooded Northeast. Being ever curious and something of a craftsman himself, Champlain examined some of the
boats in detail and through his interpreters asked endless questions
about their construction. What he learned would eventually have
great bearing not only on his own career but on the whole course of
Canadian history.

An Indian desiring to build a canoe that in normal service would
last ten years selected his raw materials scrupulously. He might
spend a week looking for just the right birch tree—a big one, perhaps thirty inches in diameter, absolutely straight as high as the
lower branches, and as free as possible from the horizontal "eyes"
that always spot parts of the creamy white outer bark. During a
long thaw in winter or, more commonly, early in the spring he used
a crude ladder to climb as high up the tree as the length of the
canoe-to-be dictated, generally ten to twenty feet in the early days.

Using a flint knife flaked to a sharp edge, he made a vertical slit through the pungent bark as far down as the average snow line. Bark lower than that was wrinkled and of poor quality.

After the requisite length of bark had been peeled from the tree, he rolled it up the short way with the grain. (Because the grain of birchbark runs horizontally around the tree, it never splits along the full length of the canoe, an important safety factor.) He then carried the bundle to a building bed near a stream and stored it in quiet water so that it would not lose its flexibility by drying out.

Other materials included long, thin roots from a black spruce. This tree grows in moist spots, and its shallow roots can be easily pried up with a stick or dug up by hand. The fiber can then be split by teeth, flint knives, and thumbnails into stout twine for lashing the parts of the canoe together. Maple wood was collected for thwarts. White cedar, which splits easily when dry, came from old deadfalls.

The building bed where these materials were collected probably had been in use for generations. No stones or roots flawed its smoothness. The surface either contained a shallow depression or a slight crown, according to how much curve, or rocker, the builder wanted the bottom of his canoe to have. The bed was shaded by trees to protect the bark from sun. There was water nearby not only for ease in launching the finished craft but because quantities of hot water had to be used in the building process.

With stone scrapers and knives made from beaver teeth, the worker first fashioned a flat center thwart. Widest in its midsection (perhaps three inches), the thwart narrowed toward its ends and then flared out again into a shoulder that could be inserted into a mortise in the inwale, as the inner strip of a gunwale is called. The length of this carefully constructed thwart determined the maximum width of the canoe and hence, to an extent, the overall dimensions of the craft. Other thwarts, their number depending on the size of the canoe-to-be (most commonly four in addition to the center piece) were then whittled out according to the scale the builder carried in his mind.

Cedar, split by stone wedges and wooden mallets into strips of desired thickness and width, was used for ribs and gunwales. A twenty-foot canoe might require as many as fifty ribs each two inches or so wide. They were shaped like U's, except that the upper parts curved slightly inward. The bottom curves in the ribs to either side of the center grew progressively tighter as they neared the bow and stern. Bending was accomplished by placing the slats, already cut to the desired length, against a tree trunk, pouring hot water over the wood to soften it, and then pulling on both ends. As soon as the desired curve had been attained, the rib was removed from the tree and its tips were tied into place with strips of cedar bark so that it would keep its form as it dried.

Gunwale strips were shaped in much the same way, though of course the length was greater and the curve much more shallow. Stem pieces, which fitted over the points where the gunwale strips came together at bow and stern, were more complicated. In making the simplest form of stem piece, the worker split about half the length of a narrow, yard-long piece of cedar into several laminations. He softened these laminations with hot water and carefully bent them into the curve that would run from the prow (or stern) of the canoe to the bottom. The straight upper part of the prow was formed by the unlaminated section of the wood.

So much for the simplest stem piece. Sometimes, however, the prow was not straight but curved outward or rose well above the level of the gunwales before tumbling back in a graceful swoop to meet them. These variations were determined partly by the uses for which the canoe was destined—for example, high, sharp prows were preferred for white water—and required additional care and skill on the part of the builder. More than any other feature of the canoe the stems embodied tribal characteristics that enabled connoisseurs to tell in what part of the country the craft had originated.

As soon as the materials were shaped, the worker built the upper part of the frame. The thwarts were seated in mortises cut from the inwale by drilling two shallow holes with bone awls—often the awls were rotated by a bowstring—and then knocking out the wood between the perforations with a bone chisel. Firmness was provided by lashings of root twine and the inwale was then laid flat on the building bed. Stakes were driven into the ground at fairly close intervals around the elliptical outline and then removed. The bark was unrolled over the holes, whose position was fixed in the memory of the builder. The side of the bark that had been next to the tree rested on the ground and hence would become the outside of the canoe.

The next step was to fold the edges of the bark upward in the general shape of the canoe. To eliminate puckering, the bark was gored almost to the edge of the remembered outline of holes. The different flaps were then turned up one by one and the stakes were replaced in the ground, so that the loose bark curled upward like an elongated tan basin inside its gently curving cradle of stakes. The gores were then laced together with spruce thread and short pieces in the midsection were pieced out as necessary from a spare roll of bark.

The complex procedure of placing the inwale frame at a pre-determined height between the stakes and the bark came next. That done, an outer strip, the outwale, was attached to the frame by wooden pegs that reached through the outwale and the bark into the inwale. The pegs were reinforced by lashings of roots wound around and around the gunwales through holes drilled into the bark by awls. Separations were left between the clumps of lashings wherever a rib was to be inserted. The canoe was then turned upside down on wooden supports, and the stem pieces were lashed onto the bow and stern. All seams were next waterproofed with melted spruce gum to which animal fat and powdered char-coal had been added to keep it from cracking in cold weather.

Finally, the canoe was replaced on the ground and its interior sheathed with thin slats of cedar. The ribs were put into place, curved parts down and sides canted a little off vertical. The upper tips were inserted between bark and inwale in the spaces between the clumps of lashing. The worker straightened the rib by hammer-ing on the uprights with a mallet. If the rib fitted properly, and a good worker made sure that it did, it pressed the sheathing tight against the bark without splitting it, and the canoe, its sides gently curving and its flat bottom rocking slightly upward at either end, emerged with its bark covering as smooth as the cheeks of a young girl.

If the builder wished, he could create designs on the stem pieces by scraping away a thin layer of the brown outside bark to reveal the lighter hues beneath. He could use porcupine quills, and some-times he inlaid his paddles with bits of deer horn. Generally speak-ing, however, the contrasting colors of the lashing and seams and the quilted look of the pieced-out bark were decorations enough, and additional designs were seldom added until European paint became available. Canoes made in later times by Indian workers for the fur traders were then often fancifully bedecked.

Seams had to be regummed frequently, and the bark could be easily punctured by a sharp rock or snag, particularly if the bottom were pushed down on the protrusion by a heavy weight from above. For that reason the Indians generally loaded and unloaded their canoes in a foot or so of water before dragging them ashore and canting them nearly upside down as nighttime shelters.

The acquisition of steel tools enabled the builders to complete their work more quickly but did not improve on quality. That was built in by the care of the worker and the nature of the materials. The natural oils and waxes in birchbark kept it from becoming waterlogged. It was highly resilient, as were the cedar ribs and sheathing. Consequently the canoe could withstand heavy blows from rocks in white water and considerable pummeling from waves in open lakes or even the ocean as long as those waves did not quarter in on them, either breaking the frame or swamping the craft.

There were no seats in Indian canoes. The paddlers knelt in the bottom, a position that gave them better leverage than they could obtain when seated. Passengers rode as best they could on baggage. As Champlain would learn in time, even heavily loaded canoes could cover sixty miles or more in a single day.

Europeans, he argued, could put the versatile craft to good use. Merchants leaving France early in the spring could reach Montreal Island in longboats by the middle of June. There they could hire Indian travelers to take them on into the interior. They would carry samples of goods with them which they would use in persuading the inland tribes to leapfrog past the middlemen along the upper rivers and bring their furs directly to an agreed-on rendezvous beside the St. Lawrence. By eliminating the charges of the middlemen, profits would be higher for everyone—especially for the monopoly. This could all be accomplished quickly enough, he thought, so that the rejoicing merchants could return to France before the onslaught of winter.

So much for business. But always in the back of Champlain's mind was the tantalizing vision of those two saltwater seas, one in the north, one in the west. As soon as a French colony had been established in the New World, explorers using it as a base could drive deep into the unknown, searching for the waterway to the

Pacific that he was sure existed. And perhaps he would be the one to lead the way.

The opportunity was long postponed, however. On returning to France in the fall of 1603, Pontgravé and he learned that the financial head of the monopoly, Amyar de Chastes, had died. Control now rested in the hands of Pierre du Gua, Sieur de Monts. De Monts was an old hand at the trade. He knew the bitterness of the winters on the lower St. Lawrence, and since his charter depended on his founding a colony somewhere in America, he was wondering about placing it farther south.

Captain Prévert, who, it will be remembered, had left the outward-bound fleet to sail south to Acadia, clinched matters. He had circled the lower end of Nova Scotia into the Bay of Fundy and was excited by the potentials there. He was convinced that he had found copper, and the Indians, who had many furs to trade, had assured him that the winters were mild. The colony, he argued, should be planted somewhere on the shores of the Bay of Fundy. The trade monopoly of the St. Lawrence could then be reinforced by patrol ships based at the settlement.

De Monts agreed and asked Champlain, whose reports had impressed him, whether he would continue to serve the monopoly by exploring and mapping the coast southward as far as Florida. Champlain assented, apparently with no great pang of disappointment. Exploring was what he liked best. And in spite of all he had said about the virtues of Indian canoes for inland travel, he had seen those awesome rapids at the foot of Mont Royal. They were certain to be a major obstacle to heavy traffic, and perhaps he could find some easier river that would lead by various interlocking headwaters to the western sea of his desiring. If not, well, the monopoly still held the key to the St. Lawrence. Some day, if necessary, he would be back.

V

Breakthrough to the Lakes

*F*or four and a half years Breton and Basque merchants clamored to Henry against the monopoly that the king had issued de Monts. They were supported in Paris by the owners of felting and hat factories, who hoped that free trade would drive down the cost of North American beaver pelts. More backing came from France's minister of finance, Maximilien de Béthune Sully. Sully argued that hungry free traders would prove more effective than smug monopolists in meeting the competition along the coast and in the lower St. Lawrence of increasing numbers of rivals from Holland and England.

At first only rumbles of these threats reached Champlain. He spent four summers, 1604–1607, exploring the coast from the upper reaches of the Bay of Fundy (Prévert's copper mine there turned out to be worthless) on south past Cape Cod. He pushed up whatever rivers seemed to open a way into the interior, and he developed his latent skill for dealing with Indians.

When winter forced a halt to exploring, he rejoined the Acadian colonists and did what he could to maintain morale. The first year was dreadful. The original settlement had been placed on an exposed island in the mouth of the St. Croix River, now part of the international boundary between Maine and New Brunswick. The weather proved unusually severe, and in the spring the surviving residents moved southeast across Fundy to a more protected site in what today is known as Annapolis Basin, Nova Scotia. There matters improved, but in France in the spring of 1607 de Monts' enemies finally prevailed on Henry to revoke the monopoly.

On learning the news Champlain hurried across the Atlantic to Fontainbleau with a new plan. The monopoly, he told both de Monts and the king, had been spreading itself too thin. The company merely annoyed its enemies by trying to patrol, with limited resources, the maze of rugged inlets between Gaspé Peninsula and Cape Cod. They should concentrate on the St. Lawrence. The river was a giant funnel into which a still-unknown number of tributaries poured, each one an avenue for furs. The upper reaches of any of those tributaries, or of the main river itself, might lead as far as the gateway to the Western Sea. If the king would relieve the company of the burden of supporting the Acadian colony and would let its men concentrate their exploring and fur-gathering activities on the great river alone, results almost surely would benefit France as well as the company.

After wavering, Henry agreed to relieve the company of its colonizing obligations and to extend its monopoly for one year. A year was not much time, but perhaps energetic expansion above Tadoussac would persuade the king to relent again the following season.

With that hope buoying him, de Monts appointed Champlain lieutenant-governor in charge of all company activities on the St. Lawrence. The new official extemporized his plans on the basis of what he had seen during his trip up the river in 1603. First he would build a trading post where the river narrowed at Quebec. It would not be the fort he had originally envisioned—there was neither time nor money for that—but it would intercept Indians journeying downstream with their furs toward Tadoussac. Moreover, Champlain had no intention of simply waiting for the Indians. As soon as the post was secured, he would range out as far as he could to acquaint the distant tribes with the new state of affairs and urge them to bring their furs to this new, much handier mart. And always as he roamed—it was a passion with him now—he would try to find a way that canoes could use for crossing the continent to the Pacific.

Meanwhile, François Gravé, Sieur du Pont, was to continue the trade at Tadoussac for the Montagnai Indians who each year descended the Saguenay River. Pontgravé reached America ahead of Champlain, and was straightway fired upon by Basque ship captains who doubted that the monopoly had been restored. Champlain's first job on reaching the rendezvous was cooling off the feud while reasserting the company's charter. He managed by letting the rivals keep the furs they had collected to date. In exchange the Basques promised, probably with their fingers crossed behind their backs, to recognize the king's will. Then off the governor went by pinnace—no one had taken a ship past Tadoussac since Cartier's time—to the site of Quebec. There between the base of the cliffs and the river he put twenty-three men, some of them lads in their teens, to work building the St. Lawrence Valley's first "habitation," as he called it.

The principal feature was a cluster of three small (nineteen by thirteen feet) structures two stories tall, each topped by a loft. A cellar, a dovecote, a warehouse, and garden plots completed the tight little community. Fortifications consisted of a moat and connecting galleries ranging along the sides of the buildings.

Champlain pushed the men hard. Mosquitos were a torture. The passing days brought with them an increasing sense of isolation and dread of winter. Breaking under the strain, five men led by one Jean Duval decided to kill Champlain and surrender the post to the Basques in return for, they hoped, generous rewards. But then one of the plotters lost his nerve and warned the governor. Duval was thereupon executed and his head elevated on a pike for other would-be schemers to contemplate. The remaining conspirators were taken in chains to France.

The rewards of those who stayed loyal were grim. During the winter scurvy felled them all. It was the first time Champlain had suffered personally from the affliction, although he had seen much of it in Acadia. It was caused, he theorized, by noxious vapors from the earth, by lack of exercise, and by an unrelieved diet of salted meat and salted fish. He was close to correct in the latter part of his diagnosis, if one takes it to mean lack of fresh fruit and vegetables. Desperate, he ordered the ambulatory to creep out into the bitter cold and look for the curative tree that had saved part of Cartier's crew seventy-three years before. The searchers failed. Only eight of nineteen men survived the winter. Two were teen-age boys of whom we shall hear again, Étienne Brulé and Nicolas Marsolet.

Shortly after the breakup of the ice, Algonkin Indians from the St. Maurice and Ottawa rivers appeared with their furs. They were pleased to see the post beside the gray cliffs, but they predicted that the Iroquois would destroy it if possible. Deciding to move first and secure his southern flank by giving the enemy a blow they would not forget, Champlain and the Algonkins sought reinforcements from Tadoussac, where Pontgravé was now conducting a flourishing trade.

If the annual supply ship had arrived by then, as seems likely, Champlain learned that the king had refused to renew the company's one-year monopoly. But Henry did not know yet that Quebec was a reality and that as soon as the Iroquois were cowed, the thrust into the interior could begin. When informed in the fall, his mind might change. Carrying that hope with him, Champlain picked up as many stout young sailors as Pontgravé could spare. Four or five of them were armed, like Champlain, with harquebuses, primitive, muzzle-loading muskets that discharged with a horrifying roar and clouds of smoke. The effect on Indians who had not seen firearms was shattering.

Confident of their strength, the combined forces started back up the river. Just short of the Richelieu (then the River of the Iroquois) they came upon an encampment of Algonkin and Huron families. These Hurons were the first members of that tribe that Champlain had met. He was delighted. They lived by the shores of one of the western seas of which he had been told, and they traded with tribes who lived still farther on toward the Pacific. If he could persuade them to undertake regular trading trips to Quebec, they would fatten the company's annual harvest of furs considerably. They might also guide him, sometime in the future, to the unknown lands he ached to see.

The Hurons were equally delighted to meet the whites. They lived in terror of the Iroquois, who occasionally raided their villages during the dead of winter and who tried to ambush their fur canoes in the spring. In spite of that they were so hungry for European goods that, when middlemen were unable to satisfy their needs, a few of them occasionally risked their lives trying to reach

Tadoussac. A post at Quebec would shorten their journey by scores of miles, while a defeat of the Iroquois would cap that gain by rendering the trip safe and relatively easy.

From a modern point of view the next logical step would have been to add a few Huron braves to the war party and keep going. That was not the way one dealt with Indians, however. Back to Quebec the entire crowd went for a boisterous session of feasting, dancing, and trading. When the flotilla at last moved upstream again, the majority of the sated Indians went right on past the Richelieu, headed for home with their families and new wares. They'd worry about the Iroquois another year.

For reasons Champlain does not explain some of the whites also dropped out. The army that moved up the Richelieu consisted of three French in a small shallop and about sixty Indians in twenty-four small canoes. Unable to take their rowboat past the first rapids, the whites switched to canoes. For the first time Champlain experienced a sustained ride in one of the craft he had recommended six years earlier.

Seventy-five miles up the Richelieu in what is now New York state the warriors entered a long lake dotted with islands and surrounded by fine trees through whose branches the expedition members caught the gleam of silver waterfalls. Entranced, Champlain named the body of water for himself.

At twilight on July 29, 1609, near the lake's southern end and hardly a long rifle shot from the headwaters of the still unnamed Hudson, they encountered Mohawks traveling in clumsy canoes of elm bark. (Birch trees satisfactory for making canoes did not grow in Iroquois country.) The startled enemy fled ashore and built a rough barricade by chopping down trees with axes they had obtained through intertribal trade. The attackers grouped their canoes in deep water off shore and held the craft together with long poles. Throughout the night both groups sang war songs and traded insults.

Rituals left over from a time when fighting had been less deadly still prevailed in part. Ambassadors from the enemy contacted the leading Indians of the invading fleet and worked out an agreement under which fighting would begin on land at daybreak. (During this time the whites stayed out of sight, and the Mohawks sent for reinforcements.) As dawn approached, the French donned armor and plumed helmets, and poured powder and ball into their harque-buses; Champlain stuffed four bullets into his. The attackers then landed unopposed, the three whites concealed in the rear ranks.

Two hundred Mohawks advanced with slow dignity toward them. Dramatically the invaders drew apart, leaving room for Champlain to stride ahead. Recovering from their momentary astonishment, the Mohawks let fly a cloud of arrows. Champlain fired at the leaders of the jammed wedge. Two chiefs and a warrior dropped. The two other Frenchmen, who had slipped through the trees to the flanks of the enemy, also fired thunderously. The Mohawks stampeded, the Algonkins and Hurons in ecstatic pursuit. They killed several, captured ten or twelve, found and looted the Mohawk camp, and then started home with the prisoners.

That evening the French witnessed one of the episodes for which the tribes of the northeastern woodlands achieved lasting notoriety —the torture of captives. But that is a white reaction. In the Indian view the ceremony—for it was that—involved respect. It gave the sufferer a chance to show the kind of courage that would make him remembered. Perhaps, if he was brave enough, he would be freed. Using brands taken from their campfires, Champlain's Algonkin and Huron friends slowly burned great welts across the bound torso of one prisoner while the others watched in anticipation of their turn. "Then," Champlain wrote, "they tore out his nails and applied fire to the extremities of his fingers and private member. Afterwards they flayed the top of his head and had a kind of gum poured all hot upon it."

Revolted, Champlain put an end to the man's misery with a shot. The victors assuaged their disappointment by cutting the body into pieces and trying to force the other prisoners to eat hunks of the dripping flesh.

It had been a notable victory. Confident that the Iroquois would think carefully before raiding the St. Lawrence again, Champlain busied himself improving the habitation at Quebec so that next year he could take full advantage of the increased trade he envisioned. What he had no way of knowing was that Henry Hudson, working for the Dutch, was at that very time nearing the river that now bears his name in present-day New York state. Within another five years merchants from Holland, already skilled in the ways of the trade by their dealings along the coast, would have pushed upstream as far as today's Albany. There they would enter into alliance with the Iroquois, whom they would solicit to bring them more and more furs, no matter what the source.

Leaving seventeen men at Quebec, where they passed an easier winter than the one experienced by their predecessors, Champlain and Pontgravé returned to France in the hope of persuading the king to renew the company's monopoly. Henry refused. In spite of that, de Monts decided to continue operations. His company's position was strong. It owned the most advanced post in North America. Champlain had won the respect of the Algonkins and Hurons. If canoe routes to the west could be kept open and the swarms of independents at Tadoussac be outdistanced, the firm should do well.

In his eagerness to prove himself, Champlain in 1610 left France ahead of the normal season, risking the icebergs of the Gulf of St. Lawrence in order to reach Canada as soon as possible.

When he disembarked at Quebec on April 26, he found several Montagnais waiting for him. They'd had a good hunting season, and in their euphoria they were spoiling for another fight with the Iroquois, who, they said, had not been chastened by their defeat the year before. What they wanted, Champlain sensed, was an excuse to celebrate another easy victory produced by firearms. He tried to bargain. If he helped them once again in their interminable war, would they guide him to the great gulf in the north?

Yes, certainly . . . next year. Champlain had no way of knowing, of course, that Henry Hudson, employed that season (1610) by the English and ranging the coasts far to the north, was even then working his way into the great Canadian bay that eventually would be named for him. Thus the "discovery" would not be Champlain's, no matter what the Frenchman did.

In due time—one seldom hurried Indians—Champlain and a handful of other whites moved up the St. Lawrence with the Montagnais. Their immediate goal was St. Ignace Island near the mouth of the Richelieu River, where Champlain the year before had proposed to rendezvous with Algonkins and Hurons from the upper country. To his exasperation several other traders, having somehow learned what was afoot, followed close behind.

They had scarcely reached St. Ignace when an express canoe arrived with an urgent message. As the Algonkins had been approaching the island, their scouts had discovered an encampment of a hundred Iroquois a short distance up the Richelieu. The enemy had taken refuge in a hurriedly erected fortress of logs, and the Algonkins, though superior in numbers, could not dislodge them without help.

Champlain was bound by his promise to the Montagnais to join the battle, but when he called for volunteers from among the dozens of French assembled on the island, only five stepped forward. The clash they entered proved to be long and furious. During it a few more shame-faced French appeared. By chopping down trees in such a way that their falling helped collapse the barricades and by pouring shot into the enclosure, the attackers, who suffered three deaths and many wounded, at last put the Iroquois to flight. Many were slain and fifteen were taken as prisoners back to St. Ignace Island.

There a great torture ceremony was launched amid poles hung with fluttering scalps. During it a belated, fur-laden flotilla of Huron canoes arrived. The disappointed occupants joined the celebration. As the fires burned smokily and the victims tried to stifle their screams, the French spread out their wares and invited the Indians to trade. Their eagerness opened the way to another triumph. By holding back their skins, the Indians drove prices so high that the competing whites had to give from eight to sixteen times as many knives and axes for a beaver as had been the case a year or two earlier.

Seeing that his company's expectations for that season were ruined, Champlain began preparing for the future. Moving quietly among the influential Algonkins and Hurons, he suggested that next year the rendezvous be moved still farther up the river, to Montreal Island so that the Indians' journeys would be shorter. He asked that the other whites not be told. Though such secretiveness ran counter to the Indians' own advantage, they agreed. Champlain also prevailed on an Algonkin chief to take home with him for the winter, to learn the land and the language, eighteen-year-old Étienne Brulé, one of the eight survivors of the first appalling winter in Quebec. In exchange Champlain agreed under pressure from the Indians to take to France with him an Algonkin youth he nicknamed Savignon. In a sense Brulé and Savignon were hostages for each other. Because both were vulnerable, neither was likely to be mistreated. Or so the Indians reasoned.

In the story he published of his adventures Champlain does not reveal why he did not stay in Canada that winter. Perhaps he hoped to take the sting from the year's poor showing by telling de Monts of the new victory over the Iroquois, of the potentially lucrative new rendezvous at Montreal, and of his placing deep in the interior a white youth who, while influencing the Indians in favor of the company, could also pick up valuable geographic secrets. Possibly, too, Champlain had learned from late arrivals in Canada that Henry IV had been assassinated on May 14, 1610, and he wanted to be on hand to learn what effect the death would have on the fortunes of the company. Could the widowed queen, ruling as regent for her nine-year-old son, Louis XIII, be persuaded to grant de Monts a new monopoly?

There was, in addition, this curious matter. In 1610, Champlain was between forty and forty-three years old. Unmarried, he had no heirs and evidently was beginning to think about his future. At any rate, shortly after reaching France he married, under a stiffly formal contract complete with complex dowry provisions, a girl named Hélène Boullé. She was twelve. The middle-aged bridegroom agreed not to consummate the marriage for two years unless Hélène's parents and their friends, after due consultations, decided that such activities would be acceptable.

In 1611, leaving his bride behind, he again returned early to Canada. When his longboats reached Montreal Island, no Indians were there. He used his free time selecting a site for a trading post a mile or two below the great rapids.

While his men were hewing logs, homesick Savignon, together with another Indian and a French youth named Louis, set out to meet the Hurons, who were expected to arrive by way of the Ottawa River. They carried a canoe around the rapids, paddled along the shore of the lake that the St. Lawrence forms on the south side of the island, and pushed a few miles up the lakelike mouth of the Ottawa. As the distance separating them from their friends increased and the silence of the forest closed about them, they began invisioning Iroquois war parties. Losing their nerve, they swung the canoe back toward the new post.

Hoping perhaps that they could forestall teasing by completing a significant adventure, they tried to run the rapids. The canoe capsized. Only Savignon managed to drag himself ashore. He fetched Champlain, to show him where the accident had occurred. The roar of the torrent and the fury of the cascades, Champlain wrote later, "made my hair stand on end." In memory of the dead Frenchman's patron saint, he named the rapids Sault St. Louis and the lake above them Lac St. Louis.*

By this time another horde of traders had arrived at the "secret" rendezvous. When the Indians began coming in, the eager competitors were ready with the most sophisticated display of trade goods yet seen in North America—shirts, hats, blankets, tools of many kinds, swords, dried prunes and raisins, hard tack, and even vegetable seeds. (The Hurons, it will be remembered, were an agricultural people.) Apparently brawls broke out during the haggling, and some of the chiefs told Champlain that they were worried by the presence of so many traders and unruly boatmen in their country.

To calm the Indians, and also to make arrangements for the future, Champlain proposed a private council on the upper side of the rapids. There he asked innumerable questions and watched intently as the Indians smoothed off a patch of forest ground and drew rough maps of distant lakes—probably Michigan and Superior —of which he had not yet heard. His ambition leaped. Recklessly he said that when he went to France that winter he would work out with the government means of eliminating some of the traders. Moreover, he would bring back to Canada forty or fifty soldiers with guns to keep order at the trading fairs and to complete the crushing of the Iroquois. He would bring priests to prepare the Indians for eternal life in heaven. He would also lead in settlers to live at Quebec and on Montreal Island, where the Indians would be welcome and where there would be factories to make the sort of things they wanted. Would the Hurons on their part show either him or his young men the way to the Western seas?

The Hurons said they would . . . some time.

The bargain was sealed with a feast. Afterward the Indians proposed to take Champlain back to his Montreal trading post in a

---

* Half a century later the rapids became known as Lachine in mockery of another great explorer, Robert Cavelier, Sieur de La Salle, who also thought for a time that the road to China might begin there.

canoe, running the same rapids where Louis and the Indian youth had died only days before. Perhaps it was a deliberate test: only courageous men could reach the Western Seas. Anyway, though Champlain could not swim, he dared not lose face now. With pretended calm he stepped into one of the fragile-looking craft.

Eight canoes made the run. The Indian paddlers, two and three to a canoe, were stark naked. They knew how to rise from kneeling to standing position in order to read the water ahead, how to slide with gathering speed down slick tongues of current that led into tumults of foam; how to distinguish between haystack waves that concealed no harm and ragged crests that hid boulders on whose lower sides were disastrous holes; how to veer bow or stern by digging their paddles against the current or with it, by stroking on the right side of the canoe or on the left. Champlain came to the landing place soaked through, shivering, and filled with renewed respect for the native craft and their navigators.

Two years later he took to canoeing in earnest. The events of the intervening months, most of them spent in France, demanded that he do so. First, the French government had finally allowed him and de Monts to form a stock company whose shares could be purchased by merchants interested in trading in Canada. Those who did not participate were barred from the traffic. To keep jealous outsiders from upsetting the arrangement, the company chose as its president an influential nobleman, the Prince de Condé. The regency also named de Condé Viceroy of New France. Since he had no intention of going there, he appointed Champlain his resident commander. Thus for the first time Champlain became responsible to the government as well as to a private company for his actions.

His headquarters were to be in Quebec. Financed by money obtained through the sale of company stock, he was to build whatever forts he deemed necessary, and enter into alliances with native tribes, whose members he should endeavor to convert to Catholicism. During such time as he had left over from supervising the trade, he was to search for a good road to China.

Arranging the many details kept Champlain in France throughout 1612. That fall, however, he did receive full reports from Pontgravé. More independents than ever, the Tadoussac trader said, had swarmed up to Montreal Island. There, swaggering and bullying, they had told the Indians that their friend Champlain, the one white they trusted, had not appeared because he was dead.

Even more unsettling was the story brought to France by a young passenger aboard Pontgravé's ship, Nicolas de Vignau. During the 1611 rendezvous at Montreal, Champlain had persuaded the Algonkins to let Vignau spend the winter with them along the Ottawa River. Their previous guest, Étienne Brulé, was thus freed to push still farther west with the Hurons.

Vignau, Pontgravé continued, had returned from the Ottawa with an extraordinary tale. He claimed that he had traveled by canoe to the shores of the great gulf of the north—a mere seventeen-day journey from Montreal Island. At the gulf he had seen the wreckage of an English ship. The local Indians, moreover, had shown him several scalps taken from the victims of the shipwreck. One young English boy still lived; the savages would deliver him to Champlain if ever the Frenchman visited their country.

Champlain's first thought was of Henry Hudson. Like every other educated man in western Europe, he knew by then that in the spring of 1611, after a winter in the frozen bay, a mutinous crew had cast the explorer and eight other men adrift in a small dinghy. The mutineers had then made their way home through ice floes and past embattled Eskimos to tell wild tales of a Northwest Passage reaching toward the Orient. The yarn created enough excitement so that instead of being punished, the sailors had been hired by a company of English speculators and sent out under Captain Thomas Button for another look at the bay. As all French navigators knew, Button had sailed west in April, 1612.

What a Pandora's box that man Hudson had opened! Already Dutch traders were on the river he had discovered south of the Richelieu in 1609—a river whose mouth, unlike that of the St. Lawrence's, was rarely closed by winter. Now the English were pushing into the bay on the north.

The dangers to New France were obvious. By allying themselves with the vengeful Iroquois, the Dutch could apply unremitting pressure from the south. In the north the English could take full-sized ships across Hudson's Bay into the very heart of the continent and intercept the flow of furs that once had traveled to the St. Lawrence.

The only way for the French to counter the dangers was to break out of the St. Lawrence Valley to the west and then swing north and south in an effort to contain these infections.

Sensing some of the implications, Pontgravé had brought Vignau to France so that the young man could report in person. By the time the lad arrived, he was well rehearsed. And yet, as Champlain listened, he was troubled. Vignau could hardly have mistaken the wreck of a dinghy for the wreck of a ship—but perhaps he had exaggerated in order to swell his importance. Equally questionable was his insistence that he had reached Hudson Bay by means of a short seventeen-day canoe trip from Montreal Island. Such a journey by no means accorded with what the Indians had told Champlain of distances. Still, Indian middlemen customarily exaggerated difficulties in an effort to keep whites from interfering with their inland customers. So perhaps Vignau was not as shifty as he seemed. In any event, it behooved Champlain to investigate.

With Vignau firmly in tow he reached Montreal Island during the last week of May, 1613. The few Indians who were there told him that the majority of the Hurons and Algonkins thought he was dead and were not coming to the rendezvous. In view of the Indians' longing for European goods the statement seems unlikely, but Champlain used it as another reason for venturing into the interior. He must round up customers.

The Indians at Montreal declined to cooperate. He could hire only one to serve as combined guide and paddler. Refusing to give up, he determined to man his two twenty-foot canoes with French —five of them, himself included. It was a reckless decision. Except for Vignau none of the whites had had more than minimal experience with the craft.

Predictably the journey up the Ottawa turned into a nightmare. Almost immediately the tyros ran into the Long Sault, a set of three closely spaced rapids that whitened the river for twelve miles. Where the nature of the shore allowed, the travelers moved forward on foot, dragging the canoes, laden with equipment, gifts and samples of trade goods, behind them with cords of braided rawhide. Where footing on land was impossible, they took hold of opposite gunwales of the canoes and waded ahead. In swift water, it was a stumbling agony. At one point Champlain, his muscles still soft from the long ocean voyage, sprawled headlong into a deep eddy and nearly lost both his life and the canoe.

Where travel by water was impossible, the men had to carry canoes and goods on their backs. Each portage required several trips back and forth. One devoured three days. Insects tormented the travelers; their beds were stony and miserable; food was hastily prepared and tasteless. Only the Indian, his eyes often contemptuous, seemed untroubled.

After seven days of toil they met fifteen canoes of Algonkins headed down stream. The Indians clucked in astonishment. The whites had done amazingly well to come this far, but they could not possibly navigate what lay ahead. It was the old ploy—too hard. Champlain turned it aside and even persuaded one of the Algonkins to join the party in the place of the least useful Frenchman, who was sent downstream with the Indians.

Thanks to their guides, they were able to avoid a twisting, rapid-torn section of the Ottawa by turning up a side stream. They crossed twelve small lakes, separated from each other by difficult portages through down timber, and scrambled with their loads over a small hill to another tributary. This carried them to a wide stretch of the Ottawa later known as Lac des Allumettes. On an island in the lake stood the major village of the Algonkins, placed there so that the inhabitants could exact toll from all who passed.

The villagers, fine-looking people handsomely dressed and garishly painted, greeted the French warmly but refused to help them go farther. Too hard. Champlain scoffed: Vignau had gone farther. The statement put the Indians into a passion. Vignau was a liar. He had never traveled past the lake where they now were.

Confronted by Champlain and the glowering chiefs, Vignau confessed. Yes, he had lied.

In his memoirs Champlain implies that the lad had made up his story out of whole cloth. But the correspondence between his invention and Henry Hudson's fate is too remarkable to be mere coincidence. One suspects that during his stay with the Algonkins he had heard tales of the wreckage of Hudson's dinghy—he might well have understood the Indians to mean "ship," a conveyance unfamiliar to most of them—and of the lifting of the scalps. Perhaps one Englishman did survive as a captive for a time. Of such hearsay he spun his tale, the hero of his own melodrama. It worked better than he thought, and by the time he reached France he was so afraid of consequences that he concentrated simply on being convincing.

Now he was disgraced, and the whites with him shared his humiliation. Venturing farther was no longer possible. But at least Champlain knew that Hudson Bay could not be reached by canoe from Montreal Island in seventeen days. More important, his two-hundred-mile trip up the Ottawa had given him a clear insight into the nature of travel into the interior. The next time it would not be so hard to go still farther.

Better still, he found customers ready to bargain and descended the Ottawa at headlong speed with a flotilla of sixty fur-laden canoes. There were Hurons in the group, and during the trip they complained to him about the Iroquois. Now that the ancient foes were in contact with the Dutch, they were growing bolder than ever. What of the white soldiers and the priests Champlain had promised? He found lame excuses and said that when he next returned from France he would help his friends without fail.

Two more years passed before he could keep that agreement. Again he spent the time in France. The company needed reorganizing so that its financial base could be broadened. Some of that new money Champlain wanted to use for strengthening Quebec. Quebec, he argued, *was* New France, for in 1613 sea raiders from England had destroyed the tiny habitations of Acadia. That left the cluster of buildings beside the gray cliffs of the St. Lawrence the only French settlement in North America—if "settlement" was the proper word for so meager a place. No families lived there; no farmers tilled the soil. The inhabitants consisted solely of traders, clerks, and artisans whose numbers dwindled each winter to a handful of disgruntled exiles who scarcely bothered to keep the buildings in repair.

Champlain hoped to change all that. He wanted to install husbandmen along with their wives and children. He urged the company to build one fort atop the Quebec bluffs, another at the mouth of the St. Maurice River, and a third on Montreal Island. A devout Catholic, he recommended that missionaries be sent along with the Indians, a move that would help bind them more strongly to the French.

He received only crumbs. As soon as the stockholders realized that the government would not help and that all improvements would have to be paid for out of the profits of the trade, they dragged their feet. Although Champlain was authorized to take out six settlers in 1615, no money was appropriated for sustaining them until they became self-supporting and so none came. He received no money for forts, and in place of soldiers he was given only the right to impress for short periods of time five men from each of the company's ships. At best he could hope for a grand total of twenty, none of them trained in military procedures. But he did have one cause for rejoicing. In 1615 the Bishops of France agreed to provide four missionaries—three ordained priests and one lay helper—from the Récollet brotherhood, an austere order of Franciscans.

The friars made up in enthusiasm what they lacked in numbers. After landing in Quebec in May, 1615, the one who concerns us here, Joseph Le Caron, rushed off ahead of Champlain to Montreal Island, where he prevailed on the Hurons at the rendezvous to let him accompany them to their homeland, by then commonly called Huronia. When Champlain appeared a little later, they demanded that he fulfill his promise to help them defeat the Iroquois. They said that as soon as they were home they would gather a war party of 2,500 men. If the French supported them with their thunder tubes, victory would be assured.

Thus beset, Champlain agreed, although affairs at Quebec were in grave need of attention. He sent twelve "soldiers" off with several score Indians and Le Caron, the latter ill-equipped for canoe travel in his long gray cassock and wooden sandals. After a flying trip to Quebec, Champlain followed. His companions were ten Hurons, plus his personal servant, name unknown, and Étienne Brulé. Only two canoes were available. Though they were as large as any the Indians made, perhaps twenty-five feet long, thirteen men, their equipment and the inevitable gifts for the chiefs of Huronia overcrowded them badly.

In spite of that the journey did not seem as physically galling as before. Champlain knew what to expect and this time he was traveling with experts. But living conditions were difficult. Meals consisted of a mush called *sagamité*. Its basic element was pounded corn taken from caches the Hurons had left in the forest when journeying to Montreal earlier in the summer. Into the bubbling gruel they tossed chunks of whatever game they managed to catch around the camp, often muskrats, and whatever fish they hooked by trolling from the moving canoes. The meat was never washed, the fish seldom gutted, the crusted kettles rarely cleaned. Because the Indians disliked stopping once they were underway, they urinated either into the kettles or into the birchbark bowls from which they ate and, if it was convenient, tossed the liquid overboard, indifferent about whether or not they rinsed the receptacles afterwards.

They passed Lake Allumettes, near whose upper end pine-topped cliffs rose five hundred feet above water that to the travelers was unfathomably deep. They portaged around the wild Des Joachims rapids and, where the Ottawa begins to bend northward, entered the east-flowing Mattawa. During the next forty rugged, rocky miles they made eleven portages before reaching Trout Lake. From there they lugged their gear and canoes over the granite ridges that separate Ottawa drainage from that flowing into Lake Huron.

A short paddle brought them to Lake Nipissing, nearly forty miles long but shallow. Here they found a village of Nipissing Indians, sharp traders whose quest for furs took them north to Hudson Bay and west as far as Lake Superior. The travelers paused with them for two days, talking geography—Champlain was fascinated—and feasting on the huge sturgeon and trout the Indians netted from the lake. Then, following the southern shore, they made their way to what very early became known as the French River, a seventy-mile run through tortured granite to the northern protrusion of Lake Huron that is now called Georgian Bay.

The trip opened Champlain's eyes to many things. One was the nature of the Canadian Shield. In following the Ottawa they had skirted for upward of three hundred miles one small edge of that enormous mass of ice-polished rock. Now they were encased by it and by its dense, shallow-rooted forests. The one relief was water— endless streams, bogs, ponds, lakes. Already Champlain was beginning to sense, half intuitively, what modern statistics later confirmed —that 25 percent of all Canada is covered with water. Forget wagons, horses, and pack trains. Summertime travel in such a land was impossible except in the remarkable canoes the Indians had invented.

Another essential was lightweight food that would not spoil. The distances that travelers had to cover in a limited time was such that they could not pause for hunting or fishing, activities that all too often were unproductive anyway. As a solution the Indians south of the Shield had discovered dried corn, a valuable item of trade with tribes that dwelt farther north where furs were plentiful but agriculture out of the question. The Iroquois tilled miles of such cornfields. So did the Hurons. But since the days of Jacques Cartier, there had been no corn in the St. Lawrence Valley—a defect that added still more force to Champlain's argument in favor of introducing settlers.

At the many-channeled mouth of the French River, Champlain at last came upon one of the huge inland seas, Lake Huron, that since 1603 had occupied so much of his thinking. Afterward he said very little about what he felt. But it was a bright day in August, and he must have been able to look across miles of glinting blueness broken by a multitude of islands, some huge and some mere dots with only a single twisted evergreen on their tortoiselike backs. Probably, too, he scooped up a handful of the cold water. Once he had supposed that it would taste salty, but from Brulé and perhaps even earlier from the Indians he had learned better. Still, there was a certain significance in the gesture and the tasting. Wtih them he accepted the enormousness of a continent that could hold such a lake, which he named Mer de l'Eau Douce, "sea of sweet water." And there were more seas beyond. How far they extended not even the Indians could tell.

Yet lakes can be crossed. One imagines him exchanging glances with Brulé. Thanks to the Indians, they had found their way this far by a route that avoided both the Iroquois and the rapids of the upper St. Lawrence, including Niagara Falls. Some day . . . but right now priorities lay to the southeast, in Huronia.

VI

Defeats

To Champlain Huronia was a delight. The nation embraced about 800 square miles of stream-laced forest and meadow between the sparkling waters of Lake Simcoe and the southeastern tip of Georgian Bay. The fertility of the soil was evident in broad gardens of squash, pumpkins, melons, and beans and in such enormous fields of corn that a stranger wandering along the intersecting paths among the stalks could easily become lost.

Four related tribes made up the Huron confederacy. The two largest and strongest were the Attignaouantan, or Bear People, and the Attigneenongnahac, the Cord People. Relative newcomers were the Arendahronon, or Rock People, and the Tohontaenrat, the Deer People. Altogether the bands occupied some twenty villages that were duplicates of those already described in connection with the Iroquois. Their combined population lay somewhere between 30,000 and 35,000.

To priests brought up in the quiet of seminaries, the towns were appalling. Garbage and human waste stunk in the streets. The smoke-filled longhouses swarmed with fleas, noisy children, and yapping dogs that contested with human occupants for sleeping space and food, sometimes even snatching morsels from the dishes of the eaters.

It was different with secular whites brought up in the poverty and squalor of France's overcrowded cities. They enjoyed the Indian towns. They were treated as equals by a hospitable and generous people. They could hunt and fish as they liked, pursuits closed to their class by the great estates that blanketed Europe. Best of all, in their eyes, was the eager sexuality of unmarried girls willing to experiment, in return for trifling gifts, however a man wished. The Indians as a whole, moreover, were happy, playful, and ingenious. They sang and danced at the least excuse, and were much given, when circumstances were appropriate, to theatrical ceremonies. To the young Frenchmen who had come along as housebuilders for missionary Joseph Le Caron and as soldiers for Champlain, the experience was a revelation.

The villages were not permanent. The wooden houses often caught fire from the open hearths inside, and, if the wind was up, much of the town might have to be rebuilt. Eventually sanitation problems forced a move to a clean site. The fields were another cause of mobility. Corn is a notorious depleter of soil, and because the Indians did not fertilize the ground, they had to search out fresh fields every ten years or so. First they killed the trees in a convenient area by girdling the trunks with axes and building fires at their bases. After the dead limbs had dried, climbers broke them off to let in more sunlight; then the women planted the newly opened area and, as the crops took root, the village was moved nearby—no great feat inasmuch as the houses consisted of little more than poles and bark. Palisades were more difficult to erect, and occasionally a village would go a dangerously long time without protection.

In view of all the building, planting, harvesting, fishing, hunting, trading, and fighting that filled each year, it is hard to believe that the Hurons were as lazy as some observers portrayed them. Still, Champlain found it hard to set them into motion against the Iroquois. Chiefs had to be summoned into council. There were feasts, dances, and bragging speeches designed to generate courage. Emissaries, including young Brulé, were sent south of Lake Erie to bring a force of friendly Andastes (Susquehannans) to a rendezvous near the Hurons' target, an Onondagan town located in the vicinity of present-day Syracuse, New York.

Early in September the Huron army—it numbered far fewer than the 2,500 men promised—began its eastward journey through the maze of streams and lakes north of Lake Ontario. Accompanying it were a few Nipissings and Algonkins, and a dozen or so whites led by Samuel de Champlain. Twenty-five days of hard paddling and portaging brought them to Ontario's eastern end. Slipping from island to island, they crossed the lovely entrance to the St. Lawrence and then journeyed some distance south along the lake's eastern shore. Scouts found suitable coves where they hid their canoes before beginning a stealthy march through hardwood forests festooned with grape vines and blazing with the reds and golds of autumn.

They reached the Onondaga village on the afternoon of October 10, 1615. Surprise failed when the enemy spotted and skirmished briefly with the Huron advanced guard before fleeing inside the town. Storming the walls then became necessary, a formidable undertaking because, Champlain wrote later, the defenses consisted of "four good palisades, which were made of great pieces of wood, interlaced with each other . . . and thirty feet high." Inside were galleries from which the Iroquois could rain arrows and stones on anyone approaching the town.

Under the supervision of the French the Hurons built a movable wooden cavalier, or tower, high enough to overlook the walls. They also constructed several parapets which, when the time came, could be advanced against the base of the palisades so that the latter could be set afire. The first part of the plan worked perfectly. On a cold, windy morning two hundred Hurons strong-armed the tower up close to the village. While arrows flew and a hideous yelling arose from both sides, three Frenchmen armed with harquebuses climbed the cavalier's sheltered side to the top and poured such a volley over the wall that the defenders on the galleries inside dropped in consternation to the ground. Unbearably excited, Huron sappers then pushed their parapets to the base of the walls and kindled fires—but in the wrong places, where the strong wind blew the flames away from the wooden pilings. When small fires did take hold, the Onondagans were able to extinguish them with water dumped from above.

Champlain stood in the middle of the melee, bellowing orders that went unheeded in the din. After three hours of confusion the attackers withdrew. Unbelievably, their casualties numbered only eighteen wounded, including Champlain, whose leg and knee had been painfully injured by arrows. In spite of his hurt, he tried to rally the forces for another attack, but the Hurons demurred, saying that they wanted to wait for the Andastes whom Brulé was supposedly leading to their assistance.

Four days dragged by. Emboldened by the attackers' lethargy, hit-and-run Onondagan war parties harassed the camp. Losing heart, the Hurons decided to retreat without further waiting. Those who could not walk, and Champlain was among their number, were lashed into wooden backpack frames, hoisted on the shoulders of stout warriors, and carried. "It was impossible," the captain declared in his account, "to move any more than a little child in swaddling clothes. . . . Never did I find myself in such hell."

Two days after their departure, 500 Andastes reached the rendezvous. After reading in the litter strewn everywhere the story of what had happened, they prudently withdrew—a useless errand.

On reaching the canoes, Champlain tried to borrow one so that he and some of his French could hurry straight down the St. Lawrence to Montreal and Quebec before the freeze-up. In a pet because of their defeat, the Hurons refused to let him have one. Their excuse was that if the French were not drowned in the rapids, they would be captured by the Iroquois. It was much better, they said, for them to return to Huronia.

It was too late in the year to use canoes on the return journey. After reaching Lake Ontario's northeastern shore, the bedraggled force went into camp, waiting for enough snow to fall so that they could travel on snowshoes, dragging their equipment on sledges. For Champlain, wounded and unused to snowshoeing, the journey was another hell.

Nothing in his writings indicates that he ever realized how portentous the defeat was. Dismissing it from his considerations, he spent hours of the long winter nights asking his usual questions about the west. He heard more about Lake Superior, which at times (his accounts and maps are by no means clear) he seems to have confused with a western arm of the North Sea, or Hudson Bay. He was told of a people in the remote west who were "like Frenchmen in color and other respects." Could this tale, which the Hurons related only as hearsay, be true? "Only time and the courage of some person of means, who can or will undertake this project, can decide." Meanwhile there was much to do closer at hand. As soon as the weather allowed, Champlain struck out along the shore of the lake to visit a nearby tribe that was new to him, the Ottawas, adept traders whom he called *les Cheveux Relevés*, "high hairs," because of their upswept hairdos.

Throughout his stay in Huronia, he studied his hosts closely. Elements of real strength were there, he decided. But to realize their potentials, the Indians would need a large number of missionaries to teach them, and good French settlers to live among them and by example "wean them from their filthy habits, loose morals, and rude licenses." Settlers, note, including young whites married to Indian girls. These stable people, supported by fields of great fertility, could build beside the Sweetwater Sea a base from which the fur trade could spread and the route to the Pacific be found.

In his calculations he should not have dismissed the Iroquois so cavalierly. In their minds they had decisively beaten the French and Hurons in spite of the white men's noisy harquebuses and movable wooden tower. Moreover, the Dutch were now solidly established at Fort Nassau, where the Mohawk River runs into the Hudson. (Later Nassau would become Fort Orange and then Albany.) Their sloops supplied the post at lower cost than the French could supply Quebec. Their demand for furs was as intense as that of Champlain's company. To the Iroquois the logic was plain: divert the flow of furs from the Ottawa and St. Lawrence rivers to the Mohawk and the Hudson. If that meant removing the Hurons, Algonkins, Nipissings, and Ottawas as the dominant middlemen of the fur trade, so be it. Even when allied with the French, those tribes, it was evident now, could be handled. And so, undetected still by Champlain, the 150-year war for the control of the upper half of North America began to take shape.

The flotilla of fur-laden canoes that Le Caron and the governor accompanied eastward reached Quebec without incident on July 11, 1616, to the joy of friends who had given them up for dead. Champlain spent three weeks catching up with the affairs of the tiny settlement and then, on August 3, sailed for France to urge his plan for expansion on the company. As he must have expected, the directors only smiled sourly. They had no intention of spending money then or in the future on pursuits not related to immediate profits.

Champlain never again went into the interior, although he often talked to the Indians about doing so. He was chained by administrative chores. Each year the volume of trade increased. Beginning in 1618, young Canada exported between 15,000 and 20,000 beaver skins each year, to say nothing of other furs. Giving gifts to and holding feasts for the chiefs whose people brought in the pelts used up much of each summer. Meanwhile the furs had to be beaten free of dust, graded, inventoried, pressed into bundles, and loaded on shipboard. Estimates had to be made of the quantity and kind of trade goods that would be needed the following year, and long lists of orders drawn up. The requirements of the settlement, which still produced no food for its own use, had to be prepared for.

The burden of overseeing all this fell on Champlain's shoulders. Increasingly they were tired shoulders. He had never spared himself physically. Not the least of his trials were his repeated crossings of the Atlantic in the stinking, tossing, wretchedly uncomfortable little ships of the day. Few journeys to and from Quebec lasted less than six weeks; most were longer. Between his first visit to the St. Lawrence in the spring of 1603 and the fall of 1618 Champlain made sixteen crossings—eight round trips. He yearned to settle down, and in 1620 he tried, bringing his wife, Hélène, to Quebec to live.

He was at least fifty then; she was twenty-two. The "habitation" at Quebec, never cared for during the winters when Champlain was absent, was in deplorable shape. Including the three servants Hélène brought with her, there were no more than half a dozen white women in all New France to whom she could talk. Yet she bore herself well until finally she was able to return to France in August, 1624.

Like Hélène, Governor Champlain needed patience. The company not only refused to foster expansion into Huronia, but also vetoed his repeated urgings that the directors authorize a fort at Three Rivers and plant a settlement on Montreal Island. Because the directors feared (accurately as matters developed) that a resident population would compete with the company for the furs of the Indians, they refused to take more than a token number of settlers to the St. Lawrence. In addition, several of the principal stockholders were Hugenots and were opposed to anything that might help the Récollet brothers win new Catholics in the Indian villages.

Limited thus by niggardliness, routine chores, and flagging

energies, Champlain had to depend on his famed young men to act as his eyes in the wilderness. The first and farthest traveled of them was Étienne Brulé. After the fiasco at the Onondaga village, Brulé had wandered with a party of Andastes down the Susquehanna River to Chesapeake Bay and back again. Afterward, while trying to return to Huronia, he had been captured by Senecas and had endured the beginnings of torture before providentially escaping during a violent thunderstorm. After recuperating in Huronia, he accompanied the Indians in 1618 to the rendezvous at Three Rivers, where he reported in full to Champlain.

Brulé liked his life. According to the missionaries, he was a notorious womanizer. Without objection he returned at Champlain's behest to Lake Huron and during the next five years spent as much time as he could on the islands and inlets of Georgian Bay, learning the lie of the convoluted land and acting as company salesman among the bands of Indians he encountered, especially the Ottawas. In 1623 he and another of the young men, this one remembered simply as Grenolle, set out at Champlain's request to find the sea now known as Lake Superior and examine the copper mines that provided the metal valued so highly by the Indians. Still more important, the pair were directed to bring about peace among the warring tribes and then to urge the western Indians to come with their furs to the great trading fairs beside the St. Lawrence.

Presumably Indians accompanied the two Frenchmen on their long cast westward, although the scanty references to the trip that survive in fur trade literature make no mention of red companions. In any event, with or without guides, the whites worked their way into Lake Huron's North Channel, a breathtakingly beautiful passageway that stretches 150 miles or more between the rugged mainland and a long chain of sheltering islands, big and small. The Channel brought them to the wild jumble of boulders over which the outlet stream of Lake Superior foams as it rushes down into Lake Huron—the famed Sault Ste. Marie of later times, relished by the Indians for its delicious whitefish and its strategic location. Here was the hub of some of the continent's principal waterways. After negotiating the rapids, paddlers could go west into Lake Superior, east into Lake Huron, or south into Lake Michigan, all of them gateways to enormous territories.

Did the two Frenchmen venture past the Sault into Lake Superior? No one really knows. They did bring back an ingot of copper, together with new geographic data that Champlain incorporated into later maps. One important item was the revelation that Superior (Champlain called it simply Grand Lac) was not connected directly with Hudson Bay. Westward, the explorers reported, were the hunting grounds of tribes, probably Sioux and related Assiniboines, of whom the Indians at the Sault were deathly afraid. Beyond the lands frequented by those awesome Indians, it was said, were more huge lakes—always lakes, beckoning endlessly. And yet, ironically, Brulé and Grenolle completely missed nearby Lake Michigan, probably because they assumed from talk they heard that it was no more than a southern extension of Lake Huron.

Another of Champlain's young men, greater than Brulé—eventually he would find Lake Michigan for the French—was Jean Nicolet. Nicolet had reached Quebec as a company employee, aged twenty, in 1618. Because he had an unusually retentive memory and a quick ear for language, Champlain sent him to Lac des Allumettes in the Ottawa River to serve his wilderness apprenticeship with the Algonkins. The tribe took to him immediately, and it was as a diplomat rather than as an explorer that Nicolet rendered his first notable services. When the Mohawks astounded Quebec by asking Champlain to arrange peace between them and the Algonkins and Montagnais, it was Nicolet who led the delegation of northern Indians to the conference.

Peace sealed, he began a nine years' residence with another Algonquian people, the Nipissings. He married a Nipissing woman, raised children in the principal villages beside the lake that bears the tribe's name, and was accepted as an Indian during council meetings. No white man ever mastered the widespread Algonquian dialects and the Algonquian view of the world any better than did Jean Nicolet.

The peace treaty he helped formulate was shakily founded, through no fault of his. The Mohawks had sought it as a matter of strategy, to protect their northern flanks while they dealt with the Mohegans (or Mohicans, still another Algonquian tribe) in a struggle to control the fur trade in present-day New York. Champlain nevertheless had high hopes for the pact. As long as it was observed, the Hurons and Algonkins would not have to fear ambush as they carried their furs to the St. Lawrence. He was dismayed, accordingly, when the company directors told him sharply that they did not approve of peace with the Iroquois confederacy. For, if fighting ended, then the western Indians might start dealing through the Iroquois with the Dutch, who had cheaper goods than the French, and then their furs would be lost to the company.

Cynicism like that ruled too many of the firm's decisions, and in the end it brought about the company's downfall. The Récollet friars, who had received scant cooperation from any of the directors except Champlain, found that their order's vows of abject poverty prevented proper maintenance of their mission stations. They therefore asked help from the wealthier Jesuits, who acceded gladly. The first black robes reached Quebec in 1625. They sized up the state of affairs there very quickly and at once achieved what the Récollets could not—they reached the ear of Cardinal Richelieu, chief minister to King Louis XIII. In their letters they excoriated the company's opposition to peace, to missionary activity, and to settlement, but absolved Champlain from blame, stating that he had tried in vain to further constructive policies.

Richelieu's response was immediate. He canceled the charter of the old company and in April, 1627, personally formed a new one that he hoped would meet the obligations its predecessor had ignored. Officially the creation was called the Compagnie de la Nouvelle France. More commonly it was known as the Hundred Associates, since 100 wealthy men were invited to subscribe 3,000 *livres* each in order to share in the company's sweeping privileges. As a firm the associates were to hold seigneurial title to North America from the Arctic Circle to Spanish Florida—Dutch claims were ignored—and from Newfoundland to the Sweetwater Sea. Seigneurial title meant that the company could grant ownership of generous tracts of land to whoever agreed to clear part of it for agriculture and bring in settlers to till it. More practically, the Compagnie de la Nouvelle France also received a permanent monopoly to the fur trade.

In exchange for these privileges, the Associates agreed that by 1643 they would transport at their own expense 4,000 settlers to New France, two hundred of them the first year. No provisions were made for any kind of self-government. Neither foreigners nor Protestants were to be allowed inside the colony. Missionary work was to be pressed, a stipulation arising from the strong religious revival then shaking France. Again Champlain was named governor of both the colony and the company.

Prodded to unusual speed by Richelieu, the Hundred Associates in April, 1628, started 200 settlers, an unknown number of employees, and ample supplies across the Atlantic in a fleet whose size is disputed by historians. Protection, however, was inadequate. England and France had gone to war again, and two half-French, half-Scottish adventurers named Kirke, deciding to capitalize on the trouble, obtained letters of marque from England's monarch, Charles I. With next to no effort their warships captured Tadoussac and then forced the surrender of the approaching fleet.

David Kirke next pushed his way as far up the St. Lawrence as he dared and sent a polite note to Champlain, asking him to surrender. With equal politeness Champlain declined. The Kirkes thereupon returned to England with their booty, confident that Quebec's hungry residents, deprived of their anticipated supplies, would sing a different tune in the spring.

It was a rough winter. About seventy-five whites, mostly males, gathered inside the decrepit habitation. The strongest of them Champlain sent into the forest to live with the Indians. The rest, who had to haul firewood from long distances, subsisted on a few ounces of gruel a day, enlivened now and then by a moose steak or a smoked eel purchased from the Indians. By spring the few children in the town were crying from hunger, and adults who still had strength enough to do so were scouring the woods for edible roots. Matters were not helped when Jesuit missionary Jean de Brébeuf and several French laymen arrived from Huronia with the fur canoes—but without food for either themselves or their Indians.

Among the newcomers from the west were four of Champlain's young men, Étienne Brulé and Nicolas Mersolet, who had survived the scurvy-ridden winter of 1608 with him, and two of whom nothing is known except their names, Baillif and Rayé. Thinking perhaps that they could fare better on their own, the quartet headed downstream in canoes. En route they met three of the Kirke brothers' ships groping upward for the coup de grace and having all kinds of trouble finding the right channel among the river's many islands. The famished Frenchmen promptly signed on as pilots.

The ships dropped anchor at Quebec on July 19, 1629. Convinced at last that aid was not going to reach him and stunned by the defection of his young men, Champlain capitulated.

Unhappily for themselves, the Kirkes had been too leisurely. Quebec's surrender occurred after England and France had signed an armistice on April 29, 1629. When the peace treaty of Saint-Germaine-en-Laye was ratified in the spring of 1632, Acadia and Canada were returned to France in exchange for Louis XIII's payment of 400,000 crowns to Charles I, the dowry promised Louis's sister on her marriage to the English king.

A few French traders reached the St. Lawrence that same year, 1632. They found Quebec in ruins and the Indians debauched by English rum. They also learned from the Hurons who came to the shrunken rendezvous that in the spring Étienne Brulé had committed some offense, its exact nature never revealed, that had led the Hurons to club him to death, dismember his corpse, boil it, and eat it.

An aftermath of the grisly deed caused some trouble to Champlain. He reached Quebec in May, 1633, with three ships carrying supplies, a few soldiers, several settlers, and Canada's first livestock —ten cows, two heifers, and one small bull. The Indians whom he met at the annual rendezvous greeted him joyfully. The Hurons, however, were conspicuously absent. He soon learned why. The Algonkins had stopped the western flotilla—140 canoes filled with furs—at Allumettes Island by saying that Champlain intended to punish the tribe for the murder of Brulé.

The trick was transparent: the Algonkins hoped the Hurons would be so frightened that they would sell their furs at a bargain price and go home. Champlain countered by rushing an emissary up the Ottawa with word that he longed to see his old friends. They need not worry about Brulé; because of the young man's treachery he was no longer considered a Frenchman and no reprisals would be exacted from the beaver-laden Hurons because of his death.

The outcome was the finest collection of furs yet dispatched from Canada. The hope it bred for the future added zest to Champlain's sixty-three (possibly sixty-six) years. Eagerly he reconstructed Quebec and then, aided by several newly arrived Jesuits, began clearing land atop the cliff for a chapel expressing thanks for the deliverance of New France. He ordered work begun on the long-deferred fort at Three Rivers, and nodded approval as the Associates began offering fine seignorial grants along the river to employees who would bring their families across the ocean to join them.

Now for the West. He went into conference with Jean Nicolet, who had been persuaded to leave the Nipissings in order to act as the company's chief agent and interpreter at Three Rivers. Would Jean travel to the farthest of the inland seas, taking Hurons with him so that he could make peace between those Indians and a distant tribe, the Puants (or "stinkers") with whom they had once dealt but with whom they had lately gone to war, to the detriment of their fur gathering? On top of that, would Jean stay alert for information about the remote people who were rumored to look like Frenchmen and also about possible routes to China? The constant wings of hope: the name "stinker" just might derive from the salty, seaweed smell of an ocean.

Nicolet agreed to go. Both men must have been sanguine of success, for when the explorer packed his gear he included a grand robe described by the *Jesuit Relation* for 1642–43 as being made "of China damask, all strewn with flowers and birds of many colors." When meeting Orientals, as he obviously expected to do, Jean Nicolet wanted to be dressed not as an Indian or even as a Frenchman, but as a proper Chinese dignitary. That famous robe, mentioned in all frontier histories, could hardly have come from any other place than Champlain's own trunk. With what pangs, one wonders, did the aging father of Canada give up his own hopes of some day wearing it himself at a meeting with the Grand Khan?

Nicolet's western push coincided with the return of three Jesuits to Huronia. They, too, were filled with high hopes. Richelieu had given their order an exclusive spiritual monopoly over New France, and after talking with Champlain they envisioned, as he did, a Christianized Huron nation serving as an advanced base for both the spread of Catholic doctrine and the fur trade. The unfriendliness of the Indians who took them along did not dim their enthusiasm one bit.

Father Jean de Brébeuf, who had worked in Huronia in 1626–28 excused the ill-nature on the grounds of "sickness among our Savages." Some sort of plague had visited Huronia the previous fall, curtailing essential harvesting and fishing. The sickness, he reported in the *Jesuit Relation* of 1636, "began with violent fever, which was followed by a sort of measles or smallpox," but how serious the epidemic was or how it would affect his fortunes and those of New France he could not yet realize.

Nicolet traveled with Brébeuf as far as Lake Nipissing. There the peacemaker paused for personal reasons. When he resumed his journey, seven Huron Indians were with him. Because the travelers carried trade goods, they probably used at least two canoes for retracing Brulé's route through the sparkling waters of North Channel.

At Sault Ste. Marie they gave a new direction to the French exploration of upper North America. They bent south. After skirting more islands, they entered a forest-bordered strait so narrow that today a mighty bridge soars across it in a single span. Commanding this narrow waterway was one of the loveliest of all islands, oval shaped, two miles across by three long, humped so that it looked like a turtle floating lazily in the sun. "Green Turtle," indeed, was its name or, as the Ojibway (Chippewa) Indians said, Michilimackinac.

Michilimackinac Strait (it was named later for the island) opened into Lake Michigan. The lake curved far to the south, but at first the explorers did not realize that. They had to keep close to the upper shore, which there runs west, while they watched the horizon warily for the fast-rising thunder squalls that could bring disaster to birchbark canoes. Coasting thus, they were not aware of leaving the main lake and entering an arm of water that later men would name *La Baye Verte*, Green Bay.

Bordering Green Bay was the land of the Puants, the "stinkers," or, as the tribesmen called themselves, Winnebagos. No one today is sure why outsiders referred to them as "stinkers"; some anthropologists speculate that the name may have been a consequence of their predominantly fish diet and of the fish entrails that littered their villages.

The Winnebagos were a Siouan tribe, inclined toward belligerence. Nicolet and his fellow explorers paddled cautiously. Now and then they landed, set sticks into the ground, and dangled gifts from them. They felt eerily that they were being watched, and the offerings they displayed were designed to inform suspicious war parties that they came as friends.

By means that Nicolet never bothered to record, they eventually made contact with a few Winnebagos somewhere near the mouth of the Fox River at the southwestern tip of Green Bay. Communication was stumbling, for the Siouan tongue was strange both to the Hurons, who spoke an Iroquoian dialect, and to Nicolet, whose forte was Algonquian. (The famed sign language of the American Indians was used primarily on the Great Plains.) But somehow introductions were completed, and then the Puants, accompanied by one Huron, hurried ahead to prepare the main villages for the new arrivals.

Four thousand Winnebagos marched out to greet them. As they approached, Nicolet donned his robe of Chinese damask and, for show, gripped a pistol in either hand. Did he really expect to be met by people who would at least have heard about Chinese clothing? Or, knowing the Indians love for flamboyance, was he simply hoping to impress them with an exotic display?

Certainly he did impress them. Each chief held a great feast for him—the main course at one banquet consisted of 120 beaver—and at each ceremony the visitors had to endure sonorous speeches they scarcely comprehended. Afterward there were peace talks and promises of renewed trade with the far-ranging middlemen of Huronia. Whenever he could, Nicolet scratched maps in the earth and asked persistent questions. Was there a sea—Big Water may be the term by which he tried to express the concept—somewhere in the west? The Puants nodded vigorously. They were thinking of the Mississippi River, truly a Big Water, but that wasn't what Nicolet understood.

In the fall of 1635, after a trip that possibly took the explorers as far down Lake Michigan as the Illinois country, Nicolet carried the word of his findings back to Quebec. Did he converse with Champlain? We do not know. The governor suffered a stroke in October and died on Christmas day. Between times he was probably lucid only at intervals. Still, one likes to think that the young man sat beside his bed during one of those moments of clarity and told the governor what we know he later told Jesuit Father Paul Le Jeune: if circumstances had allowed him to travel a few days more along the rivers of present-day Wisconsin, he would have reached the sea.

And so perhaps Champlain died with the joy of accomplishment in his heart. The difficult days of launching the colony were over, he thought, and substantial growth was beginning at last. His work and that of the young men he had inspired had opened vast new areas to European civilization. The missionaries could bring new tribes to Christ; the Hurons, their canoes laden with fresh supplies of western fur, could bring increased prosperity to his company. That wealth in turn would help create for France a colonial empire rivaling Spain's. Best of all was Nicolet's assurance that Champlain had been right: Frenchmen would soon be traveling to the Pacific by means of a relatively short water route through the heart of North America.

For those who survived Champlain, the hopes of colonial betterment proved as illusory as the notion of a sea at the western edges of Wisconsin. The exceptional fur harvest of 1633 proved insufficient to erase the debts the Hundred Associates had incurred first from the loss of their fleet to the Kirkes and afterwards from three tradeless seasons during the time the English held Quebec. Even more discouraging, the anticipated increase in the number of furs transported out of the Lake Michigan area following the Huron-Winnebago peace failed to materialize, for reasons soon to be noticed.

Needing cash to stave off its creditors, the company leased its charter to a tight little syndicate composed of a handful of its own members. This syndicate sought to recover its investment by concentrating on the fur trade while ignoring settlement. By 1640 the entire white population of New France amounted to only 359 persons. (By contrast, consider Massachusetts. Of the 102 persons who landed at Plymouth in 1620, fifty-eight perished, an attrition rate comparable to Quebec's in 1608–1609. Yet by 1640, nearly 14,000 people lived in the English colony.) Indeed, the only substantial single addition to Canada's population during the decade following Champlain's death was produced not by those legally responsible for it, but by fifty-odd zealous Catholics who in 1642 established what they called Ville Marie on Montreal Island, forerunner of the more secular city of Montreal.

Comparable zeal fired the work of the Jesuits. They acquired the support they needed not from the government or the company but by means of an effective propaganda device known as the *Jesuit Relations*. Published once a year in France, the *Relations* consisted of carefully edited letters from the different Fathers telling of their work and experiences in the wilderness. The money that flowed across the Atlantic in response to the pleas in those letters was used for founding, among other things, five mission stations in Huronia.

Devotion to the Hurons was partly pragmatic. If those far-ranging red traders could be converted, so the Jesuits reasoned, then the spread of Christianity to wild tribes living still farther inland could be greatly facilitated—an accomplishment that would also benefit the fur trade. Motivated thus, the toilers in the Lord's vine-yard managed to carry plows, pigs, poultry, and even calves in canoes to Huronia. Assisting the missionaries in the back-breaking work of transporting supplies, clearing fields, building habitations, and growing vegetables to use in the mission hospitals were dedicated laymen known as *donnés,* whose only pay was food, care when they were sick, and spiritual satisfaction. We shall look more closely at one of those remarkable men, Médart Chouart, Sieur de Groseilliers, a little farther on.

In spite of these outpourings of energy, however, all was not well in Huronia. For five years the epidemic that Brébeuf had first no-ticed during his western journey of 1634 raged through the crowded, unsanitary villages. By the time it abated in 1639, an estimated 15,000 people, half the population of Huronia, were dead. Even Paris felt the economic impact of the disaster, for the afflicted Indians were unable to gather the furs that had been antic-ipated as a result of Nicolet's journey to Lake Michigan.

Meanwhile the Iroquois, untouched by the sickness, were grow-ing stronger. In 1626, they had traded 8,000 beaver skins to the Dutch. In 1633 the number had risen to 30,000. By 1640 their country was stripped of beaver. In order to maintain their purchas-ing power, the confederation had to find fresh sources of fur. Unable to match the Hurons as traders—for one thing they were in-capable of duplicating in their elm-bark canoes the trips the Hurons made in their more substantial craft—the Iroquois turned to plunder.

The pace of their raids on the St. Lawrence Valley increased. Sudden attacks at some single target gave way to continual harass-ment by small bands that lurked everywhere from the Saguenay River to the lower reaches of the Ottawa. Montagnais, Algonkins, Hurons, French—all were attacked indiscriminately. Deadliness was increased by muskets obtained from the Dutch. The French, by contrast, seldom sold guns to Indians, and so when a party of Hurons was ambushed, they had little recourse but to flee, leaving their canoes in the hands of the marauders.

One incident, told in the *Jesuit Relation* for 1643, will suffice to describe many. On June 9, 1643, sixty Hurons traveling toward Three Rivers in thirteen canoes paused to talk with five Frenchmen who were cutting wood within plain sight of the new log palisades of Ville Marie (Montreal). Forty musket-armed Iroquois leaped on them from the nearby forest, captured most of the Hurons and all of the whites, clubbed several to death on the spot, and then, while the residents of Montreal watched in helpless horror, made off with a number of prisoners and all of the fur.

Stirred by the outcries from the colony, the French government sent a handful of soldiers to Canada. The Hurons, their strength returning now that the epidemic was over, entered into fresh alliances with the Eries and Susquehannas, who lived west and south of the Iroquois. Subdued by the mounting threats, the Iroquois sued for peace, thinking that a show of contrition would lead the Hurons to divert some of their furs southward. The Hurons, however, stayed loyal to the French traders—and, as we shall see, suffered the consequences. First, though, we need to backtrack for a moment.

During the times of turmoil, the syndicate that had leased trading rights from the Hundred Associates had despaired of ever making enough money to support the colonial government, as demanded by their charter. In 1645, accordingly, they surrendered their privileges. Their place was taken by a small group of Canadian residents banded together as the *Compagnie des Habitants*. In exchange for the right to act as the sole buyer of furs in Canada, the *Habitants* promised to support the government financially and to pay the holders of the original charter, the Hundred Associates, one thousand pounds of beaver fur each year.

The first year's operations were so successful that all Canadian males demanded the right to participate. (The total population was still less than 1,000 souls.) Seeing an opportunity to increase its revenues, the *Compagnie des Habitants* yielded. Every citizen—but no foreigners and no Protestants—could trade with the Indians provided that he pay heavy taxes on the furs he collected and then turn the pelts over to the monopoly at prices fixed by the government.

A small stampede of meagerly financed, independent traders immediately poured into the back country. They benefited very little, however. The Hurons, feeling that their alliance with the Eries and Susquehannas had made them invulnerable, declined to deal with the Iroquois. Furious, the confederacy decided to break the ring that was tightening around them. In the summer of 1648 and again in the spring of 1649 they unleashed a series of well-planned, admirably executed attacks on their enemy. They put three large Huron villages to the torch, fiendishly martyred three Jesuit priests, killed hundreds of Hurons, captured more (many of whom they adopted), and sent the survivors into panicked flight. A winter of starvation on islands in Lake Huron increased the fugitives' despair, and when they went on west into what is now Wisconsin they were little more than a rabble. Meanwhile the Iroquois were following up their Huron victories with equally slashing triumphs over every tribe they could reach—the Algonkins, Nipissings, Ottawas, and the Indians who lived around the shores of Lake Erie.

The next blows fell on the colonies. The independents, who only recently had won the right to participate in the trade, dared not leave the stockades. In 1652 not a single fur reached the ships waiting at Quebec. New France, which depended utterly on the fur trade, was prostrate.

The terror was running out of momentum, however. In the spring of 1653 the Iroquois overextended themselves by attacking Indian encampments at the southern end of Lake Michigan and at Sault Ste. Marie. Their intent was, first, to punish the tribes that had given refuge to the fleeing Indians from the East and then, that lesson delivered, to persuade the chastened victims to deal with the victors. Unhappily for the plan, the Iroquois were operating too far from home and the attacks were beaten back.

A handful of bold spirits among the disorganized tribes were quick to take advantage of the lull. Their people badly needed new European goods to replace articles lost and broken during the flight. Moreover, in the forests of Wisconsin they had come into contact with Indians to whom manufactured items were still such marvels that they were willing to pay fantastic prices in beaver to obtain what they wanted. The opportunity led a few Ottawas and a Huron or two to load three canoes with such furs as they had and start for the St. Lawrence in quest of merchandise.

It was an extraordinary journey. Fearful that Iroquois war parties might be lurking along the regular trail to avenge the defeats of the spring, the young traders followed a roundabout way of almost unimaginable difficulty. They paddled through Michilimackinac Strait and portaged around the rapids of Sault Ste. Marie into Lake Superior. They then went west, away from their goal, along the lake's cliff-girt northern shore as far as the granite mouth of Nipigon River. This led them to Lake Nipigon, where they encountered still other fugitives from the Iroquois thunderbolt, the Nipissings. After a brief rest with those sorely wounded allies, they turned their canoes eastward into the tumultuous rivers of the Canadian Shield. Backbreaking portages from stream to stream brought them to the headwaters of the St. Maurice, which they followed southward to the St. Lawrence. By the time they reached Quebec, they had covered well over a thousand miles of some of the harshest country on the continent.

While they were still in the settlements, the French were astounded by the arrival of a peace delegation from the Iroquois. The long raids the Five Nations had launched against the western Indians had left them exposed to attack from the Eries and Susquehannas. In order to fight off that threat and consolidate their gains in Huronia, the Iroquois needed quiet in the north. To prove their sincerity, the Onondagan part of the confederacy even agreed to receive Jesuit missionaries and lay helpers. Overjoyed, the Black Robes made ready to accept the invitation, although cautious settlers warned that this was another Iroquois trick and that peace would not last.

But at least the trail west was open again. The Ottawas hurried the news back to the tribes still wandering disconsolately through the lands beyond Lake Michigan. The Hurons, fearful of the Sioux ahead of them and the Iroquois behind, were too crushed to listen. Consequently the canoes that started with a few score bales of hastily gathered furs for the St. Lawrence in the spring of 1654 were manned mostly by Ottawas.

Their reports made the officials in Quebec realize that if the broken tribesmen were to become good providers of fur again, they would need help in reorganizing their lives. Several young French-men, eager to get back into the trade, volunteered to undertake the task.

The *Compagnie des Habitants* objected. Scarcity had raised the price of furs on the continent. A host of small traders, each coming home from the unexploited country with a bundle of furs to dispose of, might seek smuggling connections with sailors or, worse, might let the now peaceful Iroquois take the catch to Fort Orange.

The argument prevailed, and the governor decreed that no one could visit *les pays d'en haut,* the upper country, without an official license. He then chose two stout men to accompany the Ottawas west to discover where the fragmented tribes were regrouping and to encourage them to resume their trips to the marketplace.

The identity of one of those two wilderness delegates is a tanta-lizing mystery. The other, already on his way to becoming one of New France's most famous pioneer traders, was Médart Chouart, Sieur des Groseilliers.

PART TWO

The Irrepressible Coureurs

VII

The Farthest Lake

*M*édart Chouart, born in Charly-sur-Marne, France, in July, 1618, had migrated to Canada in 1642 or so, when he was about twenty-four. His motives were partly religious, for he went at once to Huronia, perhaps as a soldier, more probably as a *donné*, a lay assistant to the missionaries. Because he showed a natural aptitude for canoeing, hunting, and fishing, he soon became involved in transportation to and from the St. Lawrence.

It was a demanding assignment, for this was the period during which the Iroquois were stepping up their strikes on the canoe routes and the settlements. Young Chouart learned to be as wary in his responses as a lynx. When fighting, he was merciless, for like every other Frenchman in Canada he knew that being taken prisoner by the Iroquois might lead to slow death by burning.

Each trip he made involved agonizing dilemmas—whether to risk potentially fatal rapids in a loaded canoe, or to avoid the white water by portaging along forest trails where Iroquois raiders liked to lie in ambush. In between those decisions came routine difficulties. Every so often he and his companions encountered turbulent stretches of river where they had to jump overboard into waist-deep water and, slipping and falling on hidden boulders, drag their balky canoes ahead against the current. More times than he could remember he sloshed through the spring mud laden with burdens while clouds of black flies and mosquitos stung him until blood coursed down his skin. In the meantime he learned to love like brothers the temperamental Huron paddlers on whom success depended.

When the fur trade was opened to all citizens, Chouart joined the rush to the back country. Details of his movements are unknown, but his life was undoubtedly much like that of his fellows.

The first of the independents did not go very far into the Shield. Of necessity they spent their summers working around their farms or in the little shops that made shoes, furniture, and rough tools for sale to the colonists. Then as autumn neared and maple leaves showed scarlet, two or three men would pool their slim earnings and buy a canoe from the nearby Indians. Into it they loaded packs of lightweight merchandise—beads, vermillion, knives, needles and thread, awls, kettles, hatchets and small kegs of the French brandy that in early days was passed out in small quantities as a gesture of friendship before trading began.

With these supplies the neophyte traders pushed up the rivers into the dark forests of the back country. When they found a band of friendly Indians that other traders had not reached, they settled in with the *sauvages,* sharing their feasts when fish could be taken in nets under the ice or when moose could be run down in deep snow. In between times they suffered the same famines the Indians did. Unlike the Anglo-Americans farther south, they made no effort to take furs themselves, for that was a trespass the Indians would have resented.

Because the Indians kept moving about on snowshoes, so did the traders. They watched the glitter of the aurora during nights of such intense cold that tree trunks sometimes exploded with sounds like cannon shots. They experienced the joys of warm firelight and elemental companionship. Those who had no wives in the settlements, and many who did, wooed Indian women as mates, partly for convenience in daily living and partly because Indian in-laws linked them to the band and they could count on a welcome year after year.

Among those early traders, prototypes of the *coureur de bois* of a later date, none could outdo Médart Chouart. In spite of ambushes, taxes, and jealous rivals, he pried out of the lonely land north of the St. Lawrence enough fur so that he was able to obtain a seigneury that fronted on the St. Lawrence near Quebec.

The possession brought duties with it. First he was supposed to find tenants to occupy part of his holdings—this was a government device for luring immigrants to Canada—and to build grist and sawmills for their use. He had to make sure that the men who dwelt on his domain served their prescribed time in the militia and on public work projects. He held court at intervals to settle disputes. Because the rent and fees he could charge his tenants were controlled by the government, he could not possibly make as much money from his seigneury as from the fur trade. But he did gain what many valued more than money—social prestige. As a symbol of his status he was called *sieur,* a title followed by an appropriate phrase of identification.

Médart Chouart became Sieur des Groseilliers. *Groseillier* means gooseberry and was the name of his parents' farm in France. Stirred by memories, he attached the name to his Canadian estate and thus became Médart Chouart, Sieur des Groseilliers—Esquire of the Gooseberries. His tenants touched their hats when he passed, and officials recognized his step upward by calling him "des Groseilliers" in their documents. History records him by that designation, and from here on so will this account.

As befitted his station, the new Sieur des Groseilliers took a wife. Her name was Hélène. The marriage was short, for she died in 1651 after giving birth to a son. A little more than two years later, on August 24, 1653, des Groseilliers wed again. His new wife, Marguerite, aged twenty-one, had also experienced bereavement. Her first husband had been slain by raiding Iroquois, and in 1651 her half-brother, Pierre Esprit Radisson, aged sixteen, had been captured by a war party of Mohawks. Since his body had not been found, the family nursed a hope that somehow Pierre had managed to stay alive.

In the summer of 1654 Marguerite's new husband either received a summons from the governor or went on his own initiative to call on that dignitary. Their subject: the Ottawas and the few Hurons who in 1653 and 1654 had reached the settlements with furs gathered from Indians living in what is now Wisconsin. Could des Groseilliers visit—or would he visit, the case of the verb depending on who broached the subject—his old friends as an emissary of both the government and the *Compagnie des Habitants?* As a reward for undertaking the long, arduous trip des Groseilliers and an unnamed companion were to be given exclusive licenses to trade in the West during the duration of their journey.

Who was the companion? The question has perplexed historians ever since the discovery, among papers once belonging to Samuel Pepys of the court of King Charles II of England, of a series of narratives composed by Pierre Esprit Radisson. As his family had prayed, that young man had survived captivity among the Mohawks and had returned to New France in time to leave for the West with his new brother-in-law. Or so Pierre wrote in 1668–69 while loafing around England trying to impress potential investors in a new fur company.

As historians have pointed out ever since the narratives were published, Radisson's tales abound with inconsistencies, contradictions, improbable dates, and boasts of impossible journeys. Still, he did go west with Groseilliers at some point. He loved the new lands that he helped bring to the world's knowledge; he studied new tribes of Indians with a discerning eye; and he wrote of his experiences with an infectious fervor.

For those reasons Radisson's defenders have sought to explain away the confusions in his narratives. They suggest that he dictated his stories in English, a language that he learned imperfectly when he was more than thirty years old. His secretary, so the hypothesis runs, was confounded by descriptions of a trade, a people, and a continent of which he knew nothing. Uneasy in English, Radisson never checked the manuscript. As a result his slips in memory, the secretary's muddles, and even transpositions of major segments of the material went unchallenged. By rearranging the text, as various revisionists have done, some of the contradictions can be made more palatable, at least to Radisson fans. And even those who sniff at his pretensions still must use his journals, for no other account of one of North America's great adventures has survived.

A native of Paris, teen-aged Pierre Radisson had been in the New World only a little more than a year when Mohawks fell upon him and two companions while they were hunting ducks. The Indians beheaded Radisson's friends—heads carried home on pikes were a favorite trophy—but some spark of defiance in Pierre's stance led his captors to spare his life.

He was adopted by a famed warrior, slayer of nineteen foes, who lived in a village near Lake Champlain. Although life was not unpleasant there, memories of home were sweet enough that Radisson let a Huron captive whom he met during a hunt talk him into trying to escape. With hatchets they crushed the skulls of Radisson's three Mohawk companions as they slept beside the campfire. Appropriating the dead men's weapons, they fled northward for fourteen days, until only the St. Lawrence stood between them and the town of Three Rivers. There they were recaptured by a raiding party returning from the settlements with a bag of seventeen Huron and three French prisoners. Radisson's companion was executed but again the boy was spared.

The trip back to the Mohawk village was disagreeable. Each night the prisoners were stripped, tied to posts in such a way that they could not move their hands, and left to swarming mosquitoes. On reaching the village they were placed on scaffolds so that each could watch the torments inflicted on the others, a scene that Radisson's first narrative describes in almost unbearable detail. Procedures were almost routine. Radisson's soles were seared with irons fresh from the fire, and a red-hot sword was driven through one of his feet. His fingernails were pulled off with exquisite slowness and the sore tips tested with live coals. Children shot him with toy arrows and were beginning to chew on his fingers when his adoptive parents, who had accepted him as the son they had lost, halted the sport. After a month of care in their lodge he was almost as good as new again.

For an indeterminate time thereafter he shared happily in the strenuous life of the Mohawks. But underneath his surface content was a lurking dread of his captors' fickleness. If Mohawk raiders happened to be defeated with loss of life in an attack on one of the settlements, the families of the slain might seek revenge on Radisson just because he was French. And so, though he says he learned to love the Mohawks "entirely well," he contrived to escape to the Dutch trading post of Orange (today's Albany, New York). From there he managed to reach Amsterdam. Obtaining money somehow, he hurried to France and caught a fishing boat back to Canada.

He says that he arrived from his three years' absence in time to go west with his sister's new husband, des Groseilliers. The brother-in-law's most astute biographer, Grace Nute, has pretty well shown that this is not true. Still, Radisson heard details of the trip from des Groseilliers later on and appropriated them, with embellishments, for his own glorification. In lieu of anything else, we must use them as best we can.

According to Radisson, several Frenchmen—not just the two licensed by the governor—left the settlements with the returning Ottawas in the spring of 1654. They took the usual route up the Rivière des Prairies, as the Ottawa was then called, but the difficulty of keeping up with the hard-paddling Indians and then an unexpected fight with lurking Iroquois turned all but the brothers-in-law back. Dramatically those two vowed "to finish that voyage or die."

At times the two whites must have regretted the decision. Out of fear of another Iroquois attack the party traveled most of the way to Lake Nipissing by dark, a desperate expedient on rough water. Because the Indians in the group had not left caches of food to help on the return journey, starvation was a constant threat. At times the famished wayfarers had to plunge into dense thickets and scratch their thighs bloody in a search for wild blackberries. When their harvests proved insufficient to maintain strength, they scraped lichen off the boulders—the *tripes de roche* of later voyageurs—and boiled the paltry gatherings into a black, sticky mess. Only after they had reached the French River did they feel free to fish openly, with rewarding luck.

On reaching Lake Huron, they seem, surprisingly, to have left the North Channel route to Michilimackinac and to have turned south past deserted Huronia to the site of today's Detroit—a journey often impeded by contrary winds and waves that pinned them to the lake's shores for "long and tedious waits." Perhaps they took this detour in order to see lands hitherto closed to French penetration by the Iroquois, and so they became the predecessors of that other great self-server, Robert Cavelier, Sieur de La Salle.

From the narrows (the *détroit*) at the foot of Lake St. Clair, so Grace Nute speculates, the party worked westward from stream to stream across the southern part of present Michigan. They may even have dropped a little distance down the Illinois River through a country that roused Radisson, via des Groseilliers, to rhapsodies, for here "whatever a man could desire was to be had in great plenty." If only Europeans would cease fighting over barren rocks in the sea and instead come in peace to this heartland of the continent, then "what laborinth of pleasure should millions of people have."

A fair enough prophecy. But the rest is confusion. About all we can say is that the two whites and their red guides eventually reached Green Bay on the western side of Lake Michigan, wintered there, and then spent another summer traveling far and wide. By the time they had returned to Green Bay during the closing months of 1655, another winter was at hand. Undeterred, they joined a large group of Hurons and Ottawas on a snowshoe trip through the forests of Wisconsin to a river that may have been the Mississippi. If so, they and not Jolliet and Marquette were the first whites to see its northern reaches.

While des Groseilliers stayed beside the Mississippi planting and harvesting corn for the long trip home, Radisson moved, he says, west to . . . it is impossible even to guess where. Anyway, during spring and summer the two Frenchmen made contact with important new tribes. One was the Sioux—Radisson called them Nadaoueceronons, the "nation of the beef" (i.e., buffalo)—who lived where the forests feathered out to the plains of Minnesota and Dakota. The other and more significant contact was the Crees.

Having learned somehow that white traders were about, Cree hunters came to Wisconsin from the north in tiny one- and two-man canoes loaded with the glossiest beaver pelts that the veteran des Groseilliers had ever seen. During the bargaining that followed, the Crees told of rivers flowing northward into a saltwater sea across which ships with great white sails had ventured some years before. As the two Frenchmen eventually realized, the sea was Hudson's Bay and the ships were manned by Dutch and English explorers searching in vain for a Northwest Passage to the Orient.

The significance of the revelation did not dawn immediately on the white traders. They were too excited by the furs, which they bought for trifles from the unsophisticated Indians and which would bring a fortune in the settlements. They obtained as many for themselves as their wares allowed and then began urging the middlemen who had handled the trade before the Iroquois wars to take over the rest.

Again the Hurons proved reluctant, and so the fleet of fifty or more canoes that the emissaries put together in the spring of 1656 was once more manned primarily by Ottawas—about 250 of them. They handled the job masterfully—so masterfully that from then on Ottawa Indians were the principal carriers of western furs, whether working on their own account or assisting the French *coureurs de bois* who often accompanied them. Soon the tribe claimed that *they* owned the erstwhile Rivière des Prairies, the St. Lawrence's principal tributary, and that other tribes could travel it only with their permission. From that arrogant assumption the river (and hence, in time, Canada's capitol city) acquired the name, Ottawa, that it has borne ever since.

The arrival of the Ottawa fleet of 1656 made local heroes of des Groseilliers and his companion—Radisson, according to Radisson. The ships at anchor off Quebec fired their cannon in salute, and the governor himself entertained the pair royally for three days. After that . . . again we don't know. The next firm date we have is July, 1657, when Radisson was preparing to accompany a colonizing expedition to the country of the Onondaga Indians. As was noted near the end of the preceding chapter, the Onondaga branch of the Iroquois confederacy had been so eager for peace with the French that its council had agreed to let Jesuits establish a mission near the tribe's principal village. Building began shortly thereafter, and in 1657 Fathers Paul Ragueneau and Joseph Duperon led a mixed group of reinforcements up the once-interdicted St. Lawrence toward the spot where Samuel Champlain had suffered his decisive defeat four decades earlier. Radisson went along out of nostalgia, hoping that he might see friends he had acquired during his years as a prisoner of the Mohawks.

As usual, he makes a bloody adventure out of the story. The mission party consisted of about twenty French lay helpers and more than a hundred Huron Indians. Most of the latter were women who had been persuaded to join male Huron captives adopted by the Onondagans. The Onondagans' hope, of course, was to rebuild population losses suffered during the long years of warfare.

Their own touchy tempers defeated the plan. As a large fleet of Onondaga warriors was coming down the St. Lawrence to meet the colonizers a canoe capsized and seven men drowned. Primitive logic declared that the Hurons were to blame inasmuch as the tragedy had occurred as part of the welcome being extended them.

Therefore, to assuage the grief of the dead men's families and friends, the Onondagans seized a moment when the French were in a different camp and slaughtered every one of the migrating Huron females—or so Radisson writes.

In spite of this example of Indian unpredictability, the French continued to the new mission, "a most fair castle," on an island in a lake near present-day Syracuse, New York. Newly planted crops were thriving in fields cleared just that spring, and a sanguine visitor might have supposed that the civilization the Jesuits had hoped to establish in Huronia might yet take root in the environs of the Iroquois.

Rumbles of trouble were abroad, however. The whole thrust of the merciless wars of the late 1640s and early 1650s had been to crush the Hurons and thus shift the northern fur trade from the St. Lawrence to the Hudson, with the Iroquois confederacy assuming the lucrative role of middlemen. The strategy had been spoiled by the French breakthrough to the west and the rise of the Ottawas as the new carriers. Accordingly the Mohawks, the most belligerent tribe of the confederacy, had argued at the annual council in Onondaga that the peace of 1653 would have to be broken and the war of extinction resumed. The logical and easiest place to begin, they added, was the new mission.

Friendly Indians leaked word of the plot to the French. Quietly they readied boats, food, and arms so that they could attempt to escape as soon as the ice left the rivers in the spring. To delay pursuit they invited the principal warriors of Onondaga to a feast inside the French stockade. There they plied their guests with Indian corn spiced with mincemeat, with water fowl, eels, fish, and "the oil of bear, venison."

Indian etiquette demanded that each diner down everything placed before him. As the feast dragged on and on, with the French delaying its conclusion by singing, dancing, and performing sleight-of-hand tricks—Radisson, it is said, played the guitar—the Indians grew sleepier and sleepier. As soon as all were snoring, the people in the mission slipped away to their hidden boats. Using poles prepared in advance, they broke through the spring-rotten ice of the neighboring river to Lake Ontario. After a miserable journey through "high winds, snow and every day rain on our backs," they gained the St. Lawrence, whose rapids they ran at night, trusting to the spring flood to boost them over the rocks.

The desperate ruse worked. Before long young Radisson was again toasting his feet beside his brother-in-law's fireside while they discussed a canoe journey to the far end of Lake Superior, an area known to the French only through Indian accounts. There they hoped to make contact with the Crees again and develop a flourishing trade in the kind of superb pelts des Groseilliers and his companion had acquired from those Indians three years before.

The trip that resulted may well have been the only journey that Pierre Esprit Radisson actually made with des Groseilliers—a suspicion that should not obscure his remarkable skills at outdoor survival. And, even if this were his only long canoe journey, it was a climactic one, for from it came concepts that changed the course of North American history.

The beginnings were unpropitious. The two dominant groups of New France, the *Compagnie des Habitants* and the Jesuits were dismayed at the course the fur trade was taking. From the standpoint of the *Habitants* too many *coureurs* were roaming the woods and then, as had been feared from the beginning, were smuggling their furs to buyers other than the company. To these economic complaints the Jesuits added a moral one. The more aggressive *coureurs,* the priests charged, were seeking advantage over each other by plying the Indians with liquor. Both groups demanded that Canada's popular new governor, the Vicomte d'Argenson, attack the abuses by continuing to restrict the trading privileges that had been briefly extended to all Canadian citizens only a decade earlier. When Radisson and des Groseilliers applied for licenses to go west either in 1658 or, more probably, in 1659, they were refused, victims of policy rather than of animosity.

Radisson, however, saw the rejection in a different light. According to him, d'Argenson, like most of the governors of French Canada, wanted to use his control over the fur trade as a path toward personal enrichment. He refused to issue the licenses unless the traders took two of the governor's agents and two Jesuit priests with them to the Great Lakes.

Unwilling to share the profits of the dangerous trip with parasites and reluctant to waste time trying to move Jesuits beyond the limits of feasible support, the brothers-in-law refused. Then, un-licensed, they slipped out of Quebec under cover of darkness to meet, by prearranegment, certain Ottawas and Chippewas bound back to the Superior region with canoes filled with manufactured goods.

Again they ran into an Iroquois ambush, but this time the French and their Indian allies were victorious, slaying eleven of the enemy and capturing four. In doing this they suffered casualties. To avenge the loss "we plagued those unfortunates [the captives]. . . . We plucked out their nails one after another," before finally killing them and feasting on their broiled flesh.

The south shore of Lake Superior stirred Radisson to eloquence. He rhapsodised over the sand dunes of Grand Marais, the forested cliffs and sparkling waterfalls farther on, the huge fish swimming in water clearer than glass, and one promontory through which the waves had cut an arch big enough to pass a 500-ton sailing ship. Using well-trodden Indian trails that led from stream to lake to little stream, the travelers portaged across the peninsula, now named Keweenaw, that thrusts like a horn out from the southern shore. Finally, as fall colors were beginning to blaze on deciduous trees mingled with the evergreens, they entered Chequamegon Bay (pronounced *She-wám-egun*).

It was a lovely spot, sheltered from north winds by a cluster of islands later called the Apostles. Entranced, the two Frenchmen decided to rest there a time while the Indians went off about per-sonal business. The hut the traders built, its exact location disputed today, was probably the first white habitation on the shores of Lake Superior. They passed several idyllic days there. Des Groseilliers tended camp; Radisson provided ducks, venison, "sturgeons of a vast bigness and Pycks [pike] seaven feet long." In writing about the interlude years later, he coined a phrase that still stirs canoeists seeking the last remote parts of the Quetico-Superior Wilderness Area: "We were Caesars, being nobody to contradict us."

But they were not there to rest. As soon as winter had closed in, they undertook a hungry snowshoe trip to certain Ottawa villages beside Lac Court Oreille, Wisconsin. Radisson has left, in his quaint way, a description of what such trips were like; "worke whole nights & dayes, lye down on the bare ground, & not allways that hap, the breech in the water, the feare in the buttocks, to have the belly empty, the weariness in the bones, and drowsiness of the body by the bad weather that you are to suffer, having nothing to keep you from such calamity."

Traveling so, they reached the villages, passed out samples of merchandise, and then managed to arrange an impressive meeting with bands of Sioux who arrived at the rendezvous in barbaric splendor—copper ornaments on chests and arms, crow skins hanging from their belts, the tufted ends of buffalo tails dragging from moccasins decorated with porcupine quills. To impress the visitors, Radisson threw a handful of gunpowder into the campfire and reveled in the cries of wonder that resulted. More important, the traders guaranteed a flow of furs eastward by persuading the Sioux to end, temporarily at least, their traditional warfare with the Crees.

As spring neared, the two men returned to Chequamegon Bay. There Radisson so injured one of his legs while dragging a sled load of goods across slushy ice that des Groseilliers had to spend eight days alternately massaging the torn ligaments with hot bear's oil and then binding them tightly in bits of woolen cloth.

Only one clue exists to suggest how far they may have wandered after Radisson was mobile again. Maps published a few years after the trip show a "Groseiliers" River—one "l"—flowing into the northwestern part of Lake Superior. (Today the same river, now called the Pigeon, forms a section of the international boundary between Ontario and Minnesota.) A canoe hugging the rough coast on a round trip between Chequamegon and the Groseiliers River would have to travel about 600 miles—this on top of the 500 or so the *coureurs* had already paddled on their journey from Sault Ste. Marie. A taxing trip—but for Radisson, the tale-teller, it was not enough. He says, without indicating what route they followed, that des Groseilliers and he went north of Lake Superior to rivers that they followed to Hudson Bay and back. Even Radisson fans have trouble swallowing that one; there simply wasn't time enough for such a journey.

Somewhere, however, the brothers-in-law did find the Crees for whom they were looking and in so doing heaped up the richest collection of furs yet gathered by any Frenchmen. The next step was to try to find enough canoes and canoemen to take the treasure to the settlements.

The problem was complicated by rumors of a catastrophic battle recently fought beside the Ottawa River—a story that is now part of the cultural baggage of every Canadian. What had happened was this. In the spring of 1660, seventeen Frenchmen accompanied by several Hurons and Algonkins and led by a *coureur* named Adam Dollard had discovered a band of Iroquois returning from a trading and trapping trip on the upper Ottawa. Hotly Dollard urged a reversal of the usual course of events. *They* would ambush the Iroquois rather than the other way around.

Easy enough beside the campfire. But the Iroquois turned out to be more numerous than anticipated. All but five of Dollard's Indian allies vanished. Those five forted up with the seventeen French in a crude barricade beside the portage trail. For five days they withstood a siege by an estimated two hundred enemy. Then more Iroquois arrived and the defenders were overrun, horribly, but not before they had inflicted heavy casualties.

The Indians whom des Groseilliers and Radisson were trying to employ were terrified by the story, which crackled like fire from tribe to tribe. On hearing it, the demoralized Hurons and even the Ottawas sat on their hands. The Iroquois would be swarming along the trail, eager to avenge the heaviest losses ever inflicted on them. No, the risks were unacceptable.

Groseilliers responded with a long speech of scorn. If the Iroquois felt that no one dared challenge them, they would resume attacks like the ones they had made earlier against Sault Ste. Marie and around the southern shores of Lake Michigan. By being too timid to go in search of knives and guns for defending themselves, the western Indians would be surrendering their families to horror.

To drive the point home, Radisson jerked a beaver robe off one of the listeners and struck him across the face with it. "For my part I will venture, choosing to die like a man. . . . Farewell! I have my sack of corn ready . . . I shall live without you." And off he stalked.

Abashed by men willing to risk everything they valued for the sake of a goal they believed in, the Indians capitulated. By Radisson's count, 360 canoes made ready to leave Lake Superior for the settlements. A hundred may be nearer the truth, but whatever the number the departure brought forth a tantalizing tableau. The women left behind, so says the narrative (its spelling modernized by Loren Kallsen), paddled stark naked out among the canoes of the flotilla. "They sang loudly and sweetly. They stood in their boats and remained in that position half a day . . . not ashamed to show us all, to entice us and animate the men to defend themselves valiantly and come back and enjoy them."

During their long journey home, Radisson and des Groseilliers held animated discussions about the future of the fur trade. Their probings had taken them to the limits of the Great Lakes basin. Yet, in a sense, those limits were just a beginning. Beyond the grim heights of land that encompassed Lake Superior's northern shore were other drainage systems roamed by unsophisticated Indians able to tap, at cheap rates still, seemingly endless supplies of prime pelts.

Reaching those Indians in the normal way, winning their friendship, and persuading them to step up the pace of their hunting would require prodigious journeys along a trail whose lower end was menaced by plundering Iroquois. But perhaps another route was possible. If the Crees spoke truly, the western shore of Hudson Bay—Champlain's Northern Sea—extended as far into the heart of the continent as did Lake Superior. Might it be possible to bring sailing ships into strategic parts of the Bay, build posts at the mouths of rivers that led into the virgin fur preserves—rivers the Crees described in some detail to the brothers-in-law—and use those waterways as routes to the interior? Distances over which small craft would have to travel would be more than halved, the Iroquois would be circumvented, and the men who brought the gains to pass would surely be rewarded with a monopoly in the new trade. Or so Radisson and des Groseilliers assured themselves as they descended the Ottawa River, nervously alert for Iroquois war parties that failed to materialize, thanks to the hurt inflicted on the Confederacy by Adam Dollard's fabled stand.

Loaded with enough furs once again to save the economy of Canada, the traders swept into the settlements, expecting a welcome like the one des Groseilliers' party had received in 1656. Instead, Governor d'Argenson gave des Groseilliers a brief jail sentence for trading without a license and as a further penalty confiscated most of the furs that belonged to the brothers-in-law personally.

Their proposed new trade route through Hudson Bay received equally short shrift. The directors of the *Compagnie des Habitants* wanted no watering down of the firm's monopoly on the St. Lawrence, and the governor heeded them; after all, the company did pay his salary. The Jesuits joined the opposition out of fear that if the unruly, liquor-trading *coureurs de bois* of the St. Lawrence found an outlet for their furs that was uncontrolled from Quebec, they would riot unrestrained among the Indians. The concensus was clear: forget the Bay.

Enfuriated, des Groseilliers sailed to France to seek redress. He was brushed aside. Anger climbing still higher, the brothers-in-law turned to New England for help. Although they found shipowners willing to underwrite expeditions to the Bay, the efforts failed because of bad luck and timid ship captains. Nevertheless, they did manage to hurt their motherland, at least in the minds of certain high-placed Canadians, including the Jesuit Paul Ragueneau, who had known Radisson at the short-lived mission to the Onondagans. According to these detractors, Radisson and des Groseilliers encouraged the English to wrest New Netherlands from the Dutch by telling them of the profits that could be gained by helping the Iroquois take over the western fur trade.

Perhaps the pair did talk that way, but their influence was hardly conclusive. The Dutch enclave, confronted on two sides by aggressive Anglo-Americans, was doomed in any event. Its governor, Peter Stuyvesant, capitulated to an English fleet in 1664. New Netherlands became New York; Fort Orange was renamed Albany; and the southern flank of New France was now threatened by a potentially more dangerous enemy than Holland had ever been.

The changeover was equally significant for Radisson and des Groseilliers, still searching for a way to Hudson Bay. Somehow they fell in with the royal commission that crossed the Atlantic to examine England's new possession. Through these commissioners the Frenchmen were introduced, after many vicissitudes, to the court of King Charles II and, more important, to the king's cousin, Prince Rupert. The upshot, delayed until 1668 by outbreaks of bubonic plague and by the great fire of London, was an exploratory journey to the Bay of the North.

Of the two ships that sailed that year, only the little ketch

Nonsuch, thirty-six feet long, reached its destination, with des Groseilliers aboard.* Instead of halting at one of the river mouths that opened a way into the land of the Crees, the ship continued to James Bay, the nipple at the southernmost extremity of the great inland sea. There, beside a stream the travelers named Rupert for the King's cousin, they built a post called Fort Charles after the King. Strikes delivered from such a location would injure a trade that had long been flowing toward Tadoussac. In short, des Groseilliers' commercial attack on New France was going to be complete and not limited just to a race for new territories.

After enduring a winter of intense cold, the crew of the *Nonsuch* returned to London with a load of furs so enticing that eighteen wealthy investors promptly banded together as "The Governor and Company of Adventurers of England Trading into Hudson Bay." On May 2, 1670, these Adventurers obtained from Charles II a grant to what was designated as Rupert's Land.

Rupert's Land was defined in the company's charter as all the country draining into Hudson Bay. Surveyors eventually determined that the area embraced by the sweeping clauses reached from Labrador to the crest of the Rocky Mountains, from the St. Lawrence drainage system to the icy tundra beyond the Arctic Circle. In round figures the territory covered 1.5 million square miles, ten times the amount of land embraced by England, Wales, Scotland, and Ireland combined.

In 1670 no one had any idea that so much land was involved. Indeed, no one had yet grasped how big North America was. As part of their promotion, Radisson and des Groseilliers (Mr. Gooseberry, as the English insisted on calling him) had assured their backers that an expedition based on Hudson Bay could easily take canoes to the Stinking Lake (probably Green Bay, but possibly an early reference to Lake Winnipeg). From there another "7 daies padling or sailing" would bring the travelers to a strait that led to the Southern Sea.

So there it was again: the hope of an easy ship and canoe route across a continent deemed to be no bigger than Europe. It would be

---

* The *Eaglet,* on which Radisson sailed, was driven back to England by storms; to fill his time Pierre, contemplating investors rather than history, compiled his narratives.

an English route, too, the promoters declared, for the French were now in a vise, their long trail to the West vulnerable to thrusts from either north or south. Sooner or later, the St. Lawrence would have to succumb.

VIII

Rebirth

*A*lthough des Groseilliers and Radisson were personally rejected in both Canada and France, their discoveries were not. On their arrival from the West in the summer of 1660, traders and Jesuits sought them out with questions about the displaced Indians who were seeking new homes south and west of the upper lakes, and about more distant tribes that might be absorbed into the colony's web of commercial alliances. How did one manage the long distances? Where could supplies of food be obtained? Could canoes as large as the ones with which the *coureurs de bois* were experimenting be handled without undue risk in the rapids and on the portages? Did birch trees grow throughout the distance so that bark would be available for repairs, or should reserve rolls be carried, together with spruce gum and spruce roots, in canoes already overloaded with merchandise?

In addition to questioning the pair, the traders and missionaries wandered through the trading fair outside Montreal, watching the Indians who had come east with the brothers-in-law barter their furs. Merchants displayed tempting wares in booths of canvas and evergreen boughs; barkers cried their singsongs; interpreters were busy with the endless haggling. Eventually every pelt would end in the hands of the government-licensed monopoly, for it had the sole right to carry furs outside the colony for marketing. But along the way every Canadian was entitled to dicker with the Indians in the hope that he could pick up a few skins for resale to the *Compagnie* at prices that would allow a small profit. To the distress of the Jesuits and in spite of prohibitions of varying severity laid down from time to time, brandy too often was the most successful medium.

The bustle did not stop with merchandising. At nights the *coureurs* roistered and sang while the Indians performed their dances beside towering bonfires. Priests held high mass, fully aware of how the elaborate rituals appealed to *les sauvages'* sense of color and tradition. Meanwhile the colony's leaders, secular and religious, argued about the meaning of what they saw. What kind of offerings most appealed to their visitors? How could their friendship and hence their aid be best obtained? Above all, how could their chronic dread of the Iroquois be allayed, so that the commerce that was life to New France might flow unrestrained?

These were critical questions. Until des Groseilliers and his brother-in-law started them flowing as a result of their bold journey, some pessimists had even been advocating the abandonment of the tiny, thin-spread colony. Now the very asking showed that there was hope again. If that hope in all its ramifications could be transported to Paris and used to elicit concrete government help, then Canada might yet experience what historian Marcel Trudel many years later called "a new founding." Certainly the effort was worth making. With an eagerness they had not felt for years, the more responsible men of the settlements began searching for a delegate to convey the message across the Atlantic. The man they chose was Pierre Boucher, recently ennobled for his work as governor of little Trois Rivières—but more of him and his mission later on.

Hungrier men, unable to wait for France's response to the emissary's pleading, decided on more direct action. In their van were six traders who arranged to travel with the returning Ottawas to Chequamegon Bay on the southwestern shore of Lake Superior. There, so they hoped, they would find salvation by duplicating the commercial success achieved by des Groseilliers and Radisson— but without the attendant penalties. Their leader was Adrien Jolliet, eldest brother of one of Canada's best known fur-trading families. No doubt other *coureurs* would have liked to go along, but presumably those six were the only ones who managed, within the short time available, to obtain licenses and financing.

Then the Jesuits appeared and asked the Ottawas to add two priests and a lay helper to the party. One candidate was Charles Albanel, forty-four, vigorous, enthusiastic, and toughened to wilderness living by several hard winters spent with the Montagnais on the bleak upper reaches of the Saguenay River. The other was René Ménard, fifty-six and worn out by the rigors of his career. He had survived the Iroquois massacres at Huronia and after that experience had still had enough fortitude to participate in the short-lived mission to Onondaga, where Radisson, too, had been for a time.

The Ottawas declined at first to transport any priests. Jolliet's *coureurs* probably instigated the surliness. A natural antipathy existed between Canada's fur traders and the Jesuits, softened on the traders' part only by the priests' usefulness in collecting geographical information and helping maintain peace among the tribes. The Jesuits objected to liquor in the Indian country. They urged agriculture on their charges. If either policy took hold, it would reduce the number of pelts available for trade. Indeed, the Jesuits would have liked to isolate the pagans completely, so that they could be taught to worship the one true God uncontaminated by the influences of civilization. Naturally the traders had scant use for them.

On the whole the Indians, especially the men, preferred the *coureurs*. True, the forest runners were rapacious and resorted to contemptible tricks in order to beat competitors to a pelt. But they accepted the Indians' way of doing things, married their daughters, and enjoyed to the full the happier aspects of village life. The lust of most, but by no means all, of the Indians for the brandy that the *coureurs* managed to bring them was another bond.

By contrast, the Indians found the ideals of Jesuits incomprehensible in many ways. Their celibacy and daintiness about morals in general seemed ridiculous. Although Catholic ritual was attractive from the standpoint of theatricals, the Jesuits' demand that native forms of worship be abandoned as a prerequisite to participating in the ceremonies stirred resistance. Nor did the white man's heaven seem to offer adequate recompenses for the restraints required on earth. Besides, if the way of life preached by the Jesuits was as good as claimed, why did so many Frenchmen fail to follow it?

But the Jesuits could be persuasive. After hours of argument, a few Ottawas said that they could find room in their canoes for one priest and the lay helper, Jean Guerin. Beyond that they would not budge.

The assignment fell not on Albanel, who was better equipped physically for the trip, but on René Ménard. Ménard knew the Hurons and their language. It was hoped that he would find among the demoralized bands in Wisconsin a few converts who remembered him and might help him establish a new station from which, in the fullness of time, the Word could be spread to tribes still lost in superstition.

Ménard was not overjoyed. At midnight, just before his departure, he wrote a friend, "In three or four months you may include me in the Memento for the dead." And yet his conscience would not let him ask to be relieved. "If I failed to respond to this opportunity I should experience endless remorse."

Of necessity he and Guérin traveled with Indian paddlers, each white in a different canoe. Probably Radisson and des Groseilliers had also gone west in vessels manned chiefly by Indians, though at times they may have used a small two-man canoe for side trips. But from the number of traders involved in the journey of 1660 and from circumstances connected with the sketchily known adventure, it seems likely that Adrien Jolliet and his fellows used their own craft. One wishes it were possible to be sure, for if the assumption is correct, this was another trail-blazing trip. So far as records show, whites unaided by Indians had never before driven canoes across such distances and through such water.

Jolliet's group did not begin from scratch, of course. Ever since the trade had been liberalized during the late 1640s, young Canadians working the nearer lakes and streams had learned the rudiments of managing canoes devoted to the hauling of freight. As they labored they had slowly systematized, in ways the Indians had not done, the structure of the craft and the procedures for handling cargo. The standards were not rigid and never would be, but already they were pointing the way toward the elephantine freight canoes of later times.

Jolliet's people probably used canoes like those described in 1684 by Louis Armand Lom d'Arce, Baron de Lahontan, a soldier, explorer, and literary scribbler who spent a decade or more observing the new civilization being created in Canada. According to Lahontan, the vessels most commonly employed in the trade at that time averaged between twenty-eight and thirty feet in length. They were between four and five feet wide and twenty-one inches deep amidships. Although these dimensions were considerably smaller than those of the *canots de maître* that would be developed during the following century, they could carry 2,000 pounds of freight each— or, when impressed for military use, up to fourteen soldiers.

Three men managed each canoe—the *avant* in the bow, the *gouvernail,* or steersman, in the stern with the longest paddle, and the least experienced man, the *milieu* in between. In quiet water the paddlers generally sat on bales of merchandise. When running rapids they usually knelt, although the *avant* or *gouvernail,* or both, might stand if that precarious position commanded a better view of the perils ahead. They also stood when using long setting poles to thrust the craft up a swift stream that had a firm and relatively shallow bottom. Poling was an exhausting procedure and required marvelous exactness in timing and balance.

If the river banks were open and the water free of snags, the canoes could be dragged upward with a *cordelle,* a braided rope sixty or more feet long. (The ropes were braided so that, if one strand broke, the whole canoe would not be lost—an uncomfortable prospect for the steersman, who remained in the craft to keep its nose from veering in against the bank.) Another device for overcoming fast water was to remove half the load from the canoe —a *demichargé*—and then paddle the lightened craft past the barrier to a safe landing place. There the remaining goods were deposited on the bank, and the men returned in the empty canoe for the packs they had left at the foot of the rapids. To preclude injuring the canoe on the rough river bottom, loading and unloading were always carried out in hip-deep water.

Sooner or later a roaring *sault* appeared that could be by-passed only by portaging. Over the years this need led to uniformity in packaging. Merchandise on the upper journey and furs on the return were pressed into compact bundles that weighed on the average ninety pounds each and were protected by water-proofed coverings. At the start of a portage, two pieces were strapped together into a *pacton.* Other members of the crew, who would be similarly served in their turn, lifted the *pacton* onto the carrier's back in such a way that the bulk of the weight was borne by his hips. The burden was held in place by a *collier,* or tumpline, whose central portion passed around the porter's forehead. Often a keg of liquor or a casette, a tight wooden box in which articles of exceptional value were carried, was placed on top of the *pacton.*

Leaning forward against a load that always weighed at least 180 pounds, often 270, and sometimes more, the *coureur* went ahead at a kind of shuffling trot that on a smooth trail averaged five miles an hour. The average portage was by no means five miles long (though a few exceeded that length), but with only three men to handle twenty to twenty-two packs and the canoe, even a short portage added up to a lot of running back and forth.

Summer days were long, and the traders were generally up before dawn. Until dark their only rest came during brief pauses each hour when they were allowed a few pulls on a pipe. Food was uncertain. In order to have as much space for merchandise as possible, the travelers left the settlements with only a little hardtack, some dried peas, and corn leached by lye into a kind of hominy—but with at least one good gun per canoe, ample powder, fish lines, and nets. If game proved scarce, one went hungry, for as distances increased and the agricultural productivity of the displaced tribes decreased, the old Huron practice of leaving food caches along the way for the return journey was abandoned. Throughout the history of the trail this problem of food remained, as we shall see, a paramount concern of the trade's organizers.

Another respite was occasionally provided by the use of sails, a French innovation. The device worked well only on relatively quiet water and with a following wind—but the relief that followed such a conjunction was blessed enough to compensate for the inconvenience of carrying mast and canvas over the portages. The sail, moreover, could be used, along with brush, poles, and the canoe itself for creating nighttime shelters. On such occasions wind was never a friend, for then the canoes had to be staked down tight lest they suffer injury from being blown against rocks or trees.

Although the Ottawas of the 1660 flotilla did not move with the precision that the French were attaining, the lateness of the season allowed no loitering—and no dead weight. Despite his age, Ménard was forced to labor with setting pole and paddle, and to bend under heavy burdens at the portages. Any show of pain, even when the rocks cut his feet, brought jeers from his companions, and when he dropped exhausted beside each night's campfire he was given the poorest remnants of the food. The other French, traveling with the advanced part of the flotilla, did not see and hence did nothing to alleviate his miseries. Quite possibly they made sure they would not see.

For six weeks he held. Then, a few miles east of the Keewenaw Peninsula an accident demolished the canoe in which he was riding. Sagging with weariness, he followed the three Indians who had also been involved in the shipwreck west along the sandy beach. On October 15, near the mouth of the stream that marked the beginning of the portage across the Peninsula, they found a winter camp of Ottawas. Canoes could have been obtained there, but Ménard's Indian companions decided against continuing to Chequamegon Bay that winter, though it was less than 150 miles away. The Jesuit was too tired to protest.

He was not too tired to be objectionable. The chief of the band was a warrior named Kinongé, which the French translated as Le Brochet, or, in English, "the pike." Kinongé had several wives. To the Indians polygamy was common sense, if a person could afford it. Frequent battles with enemy tribes had left an imbalance between the sexes, and, if widows and children were to be protected, some men were going to have to accept additional women into their households. Besides, extra women enabled a man to cure more pelts and to have bigger gardens.

Sensing none of this, Ménard plagued Kinongé about his sinfulness until the chief lost patience and drove him out of the village. The rest of the winter the missionary spent in a hut of fir boughs, to which compassionate women occasionally brought food.

Fortunately the winter was one of the mildest the region ever knew. By early April, 1661, ice was gone from the lake. Troubled by their consciences, fearful of Jesuit power in Montreal, and desirous of picking up whatever furs Kinongé's people had accumulated during the winter, Adrien Jolliet's French decided to hunt up the stranded father and transport him to Chequamegon Bay. It was a lovely spot, cobalt water protected by islands and a sandy needle of land called by the French La Pointe du Chagaoumegan—or, more simply, La Pointe.

The land around the shores of the bay was flat and open, well suited to the growing of maize and squash. Several thousand Ottawas and related bands (probably Ojibwa, or Chippewa in English) had moved in following the departure of Radisson and des Groseilliers and were building a village of bark huts. Here was a fertile field for Ménard's own sowing. But again he was not content. A handful of emaciated Hurons had just arrived at the village with a report that a band of their people were starving on what is now the Black River in central Wisconsin. They were terrified of the Sioux to the west, and they needed good soil for the few precious bags of seed to which they still clung. Would the Ottawas give them permission to move to Chequamegon?

The Ottawas would. As the joyful Hurons prepared to return home with the tidings, Ménard asked to go along in the hope that he could save a few souls by baptizing the dying. Reluctantly the Indians agreed, and the priest then prevailed on one of the French traders to accompany him as a helper. Why he passed over his lay assistant, Jean Guérin, is not a matter of record.

Because of Ménard's enfeebled condition, the proselytizers could not keep up with the Indians. One day they were left stranded. Still the Jesuit persisted. By chance his companion found a small hunting canoe beside a lake, and they appropriated it. By then, however, Ménard was too exhausted to paddle. To lighten his friend's work, he left the canoe at the foot of a long stretch of rough water and said he would walk ahead through the thick forest. He was never seen again, though the *coureur* searched as best he could. The probability is that Ménard, having forced himself beyond his limits, simply laid down and died. Later his *donné,* Jean Guérin, also died from what the traders all swore was an accident with a gun.

The *coureurs* were not too disconsolate. Having collected more furs than they could pile into their two canoes, they entrusted the surplus to the Ottawas, who had been chosen to make the regular run to Montreal with the pelts the villagers had collected during the winter. At that point, just before departure time, the whites learned how uncertain Indian transport could be.

Ottawas roaming west of Superior had recently clashed with a band of Sioux. Shortly after their return, rumors of retaliatory raids swept through the camp. Promptly the canoeists dropped their paddles and picked up their bows and such guns as they had. It was their duty as warriors to stay at home to defend their women and children.

No Sioux appeared; the shortening days grew hazy with the promise of autumn; but still the paddlers would not budge. As the first sleet storms rattled onto the empty bark canoes, the Frenchmen went mournfully out onto the choppy water, black-looking under steely clouds, to catch enough whitefish to carry them through the winter.

The next year they were frustrated in similar fashion, except that this time the panic was caused by a war party of Iroquois raiding past Sault Ste. Marie to Lake Superior's eastern shore. A mixed group of allied Ottawa, Ojibwa, and Nipissing hunters surprised the camp at dawn, killed several, and put the rest to flight. In spite of the victory the dread of Iroquois vengeance somewhere along the trail was such that Adrien Jolliet, lacking the forcefulness that Radisson and des Groseillier had shown in a comparable situation, was unable to get the flotilla underway.

Finally, in 1663, thirty-five canoes made the run to Montreal. This was fewer than half the number des Groseilliers and Radisson had brought down, and the three years' interest that had accrued on the debts the traders owed their suppliers kept them from realizing a satisfactory profit for their time and trouble. Still, the trip had not been wholly unproductive for the future. Along with their furs the men brought back an ingot of pure native copper and tales of great boulders of the same metal that the Indians mined by building fires on the huge stones and hacking off the softened edges with their hatchets. The *coureurs* also provided data about tribal alignments, enmities, and attitudes that would be helpful to anyone else entering the area. Probably, too, they were the source of some of the rumors, rapidly gathering fresh headway during the decade of the 1660s, of usable waterways to the Western sea.

It is even possible that during their enforced stay in the *pays d'en haut* they wondered a little about the limitations placed upon them by their way of doing things. They had conducted a "fugitive" trade. That is, they had created no permanent base, but, like their predecessors, had simply gone to a spot that had sounded promising and then had left with no indication that they might return. Shorthanded, they had relied on Indians for much of the work they needed done, particularly transport. But if ever the trade were to be institutionalized—and it would have to be if the distances opening out of Superior were to be conquered profitably—then the *coureurs* would have to free themselves from the caprice of the Indians. They would have to hire *engagés* to do the paddling, so that cargoes big enough to be profitable could be moved on schedule. They would need to establish supply depots where food for workers could be stored and where the middlemen who supplied the distant tribes of the interior could count on finding whatever merchandise they needed to meet the demands of their business. But payrolls and posts implied more permanence than the resources of New France had yet been able to achieve.

Change was on the way, however. On arriving in Montreal, the traders were interviewed by Pierre Boucher, the emissary who had recently returned from France. He had found so much interest there that he was preparing for publication in Paris the colony's first propaganda booklet, "The True and Genuine Description of New France Commonly Called Canada." Eagerly he pumped Adrien Jolliet for information about the copper, furs, and other resources of note in the Superior country.

During those interviews Jolliet learned more than he imparted. Boucher, he discovered, had arrived in Paris just as the twenty-three-year old king, Louis XIV, was beginning to shake off the bonds imposed on him by the regents who had ruled France in his name since his ascent to the throne at the age of five. Among a multitude of other things, the monarch and his new Minister of Marine and of Colonies, Jean-Baptiste Colbert, were concerned with building a colonial empire powerful enough to match those being created by England and the Netherlands. Accordingly the two men had listened carefully to Boucher and responded more decisively than the supplicant had dared hope.

The government was taken from the Hundred Associates and the firm that was currently leasing its rights. In its place the King instituted a provincial-type regime somewhat like those that prevailed inside France. Duties were split between two men. One, the governor-general, was to oversee the army in Canada and handle external affairs, including Indian relations. The other, the intendant, supervised internal finances, justice, and law and order.

The minister, Colbert, meanwhile laid out a new economic program. At its heart was an insistence that the potentials of the St.

Lawrence Valley—agriculture, fisheries, timber, shipbuilding, iron works and commerce with the French West Indies—be developed before the fur trade was extended and drew still more able-bodied men from the colony. But whether or not such a program could be successfully launched was something else. New France possessed no industries for attracting skilled labor. The short growing seasons discouraged most farmers. Only the fur trade held forth hopes of advancement to the ordinary man.

Determined to overcome these limitations Colbert promised to search for and send to the colony special strains of cold-resistant grain. He dispatched shiploads of fine dairy cows, sheep, and, it is said, the first horses in Canada. Because the colony's population was predominantly male, he had his agents scour French orphanages for marriageable girls of sound morals, and used government funds for paying their way across the Atlantic. He sought to stimulate fecundity by small subsidies and barrages of propaganda extolling early marriages and large families. The collection and marketing of beaver was placed in the hands of a new monopoly, the *Compagnie de l'Occident*. It had no governmental responsibilities, and since it also controlled the commerce of the West Indies, its managers, Colbert hoped, would not be inclined to push the Canadian fur trade at the expense of other projects.

Best of all, so far as New France's immediate worries were concerned, Colbert promised Boucher substantial aid against the Iroquois.

Because of troubles elsewhere, the first soldiers did not reach Quebec until 1665—the same year that saw the arrival of a new governor, Daniel Rémy, Sieur de Courcelles, and the first intendant, Jean Talon. (An earlier appointee as intendant had failed to show up.)

Breathing fire, Courcelles launched and bungled a winter campaign against the Mohawks. The regimental commander, the famed Marquis de Tracy, did better on a second attempt late in the summer of 1666. As soon as the Mohawks' crops were ready for harvest, he marched south with 1,600 men. Stunned by the size of the force, the Indians avoided a pitched battle and let the invaders burn their fields and their wooden towns.

The damage was not permanent, but what was to prevent similar invasions in the future? Disheartened by the prospect and the three forts Tracy's engineers were building on the Richelieu River, the route the Iroquois traditionally followed when striking at the settlements, the entire Confederacy sued for peace. This time even Canada's skeptics hoped that the relief would last.

In gratitude the Canadians expanded the name of the farthest lake, originally called Supérieur because of its geographical position, to Lac Supérieur au Tracy. Considerable irony underlay the designation. To a large segment of Canada's small population (3,125 civilians in 1666) Superior meant furs, and Tracy was the one who had made Superior attainable again. But Colbert had wanted the victory for the sake of a more stable settlement along the St. Lawrence—one that would not be dependent on a single commodity. Resolving that split in attitudes was the almost hopeless task assigned the new intendant, Jean Talon, the first strong leader New France had had since the death of Champlain.

IX

Grasping for a Continent

*J*ean Talon, the man charged with transforming a fearstricken outpost into a thriving colony, hardly looked suited to his task. He adorned himself in the ruffles and satin favored by the court of Louis XIV and let the curls of his powdered wig cascade over his shoulders. But for ten years he had served well as the intendant of a province in France, and he possessed a vigorous, creative imagination. In one sense the characteristic proved to be a drawback in the New World. It lifted his eyes from the confines of the St. Lawrence Valley, to which he was officially restricted, and let him glimpse the dim shape of a continent that some power sooner or later was going to seize. Why not France?

At first he confined himself to his assigned tasks. He compelled the recipients of seigneury grants to speed up the clearing of their land. He awarded medals to persons achieving distinction in agriculture and inaugurated such small industries as making tar, potash, and ship's masts from local timber. He had an ocean-going ship constructed and started a brewery in the hope that it would reduce the colony's imports of ardent spirits, much of which was carried to the Indians by the *coureurs de bois*.

The tasks bored him. The West was where things were happening, a point driven home to him when he interviewed Father Claude Allouez, fresh back from the first circumnavigation of Lake Superior.

Allouez was a tiger of a man, tireless, an accomplished linguist, fanatically patriotic, and convinced that God was on the side of the Jesuits, both in the wilderness and in King Louis's hostile court. In 1665, while the war with the Iroquois was still raging, he and six traders had accompanied 400 Ottawas—enough to give pause even to the Iroquois—to the new Huron and Ottawa villages at the base of Chequamegon Bay. There he built a small, bark-covered chapel that he named the mission of Saint Esprit. A group of young warriors tore it down and threatened his life. Coolly Allouez rebuilt. Impressed by his courage and fearful that if they drove him away the traders might desert them, the Indians let the new structure stand.

On May 6, 1667, after nearly two years of lonely labor, Allouez started for Quebec to report and ask for a helper. Characteristically he decided that he might as well explore new areas by swinging around the western tip of the bay and then travel east along the north shore. He took only one companion with him, an Indian. Like Adrien Jolliet before them, the two carried as part of their baggage a chunk of raw copper.

It was a gorgeous trip. After passing the tip of the bay, later called Fond du Lac, the paddlers turned their canoes northeast past giant headlands and across deep bays, using the lee sides of the numerous coastal islands as shelter from the lake's unpredictable winds. In places the shore was fringed with dense stands of sugar maples, prized by the Indians, who had learned to tap the rising sap in the spring and boil it down into hard, sweet chunks that they stored in bark containers. Behind the maple groves, in which aspen and birch also grew, were somber forests of white and red pines, twisted black spruce, and tamarack climbing to the top of rounded peaks whose reflections at dawn and sunset shimmered in water of purest crystal.

At Nipigon Bay, Superior's northernmost point, the explorers encountered a big, grayish river flowing from the north. A day's paddling away, the Indian said, was a ruffle-shored lake, Nipigon, that anywhere except in the vicinity of Superior would have been regarded as big. Allouez insisted that they detour to look at it. Then back they came to the bay, dotted with islands eroded to singular shapes, and on east past broken tiers of cliffs over which streams cascaded in long silver ribbons.

A gorgeous trip, but frightening at times. Rain squalls were frequent and sometimes furious. The waves they created dashed against the shore with such violence that in places no vegetation had been able to take root within twenty-five feet of the lake's edge. Fortunately, the many coves offered protection. In some, however, the granite banks were too steep to permit landing, and then Allouez and the Indian had to sit hunched and miserable in their rocking, rain-lashed canoe until the storm had passed. Later voyageurs coasting Superior's north shore estimated that, on the average, the lake's temperamental wind—*la vieille,* "the old woman," they called it—kept them pinned to the shore one day out of each three.

On reaching Quebec, Allouez showed Talon the copper he had brought and told him about two great rivers the Indians had frequently spoken of. As nearly as the priest could make out, one of the streams arose to the south in the land of the Illinois; quite possibly, Allouez speculated, it flowed into the Atlantic somewhere near Virginia. West of Superior, he continued, was another river that the Sioux called, as he remembered, "Messipi," the first known use of the word by a white. What he did not realize, understandably enough, was that the two rivers, described to him separately, were in fact one—the "Big Water" Jean Nicolet had learned of in 1634.

Talon's imagination was gripped. Allouez's report seemed to confirm earlier rumors, first printed in the *Jesuit Relation* of 1662, of remote tribes that paddled long distances southward to a seacoast where they traded with people who prayed as the French did. Presumably these were Spanish and therefore, the writer had concluded, the sea must be "either the Gulf of Mexico . . . or else the Vermillion Sea, on the Coast of New Granada, in the great South Sea." Hope swung conjecture toward the latter. New Granada was Mexico; the Vermillion Sea was the Gulf of California; and as Talon knew from maps circulating in Europe, the Gulf was fed by a river laden with red silt (our Colorado) that rose somewhere in the northeast. Might its upper reaches be Allouez's "Messipi"?

The question had international implications. By acquiring New Netherlands, the English had gained the only easily traveled water gap through the Allegheny Mountains. They could row their bateaux up the Mohawk River and portage without difficulty to Lake

Ontario. Aided by Iroquois eager to find new sources of fur for replacing the plundering expeditions now closed to them by Tracy's peace, traders from Albany might reach the "Messipi" and eventually the South Sea ahead of the French. Nor was that all. Any big river flowing as far south as New Granada would probably offer better agricultural possibilities than the St. Lawrence. The harbor at its mouth would not freeze five months of every winter. In such a country a colony of the sort Colbert envisioned could be firmly rooted—a colony, moreover, that would face toward both the silver mines of Mexico and the sea lanes to China.

There was still another reason—a ticklish one—for secular Canadians to move more rapidly west than Colbert wished. That was the Jesuits. Talon and Governor Courcelles, often at odds with each other, quarreled still more frequently with the head of the Society in New France, Bishop François de Laval de Montigny. Laval insisted that he was responsible only to the Pope and not to the church in France—that is to say, to neither King Louis XIV nor to the king's representatives in Canada. The argument made Talon and Courcelles bristle, for it confirmed their suspicions that the Jesuits of New France intended to elevate their spiritual authority above the king's temporal prerogatives.

Such a scheme, Talon believed, helped explain the eagerness of the Black Robes to get west as fast as—or even faster than—the traders. The priests wanted to dominate the Indians and confine the fur trade within narrow bounds they would prescribe. They were already making alarming progress. Allouez had a mission at Chequamegon. Another was planned for Sault Ste. Marie. The king would want to counter those thrusts . . . and yet Talon's orders from Colbert were to avoid extending the colony.

Caught on the horns of that dilemma, the intendant resorted to jesuitical reasoning of his own. Arguing that the development of copper mines was so essential to the well-being of the colony that it would not constitute an extension, he summoned to his office a noted *coureur* named Jean Péré. He equipped Péré with goods and directed him to go to Lake Superior as soon as the ice broke in the spring of 1668. There the *coureur* was to make friends with the Indians in the king's name and enlist their help in compiling information about the area's mineral resources. Though the point was not emphasized, he obviously would take note of fur resources as well. In order that he could stay on the job as long as necessary, Talon would direct husky, black-bearded Louis Jolliet, aged twenty-three, one of Adrien's many younger brothers, to carry fresh supplies to him in the spring of 1669.

A useful discovery would mean handling ores whose bulk would preclude their being transported over the rough Ottawa-French River route to the St. Lawrence. Therefore Péré and Jolliet should examine a possible alternative through lakes Ontario, Erie and the southern part of Lake Huron, a way to the west that had been opened to the French for the first time by the Iroquois peace. The arc would add 200 miles to the journey to Superior, but greater ease in travel might well compensate for the difference.

Talon did not wait to see Jolliet leave. His patience worn thin by the frustrations of his job, he had written Paris again and again, asking to be relieved. Late in the fall of 1668 a replacement arrived, and Talon returned joyfully to France on the last ship to leave the St. Lawrence before the freeze-up. There, to his surprise, his report about south-flowing rivers, fertile lands and possible water links to the Pacific caused Colbert to execute an about-face in policy.

The Minister had learned that earlier in the year the English had sent two ships to Hudson Bay with Radisson and des Groseilliers abroad. (It will be recalled that on this exploratory mission only des Groseilliers reached his destination.) In all probability, Colbert surmised, one of the arguments the brothers-in-law had used in gaining English support was a repetition of a point they had advanced vehemently in both Canada and New England: journeys between Hudson Bay and the lands beyond Lake Superior could be easily accomplished by following the north-flowing rivers the Crees had described. Now suppose, Colbert continued, that the headwaters of those rivers interlocked with the sources of Allouez's "Messipi." * The way would then be open for England to outflank Canada.

Straightway Colbert ordered Talon back to New France. No skimping this time. The intendant was to take every measure neces-

---

* As indeed they do. Using those waterways, Vikings from Norway may have reached Minnesota a thousand years ago. In 1930, two teen-age boys, Eric Sevareid, later of the Columbia Broadcasting System, and Walter Post canoed 2,500 miles from Minneapolis to York Factory beside Hudson Bay. Although Indians left no records, they certainly duplicated the feat many times.

sary to anticipate both the English and the Jesuits in the west—but without offending either, for France and England were at peace, and the king had no desire right then to cross swords with the powerful Society of Jesus. At Talon's request, the term of his appointment was limited to two years.

His start was unpropitious. A gale drove his ship south to Portugal, where it grounded and went to pieces. Talon, who survived, was not able to risk the Atlantic again until the spring of 1670. He brushed disaster once more when his vessel struck a rock off Tadoussac. Thoroughly shaken, he reached Quebec on August 18, 1670. Almost simultaneously des Groseilliers and Radisson, traveling again on separate ships and acting this time as advisers to the newly chartered Company of Adventurers Trading into Hudson's Bay, disembarked at the mouth of Rupert River, six hundred miles north of the St. Lawrence. There, with emotions never described, the two Frenchmen watched the officials in the party lay claim to the Bay's vast drainage system for England.

Immediately after landing at Quebec, Talon set about gathering data on what had been happening during his absence. Very little that he learned pleased him.

First there was the matter of the copper mine. The reports Péré had sent in were, so Talon wrote Colbert, "very obscure," and little more could be pried out of Louis Jolliet. Jolliet had not contacted Péré in 1669, as instructed, but had left the supplies intended for him at the new mission just then being built on the south side of foaming Sault Ste. Marie. His reason: the whites in the area had ransomed several Iroquois prisoners from the Ottawas and wanted the men transported home—by French, to prove French friendship —before the Confederacy declared war on the northern Indians and disrupted the accelerating fur trade. One of the ransomed Iroquois was stranded at the Sault, and Jolliet had agreed to rush him east instead of continuing in search of Péré.

According to surviving records, this trip with the erstwhile captive and an unknown number of voyageurs is the one that blazed New France's main alternate to the Ottawa River route. (Actually both Péré and Jolliet, obedient to Talon's instructions may have followed the same path up country.) Be that as it may, Jolliet saw no advantage in the route. His canoe, he told Talon, had been constantly battered by the winds that swept the lakes. The crew had been forced to circumvent "a vast and prodigious cadence of Water" (Lahontan's description of Niagara Falls) by means of an arduous ten-mile portage. Afterward, between the lower end of Lake Ontario and Montreal they had run four sets of rapids that as late as 1818 led tourist John Duncan to exclaim nervously about tempestuous currents "dashing furiously over the rocks, sweeping around insulated fragments with the velocity of a whirlpool, and heaving even in the less agitated spots with a broken and fearful commotion." Ore could not come down that way unless sailing vessels were built for carrying it through the lakes and a wagon road was constructed for skirting Niagara Falls. Fur traders anxious to reach the St. Lawrence before the last ship departed for France would probably prefer the original trail.

As far as the course of the trade itself went, Talon's best information came from a *coureur* named Nicolas Perrot, aged twenty-six in 1670—one year older than Louis Jolliet. Perrot had come to New France some ten years before as a lay assistant to the Jesuits. In 1665 he had made a quick trip to the interior as a hired hand. The following winter he had worked as a domestic for a Montreal widow and then for the Sulpicians, a Franciscan order that during the 1650s had received Montreal Island as a seigneury grant.

Peace with the Iroquois enabled Perrot and an illiterate friend who knew the West, Toussaint Baudry, to form a trading partnership for taking goods supplied by Montreal merchants to Chequamegon Bay. They traveled there with Father Allouez, his new, untested helper, Louis Nicolas, and a mix of Indians and other traders as opportunistic as themselves. A single winter at the mission was enough for Louis Nicolas and he returned to the St. Lawrence with the first convoy of the spring. Not Perrot. He was reveling in his freedom.

The rough post that he and Baudry built at Chequamegon lured in several red hunters from the central part of Wisconsin. From those visitors the whites learned that the refugees displaced by the Iroquois attacks of 1648–53 were at last coming to terms with their new land and their new neighbors, and were settling in semipermanent agricultural villages. Curious and scenting untapped trading opportunities, Perrot pushed south from Chequamegon to investigate.

For nearly three years he crisscrossed all but the westernmost part of what is now Wisconsin. In winter he snowshoed; in summer he preferred to canoe, but he walked with a heavy pack on his back when he had to. Sometimes he had Baudry for company, sometimes Indians. Often he traveled alone. Already competent in the Algonquian dialect used by the Ottawas, he worked hard at picking up a smattering of other languages, including the Siouan tongues used by the Sauks and their surly allies, the Foxes. He learned to be completely at home in the Indian villages. The inhabitants trusted him, and he was able to arbitrate with cool impartiality disputes between the new settlers and the established residents.

By 1670 he and his fellows had collected an enormous store of fur, and still more pelts remained in the villages for want of merchandise with which to purchase them. Yearning for the fleshpots now that they were rich, the whites decided to move the whole mass to Montreal by means of the biggest convoy yet assembled—some 900 Indians representing a medley of tribes. Many were hereditary enemies sworn to peace for this round trip of 1,800 miles. Mingling excitedly were Ottawas, Hurons, Eries, Illinois, Miamis, Mascoutens, Potawatomis, Winnebagos, Foxes, Sauks, and even a few Sioux. Among them were several women and children, as was generally the case with Indian fur caravans.

Colorful, noisy, and confused, the disorganized flotilla swept through the sparkling waters of Michilimackinac Strait, along the rocky shores of Huron's North Channel, over the French River portages, and then down the torrents of the Ottawa to what was for many in the group their first sight of a white man's village. Their carousing shocked the staid residents of Montreal and Three Rivers, but the furs that between dances and drinking bouts flowed into the warehouses warmed the blood of the merchants. Overnight the name of Nicolas Perrot, one-time domestic, was on everyone's tongue.

Gradually the Indians straggled home, their canoes laden with goods for themselves and for barter with more distant tribes. Perrot would have gone with them if the governor had not ordered him to stay in Quebec until Talon arrived. After that things moved swiftly.

First Perrot brought the intendant up to date about the new patterns of Indian settlement in Wisconsin. The Jesuits, he added, were exploiting that pattern assiduously. Claude Dablon, the Society's most talented administrator in New France, had established frontier headquarters at the new mission beside Sault Ste. Marie and from there was directing the spread of new stations with alarming zeal. He had sent frail Jacques Marquette to St. Esprit beside Chequamegon Bay and had transferred Allouez to the shores of Green Bay and the lower Fox River. In short order that indefatigable worker in the Lord's vineyard had founded and staffed four missions. A fifth, Perrot prophesied accurately, would soon go up at Michilimackinac.

That was not all. The Jesuits were also compiling geographic information against the day when they could launch new moves deeper into the interior. They had learned the exact name of the great south-flowing river—Mississippi—and speculation about its ultimate destination filled hour after hour of talk beside the smoky fireplaces. Mixed with that talk was more about a sea that supposedly lay some 200 French leagues, roughly 500 miles, west of Lake Superior. The Indians who told about that big, brackish body of water were describing Lake Winnipeg, but the French did not understand it that way. As Dablon would write shortly, "This Western Sea can only be the Japan Sea." Behind the words lay the implication that the Jesuits planned to be there as soon as anyone.

There was another problem. Even while the intendant was reflecting on what he had learned from Perrot, the Indian grapevine brought word that two ships had been sighted in James Bay, the dangling southern extremity of Hudson Bay. Immediately Talon, who had been briefed in Paris on the activities of Radisson and des Groseilliers, guessed where those ships had come from and why.

Obviously ripostes were necessary. The first step, he decided, should be a pageant of possession at Sault Ste. Marie—one impressive enough to convince both the Indians and the traders that the king's authority was superior to that of the Jesuits in all save strictly spiritual matters. The same ceremony should also serve notice on the English in both New York and at Hudson Bay that France intended to claim and defend the still unknown territories of the West.

He placed this ambitious undertaking under the nominal command of one of his protégés, François Daumont, Sieur de St. Lusson. The galvanizing force was Nicolas Perrot. The urgency that the intendant attached to the matter showed in the group's start late in October, their canoes laden to the gunwales with gifts and merchandise. (St. Lusson planned to trade on the side.) The days were short, the nights chill. When glazes of ice made landings difficult along Huron's rocky north shore, the travelers halted and set up a winter camp.

They did not suffer from boredom. A group of Indians who joined them told of huge herds of moose wintering on nearby Manitoulin, largest of the granite-wrinkled, lake- and meadow-dotted islands that form the southern edge of Huron's North Channel. Sport! Building sledges, the French and Indians crossed to one of Manitoulin's many handsome peninsulas and established hunting shelters. They found converging walls of granite that enabled them to construct one or more pens with a minimum of logs. On snowshoes and helped by yelping Indian dogs, they day after day herded moose into the enclosures and with arrows, spears, and even knives slaughtered an estimated 2,400 of the huge animals before the weather began to soften.

Talon had directed that the greatest possible number of Indians attend the ceremony at Sault Ste. Marie. Accordingly as soon as the first ribbons of open water streaked the ice, Perrot and one or two companions loaded a canoe onto a sledge, pulled it cautiously to the edge of the floes, and embarked for Green Bay. Other messengers hurried on to Lake Superior to contact and speed up the movement of the red traders who were already preparing to travel to the Sault with their furs.

The pageant was scheduled for early June, 1671, so that Indians who wished to visit Montreal and return before winter could do so. Perrot reached the rendezvous comfortably ahead of the assigned date, bringing with him Claude Allouez and delegates representing most of the Wisconsin tribes. (The few who did not come appointed proxies.) Although Marquette's delegation arrived late from Chequamegon, other groups of Lake Superior Indians—Ottawas, Chippewas, Crees, Nipissings, and a few Assiniboins—also arrived at the Sault in good season, cradling in their arms their beribboned guns and long-stemmed calumets. Fourteen bewhiskered traders were on hand to greet them, as colorful in sashes and bright capots as were the greased, heavily painted Indians, strutting in feathers, bear claw necklaces, and moccasins resplendent with beads and dyed porcupine quills.

The setting was carefully prepared. On the top of a small hill that overlooked the mission palisade lay two long poles ready for lifting. One bore a cross; the other, a wooden escutcheon on which the royal arms had been carved. Beside the poles were wrapped bundles that everyone knew contained gifts for the chiefs. Lured by anticipation of the present-giving, hundreds and hundreds of Indians ranged themselves along the slopes, leaving only a narrow lane open for the approach of the whites.

On signal the palisade gates swung open. Four Jesuit priests paced slowly out, crucifixes held high as they chanted Latin hymns. The traders followed, looking self-conscious. Behind them came St. Lusson, dressed either in armor or (historians differ) in shimmering, knee-length velvet breeches and a short jacket that covered a ruffled shirt with lace at the end of the sleeves. He held either a helmet or a plumed beaver hat (surely the latter would have been more appropriate) in the crook of one arm and carried an unsheathed sword aloft in his opposite hand. The cross went up, Dablon sprinkled holy water. During the momentary stilling of the voices that accompanied the action, the roar of the rapids twined with the sigh of wind through the pines until one could not be sure which sound was which.

The king's moment came next. Perrot gestured to his *engagés*. With knives they ripped open the bundles and held aloft samples of the presents—blankets, bolts of bright cloth, hats, swords, mirrors. Not to be outdone, the chiefs had their warriors lay heaps of beaver fur at St. Lusson's feet. Then Allouez raised his hand for silence and, in the Ottawa tongue that was at least partly familiar to most of the crowd, sought to explain to the Indians just how powerful the king of France really was. "He is more terrible than the thunder; the earth trembles; the air and sea are set on fire by the discharge of his cannon." Then, abandoning his Biblical cadences, he turned to images his listeners could more readily grasp. The warehouses of the chief of the French held "enough hatchets to cut down all your forests, enough kettles to cook all your moose [including 2,400 on Manitoulin Island?], enough glass beads to fill your cabins."

Now St. Lusson took over. A paper on which the chiefs had inked their marks—an admission of French sovereignty, though it is unlikely they understood what the declaration implied—was placed behind the escutcheon bearing the royal arms. To the chanting of more hymns the pole was swung upright, its top just a shade higher than that of the pole carrying the cross. Picking up a piece of turf, St. Lusson cried loudly that he was taking possession in the name of the king of all the lands that lay between the Seas of the North and the South and the West. *Vive le Roy!*

The whites cheered; muskets volleyed. The Jesuits retreated inside the mission, presumably aware that they had been upstaged. Moreover, so far as French lawyers and diplomats were concerned, any Englishman who henceforth strayed into these areas from either New England or Hudson Bay could be charged with trespass.

The Indians were less certain. The placing of the written declaration of sovereignty behind the royal standard and the raising of it high in the air had made them suspicious, just as Cartier's raising of a cross on Gaspé Peninsula nearly a century and a half earlier had stirred doubts among Donnacona's people. After the gathering had dispersed, a few young men quietly returned, shinnied up the pole, retrieved the paper, and burned it. Let there be no magic working their people harm.

Then, loading their canoes with the magic goods that really were destroying the ancient ways, they paddled home to their villages.

X

The Rivals

*J*ean Talon knew well enough that, although St. Lusson's airy
proclamations at Sault Ste. Marie were useful as opening moves
in the game of international chess, they would not hold up against
gestures of actual occupancy by rival powers. Accordingly he determined to send other expeditions into two critical areas as yet un-
trodden by the French. One was the southern rim of James Bay;
the other, the region south of the Great Lakes recently made ac-
cessible by peace with the Iroquois.

The northern expedition was charged with learning, first, whether
or not men from the ships reported in James Bay had actually
landed and given evidence of proclaiming sovereignty. If no signs
of such activity were found, then the explorers were to search out
some cove where French vessels dispatched around Labrador from
Quebec could winter while French workers built a post and mission station as proof of their rights.

Talon placed the expedition in charge of husky Charles Albenal,
the priest who had been left behind in 1660 when the Ottawas had
permitted only René Ménard to go with them to Chequamegon.
True, Albenal was a Jesuit and, aged fifty-four now, old for so
exacting a trip. But missionary work around Tadoussac had made
him familiar with part of the land his group would traverse and
with some of the tribes they would meet. Albenal's own hope was

that he would find new peoples to whom he could impart the Blessed Word.

Two laymen accompanied him, Paul Denis, Sieur de St. Simon, and a *coureur* named Sébastian Provencher. After a late start from Tadoussac in mid-August, 1671, the trio pushed up the cliff-girt Saguenay River as far as Lake St. John. There they encountered unfriendly Mistassini Indians from farther inland. The Mistassini, middlemen in the trade between Tadoussac and the fringes of James Bay, wanted no interference with their monopoly. They sought to turn the French back with tales of horrors waiting ahead. Divining their motives, Albenal circled around the scare stories in search of useful facts. To his dismay he learned that white men had passed the winter of 1670–71, in cabins at the mouth of Rupert River and, on sailing away in the spring, had promised that others of their nation would return later in the year to resume trading. For all the Mistassini knew, the reinforcements were already landing in Rupert Bay.

Cabins with their implications of sovereignty gave the explorers pause. They did not mind deep water, cold nights, and wretched food, but they had no desire to be arrested and transported across the Atlantic as spies. Seeking a remedy that either Talon or Albanel should have thought of earlier, the French hired Indians to go to Quebec for passports.

By the time the messengers returned with the documents, the season was too advanced for a sustained journey northward, and so the trio joined a band of wandering Indians for what the priest described in the *Jesuit Relations* as the most severe winter he had ever spent.

A painful time—but Albenal made the most of it. During the long nights in the fetid, smoke-filled bark wigwams he propounded an ominous mixture of theology and economics that he believed impressed his hearers. The strangers at the Bay, he said, "acknowledge the Demon for their master." That is, they were Protestants, and it would be fatal to the Indians' hope for salvation to deal too closely with such people. "Resume your old route to Lake St. John, where you will always find some black gown to instruct and baptize [you]." Scare stories, it would seem, were not limited to Indians.

On June 1, 1672, the French started north again, accompanied by sixteen suspicious Mistassini hunters. It was a taxing journey beside mountains half a mile tall, over majestic lakes, past forbidding headlands. On June 6 they portaged across a rocky hill and descended to a lake that drained into Rupert River and Hudson Bay. On the twenty-eighth, shortly after the longest day of the year, they reached the bleak coast and with awe watched dawn color the waters to the northeast before twilight had vanished from the northwest.

Near the mouth of the river they found a sloop-rigged coasting vessel anchored in a sheltered inlet near two empty cabins. They spent a week examining the beaches on either side of the "settlement" mostly so that Albanel could find Indians he could proselytize. On July 6 they started home. Three days inland, on an island in Lake Nemiskau, they took possession of the country by raising a cross and the king's arms. As for the validity of their action as opposed to the English claim, that would be up to others. Their own hearts were light. They had served their country, Albanel by his own count had baptized 200 heathens, and his companions had filled their canoe with furs.

Less is known about a potentially more important expedition that was commanded during those same years by a hard, selfish, arrogant, and unusually capable young man named René Robert Cavelier, Sieur de La Salle. Cavelier, incidentally, was an ordinary name, not a title.

As a schoolboy in the College of Jesuits in Rouen, France, La Salle had pored over each *Jesuit Relation* as it arrived from Canada. One recurrent theme, the possibility of a transcontinental waterway to the Pacific, fired his imagination. Why should he not be the discoverer—and the inheritor of the riches that would attend success?

Fortunately for the dream, an older brother, Jean Cavelier, served as a lay priest at the Seminary of St. Sulpice in Montreal. In 1666, René Robert, not quite twenty-three, journeyed to Montreal to visit Jean. Almost at once he decided to stay. From the Sulpicians he obtained (his parents were wealthy) a seigneury fronting the thunderous rapids that Champlain had named Sault St. Louis. There, eight miles from the docks of Montreal, La Salle built an austere manor house enclosed by pickets.

The site was strategic for his purpose. To avoid battling the rapids, merchants and *coureurs* carted their wares and furs along a road that connected the warehouses in the village with the canoe landing places above the stormy water. Each spring and again late in the summer and early fall throngs of Indians, woods runners and priests walked or rode past La Salle's seigneury. Legend insists that the young owner asked the travelers so many questions about routes to the Western Sea that his manor and the rapids both became known derisively as La Chine, the starting point for the trip to the Orient. Though the spelling was soon changed to Lachine, the name remains attached to the area.

Accompanied by fourteen *engagés,* the seigneur of La Chine made his first venture into the interior in 1669. His destination was a west-flowing river, presumably the Ohio, of which Seneca Indians had told him. Tagging along were seven Sulpician priests and helpers intent on establishing a station among the Senecas. On their way the combined groups met Louis Jolliet returning from Sault Ste. Marie with his ransomed Iroquois brave. The *coureur's* report of throngs of unconverted Indians in Wisconsin (an area Jolliet had not yet seen in person) led the missionaries to shift destinations. They split from La Salle and after a miserable winter on the northern shores of Lake Erie reached Sault Ste. Marie only to discover that Jesuits had preempted the Wisconsin field ahead of them. La Salle meanwhile swung south into Ohio on a journey whose details have been lost.

Both the Sulpicians and the explorer were back on the St. Lawrence when Talon returned with Colbert's instructions to press the search for the Western Sea. After interviewing the travelers, the intendant directed La Salle, "who," he wrote the king, "is very enthusiastic for these enterprises," to continue southwest until he located the Mississippi. These orders were delivered at the same time that St. Lusson was sent to Sault Ste. Marie to stage his pageant of possession.

Again there is no telling where La Salle went. He returned to Montreal in 1671 for supplies and, strangely, hurried back into the Ohio wilderness without reporting to Talon. As 1672 dragged by with no word from him, the intendant, whose two-year term was nearing its end, grew impatient and decided to send out another expedition to descend the Mississippi far enough to learn whether it emptied into the Gulf of California or the Gulf of Mexico. The decision was approved by another famed figure in the turbulent history of New France, Louis de Baude, comte de Frontenac, who had just arrived to replace the Sieur de Courcelles as governor-general of the colony. The man that Talon and Frontenac put in charge of the Mississippi adventure was Louis Jolliet.

Pressures for speed must have been heavy. Jolliet hired the best paddlers he could find, filled his canoe with supplies and trade goods, and in mid-October began a race with winter. Thanks to a late freeze-up he managed to reach the new mission of St. Ignace on the northern shore of Michilimackinac Strait early in December. At St. Ignace he found Father Jacques Marquette, who was there as a result of a disaster.

In 1671 Sioux Indians had fallen savagely on the Huron and Ottawa villages at Chequamegon Bay. In shambling panic the victims had fled east to Michilimackinac Island, which had been one of their havens after their routing by the Iroquois two decades earlier. Marquette, who had been stationed at Chequamegon at the time of the rout, followed his charges. As he knew, mission buildings had been erected a year earlier on Michilimackinac Island (a name gradually being shortened to Mackinac, pronounced Mackinaw), but many traders were also clustering there. In the priest's mind their influence was corrupting. Besides, fields for farming were limited on the island. Consequently he moved the chapel to a more secluded spot on the mainland and persuaded many of the Indians to follow.

Jolliet, who had met Marquette before, tapped him to be the spiritual head of the Mississippi expedition—a sop to the Jesuits, but one that left Jolliet in command of actual operations. Why the choice fell on Marquette is unknown. Perhaps, being at the outfitting point, he was convenient. Certainly he was zealous. But he was also in poor health for so demanding a labor.

Our concern here is not with the epic trip down the Mississippi, which the explorers followed until they were sure that it emptied into the Gulf of Mexico, but with its results. On their return north, the party ascended the Illinois River and portaged easily through the site of present Chicago to the bottom of Lake Michigan. Because Marquette was seriously ill, Jolliet took him to the Mission of St. Francis Xavier at Green Bay and then utilized the remaining good weather of fall to reexamine the southern parts of the lake.

As soon as the water was open in the spring of 1674 he headed for Quebec with his maps and journals to report to Governor Frontenac. He almost did not make it. His canoe capsized in the lower section of the Lachine rapids. His companions drowned, his papers vanished. Jolliet himself, battered unconscious against the rocks, was fished from the water by a following canoe.

None of this dimmed his enthusiasm for the Illinois country. Its resources, he told Frontenac on finally reaching Quebec, were magnificent. Moreover, cutting a short canal from the bottom of Lake Michigan to a convenient tributary of the Illinois would enable small sailing vessels to journey without interruption from Niagara Falls to an ice-free harbor at the mouth of the Mississippi.

To Frontenac the news was electrifying. He was a scoundrel, but a magnetic one. A godson of Louis XIII, he had fought in several of his country's innumerable battles, had schemed with skill for advancements he did not always deserve, had lived luxuriously, and at the age of fifty-two had found himself mired in debt. To escape his creditors, he obtained an appointment as governor-general of Canada. His overweening purpose was to restore his fortune by muscling in on the fur trade.

He had quickly seen that the alternate trails to the interior—one by the lower lakes, the other by the Ottawa River—gave him an opportunity to cut off pelts traveling along the southern route before they reached Montreal. Requisitioning labor and supplies from that town, the very settlement he intended to injure, he built a fort he named Frontenac for himself. It stood exactly where Colbert had ordered Talon not to build a post, at Cataraqui, near the point where the St. Lawrence flows out of Lake Ontario. (Kingston, Ontario, occupies the site today.) Frontenac's justification for his unauthorized act: the fort would keep the Iroquois from trapping the beaver that were making a comeback in unoccupied Huronia and taking the catch to the English at Albany.

Although the Iroquois were doing just that, no one in Montreal was fooled for long about the governor's basic intent. Frontenac meant to levy tribtue on all furs flowing through the Lakes from the West—an unimaginative form of graft that took on added dimensions as soon as La Salle returned from the southwest.

The young explorer had not reached either the Ohio or the Mississippi during his wanderings beyond Lake Erie, but he did not feel the lack. The country through which he had traveled so impressed him that he had forgotten the Western Sea and began to dream instead of creating his own commercial empire in those beneficent lands. Because he would need the governor's aid in obtaining charters from the French court, he shared his ideas with Frontenac.

At once the governor's plans leaped from a simple shakedown of passing canoes into a scheme for engrossing the entire trade south of the lower Great Lakes. In 1673 he turned Fort Frontenac, which had been built as a public defense, into a private seigneury and gave it to La Salle to use as a staging point for an advance into the proposed new empire—partly Frontenac's empire now.

Jolliet's account of his journey with Marquette added exciting new dimensions to the plan. Why, the visionaries asked each other, should their activities be limited to the areas adjacent to the lakes? By stringing forts through the Illinois country to the Mississippi River and on to the Gulf of Mexico, Frontenac and his protégé could control the heartland of the continent—a heartland filled with furs.

As word of the dazzling dream leaked out, the merchants in Montreal raised such a storm of protest that the French government decided to investigate the whole course of the trade. The result was a belated discovery that nearly all the *habitants,* and not just Frontenac and his henchmen, were bringing about the very situation Colbert had originally feared. Unburdened by dread of the Iroquois, they were overextending the colony's slender resources in a shortsighted pursuit of one commodity only. Restoring the economy—and even the morals—of New France would demand drastic reductions in the prices paid for pelts and in the number of men permitted to trade for them.

A principal factor in the problem was the unexpected concentration of Indians in the Wisconsin area, a process that had been quickened by the flight of the Hurons and Ottawas from Chequamegon to Michilimackinac. This concentration had led to the almost overnight construction of several trading posts and mission stations near the largest Indian villages, especially in the vicinity of Green Bay. The presence of whites with goods to trade attracted still more Indians. Even the Jesuits engaged in barter, partly to meet expenses and partly to lure possible converts to their doors.

Business was good. A cornucopia of furs still existed within the

Wisconsin area itself. In addition, an easy approach to the Mississippi by way of the Fox and Wisconsin rivers opened access to new territories. Certain of the tribes, notably the Reynards (the English would call them Foxes), began setting themselves up as middlemen serving what is now southern Minnesota and northern Iowa. Meanwhile, and in spite of the disaster at Chequamegon, Ottawa canoemen, the best on the continent, aided by a handful of daring whites, continued to tap the output of the native peoples who dwelt along the far shores of Lake Superior.

The result was a greater flow of pelts than the hatmakers in Europe could absorb. To make matters worse, most of the furs were of the wrong sort. The underfur, or "wool," of pelts taken south and southwest of Lake Superior was not as heavy as that produced farther north. The southern Indians, moreover, were less inclined than those in the Canadian Shield to sew the pelts they obtained into coats, and, as a by-product of staying warm, "grease" the garments with their body oil and sweat. Greased furs were an essential component in the felt needed for quality hats, but because of the rush to Wisconsin, Canada in 1677 exported only 4,000 "coat beaver" in a total output of 92,000 skins.

The law of supply and demand had no effect on the situation. The Canadian fur market was controlled by a monopoly that paid the Crown a high annual rent for its privileges. One of those privileges was the right to levy a twenty-five percent tax on all beaver pelts and a ten percent tax on all moose hides produced in New France. The presumption was that this tax would bring in enough revenue to meet the company's payments to the Crown, which in turn used the money for funding the colonial government.

The monopoly was also privileged to act as the sole exporter of furs from the colony. Although any resident could barter with the Indians for pelts, the skins eventually had to be turned over to the company at prices set by law. In theory these prices were pegged high enough so that the seller could thrive after paying his taxes, and yet were low enough so that the monopoly could make a profit when marketing the products in Europe. The European market was not pegged, however. The oversupply of furs pouring out of North America during the late 1660s and early 1670s pushed prices so low that in 1674 the Compagnie de l'Occident, established by the Crown in 1663, went bankrupt.

It was followed by a succession of lessees operating as the

Company of the Farm. To help the new *fermiers* stay solvent, the Minister of Colonies reduced the price paid for pelts in such a way as to place a premium on coat beaver. A better policy would have been a refusal to accept more than a minimum amount of poor-grade skins from Wisconsin, but French bureaucracy dared not take the step. Trade in inferior skins made up the bulk of the business of the Montreal merchants and hence of the French factories that supplied the Montrealers with merchandise. Besides, so it was argued, if Montreal did not buy parchment (sun-dried) pelts from the South, the Indians would turn to the English. New alliances would be forged and the balance of power in the Americas upset. And so the *coureurs,* assured of an unfailing market in Montreal, kept going West in search of whatever pelts the Indians chose to provide, even immature beaver caught in summertime.

By the mid 1670s the situation was critical. The total population of New France, children included, was only a little more than 7,000. From that small figure the most vigorous young males—an estimated 300 of them in 1673, and each year the number increased—vanished into the forest for long stretches of time. This was a sore drain on manpower needed for farms, service trades, and nascent factories. Stemming the flow, it was thought, was the only way in which to restore strength to home industries—and, in addition, to reduce the input of cheap furs that was so damaging to the hopes of the *fermiers*.

Even morals might be improved. According to one angry report, the frustrations that resulted from having so many young men away from home drove wives and unmarried girls who saw no husbands in the offing into wantonness. Adultery was rife, seduction easy. Each winter, nine months after the annual flotillas had returned to Montreal and Three Rivers, the number of births to un-wed mothers and to wives whose husbands had been nowhere near soared high.

In vain the clergy exhorted colonial officials to set a good example by scowling on late entertainments because of the "unseemly happenings that usually occur at nocturnal banquets." As for balls, "one must state of them, as a doctor [stated] of mushrooms, that the best are worthless." "Immodest curls" and "a baring of neck and shoulders" were to be forbidden as "a cause of perdition for an infinite number of souls." But without a stabilizing element of sober, church-going artisans and farmers at home, how could such ideals be attained?

In an effort to keep the boys down on the farm, the officials tried licensing. Only a limited number of men bearing *congés* (permits) signed by the governor or the intendant—Talon's successor, Jacques Duchesneau, had finally arrived in 1675—could go into the interior to trade. Predictably the system failed. Frontenac handed out special permits to favorites and grafters, and men unwilling to grease his palm simply went west without licenses.

Enraged by the wholesale flouting of the laws, Intendant Duchesneau the next year, 1676, revoked all *congés*. Let the Indians bring the furs to Montreal, as they had done in the old days, and to an extent still did.

The resultant increase in the number of red carriers created still fresh problems. Plied with French brandy by the traders, the Indians indulged in annual bedlams that caused the residents of Montreal to barricade themselves inside their houses until the celebrants had drunk themselves insensible. Reports of even more deplorable occurrences in the native villages led in 1678 to the summoning of a parliament to consider restrictions on the use of spirits in the trade. Hoping to bring about total prohibition, the priests told hair-raising tales of horror. "The Indians drink only to get drunk and in that state commit incest and many other crimes. Sons kill their fathers and rape their sisters. Mothers kill their children, and women prostitute themselves for a pint of spirits."

Merchants retorted that the tales were exaggerated; when isolated cases of murder and rape did occur, the underlying cause was not alcohol so much as the Indians' lack of civilized restraints. Besides, if the insatiable *sauvages* could not obtain liquor from the French, they would turn to the English, an old argument supplied with a new twist. Let the priests beware. Indians drinking happily among the heretics of Albany might end up as Protestants.

The outcome was a meaningless compromise. Traders were prohibited from carrying brandy to the interior (where *coureurs* weren't supposed to go anyway) and the Indians were to be sold only moderate amounts of drink at the Montreal trading fairs. Neither restriction was given more than lip service by the merchants in the towns and the illegal forest runners in the wilderness.

La Salle muddied the trading situation still more. After two visits to the French court he finally won a five-year royal charter granting him the right to traverse the Mississippi River and build forts throughout its huge valley. In return he agreed to pay out of his own pocket all exploratory and developmental expenses and not to trade with Indians accustomed to traveling to the fairs at Montreal. The last behest he had no intention of heeding; if everything went as planned, he would soon be diverting the entire trade of the Great Lakes area to the ice-free mouth of the Mississippi, far beyond reach of the Montrealers.

He reached Canada from France in September, 1678. Accompanying him were a Sulpician priest, Louis Hennepin, and an Italian-born French soldier, Henri de Tonti, the latter destined to be one of the few loyal friends La Salle would ever have. As a replacement for a hand lost in battle, Tonti wore an iron hook capable of cracking open the skull of anyone reckless enough to confront him. The iron streak of fortitude inside him matched that hook.

Tonti had a cousin in New France, Daniel Greysolon, Sieur Du Lhut, a man as obsessed as La Salle with reaching the untapped interior of the continent.* In many ways, indeed, Du Lhut was much like La Salle, though older by from four to seven years. (The exact date of his birth is uncertain.) After several years service in the French army he had come to Montreal to visit an uncle, a merchant named Patron who was involved in various fur trade deals with Governor Frontenac. During his stay Du Lhut haunted the trading fairs, talking to the *coureurs* and Indians. The tales he heard of a Western Sea somewhere beyond Lake Superior fired him as similar tales had fired La Salle nearly a decade earlier, and he determined to find the way there. The fact that he was a distant cousin by marriage of Pierre Esprit Radisson may also have had something to do with his fascination in distant lands.

In 1673 or 1674 he returned to France to put his affairs in order. He picked an unpropitious time. He was swept back into the army as squire to the Marquis de Lassey, commander of Louis XIV's

---

* Du Lhut, with the carelessness of the times, spelled his name various ways. American usage perpetuated the form "Duluth" in the Minnesota city at the western tip of Lake Superior. The correct usage, adopted in Canada, is "Du Lhut," a form that will be followed in this account.

personal guard, and was marched off to fight a superior force of
Spanish, Dutch, and Austrians at Seneffe in the valley of the Meuse
on August 11, 1674. During that furious engagement, in which the
opposing armies each lost one-seventh of their men in killed alone,
he may have encountered La Salle's Sulpician friend, Father Louis
Hennepin, chaplain of one of the French regiments.

Du Lhut got back to New France at about the time that the new
intendant, Jacques Duchesneau, refused to issue any further licenses
for travel to the interior. To top off his frustration, Du Lhut late
in 1677 met a certain Hugues Randin, whom Frontenac the year
before had sent to explore Lake Superior in defiance of Duchesneau's ban. Randin returned with a good map of the lake and a
report that the Ottawas and Hurons were not going to bring many
furs to the settlements from the far west because of their warfare
with the Sioux, or Nadouesioux, as the French called the tribe after
picking up the word from their enemies, the Ojibwas and Ottawas.
What was needed to stimulate trade, Randin suggested, was a peace
mission to the belligerents.

By this time Du Lhut had convinced himself that the way to the
Western Sea lay through the land of the Sioux. Acting as an emissary to the embattled Indians might be a way to reach his goal.
Then, having penetrated to the heart of Sioux territory, he would
cap his public service by proclaiming French sovereignty.

Alas for schemes. Suspecting that the plan was a disguise for a
trading expedition, Duchesneau refused the necessary permits. Du
Lhut, accompanied by his uncle, Patron, next approached Frontenac. The governor spread his hands. Duchesneau and he were at
complete loggerheads, and in the matter of permits the home government was supporting the intendant. True, La Salle had won a
special charter from the king with Frontenac's help, but that was
the limit.

Du Lhut refused to give up. The interdiction against traveling
to the interior was worded in such a way that it seemed to apply
only to furs. *Voila!* He would go without trading and Duchesneau
would have no grounds for complaint.

At the next trading fair Du Lhut bought three Sioux prisoners
from the Ottawas to use as guides and slaves (there was a brisker
trade in Indian slaves in New France than most records admit),
found seven *coureurs* willing to take the risk with him, and on

September 1, 1678, slipped quietly out of the settlements. The stealth was to keep Duchesneau lulled. Frontenac knew perfectly well what was afoot, as a letter that Du Lhut wrote to him from the interior a few months later clearly shows.

La Salle learned of the developments on reaching Quebec with Tonti and Hennepin a few days after Du Lhut's departure. Suspicious to the point of paranoia about potential rivals, the Sieur of Lachine was certain that Du Lhut was planning his ruin. Western Sea indeed! Du Lhut meant to cross directly from Lake Superior to the upper Mississippi and, by coursing its length ahead of La Salle, cut the ground from under the feet of the legitimate charter holder.

Obsessed now by a need for speed, La Salle hired as many able-bodied men as he could find and spent the fall of 1678 moving material up the St. Lawrence in huge wooden bateaux dragged from the shore by means of long *cordelle* ropes. Dividing his crew into groups he spent the winter building small freighting ships for use on Lake Ontario and a larger vessel, the *Griffon*, for journeying between Lake Erie and Lake Michigan. He hewed a portage road around Niagara Falls and protected the critical spot with a new bastion and staging point named Fort Niagara.

In August, 1679, he, Tonti, Hennepin, and thirty or so *coureurs* sailed aboard the *Griffon* to Green Bay. There he loaded the ship with furs purchased from outlawed traders and from northern Indians with whom he had promised not to trade. The *Griffon* was to take the pelts to Niagara—La Salle badly needed the money they would provide—and straightway return with fresh supplies to the southern tip of Lake Michigan. Those arrangements made, he divided his *coureurs* in half. Tonti was to lead one party down the east side of the lake while La Salle went down the west.

In due time they joined forces at the bottom of the lake. After building a post on its southeastern shore, they made their way to the Illinois River and paddled southward through floating cakes of ice to the site of present-day Peoria. There, watched by several hundred suspicious Illinois Indians, they built another fort.

During this time La Salle received catastrophic news. The *Griffon*, which had been scheduled to stop at Michilimackinac on its way to Niagara, had failed to appear. Later rumors would say that Ottawa Indians, sensing the ship's threat to their carrying trade, boarded the vessel and scuttled her, along with all hands.

More probably a storm was responsible for the disappearance. In any event, La Salle would have to go back to Niagara during the dead of winter and make arrangements for new supplies and financing. A year lost! Meanwhile, where was Du Lhut?

Late in February, 1680, La Salle directed Hennepin and two French *coureurs* to canoe down the Illinois to the Mississippi and turn up the latter stream to its source. He wanted to learn what the country was like—theoretically the area lay within his grant—and he certainly wanted to discover what his rival, as he conceived Du Lhut to be, was up to, so that he could lay plans for checking him if necessary. Then, accompanied by five companions, he struck overland through bitter weather for the shores of Lake Erie.

XI

Lost Dreams

*D*u Lhut and his ten men traveled west in three, possibly four, canoes. Each carried a ton of cargo—hulled corn and pork grease for food and merchandise for the Indians. The latter was to be used exclusively as gifts of good will to the chiefs, or so Du Lhut insisted in such public documents as survive. After wintering near Sault Ste. Marie—how easy to toss off the phrase, but what was winter really like?—the men continued to the western tip of Lake Superior, swinging their paddles through forty to sixty strokes each minute, sixteen hours a day, except when spring's fitful weather forced them to seek shelter from the long combers crashing against the beach.

Somehow—another maddeningly vague word—they made contact with bands of both Sioux and Ojibwa (Chippewa) Indians. Helped by his slaves. Du Lhut brought the hostile groups together. In a stately oration modeled after those he had heard at the Montreal fairs, he urged them to send runners to all the tribes they could reach, announcing a peace conference to be held at the tip of the lake as soon as aspen leaves showed yellow. To assure attendance, he promised wonderful gifts, samples of which—mirrors, little bells, beads, cheap knives—he entrusted to the messengers. To show their awe the Indians used their customary gesture of clapping the palms of their hands over their mouths.

Arrangements completed, Du Lhut's group accompanied the

Sioux messengers (or Dakota, as they called themselves) to their main village at what is now Lake Mille Lacs in eastern Minnesota. His hosts were, on the average, tall and handsome, dexterous with bows and arrows, but indifferent canoemen. They had come on foot to Lake Superior, and of necessity Du Lhut's party traveled in the same fashion, carrying their possessions and trinkets for the villagers on their backs.

Along the way they learned something about the wilderness warfare Du Lhut hoped to resolve. For centuries the Dakotas had been drifting north from what later became the southeastern United States. As the migrants had groped their way into the lake-brightened forests of eastern Minnesota, they had run head on into the Ojibwas, relatives of the Ottawas, who had been drifting westward from the lower Great Lakes.

A major bone of contention was the maze of shallow lakes west and southwest of Lake Superior. The muddy bottoms of those lakes nurtured long stalks of heavy-headed wild rice. As soon as the grain was plump in the fall, the Indians pushed among the tall, rustling stalks in little two-man canoes and with flails beat the rice loose into the bottoms of their vessels. At their camps they dried the harvest and put it into leather lined holes in the ground. With sticks and feet they shook loose the husks and then winnowed the grain. Because rice kept well, the gatherers were able to store it for winter use and to trade it profitably with other tribes. Both the Ojibwas and Dakotas wanted to monopolize the resource, a form of imperialism not so very different, except in scale, from that being practiced by the nations of Europe.

Because the Ojibwas received guns first through Ottawa middlemen, they were able to start pressing their rivals away from the rice lakes toward the Great Plains. The advantage disappeared when the Sioux began to get firearms through the Fox middlemen of Wisconsin. The fierce contests that resulted were complicated by a desire to control the movement of all European goods onto the prairies.

As one result of the confused rivalries, a branch of the Sioux now called the Assiniboine (Du Lhut knew them as Assenipoulacs and Assinipoets) broke away from the main tribe and moved toward the northwestern side of Lake Superior. There they entered into a loose alliance of the Crees. The latter, as Radisson and des Groseilliers had discovered, ranged as far north as Hudson Bay.

Although this information about territories, cultures, alliances, and enmities may seem picayune today, it was important to the businessmen and missionaries of New France. Hence Du Lhut's eagerness to meet as many tribes as possible that fall. The data he assembled might soften official anger over his unauthorized trip. Surely, too, he would learn something at the conference about the sea of his desiring.

On July 2, 1679, after long powwows with the chiefs, he raised the arms of France on a pole in the principal Dakota village of Kathio at Lake Mille Lacs. Wandering on south, he repeated the ceremony at two other villages. During this time he was operating within the sweeping arc formed by the Mississippi River north of today's Minneapolis, though whether or not he was aware that the stream was the same one La Salle was seeking is uncertain. Anyway, he was sure now that the Western Sea was within reach, and during the summer he sent three men toward the prairies in search of additional information. He himself returned to Lake Superior for the peace conference.

The gathering was a howling success—dances, feasts, exchanges of gifts among at least six tribes—Sioux, Assiniboines, Ojibwas, Ottawas, Crees, Monsonis. During the exchanges the Indians sought to press heaps of pelts on Du Lhut. Despite his heavy expenses in passing out merchandise to the celebrants, he accepted nothing in return, "in order," he wrote later, "that no one might tax me with having carried on an indirect trade." Meantime, hoping to cement the new friendship between the tribes with something stronger than banquet emotions, he tried to arrange several inter- tribal marriages. He failed completely. But at least he was able to persuade various young braves from the different bands to join forces for their winter hunts.

As cold weather neared, Du Lhut and his men paddled—what a relief to be in canoes again!—some two hundred miles northeast from the tip of the lake (Fond du Lac, as it became known) to a deep, island-protected, mountain-bordered inlet later named Thun- der Bay. At the bay's head was a heavily forested valley some five miles broad. Through this handsome trough flowed a river that the Cree Indians called, in Du Lhut's phonetic spelling, Kamanistigoya. (The spelling today is either Kaministiquia or Kamanistikwia.) The word means, approximately, "the place where the river divides," because a little distance back from the lake shore the stream splits into three sluggish channels, the water dyed by vegetable matter to the color of clear sherry. Somewhere near one of those channels Du Lhut's men built cabins in which to winter.

He had reached one of the key rivers of the fur trade. Radisson and des Groseilliers had perhaps seen its mouth in 1660. Randin's map may have shown it. Surely the Crees who led Du Lhut to Thunder Bay briefed him about the stream, for it was one of their favorite routes for breaking out of the Canadian Shield into the drainage system of the St. Lawrence.

A party pushing west started out by poling up the river's increasingly swift current for about thirty miles. As the banks pinched together, tinges of somber red rock broke through the prevailing hues of slaty gray. Ahead, the tea-colored river crashed in a boil of mist over a cliff 128 feet high—Kakabeka Falls, cause of a laborious portage.

Above the falls the stream became known as Dog River for a curious reason. At some unknown date Sioux Indians had tried to ambush a party of Ojibwas traveling along the river and had been defeated. Resentfully they had stripped turf and lichen from a slanting cliff of white rock in such a way as to form a giant image of a recumbent dog. The primitive billboard was supposed to proclaim to the world that the Indians who used this pathway, the Crees and the Ojibwas, were base dogs.

The startling pictograph, which became familiar to generations of voyageurs, also gave a name to the difficult Great Dog Portage that led to a major divide called simply Height of Land. Ahead lay the ragged network of streams and lakes that collected in the broad mixing bowl of Lake Winnipeg and from there plunged through the Nelson River to Hudson Bay.

Des Groseilliers' and Radisson's discovery of the outlines of that enormous drainage system had resulted in the Hudson's Bay Company. The Jesuits, picking up ill-understood information about Lake Winnipeg from far-traveled Indians, had speculated that the distant body of water might be the Western Sea. It seems impossible that Du Lhut could have wintered at a major gateway to that western world without collecting additional information about it. Yet, if he did, he paid no attention—for cause.

The three men he had left among the Dakotas returned with a

startling tale. After traveling west an indeterminate distance from Lake Mille Lacs they had encountered Indians returning from a hunt out on the prairies. From these Indians they received a few grains of salt. Allegedly the material had come from a large body of saltwater and had been recovered through evaporation on rocks or in tide pools.

That salt is another of the enigmas of western history. Some arm-chair explorers speculate that its source was Utah's Great Salt Lake. The theory seems untenable. Canoes could not have traveled there, and horses had not yet reached the plains. Salt transferred from one sweaty hand to another and subject always to curious tongues, to say nothing of rainstorms and hostile raiders, could hardly have remained intact. A better explanation may be the salt springs that still exist in the Red River Valley between Minnesota and North Dakota. The sea? Well, the French were communicating through interpreters who did not know what an ocean was. The word "water" might have come out as anything. Finally, there is always the possibility of a little leg-pulling. Why not send these strange, whiskery whites off on a wild goose chase?

That is what the touch of salt did to Du Lhut. His preconceptions, he decided exultantly, had been right. The way to the Gulf of California, or possibly the Sea of the West, lay through the land of the Sioux. As soon as the weather opened, he apparently sent three of his men and some Indians to Patron and Frontenac with a load of the furs he said he did not trade for. (The reason for this as-sumption, which impugns Du Lhut's honesty, will appear shortly.) With the remaining four Frenchmen he headed for Lake Mille Lacs.

Since the traffic he envisioned for the future could not be handled by foot, he searched for a water route. Following Indian advice, he turned his two birchbark canoes some sixty miles east along the southern shore of Lake Superior to the mouth of the Bois Brulé River. It was a smallish stream. He and his men were in the water chopping out fallen trees and beaver dams more often than they were in their canoes paddling. After they had reached the south-flowing St. Croix, things went easier—until they reached the Mississippi a little below present-day St. Paul. There the in-habitants of a small village of eight bark huts told them that a band of Sioux farther down the river were holding three Frenchmen as prisoners. One of the captives was a priest.

The information turned Du Lhut from an explorer into a diplomat. Did the Sioux have no regard for the treaties he had negotiated the summer before? In a single canoe, accompanied by a guide, an interpreter, and two *engagés,* the Pepin brothers, he paddled for two days and two nights through a broadening stretch of the Mississippi known thereafter as Lake Pepin. At its lower end he found the captives—Father Louis Hennepin and two of La Salle's employees.

Although there were a thousand Sioux in the vicinity, they hung their heads under Du Lhut's crisp scolding and readily surrendered the trio. Although the prisoners had not been seriously mistreated, at least according to Hennepin's account, Du Lhut decided to make an issue of the matter. He took his own men, the quondam prisoners, and most of the Sioux back to the main village at Lake Mille Lacs. Summoning the chiefs to a conclave, he read them the riot act. For the Indians to behave this way after accepting his presents proved that they were the serpents that the Ojibwas said they were.

As so often happened among Indians when confronted with unrelenting moral courage, the chiefs caved in. "Each one in the council," Du Lhut wrote later, "endeavored to throw the blame from himself." The peace pipes came out; there were dances of friendship. In spite of the show of contrition, however, Du Lhut decided against letting the released trio find their own way back to La Salle's forts. Instead he escorted them personally down the Mississippi and over the Wisconsin-Fox river route to Michilimackinac.

His motives are obscure. Perhaps he had already decided to seek a royal charter to the trade of the Sioux and was moving La Salle's henchmen out of the area as a notice that on the upper Mississippi his power was supreme. Possibly he was being truly humane and delaying his own ambitions in order to guarantee the well-being of his countrymen. In any event he committed himself to an unproductive though hardly monotonous winter at Michilimackinac.

A constant flow of disturbing news arrived there along the ever-active Indian grapevine. Hennepin and he learned of the loss of the *Griffon* and of La Salle's tremendous winter journey through southern Michigan to Lake Erie and Fort Frontenac. His affairs straightened out, that indominable man had then returned to the Illinois country by way of Mackinac, passing through the strait just before Hennepin and Du Lhut arrived. On reaching his establishments in the south, so the grapevine said, he had discovered them in shambles.

Part of his men had mutinied, destroying considerable property during the uprising. Shortly afterward, the Iroquois, furious at the defection of tribes they considered their vassals, had devastated the villages of the Miami and Illinois Indians. Presumably most of the French living in the razed towns, Du Lhut's cousin Tonti among them, were dead. If so, then the Iroquois must have acted with full knowledge that they faced a general war of reprisal. Perhaps they wanted a war. They were stronger now, having at last subdued the Andastes, whom they had forced into a league with them. Did this mean renewed attacks on the canoe routes—even on the St. Lawrence settlements?

Amid these speculations Du Lhut picked up word of a personal problem. Intendant Duchesneau had declared him an outlaw because of his unauthorized trading expedition.

Trade? Burning with righteous anger, or else putting on a good show of it, Du Lhut and his men left Michilimackinac in March, 1681, dragging their canoe on a sled until the ice should break, such was the leader's hurry to clear his name. Hennepin, who by then was dubious of La Salle's success, went along.

The headlong journey did not impress Duchesneau. He had already written the Ministry in Paris that during the preceding year men associated with Du Lhut on Lake Superior had brought back furs contrary to regulations. (This letter is the basis of the assumption made earlier in the chapter that Du Lhut may have traded illegally at Kaministiquia.) Nor, the intendant continued, was that the end of the law-breaking. Du Lhut and his uncle, Patron, had acquired other furs from somewhere that raised the value of their harvest to 60,000 *livres*—say $125,000 in terms of today's currency. To avoid confiscation they had arranged, with Frontenac's connivance, to smuggle the pelts to Albany. Righteousness indeed!

Du Lhut denied everything. The furs were not his. He had used his merchandise not for trade but for bringing peace to the West.

He had extended the king's dominions by hundreds of leagues and deserved gratitude, not censure.

The intendant responded by ordering Du Lhut imprisoned. The *coureur* escaped by fleeing to Frontenac's chateau, where he was treated as an honored guest. He chafed nevertheless, for he wanted to go to France in quest of monopolistic trading rights to whatever territory he discovered during his search for the Western Sea. After all, why should La Salle be the only privileged grantee in North America?

Relief came unexpectedly. For some time Duchesneau had been complaining to Colbert about the number of *coureurs* illegally living in the woods—he estimated that the total had risen above 600 —and about the impossibility of apprehending them because of the sympathetic protection extended them by the colony. Deciding finally that prohibition against trade in the interior could not be made to work, Colbert declared a general amnesty for all *coureurs* who would return to the settlements. Thereafter a new system of *congés,* or licenses, would be instituted. Twenty-five would be issued each year. Each holder would be entitled to send three men with a single canoe load of goods to specified points. No individual could hold a license two years in succession, and so on—bureaucratic restrictions that Colbert supposed would work where outright prohibition had not.

Du Lhut was freed under the terms of the amnesty, only to encounter new frustrations. La Salle had reappeared in the settlements, accompanied by Tonti and a few others who had escaped the Iroquois attacks on the Illinois villages. Again La Salle needed money to repair his losses. Some of it, so the rumors went, was provided by Frontenac out of his share of the pelts he had helped Du Lhut and Patron smuggle to Albany.

Du Lhut's connection with the money (if any) did not mollify La Salle's hostility toward his potential rival. Learning of Du Lhut's hope of setting up a commercial empire in the north, he wrote angrily to the Ministry, urging that the application be denied as an infringement on his chartered rights. Then back west he went, to complete at last his long journey to the delta of the Mississippi. Five years later he was dead, assassinated by one of the colonists he had hopefully led to the fringes of his new empire in Texas.

Du Lhut, too, failed in his bid for empire, but less drastically. Although he crossed the Atlantic to appeal in person for his charter, he was denied. La Salle's opposition was not a factor. The granting of extraordinary privileges to that doomed adventurer had been made in the hope that fortified posts strung through the Mississippi Valley as evidence of occupation would help keep English traders from crossing the Alleghenies. Another private preserve somewhere off beyond Lake Superior would serve no such purpose. In fact, it might drain strength from the St. Lawrence settlements, an eventuality the government was trying to prevent by restrictions on the fur trade. And so, to his acute disappointment, Du Lhut was turned down.

Canada was still his great love, however, and back he went, taking with him a brother more than twenty years younger than he, Claude Greysolon, Sieur de La Tourette. They reached Quebec late in the summer of 1682 to find that the government had been completely reorganized. A combination of angry Jesuits and exasperated merchants had finally forced the recall of both Duchesneau and Frontenac. The latter's replacement as governor-general was a cautious temporizer and undistinguished army officer named Joseph-Antoine le Febvre La Barre.

Hoping to find helpful advice for meeting the problems of his new command, La Barre summoned a council of the colony's principal men to meet with him in Quebec on October 10, 1682. Among those invited to attend was the onetime outlaw of Lake Superior, the Sieur Du Lhut. Possibly to his surprise—certainly to his gratification—the *coureur* emerged from the long and agitated discussions clothed in powers very different from but almost as sweeping as those he had failed to obtain in Paris.

XII

War on Two Fronts

*T*wo threats to the colony's well-being, La Barre discovered, pre-occupied his councilors—the Iroquois on the south and the Hudson's Bay Company in the north. If unchecked, both were capable of disrupting French activity in the west.

Most of the councilors believed that the ruthless blow the Confederation had inflicted on the Miami and Illinois Indians signaled a new effort to gain control of the fur trade. If so, the strategy was working. The western tribes were so fearful of attacks on their canoe flotillas that few had ventured east that year, and the Montreal trading fair was sputtering out for want of customers. Meanwhile the Iroquois were saying in effect that running the gauntlet was not necessary. They could easily bring to the Great Lakes area from their suppliers in Albany, New York, better and cheaper goods than the French offered. Why, then, should the western Indians maintain their alliances with the French?

The counter recommended by La Barre's council was the placing of military garrisons at key trading centers in the west. Behind that shield the post commanders could curry the friendship of leading chiefs with gifts, pageants, and promises of protection.

The second threat was that posed by the expanding Company of Adventurers Trading into Hudson's Bay. During the 1670s, sea-going officials of that firm, assisted by des Groseilliers and Radisson, had built two new trading forts on the shores of James Bay.

Both lay well west of the original post at Rupert's River. One, Moose Fort, was located near the mouth of the stream of the same name. The second, Fort Albany, stood beside the Albany River—repetitive nomenclature in view of the other English trading center at Albany, New York.

Attracted by the superior merchandise and cut-rate prices offered by the traders of the Hudson's Bay Company, more and more Crees and Assiniboines were going to the new establishments with their fine coat beaver. To the French, who were eager to increase their supplies of *castor gras* as a counterbalance to the surplus of parchment beaver from Wisconsin, the loss was serious.

Radisson and des Groseilliers offered a solution. Feeling underpaid and underrated by their English employers, the brothers-in-law had abruptly resigned from the company. After various vicissitudes they had fallen in with a wealthy merchant of Quebec, Charles Aubert de La Chesnaye. They informed La Chesnaye that, although ships of the Hudson's Bay Company called occasionally at the mouth of the Nelson River, far up the western side of the Bay, the English traders had made no effort to build a permanent station there. The omission was a mistake, for it left the Nelson, the main artery leading to the heart of the continent, open to exploitation. Why shouldn't the French take possession?

Excited by the prospect, La Chesnaye joined the brothers-in-law in forming the Compagnie du Nord for trading in and near Hudson Bay. When the governor's council met in October, 1682, the members learned that the invasion was already underway. Equipped with two small ships and twenty-seven men, Radisson, des Groseilliers, and the latter's son, Jean-Baptiste Chouart had sailed for the north early in the spring. Their destination was a small river called Ste.-Thérèse by the French. Today it is the Hayes, and its mouth is separated from the Nelson's by a narrow spit of marshy land.

As Radisson had learned on earlier trips, the upper reaches of the Hayes are connected by short portages to the mightier Nelson. Because the Hayes is easier than the Nelson to navigate, many Indians from the interior preferred to switch to the smaller river for the last leg of their journey. Accordingly the French proposed to locate their post on a small island in the mouth of the Hayes.

Because satisfactory bark for canoes did not grow that far north, the traders carried small craft with them on shipboard. The plan was for Radisson and young Chouart to paddle inland until they met Indians who would carry word of the new post throughout the interior. If all went well, the ships would return to Quebec the following summer, 1683, for more merchandise, leaving Chouart in charge of the new post, christened Fort Bourbon.

In time a fine trade in coat beaver should result from the activity. Meanwhile, however, the problem of the three English forts at James Bay remained unsolved. Some members of La Barre's council urged that they be seized by force. The necessary scouting had already been done, under Frontenac's orders, by the brothers Louis and Zacharie Jolliet. The forts, the pair had reported, were carelessly defended and would yield easily to a surprise attack by land. Yet Frontenac had demurred. England and France were at peace, and he had seen no gain—at least for himself—in stirring up a hornet's nest.

The same consideration—international peace—also led La Barre to reject military action in favor of commercial rivalry. La Chesnaye's Compagnie du Nord constituted one jaw of the vise he envisioned. The other was to be formed by creating a screen of posts north of Lake Superior. By sparing the Crees and Assiniboines the difficult journey to Fort Albany, these new posts would pick up whatever furs did not go down the Nelson and Hayes rivers to the French traders at Fort Bourbon. As soon as the English were convinced that they could not trade profitably in the Bay, they would leave without the necessity of physical attack. Or so it seemed within the cool gray walls of Quebec.

Du Lhut emerged from the meetings with assignments on both fronts. He was given an officer's commission in the Troupes de la Marine and directed to fortify Michilimackinac. That done, he was to survey the tribes around Lake Superior in order to determine how many red allies he could bring east in case of war with the Iroquois. He was to build two screening posts beyond Lake Superior and, if possible, he was to establish overland contact with Jean-Baptiste Chouart at Fort Bourbon, so that the left hand would know what the right was doing as the jaws of the vise began to close.

Du Lhut named his brother Claude, Sieur de La Tourette, second in command and bought a *congé* so that they could trade on the side. They went west in the spring of 1683 with fifteen canoes of all sizes loaded with soldiers, *engagés,* trade goods, and food enough so that they could reach Michilimackinac without pausing. Quite probably it was the largest flotilla manned primarily by whites yet to tackle the turbulent Ottawa River route, and the brothers must have received a thorough indoctrination in what became the western fur trade's most serious problem in logistics—carrying food enough to keep a large number of men working at peak performance throughout the long daylight hours of the northern summer. They were also devoured, as matters of routine not worth mentioning, by swarms of black flies and mosquitos.

While the bulk of the crew worked at fortifying Mackinac, Du Lhut inspected the rebuilt forts in the Illinois country. On his return he was confronted with a dilemma. Four reckless Ojibwas, members of an influential family, had robbed and killed two French traders near Keweenaw Peninsula, on the southern side of Lake Superior. The *coureurs* closest to the area, fearful of incurring the enmity of good customers, made no effort to punish the guilty. This put the problem squarely into Du Lhut's lap. The Indians must be made to respect the French—for one thing the Iroquois would capitalize on anything that looked like timidity—yet excessive severity would invite reprisals. Gingerly he set about walking the knife edge.

Aided by Jean Péré, the wisest, oldest, and most daring of the Lake Superior *coureurs,* he brought the defiant suspects to Sault Ste. Marie. There he tried them before an assembly of their own chiefs in the cabin of old Kinongé, the polygamous warrior who twenty-three years earlier had ejected Father René Ménard from his village because of the priest's moralizing. After hearing the testimony, the listeners publicly admitted what everyone knew—the four were guilty.

Inasmuch as only two Frenchmen had been killed, Du Lhut decided to execute, by firing squad, only two of the murderers. He picked those that had played the leading roles in the crime and had his soldiers carry out the sentence in front of 400 somber Indians summoned to Sault Ste. Marie to witness the spectacle. Kinongé, sick at heart over having had his cabin used for such a performance, was mollified by an elaborate feast attended by the principal men in the vicinity. During it, all concerned vowed that never again would friendship between white men and red be strained by such an incident. In the opinion of one historian of New France, Louise

Kellogg, Du Lhut's handling of the incident saved Lake Superior for the French. Possibly so, for the intense competition both to the south and the north was bringing unrest to all the tribes, and signs of weakness could have been disastrous.

The next spring, 1684, Du Lhut reoccupied Kaministiquia. From there he went with his brother and Jean Péré to the northeast corner of Lake Nipigon. At the mouth of an inflowing river, used by the Crees and Assiniboines for reaching James Bay, they and their men built Fort La Tourette. After sending Péré overland in a hazardous effort to reach Jean-Baptiste Chouart at Fort Bourbon, Du Lhut began holding conferences at the fort with traveling Indians. Results pleased him. "All the Savages of the North," he wrote Governor La Barre, "have great confidence in me, and this enables me to promise you that before the lapse of two years, not a single savage will visit the English at Hudson's Bay."

His program was interrupted by the truculence of the Iroquois. In March, 1684, war parties of Senecas and Cayugas attacked French fur brigades and a French post in the Illinois country. Although the fort's garrison beat back the assault, the very fact that it was made led the merchants along the St. Lawrence to demand war. Acquiescing reluctantly—he distrusted the extended supply lines and guerrilla tactics of wilderness fighting—Governor La Barre marshalled 1,100 troopers and Canadian militiamen. Rumor said that the Iroquois could muster 2,800. Hoping to achieve a more equal balance, La Barre rushed orders to Nicolas Perrot, the new commandant in Wisconsin, and to Du Lhut at Kaministiquia, directing them to join him at Fort Niagara with as many *coureurs* and Indian auxiliaries as they could raise. He then sent a peremptory message to the Iroquois, demanding a parley.

Except for some of the Ottawas, whose carrying trade was at stake, the tribes of the interior were loath to risk reprisals by joining the campaign. Only 400 or so *coureurs* and Indians heeded the exhortations of the western commanders, and skilful diplomacy was needed to keep the mercurial, undisciplined force moving toward its goal.

The effort was wasted. As La Barre's soldiers moved toward Niagara, more than half fell ill with influenza. The commander himself was so weak that he had to be carried in a chair to meet the Iroquois delegation. Sensing how powerless he was, the Indians silenced his petulant scolding and told him contemptuously that they would call the tunes in the west.

Fearful that defiance would jeopardize his disease-ridden army, La Barre swallowed the humiliation and started back to Montreal without waiting for the contingents from the Upper Lakes. On learning what had happened, Perrot's and Du Lhut's followers swung home in angry disillusionment. The next year, 1685, English traders from Albany, guided by renegade *coureurs,* took a heavily laden flotilla to Michilimackinac Strait, in the heart of the French fur country, and reaped handsomely. Never before had French prestige sunk so low.

There were other humiliations in the north, where at first it seemed that the French had won a stunning victory. The effort by the Compagnie du Nord to take possession of the Hayes River-Nelson River estuaries had been contested by the unexpected appearance of rivals—one a Hudson's Bay Company party, the other a group from Boston. During the winter the French managed to capture the men of the opposition. But what was to be done with them? Every ship in the vicinity except the *Bachelor's Delight* from Boston had been wrecked either by accident or by the spring breakup of the ice.

Radisson solved the problem by patching together one rickety vessel from the remnants of two. He loaded all but the leading men of the opposition aboard the makeshift craft and sent them south to the English posts in James Bay. Then, appropriating the *Bachelor's Delight,* he loaded aboard the furs gleaned during the winter by all three parties and sailed to Quebec with his important prisoners. As had been arranged earlier, Jean-Baptiste Chouart stayed at Fort Bourbon on the Hayes River to await his return.

The reception accorded Radisson and des Groseilliers in Quebec and later in France was not what they had anticipated. They were forced to surrender the *Bachelor's Delight* to its owners and pay the Canadian Company of the Farm the standard twenty-five percent tax on their furs. Des Groseilliers, sixty-five years old by then, decided against fighting and retired to his seigneury. Not Radisson. With characteristic touchiness, he sought revenge by recapturing Fort Bourbon for the Hudson's Bay Company! This he accomplished during the summer of 1684 by sailing under French colors to the post commanded by his unsuspecting nephew. The victory resulted in the confiscation of some 32,000 pelts and valuable stocks of provisions and tools—booty enough so that the Hudson's Bay Company paid its first dividend since its founding.

News of the losses reached Quebec in the summer of 1685. Hard on its heels came word of another outrage. Du Lhut, it will be recalled, had sent the famed *coureur* Jean Péré overland from Lake Nipigon to Hudson Bay to establish contact with Jean-Baptiste Chouart. Aided by companions named St. Croix and des Moulins, Péré in the spring of 1685 followed the canoe route of the Crees down the Albany River to Fort Albany on the western side of James Bay. Without revealing their purpose, they asked for and obtained fresh supplies from the English there. Then on they went, lulled into carelessness by beautiful weather and their inexperience with ocean water.

One night a high tide washed their canoe off the open beach where they had camped. Unable to locate birchbark for building a new craft, they returned on foot through muskeg and flooded timberlands to Fort Albany. Their skulking, as it seemed to the English, led to their being arrested as spies.

Péré, the leader of the trio was held at the fort. St. Croix and des Moulins were put on an island in James Bay so that they could support themselves by hunting and fishing. In trying by this means to lighten the drain on their supplies, the English underestimated the French *coureurs de bois*. Some runty birch grew on the island. From the bark the marooned men fashioned a small craft. In it they crossed ten leagues—roughly twenty-five miles—of open water, pushed up an unguarded stream, and found Indians who agreed to take them to the nearest band of Ottawas. The Ottawas transported them to Michilimackinac, and from there the commanding officer hurried word of their experience and of Péré's imprisonment to Quebec.

By this time a new governor, Jacques-René de Brisay, Marquis de Denonville, had replaced the hapless La Barre as governor-general of New France. A hot-tempered and able soldier, Denonville agreed with the merchants of the St. Lawrence that the actions of the English demanded a response. Assembling a force of thirty soldiers and seventy carefully selected Canadians under Captain Pierre de Troyes, he ordered them to seize the three English posts scattered along the rim of James Bay.

Much braggadocio about capturing Radisson and freeing Péré accompanied the preparations. Mostly this was to stir the ardor of the troops. (Radisson was out of reach at Fort Bourbon, which he had renamed Fort Nelson, and, though the Canadians didn't yet know it, Péré had been sent to England, whence he eventually reached France.) Economically, the goal was much craftier. Because Du Lhut's and La Tourette's screening posts near Lake Superior were proving very effective in reducing the flow of pelts to James Bay, there was no real need to capture the English forts. But perhaps the posts could be swapped back to the Hudson's Bay Company for Fort Nelson (née Bourbon). French control of the heartland would then be assured.

The march that was to give substance to this strategy was one of the epics of northern travel. Hoping to reach James Bay ahead of the annual supply ships from London, de Troyes assembled thirty-five canoes, large and small, at Lachine during March, 1686. Because the craft could carry only muskets and grenades for the assault, de Troyes reasoned that he must take at least one of his targets by surprise in order to obtain heavier armament from its stores for battering the other two into submission. His choice fell on Moose. As yet no white had reached that fort by land, and so the defenders might not be expecting trouble from that direction.

His route led up the Ottawa River to its head and on across the Height of Land to the Abitibi, a tributary of the Moose River. The commandos began their 800-mile trek by dragging their canoes on sleds wherever the ice was solid. The rapids, however, were seldom frozen. What then? Portages or black water? Where the current allowed, the men avoided wading through snow with their heavy loads and jumped instead waist deep into the water. Gripping the gunwales, they dragged the canoes upward among bobbing cakes of ice.

Only occasional whites had traveled the Ottawa above its main western fork, the Mattawa. As a result portage trails had not been cleared. When rapids could not be surmounted, supplies and canoes had to be strongarmed through tangles of underbrush, over rocks and fallen trees. Often the landing places at the portages would accommodate only two or three craft at a time; the jam-ups that occurred in such places snarled tempers and caused long delays. Other layovers resulted from high winds, lashing rains, and the constant need to repair the battered canoes.

One crew, warming themselves beside a fire while waiting to cross a 1,500-foot portage, let the blaze get away into the evergreens. A high wind drove the flames along the trail and sent the men scurrying, de Troyes wrote, like terrified ants. Most managed to push their canoes into marshy ponds or small lake coves and survived by pulling wet blankets over the craft. A few simply flattened against the ground and prayed. Amazingly, they lost only one canoe, some muskets, and, even worse, several sacks of corn.

Not every day was a crisis. As spring greened the land, the word "beautiful" appeared more and more frequently in the leader's journal. (Six inches of snow fell on June 13, however.) On June 20, eighty-two days out of Lachine, they reached their destination, a square palisade eighteen feet high protected by bastions at each corner. The French attacked at dawn. Covered by furious musket fire, a handful of men scaled the palisade while others smashed in the front gate with a battering ram prepared at the last camp and carried to the landing place in a canoe. The English, who had posted no sentries and had left the cannon in the bastions unloaded, surrendered without a struggle.

Leaving forty men at Moose, de Troyes led the rest in canoes to Fort Rupert, seventy-five miles away. The victory on July 3 was almost a duplicate of the first except that this time the attackers netted a fully equipped ship. After destroying the fort, the raiders loaded the vessel with cannon and, accompanied by a flotilla of canoes, swung back through thick fog, along a coast that was a treacherous mixture of squishy land and saltwater, to the west side of James Bay. Outside Fort Albany they found a patch of frozen gravel, chipped out footings for their big guns, and by pumping 140 cannonballs into the enclosure forced its capitulation.

On August 19, 1686, de Troyes started home, leaving James Bay in the possession of forty Canadians commanded by two employees of the Compagnie du Nord, the brothers Le Moyne, who had served him with dash and intelligence throughout the campaign. (One, Jacques Le Moyne, Sieur de Ste.-Hélène, was twenty-seven. The other, Pierre, Sieur d'Iberville, destined to become one of the great names of New France, was twenty-five.) In achieving its success the expedition had suffered seven casualties: four men sent home exhausted from their early struggles with the icy rapids and three killed, one by drowning when his canoe capsized.

The turn of the Iroquois came next. In 1686, while de Troyes was still absent, Governor Denonville recalled Du Lhut from Kaministiquia and had him build a fort at the strategic narrows where Lake St. Clair funnels into Lake Ontario. (Detroit stands just north of the site.) That done, Du Lhut was ordered back west to help recruit another army of western auxiliaries for a second campaign in 1687. This time there was no craven parley. Denonville swept with 1,500 men through the lands of the Senecas, largest and westernmost tribe of the Iroquois league. He burned their towns and ravaged their fields. But he could not maneuver the enemy into a decisive battle, and so his victory was not as final as he boasted when he wrote the king, stating that his work was done and he would like to be relieved.

Du Lhut returned to Nipigon with his strutting Indian allies. Profits gleamed ahead like rainbows. Very few furs had gone to the St. Lawrence following La Barre's fiasco in 1684. But now the trail looked safe again. During the next two years 800,000 livres' worth of pelts—say $2 million for a colony whose population was scarcely 12,000—poured into Montreal.

The stimulation prompted trader Jacques de Noyon to make the first reported trip by a white man up the Kaministiquia River, along the Great Dog Portage, and over the Height of Land to a maze of streams draining westward. The creeks there widened constantly into curving lakes rimmed with mottled granite and dotted with so many islands that finding the proper outlet was a long exercise in trial and error. But it was a beautiful exercise. Water sparkled over the rocks and between the trees; water fowl rose in clouds; moose fed on the yellow lilies. Black-and-white loons followed the canoe curiously, every now and then cackling derisively before diving out of sight.

Noyon and his men spent the winter of 1688–89 at Lac La Pluie (Rainy Lake), perhaps near the thunderous falls at the outlet. During the winter he met Assiniboine Indians who stuffed him with strange tales of a great lake eighty leagues farther on—probably Lake of the Woods—and then, still farther away, of a Western

Sea beyond which lived a nation of dwarfs who rode horseback with their women mounted behind. Since in 1689 there were no horses closer than the central Rockies, it is not very fruitful to wonder about the provenance of the yarn. But it made another memo for the government to file away under the always intriguing heading, *La Mer de l'Ouest*.

Meanwhile a trip that would reach even deeper into the interior was being readied by an English lad named Henry Kelsey. Kelsey had reached Fort Nelson in 1684 at the age of fourteen and had instantly fallen in love with the great barrens of the north and the Indians who roamed them. By the time he was twenty he was so adept at wilderness travel that the company ordered him to push as deep into the interior as he could, urging all the Indians he met to bring their furs to the English fort near the Nelson. (Rebuilt on the spit between the Hayes and Nelson, it had been renamed York Factory.)

It is not possible to be sure just how far Kelsey went. Because the Indians with whom he journeyed wanted to avoid the rough waters of Lake Winnipeg and the lower Saskatchewan River, they wound a long distance through pea-green marshlands before dropping down to the huge stream near today's The Pas. There Kelsey left the swampy woods behind. He crossed through verdant parklands of mixed meadows and trees and emerged eventually onto the northern edge of the Great Plains. He marveled at herds of buffalo so large that there was no way to estimate the number of animals in them. He met new tribes, and told them, through interpreters and signs, of the marvels that could be had at York Factory by anyone bold enough to make the journey. But like de Noyon, he did not actually see the long, shallow lake, Winnipeg, that for decades had been the source of so many tales of wonder.

Kelsey and de Noyon, who probably never heard of each other, were years ahead of their times. The marshalling of capital, the logistics of supply, the divisions of labor, and the means of wooing government cooperation needed for the kind of trips their efforts presaged had not been developed—and would not be until energies were freed from the long-festering drains in the east.

The years of crisis came to a head when France and England went to war again in 1689. Except for an uneasy truce at the turn of the century, the conflict lasted until 1713. Insofar as feats of arms were concerned, the Canadians by and large emerged successful. In 1689 they withstood the Iroquois' brutal attack on Lachine and an awkward land and naval assault aimed at Quebec. In Hudson Bay, Pierre Le Moyne, Sieur d'Iberville, captured and held York Factory—not an unqualified triumph, for the English regained the posts at the bottom of the Bay. Finally, in 1701, the Iroquois, worn down by unremitting guerrilla warfare, capitulated forever.

During these triumphs the fur trade collapsed. Goods laid down by French ships at Fort Albany (until its loss to the English in 1693) were cheaper than those carried by canoe to Du Lhut's posts at the far end of the Lake Superior. Because screening no longer made sense, it was halted, but not before the French had created a situation that a few years earlier would have been unbelievable— a surplus of choice coat beaver.

The situation farther south was comparable. That irrepressible schemer, doughty old Frontenac, replaced Denonville as governor in 1689. Eager to reassert his corrupt hold on the fur trade, he put so much pressure on the Mohawk villages that in 1693 another huge flotilla loaded with *castor sec* was able to push through from Wisconsin. In 1696 a worried check by the *fermiers* revealed that enough beaver pelts were on hand in Canada and France to make half a million hats. Abruptly all trading licenses were cancelled and every post in the west except one in Illinois was ordered closed.

The Jesuits applauded; the merchants wailed. As had happened during the earlier period of prohibition, the *coureurs* stayed defiantly in the west, producing as many furs as their shortage of supplies allowed. More seriously, the Indians, bewildered by the shift in policy, began listening to overtures from English traders in New York and Pennsylvania.

To meet the objections, new compromises were extemporized. A few *congés* were permitted, but the price paid for fur by the purchasing monopoly was cut drastically. Smuggling with Albany, New York, was ignored. A few western posts were reopened and their trade, subsidized by the government, was placed in the hands of the commanders of the military garrisons, in the hope that by cautious dealings they could maintain the loyalty of the Indians.

The relaxations did not extend to Lake Superior. No post that might have served as a jumping off place for the west stayed open, and de Noyon's feat of 1688–89 was all but forgotten. Fortunes shift, however. Defeated in Europe, France at the Treaty of Utrecht, 1713, sacrificed her interests in America for the sake of favorable terms at home. The right of the English to Hudson Bay was confirmed. The traders of England's Atlantic colonies were granted free access to the tribes beyond the Alleghenies.

Almost simultaneously the feltmakers in France discovered that vermin had turned the forgotten furs in their warehouses into a putrescent semiliquid. The demand for beaver promptly skyrocketed. To get it ahead of the newly aggressive English, the traders of New France were going to have to develop means for reaching beyond Lake Superior that would not cost more in time, energy, and even life itself than they were willing to pay.

XIII

A Family Affair

*W*hat *was* the Sea of the West? Occasionally the question was debated with no great heat in the Académie Royal des Sciences, founded in 1666 to further the compiling of dependable maps and naval charts for the French government. Naturally enough, the main concern of the cartographers was Europe. (The exact length and position on the globe of the Mediterranean, for example, was not established until 1700.) But colonial possessions, too, called for study, and since accurate astronomical observations for Africa and America were not available, the savants tried to fill the gaps by correlating travelers' tales with the logics of theoretical geography.

So far as North America was concerned, a primary problem lay in defining *La Mer de l'Ouest*. The concept had tantalized mapmakers since the day in 1524 when Giovanni Verrazano had peered across the sandspits of Pimlico Sound at what he thought might be Balboa's South Sea. Or possibly, as some supposed, he had discovered an entirely different body of water.

One would think that later discoveries would have erased the misconception. But no. Indians kept insisting that saltwater did lie somewhere out yonder, on the far side of the next portage, beyond the next white-toothed rapids. And so, instead of denying the concept Verrazano had bequeathed them, armchair cartographers kept moving his elusive body of water farther inland. They disputed its nature; they gave it strange shapes. But they seldom challenged the tradition.

Some thought it was a whole ocean, perhaps a northern extension of the Pacific. Others argued that it was a deep bay. Some favored an interior lake whose waters discharged into the Pacific.

Proponents of the sea as a gulf used the logic of symmetry to support their contentions. North America was ringed with gulfs: Hudson Bay and the Gulf of St. Lawrence in the north and east; the Gulf of Mexico and the Gulf of California in the south and southwest; and, it stood to reason, *La Mer de l'Ouest* on the West Coast. There was this problem, however. Indian talk placed *La Mer* at no great distance beyond the Mississippi and Lake Superior, yet men were beginning to realize that North America was very wide. Therefore the gulf, or bay, must extend far inland. This consideration led some mapmakers to represent the Sea as being shaped like the bulb of a syringe. A narrow strait, the tube of the syringe, joined the bulb to the Pacific.

The strait was narrow to account for an opening that various Spanish prevaricators, notably Juan de Fuca (1592) and Martin Aguilar (1602), claimed to have found north of present-day California. But might not the opening be a river mouth? Those who thought so argued that the Sea of the West was an interior lake larger even than Lake Superior, and that the water it released provided the true way to the West Coast. Salt? Well, perhaps that was a misunderstanding of the Indian description. Ouinipeg [Winnipeg] might mean discolored water rather than salty water. As for symmetry, consider the possibility that the sources of all of North America's great river systems—the Nelson, the St. Lawrence, the Mississippi, the Colorado, and the still-undiscovered River of the West—might lie in the same general area. If that were so, then a few portages would let men used to traveling by canoe trade anywhere on the continent. Surely such a prospect bore investigation.*

The point here is not the nature of the speculations but the airing of them in the Royal Academy. For this attracted the attention of the Duc d'Orléans, patron of the arts and sciences and regent for King Louis XV.

---

* Further complications came from theories about the Strait of Anian and the Northwest Passage, chimeras irrelevant to this account.

Thanks to the years of peace following the Treaty of Utrecht (1713), the regency had time and money for non-military pursuits, including colonial development. To the disgruntled *habitants* of Canada, however, it seemed that upstart Louisiana was receiving a disproportionate share of the mother country's attention. Canadians, too, needed help, primarily in pushing the fur trade far enough west to counter the threats posed by the English north and south of them. One way of doing this, the current governor, the Marquis de Vaudreuil, and his intendant, Michel Bégon, decided, was to exploit Orléans' interest in the Western Sea.

They exhumed from the files Jacques de Noyon's report of his 1688 thrust from Kaministiquia on the northwest shore of Lake Superior over to Height of Land to Rainy Lake. They abstracted the tales that Assiniboine Indians had told de Noyon about a Western Sea beyond which midget horsemen dwelt in cities like those of Canada. Certainly the English should not be allowed to reach so intriguing a place first. Therefore, Vaudreuil and Bégon informed the regent, they had taken it upon themselves to reactivate the post at Kaministiquia, and in 1717 had placed it in charge of a worthy officer, Zacharie Robutel de la Noue.

If the government approved, Noue would also build posts at Rainy Lake (then generally called the Lake of the Crees) and at Lake of the Woods (then called Lake of the Assiniboines). Traders operating from those posts would intercept the flow of furs toward the Hudson's Bay Company's York Factory. Meanwhile they would collect information that would allow explorers to press on to the Western Sea. Estimated time for the project: two years. Estimated cost to the government: 50,000 francs for building the establishments, hiring men to manage the canoes, and giving presents to the Indians.

The Ministry returned a qualified approval. The posts would have to be built with proceeds from the fur trade, but as soon as Noue was ready to undertake actual exploration—and he must keep France informed about all details of preparation—the king, acting through his regent, would render the necessary aid.

Noue barely got started. His excuse: perennial warfare between the Sioux and Ojibwas. The fighting had not only reduced trade, he said—warriors did not hunt—but had constantly threatened to embroil his *engagés*. In 1721, after four years of frustration, he surrendered his command.

The timing was ironic, for while he had clung to the comparative safety of his posts, French curiosity about internal North America had been soaring, mainly because of a speculative scheme later known as the Mississippi Bubble. Although most of the interest centered on Louisiana, there was carryover to all parts of New France, including the Western Sea. Hoping to unearth as much solid information as was available, the Duke d'Orléans ordered a former teacher in the Jesuit seminary at Quebec, Pierre François-Xavier de Charlevoix, to visit New France again and discover the best starting place for a transcontinental journey.

At the time of his assignment, Charlevoix was thirty-eight years old, of unflagging zeal, lively curiosity, and a keen sense of his own importance. On reaching Montreal, he provided himself with two canoes and eight *voyageurs*—more than some traders used for a whole year's work.

His route took him through the Great Lakes to Michilimackinac. There he encountered Noüe, headed toward the settlements from Kaministiquia. What the trader had to say was not intriguing enough to pull the fact-finder into Lake Superior. He turned south through Lake Michigan. Although he had hoped to travel to the upper Mississippi by way of central Wisconsin, the belligerence of the Fox Indians prevented this. Accordingly he followed the Illinois to the Mississippi, as travelers between Quebec and Louisiana had been doing quite casually for several years. Thus he ended his trip with nothing but secondhand information—and he was skeptical of most of it. Living in Canada, he said, seemed to unfit men for telling the truth.

Still, he had to make some sort of recommendation. Skipping Lake Superior as a favorable starting place for the West, he recommended either a sustained push up the Missouri or a slower advance farther north through the land of the Sioux. He favored the latter. A staging point would be difficult to establish on the remote and turbulent Missouri, where the temper of the Indians was unknown. Not so the upper Mississippi. A combined military post and mission could be maintained there from Quebec and used for winning the friendship of the powerful Sioux. Two sources of accurate information would then become available—Indian traders working west as middlemen and captives brought in from the interior by Sioux raiders. Best of all, the post could use the fur trade to finance itself during the period of preparation, and there would be no drain on the national treasury until exploration actually began.

Won by the arguments, the Ministry of Marine, which had charge of colonial affairs, ordered the establishment of the necessary post on the shores of that long, bluff-lined widening of the Mississippi, Lake Pepin. There was some delay while the Fox Indians were being quelled, but in 1727 the post builders were finally able to get underway. Two Jesuit missionaries accompanied the party, Michel Guignas, an old hand in the wilderness, and Nicolas Gonor (or Gonner), a relative newcomer. The commander was Captain René Boucher, Sieur de La Perriere, aged fifty-five. Among La Perriere's junior officers was his great-nephew, nineteen-year-old Christophe Dufrost de La Jemeraye.

And that brings us to one of the most enigmatic and remarkable families in New France, the children, grandchildren, and great-grandchildren of Pierre Boucher. Boucher, as we have seen, was the governor of Trois Rivières who during the 1660s obtained from France the military aid needed to crush the Iroquois. He also authored the first publicity book extolling the resources of Canada.

René Boucher, Sieur de La Perriere, was one of Pierre Boucher's many sons. A truculent man, he had acquired an unenviable reputation for savagery. Gossip in the settlements said that during a French-led Indian raid on Haverhill, Massachusetts, at the turn of the century, René had personally killed the village minister, had scalped his wife, and had dashed out the brains of their infant child against a rock.

René had a sister named Marie. At the age of twelve Marie wed one of the soldiers who had been sent to Canada in response to her father's plea. She bore him thirteen children. Eight of them reached maturity. Youngest of the eight was Pierre Gaultier de Varennes et de La Vérendrye—La Vérendrye for short, a famed and in some ways overrated explorer who, despite many missteps, did lay out the first long stages of a workable canoe route across the middle part of the continent.

Young Pierre's father died when he was four or five, leaving his mother hard-pressed to support her large family. Partly to ease the strain, Pierre later enlisted in the Canadian militia. In 1704, aged nineteen, he served with the combined force of Canadians and Indians that razed Deerfield, Massachusetts. From the battlefields of the new world he was shifted to the old. During the carnage at Malplaquet in Flanders in 1709 he was hacked eight times with sabers, shot once with a musket, and abandoned by his comrades as dead. Enemy troopers saw him stir, patched him up, and carted him off to prison, where he stayed fifteen months before being exchanged.

He expected a lieutenancy for his pains. When the promotion did not materialize, he returned to Canada in 1712, married a childhood sweetheart—he was twenty-seven, she seventeen—and settled down to farming. Though his family of four sons and two daughters was of no more than average size for Canada, he was always strapped for money. To supplement his income he reopened a trading post his father had once operated beside a portage trail around the first rapids of the nearby St. Maurice River. While thus engaged he added appreciably to the knowledge of Indian manners and characteristics that he acquired while fighting beside them during the colonial wars.

So he lived until he was forty-one, working hard and experiencing little of the excitement that had marked his military days. Then, in 1726, his oldest brother, Jacques-René Gaultier de Varennes, took charge of the Postes du Nord, as the forts on the northern shore of Lake Superior were called. Jacques-René asked Pierre to go with him as his second in command.

By this time the fur trade had become a quasi-military pursuit. Army officers commanded the western posts, and with their tiny garrisons tried to control the unlicensed *coureurs de bois* while keeping order among the tribes that were France's chief reliance against English expansion from either Hudson Bay or the Atlantic colonies. So that they would have the clout they needed for backing up their wilderness diplomacy, each post commander was allowed to control the fur trade in his district. Inasmuch as the privilege could be lucrative, it was eagerly sought, a situation that enabled the ever-penurious government to cut costs by leasing the forts to deserving (or influential) officers.

It was no laissez-faire operation. Each commander had to specify how many canoeloads of merchandise (brandy was strictly limited) he wanted to move west. He had to supply the government with the name and place of residence of each employee. Each *engagé* in turn was furnished with a contract setting forth his wage, destination, and length of service. The government's intent was to keep a sharp bureaucratic eye on everyone who left the settlements. Those who visited the wilderness in effect promised to behave—at least insofar as paper chains could make them behave.

In spite of the restrictions, the commanders achieved considerable flexibility. Because an officer generally held his appointment for at least three years, he could arrange long-term credits with the Montreal supply houses—an essential step in expanding the trade, for now repayment in pelts did not have to be made at the close of each trading season. In addition each commander was allowed to enter into subcontracts with duly licensed civilians. It was these civilians who did the actual work of carrying the goods the commander had brought from Montreal out among the Indians. Again credit played a major role. As a result civilians who had little to offer other than ambition and a knowledge of Indians were able to roam under a semblance of official supervision as far as they liked in search of pelts, provided that they did not encroach on another commander's territory.

They traveled with seven-league boots. Physical resources had improved markedly over the years. Primarily because of the needs of the military, canoes had grown steadily roomier, until the largest of them could carry a three-ton payload in addition to a crew of five to eight men, depending on the speeds desired. Indians no longer served as the principal builders. By La Vérendrye's time, a canoe factory was in operation in Trois Rivières. Although its plank building beds and metal tools were standardized, the finished products did not have a mass-produced look of uniformity. Too much handcrafting was still necessary in splicing the bark and lashing the gunwales, and in the fanciful designs that were painted on the high prows.

Such a canoe cost roughly $500 in terms of today's currency, but would last three or four years. Master builders earned ten times the wages of ordinary carpenters. In spite of the pay no surplus of labor developed. The skill was difficult, and new openings kept appearing at the interior forts, both for creating replacements and constructing smaller canoes for use on tributary streams and shallow lakes. And although the Indians were displaced as craftsmen, they found new sources of revenue in providing bark, spruce gum for waterproofing the seams, and split wattape roots for the lashings.

During the spring close to a hundred canoes, traveling generally in brigades of three or four, left Montreal for the interior. The need for paddlers created a new class of worker, the voyageur. Unlike the *coureur,* who traded as well as paddled, the voyageur was concerned solely with moving goods.* His pay depended on his function. Bowmen and steersmen (*avant* and *gouvernail*) earned about 25 percent more than the middlemen, or *milieux.* Hours were long—from before dawn to dark. One nineteenth-century traveler on Lake Superior, Thomas McKenney, estimated that in the course of one working day each of his voyageurs made 57,600 paddle strokes.

Each man was expected to carry at least two packs, 180 pounds, across the portages. If he carried more, he received a slight bonus. This and the vanity of many of the men led them to risk injury or even death from a strangulated hernia while struggling ahead under three or more packs. One family of noted strong men, the Bongas, part Indian and part black, reputedly carried as many as five packs each. The record, according to meticulous Edwin Adney in his *The Birch Canoes and Skin Boats of North America,* was seven—630 pounds!

The men who performed these feats were not giants. French Canadians were naturally short, as were the halfbreeds and occasional pureblooded Ottawa and Iroquois Indians who also served as voyageurs. Giants were undesirable; the space required by a six-footer was filled more profitably with merchandise. As a consequence, voyageurs averaged only a few inches more than five feet in height, bandy-legged but powerful through their chests and shoulders.

Swarthy and scarred by their arduous trade, most were illiterate, boastful, gay-spirited, and, when left to themselves, undependable. They liked gay sashes, neckerchiefs, and red-stocking caps with long tassels, adornments they generally kept folded and clean until they wanted to make a dashing entrance into some trailside fort. Otherwise their clothing was sparse and utilitarian: moccasins, leggings attached over their bare thighs to their belts, Indian-style breechclouts, and short woolen or deerskin shirts. Unlike the independent *coureurs,* they were averse to fighting Indians and venturing into unfamiliar situations. But under supervision and in the

---

* Sometimes he was allowed to carry among his personal possessions a few small articles for private barter, but the amount was insignificant.

face of accustomed hardships—running dangerous rapids, poling against swift currents, carrying burdens through knee-deep mud, enduring fogs and wind and ravenous insects—they were toilers without peers in pioneering history.

In the process they consumed prodigious amounts of high-energy food. Providing that fuel was one of the most persistent problems of the expanding fur trade. Because of the early departures from Montreal, it was impossible to send out advanced parties to make food caches, as the Huron Indians had done a century before when coming east from Huronia. Because of the long distances that had to be covered, the men could not pause to hunt and fish, after the fashion of the first *coureurs*. They had to carry their food with them —food that kept well, was easily transported, and yielded maximum nourishment.

The answer was one of the Indians had found long since—a mush made from corn hulled with lye leached out of wood ashes. The Indians flavored the mess with beaver fat, bear oil, and whatever fish they happened to have. The whites, who for the sake of variety often alternated dried peas with corn, crumbled in bits of hard ships' biscuit and added a few strips of fat salt pork, the last an item that led voyageurs on the Montreal run to be called *mangeurs de lard,* or pork-fat eaters. In the spring they were also able to scoop up eggs from the nests of the innumerable water fowl that arose in clouds at the approach of the canoes. Once in awhile they caught a fish or killed a duck to add to the mixture.

The ingredients were boiled with water in a large black pot. Rations were calculated at a quart per man per day. Eating habits were not delicate. Sometimes the men squatted around the kettle, dipping into it with wooden spoons. Many carried cups. Those utensils lacking, a hungry voyageur might use his pocket handkerchief or his cap as a receptacle, or else find a depression in a rock, pour in his share so that it would cool, and then lap it up.

It was not possible to carry enough corn for reaching the ends of the farthest lakes and still have room in the canoe for profitable amounts of merchandise. Accordingly a refueling station, serviced by the agricultural Indians living around the rim of Lake Michigan, sprang up at Fort Michilimackinac, located in La Vérendrye's time on the south side of the strait. This was convenient for canoes bound for Wisconsin and the Illinois country, as most were—an average, during the 1720s, of thirty or so a year as compared to five or six destined for the posts of Lake Superior. But for Lake Superior traders reaching Michilimackinac meant a detour of 200 miles.

The voyageurs did not mind. They had an evening's roister. Then, heavy-headed, they paddled back north to the roaring rapids of Sault Ste. Marie. After portaging around that tumult they still faced 400 miles of lake travel before reaching Kaministiquia. Inasmuch as several of the crew would be returning to Montreal that same season with the winter's furs, there was no time to waste.

For two or three days they traveled past conspicuous promontories crested with trees and pocked in places with resounding caves. About 125 miles from the Sault, the precipitous shore bent abruptly west. In the elbow, at the mouth of the Michipicoten River, was a subpost, Fort Michipicoten, that lay within Jacques-René's command. The brothers paused there to discuss arrangements with the trader and learn what success he had had in harassing the English beside James Bay. Then on they drove, past more high mountains and dense forests to the jagged islands guarding Nipigon Bay. On the west side of the broad river was Fort Ste. Anne, where Pierre de La Vérendrye was to be stationed. Jacques-René continued to the headquarters post at Kaministiquia.

England's control of Hudson Bay, gained through the treaty of Utrecht, had placed severe handicaps on Lake Superior French. Big though their canoes had become, they could not carry enough heavy woolens, axes, big kettles, and long iron chisels (used by the Indians for breaking into beaver lodges) to show a profit. To obtain those items the Crees and Assiniboines, who lived west and northwest of Lake Superior, journeyed to the Bay to trade. There they also picked up whatever finer, lighter goods they desired.

The French response was a ruthless refinement of the screening methods pioneered by Du Lhut. *Coureurs* holding licenses from the army officer in charge of the Postes du Nord pushed over the Heights of Land to the rivers that led to James Bay or York Factory. At temporary outposts or during visits to the mobile villages, they tempted the Indians with such easily carried items as pepper for seasoning tainted food, vermillion for painting themselves and mirrors in which to observe the results, and above all with as much brandy as they thought they could get away with.

In exchange they took the finest northern beaver the Indians had and also the lightweight pelts that brought premium prices in Europe—marten, otter, ermine. They urged the susceptible Assiniboines to raid caravans traveling toward the Bay and plunder them of their cargoes. After absorbing the choicest of the pelts, the *coureurs* let the rest continue to the English.

The area covered by these roving *coureurs* can be guessed at only indirectly. Before and during La Vérendrye's time, the managers in charge of English posts as far away as York Factory complained to their home office of the disruptions wrought by the French in the interior. The nature of their remarks leads to a strong assumption that by 1726, the year La Vérendrye reached Fort Ste. Anne, the *coureurs* had acquired a working knowledge of the land as far west as Lake Winnipeg. They may not have actually seen either the lake or its outlet, the Nelson River, but from what the Crees and Assiniboines told them they understood that lake and river together formed the principal highway between the heart of the continent and York Factory. If the *coureurs* possessed such information, then surely they passed it on to their post commanders.

Related to those assumptions was other crucial information. Immediately after reaching Kaministiquia, Jacques-René rounded up a contingent of Ojibwa and Cree braves and returned to Michilimackinac to participate in the war against the Fox Indians. (In all likelihood he had received his orders from the new governor, the Marquis de Beauharnois, before leaving Montreal.) This war, waged successfully during the early autumn months of 1726, was aimed at opening a way to the upper Mississippi for the party charged with founding a staging post from which explorers could search for the Sea of the West. That post, named Fort Beauharnois in honor of the governor, was erected on the western shore of Lake Pepin in 1727. Its supervisor, it will be recalled, was an uncle of La Vérendrye's. One of the group's junior officers was La Vérendrye's nephew, Christopher Dufrost, Sieur de La Jémeraye. In view of these connections it is difficult to believe that La Vérendrye was not familiar with the post's objectives.

For reasons that have not survived, Jacques-René gave up his command of the Postes du Nord in 1727, and his younger brother moved to Kaministiquia in his stead. During the winter that followed, Pierre spent a great deal of time pondering about the Sea of the West. Was the upper Mississippi really a logical starting point for reaching it? From the maps the Indians drew for him and from the talk of the *coureurs,* he became aware (as de Noyon and La Nouë had been aware before him) of the necklace of waterways leading to Rainy Lake and Lake of the Woods, and of a west-flowing river, later called Winnipeg, that roared through at least thirty major rapids on its way to the massive lake of the same name. He heard, too, of another great river, eventually known as the Saskatchewan, that ran through the country west of Lake Winnipeg.

Tantalized by the Indians' suggestions of untouched vastness, La Vérendrye grew eager to reach that distant land. If he could maintain posts there, at so staggering a distance from Montreal, their trade should be lucrative. Success would hurt the English while fortifying France's claims to the bulk of North America. And always there was the possibility of glory for himself and his country in being the first to cross the continent to the Pacific.

To gain the necessary permission and, if possible, financial aid from the government, he prepared a lengthy prospectus for submission through Governor Beauharnois to the Minister of Marine, Jean Frédérick Phélypeaux, Comte de Maurepas. Knowing that French policy was opposed to spreading Canada's resources too thin, he subordinated the motives of trade to the ideal of exploration in the interests of pure science.

In presenting himself as the man best suited for leading this westward thrust, La Vérendrye was not candid. As Professor A. S. Morton has pointed out in his voluminous *A History of the Canadian West,* the aging commander of Kaministiquia—La Vérendrye was forty-three in 1728—did not mention his predecessors, neither de Noyon, La Nouë, nor even the *coureurs* he himself had licensed. Whatever he found, he implied, would be the result of his own work.

He gave an erroneous shape to Lake Winnipeg. He said it ran toward the west, though it is scarcely credible that he had not learned better. He stated that the great River of the West, by which he presumably meant Saskatchewan, flowed westward *out* of Lake Winnipeg. But if La Vérendrye's *coureurs* realized by then, as they probably did, that Winnipeg's outlet stream, the Nelson, flowed northeast, then they also knew that there could not be another outlet flowing in an opposite direction. Any major river connecting with Lake Winnipeg on the west of necessity ran *into* it. Nevertheless La Vérendrye proposed to build a fort beside Lake Winnipeg and from it dash *downstream* with sixty voyageurs to the Sea of the West. The trip, he added in a fatal effort to add a last bit of gloss to his presentation, should not take long.

When he paddled the Mackinac in 1728 to see about fresh stocks of Indian corn, he took the proposal with him for transmittal to Montreal by some passing brigade. To his good fortune he encountered at the supply depot one of the Jesuits, Nicolas Gonor, who had helped with the building of Fort Beauharnois the year before.

Gonor was convinced that the post was a mistake. He said that the Fox Indians had not been soundly defeated and predicted that they would soon renew their efforts to keep the French from passing through their lands. The Sioux, he continued, were also sullen because they suspected that the western push proposed by the whites was really an effort to undercut their position as middlemen.

Gonor's opinion delighted La Vérendrye. He outlined his own plan, enlisted the missionary's support, and entrusted him with delivering the prospectus to the governor. Confident of eventual success, he then returned to Kaministiquia and with his successor at Fort St. Anne, the Sieur de Verchères, vigorously expanded his trade. Protests from Hudson Bay suggest that the pair continued exhorting the Assiniboines to raid Indians bound for the rival posts and then obtained the best of the plundered furs by soaking the victors in brandy. Although the charges of wrongdoing cannot be substantiated, La Vérendrye and de Verchères did make so much money during the next two years that it lifted the eyebrows of some of the bureaucrats in Paris. Should army officers be using their positions for quite that much private gain?

In 1730 La Vérendrye went to the settlements to see his family and learn why no answer to his proposal had yet come from the Minister of Marine, the Comte de Maurepas. He found no official letter but was gratified by the welcome he received from Governor Beauharnois and Canada's new intendant, Giles Hocquart. The pair disagreed with France's official policy of discouraging the fur trade because of the harm it reputedly brought to more stable colonial industries. They believed that Canada would prosper more if the trade were fostered rather than limited, and they felt that exploration should be tied to commercial aggrandizement. Nor did they have to choose between starting points. Renewed attacks by the Fox Indians had closed the road to the upper Mississippi and had forced the abandonment of Fort Beauharnois. Consequently the two officials promptly endorsed Lake Superior. Without waiting for final approval from Maurepas, they even granted La Vérendrye 2,000 livres for buying presents to give the influential chiefs he met. Beyond that they dared not go.

It was enough for La Vérendrye. Convincing himself that more support would soon follow, he spent his own money and more that he borrowed to hire fifty or so *voyageurs* and outfit six or seven big canoes. These, he hoped, would carry his initial loads of equipment as far during the first season as Rainy Lake.

As his second in command he chose his nephew La Jémeraye, aged twenty-three, just returned from the abandoned fort on the Mississippi. Also included as junior officers were three of La Vérendrye's sons, Jean Baptiste, seventeen; Pierre, Jr., sixteen, and François, fifteen. Although the youngest boy, Louis-Joseph, was wild to go along, he was the most able scholar of the four and his father said he must stay in school until he learned enough mathematics, surveying, and drawing to act as official mapmaker of the West. Meanwhile La Vérendrye's wife was to continue serving, as she had done during the past four years, as his lobbyist, purchasing agent, and dispatcher of supplies. No other major effort to penetrate the North American wilderness has even been so completely a one-family enterprise.

As soon as the ice broke, the voyageurs carted the bales of goods past Lachine, loaded the canoes, and crowded into the little stone chapel of Ste. Anne for a final blessing. That was one farewell to civilization. Another came several miles farther on at the first night's camp. There the men tapped the little kegs of brandy that were part of their pay and indulged in the trade's traditional mass drunk. Having thus paid obeisance to both the spirit and the flesh, they presumably felt ready for whatever lay ahead.

Happily for his own hangover, La Vérendrye did not know then that a letter from Maurepas had just reached Quebec. In it the Minister authorized what had already been done—the dispatching of the expedition and the expenditure of 2,000 livres for presents. But, he said, that outlay ended the government's involvement. La Vérendrye would have to support the adventure by trading as he went. To this stipulation Maurepas, suspicious at best of La Vérendrye's motives, added an almost impossible condition. The leader must never forget that he was an explorer. Trade should pay expenses, but no more. If lust for profit slowed forward motion, permission would be revoked.

All this La Vérendrye learned after he had begun his work. Scylla against Charybdis. Henceforth he would have to depend on the merchants of the St. Lawrence Valley for the credit he needed, and they would insist that he trade as energetically as he could. But, if he did, he would run afoul of the authorities. Could any family, however united in purpose and philosophy, hew to such a line?

XIV

Dead Ends

*E*ver since the days of Du Lhut, the French had reached the Height of Land enclosing Lake Superior by following the difficult Kaministiquia route past Kakabeka Falls to Great Dog Portage. But the Assiniboines said that another day's paddling on toward the end of Lake Superior would bring the whites to a trail that would save eighty miles on the way to Rainy Lake, which was La Vérendrye's goal for the season.

It wasn't an easy shortcut. First there was a nine-mile portage around the deeply canyoned lower reaches of the Pigeon River. Another forty or so carrying places interrupted the waterways that twined on the rest of the way to the lake. A constant struggle— but it saved time and there was still a post to build before snow came. La Vérendrye scarcely hesitated over the choice.

His party reached the base of the first portage, some four miles past the narrow bay marking the Pigeon's mouth, on August 26, 1731. The voyageurs climbed slowly out of the canoes, tilted their heads upward, and were dismayed. They could not see the divide, fifty miles away, and they did not know that in those fifty miles of alternating water and forest they would have to gain 900 feet in elevation. But they did sense that they faced the steepest, highest pitch of land they had encountered since leaving Montreal. And, after surmounting it, then what? Rumors picked up along the way said that the land on the far side was bleak and inhospitable. Hunt-

ing was poor; the wild Indians grew none of the corn that everywhere east of them was the staple item of a voyageur's diet. Why
labor to reach a place where, in all probability, they would starve
during the winter?

They mutinied. Like most such protests, however, this one lacked
cohesion. By playing on the vanity of men they had marked during
the thousand-mile trip from Montreal, La Vérendrye and his
nephew managed to recruit a small party of faithful stalwarts who
were willing to risk the path ahead. While La Vérendrye took the
majority of the shamefaced men back to Kaministiquia, where he
could hold them together until spring, La Jémeraye and the oldest
son, Jean Baptiste, set out with the rest to learn whether the trail
was feasible.

In later days, after the trade had become standardized, every
voyageur using this route was expected to carry eight bales across
each carrying place, including the first one of nine miles. If he
moved only two bundles at a time, he had to make four round trips
—seventy-two miles. The men did not like that much walking; their
employers fretted over lost time. It became customary, accordingly,
to pay a man an extra six livres for every extra bale he took to
the top.

Whether he carried an extra burden or not, his rest came at each
posé. *Posés* occurred every third of a mile or so, as designated
either by custom or the *bourgeois* in charge. The men dumped their
burdens there and went back for the next load. All *pactons* were
brought to each halting place before any were carried to the next.
The pattern probably was already ingrained by the time La Jémeraye and Jean Baptiste confronted those grueling nine miles that
soon became referred to as *the* Grand Portage.

Canoes were another problem. Undoubtedly the trail blazers had
learned from the traders at Kaministiquia that the big canoes used
on the Montreal run would not do for the tight bends and shallow
rapids of the streams leading to Rainy Lake. So almost surely they
used smaller Indian canoes drawn from the pool assembled over
the years by the *coureurs* stationed at Kaministiquia. Later the
canots du nord, as they were called, became as standardized as the
Montrealers. They were twenty-five feet long and could handle
3,000 pounds of freight. During portages such canoes were carried
right side up by four men. By contrast the Montreal *canots* were

carried upside down on the shoulders of six men placed in pairs along the canoe's length. Because their heads were inside the overturned vehicle, the porters could see little more than the ground at their feet, yet they were expected not to bump the bark sheathing against trees or rocks.

Although the laborers scarcely noticed, the trail was spectacularly beautiful. As they climbed from *posé* to *posé* they could look back at the glistening expanse of Lake Superior, seemingly as huge as an ocean, its deep blue or gunmetal gray water, the hue depending on the weather, broken here and there by dark islands. To the north fold after fold of timbered hills rolled to the blue-misted horizon, a hidden lake in every fold.

The views disappeared when the men entered the forest, soft carpeted with layers of needles. On either hand balsams and red-barked pines soared a hundred feet overhead in a silent struggle for light. Save for occasional golden rays breaking through an opening left by some fallen giant, the gloom beneath the canopy of boughs was deep and hushed. In wetter places the white trunks of aspen and birch stood out vividly against the somber evergreens.

Like the Kaministiquia River, the Pigeon was stained the color of tea by vegetable mold; the "white water" of the rapids frothed with a yellow tinge. Higher up, the water in the lakes was clearer. There was nothing clear about their shapes, however. They were scalloped with coves and indented with sharp-nosed promontories, some wooded and some gray with granite crags creased and scoured by ancient ice. Outlets were easy to miss.

The portage across the Height of Land proved easy, a mere 700 paces, less than half a mile, quickly covered by the shuffling dog-trot that was the customary gait of voyageurs bent under their monstrous burdens. On the western side they encountered an even greater abundance of lakes and a deeper sense of wildness, especially at night when the stars glittered in the increasing cold and the loons called across the dark surface of the waters.

By day there was the joy of floating with the current rather than fighting it, of rapids to run, of the sight of autumn's blazing colors. Near the lower end of twisting Lac la Croix, 150 miles from their starting point, they intersected the trail from Kaministiquia. Eighty miles saved! They felt good.

Only 200 more miles, most of them easy, separated them from

the mist-shrouded falls at the lower end of Rainy Lake. (The Monsoni Indians who lived in the vicinity called the lake Teca-mamiouen after their word for the swirling mists. The French called it Lac la Pluie, perhaps because of the same drenching spray.) There, on the north bank of the Rainy River, within sound of the thundering cascades, the pioneers built a pair of two-room cabins enclosed by a stockade 150 feet square made of a double row of pickets thirteen feet tall.

They named the place Fort St. Pierre in honor of Pierre de La Vérendrye. In it they survived months of intense cold on wild rice and occasional moose meat obtained from the Indians. When spring came, they returned to Kaministiquia strutting like fighting cocks. *Hommes du nord!* Later the term became a badge of honor. La Jémeraye's men would have felt they deserved it even more than most.

By early summer La Vérendrye had moved all his voyageurs, traders, and equipment to Fort St. Pierre. Only a handful of men remained at the post, however. The rest, accompanied by fifty canoes of excited Cree, Monsoni, and Assiniboine families, coasted eighty miles down Rainy River to the maze of coves, peninsulas, and broad, pike-filled waters of Lac des Bois, named for the forests that clothed its banks and, rooted precariously on the multitude of islands, seemed to float on the water itself.

About halfway up the lake's twisting western shore, La Vérendrye entered a handsome bay bordered by small meadows that let sunlight warm the ground throughout the day. There, and not at Lake Winnipeg, as he had promised, he built the first major post northwest of Lake Superior. He called it Fort St. Charles, after the Governor, Charles Beauharnois.

In Paris it seemed a curious stopping place—scarcely 120 miles beyond Fort St. Pierre. La Vérendrye had his reasons, however. Supply brigades bringing goods from Montreal and returning with furs could reach no farther west than this in a single season. Even then they would need help. He would have to improve the carrying places and build a shelter at the top of Grand Portage where small canoes could be cached to do away with the need of lugging them up the trail from Lake Superior.

He felt, too, that he must explore carefully before he advanced into blind alleys. Reports gathered from Indians and *coureurs* indicated that after traveling 1,500 miles along waterways whose axis ran east and west, he was now nearing one that ran north and south, a massive system reaching from the headwaters of the Red River, halfway down the western boundary of present Minnesota, on through Lake Winnipeg into the Nelson. Beyond this axis lay, as nearly as he could make out, a confusion of marshlands, prairies, erratic belts of timber, and still more vast lakes. False casts would be all too easy in such a region, especially when one's guidance depended on Indians speaking unfamiliar tongues.

Compounding his uncertainties were dim rumors of a big river several days travel southwest of Lake Winnipeg. The inhabitants on its banks were said to dwell in underground villages. They had light skins, fair hair, blue eyes. They reputedly traded with white men who lived at the mouth of the river. The latter, La Vérendrye conjectured, would be Spaniards, a possibility that brought him a twinge of disappointment. He wanted to reach the Western Sea at some point unseen as yet by Europeans.

A final reason for pausing beside the Lake of the Woods was his growing awareness that his route led through an area frequently raided by the Sioux. Each strike stirred the Crees, Assiniboines, and Monsonis to retaliatory raids from which they often returned with both scalps and prisoners. The situation was awkward. The French had resumed their wars against the Fox Indians of Wisconsin so that Fort Beauharnois could be reopened among the Sioux of the upper Mississippi, a tribe the whites regarded as valuable allies. La Vérendrye, who now lived among the Crees and considered them his allies, was bound as an army officer to bring about peace among the groups. Yet the Crees, Assiniboines, and Monsonis resented his attempts at restraint. Placating them may be one of the reasons that prompted La Vérendrye to buy their Sioux prisoners and send the unfortunates to Montreal as slaves. If the government chose to be altruistic, let it return the far-traveled captives to their homelands.

Conferences concerning peace were endless, and one suspects that La Vérendrye enjoyed the pomp, the feasts, the exchange of collars of wampum that served to symbolize the giver's assent to the will of the receiver. Radisson's boast comes back: "We were Caesars," uncontested representatives of the might of empire.

And so La Vérendrye paused to build, to consolidate, to plant corn (for one could not always count on wild rice and fish), to ask, and above all to listen. Preparation made dull reading in the East, however. When La Vérendrye visited the settlements on a necessary business trip in 1734, he was bombarded with criticism from Paris and his creditors. To quiet the storm he promised vigorous action during the ensuing years. To finance that action he leased the trading rights at some of his posts to a syndicate of Montreal merchants. In addition to paying fees each year, the lessees also undertook to forward supplies for their own men and for La Vérendrye's as far as Fort St. Charles—an arrangement which, if it succeeded, would take considerable weight from La Vérendrye's shoulders.

His energies, he was told crisply, must now be devoted to reaching the mysterious people dwelling on the river southwest of Lake Winnipeg. One theory held that inhabitants might be migrants from either Tartary or Japan. "If this story be true," wrote the young Jesuit, Jean-Pierre Aulneau, who had been appointed to accompany La Vérendrye on his explorations, "we have here a splendid opening for the Gospel." And then, like Charlevoix before him, he reined in on his hopes. The tale should not be given too much credence. "There is no country in the world where there is so much lying as Canada."

An intriguing goal, the financial support needed for reaching it, and the company of the last of his sons, the young scholar Louis-Joseph—only one major alarm still troubled La Vérendrye as he hurried his brigade westward during the spring and summer months of 1735. That worry revolved around his oldest boy, Jean Baptiste.

Shortly before the father's departure for the East, the Cree Indians had adopted the young man, who at the time was not yet twenty-one. The elders had then insisted that he cap his rite of passage by joining an attack on the Sioux of the upper Mississippi. When Jean professed his willingness, the excitement of the Indians had been so intense that La Vérendrye had not been able to calm them. But after long arguments he did make them promise they would avoid the Sioux of the River, who were allies of France, and direct their attacks against the Sioux of the Prairie. Then, to prove he hadn't been a timorous father coddling a grown son, La Vérendrye had joined the Crees' war dance and had stripped off his shirt to show the scars left by his own days in battle.

Had the Crees kept their promises? How had Jean fared? On

reaching Fort St. Charles, La Vérendrye learned that part of his forebodings had been accurate. The Crees had marched against the Mississippi. Faced with that dilemma Jean Baptiste had behaved well. After upbraiding the Indians for their lack of faith, he and the handful of voyageurs with him had split from the Crees and had turned west down the Roseau River to the Red. They descended the latter stream, which runs north, to a high bluff within fifteen miles or so of Lake Winnipeg. There, where they could intercept prairie Assiniboines bound for the Nelson River and York Factory, they had built a small fort that they named, for whatever good the flattery would do, Fort Maurepas. Leaving a small caretaker force in charge, Jean had then returned to Lake of the Woods to meet his father and learn what had happened in the East.

La Vérendrye was pleased. Four stout sons and a nephew without peer among the traders of New France—the future looked promising. He sent La Jémeraye, Louis-Joseph, and François to Fort Maurepas with instructions that they trade diligently (he still retained that concession) and also prepare for a trip to the people southwest of the new post.

It was the beginning of disaster. La Jémeraye died during the winter. The devastating news reached La Vérendrye in the spring while he was beset by yet another worry. The men who had leased trading privileges from him should have sent a consignment of supplies to Fort Charles late the previous autumn. None had appeared. He surmised, correctly, that the brigade had wintered instead at Kaministiquia. But why hadn't they pushed on as soon as the ice broke? The days were lengthening, and soon he would be completely crippled for want of the equipment he had promised the Indians and the saddened survivors at Fort Maurepas.

Impatience made him reckless. He suspected that Sioux war parties might be lurking in the vicinity, hoping to repay the damage the Crees had inflicted on them the year before. Yet, feeling that he must hurry the laggard supplies along, he decided to send his oldest son, Jean Baptiste, the missionary Aulneau, and nineteen voyageurs to Lake Superior.

Within days after their departure two different groups appeared from the east. Neither had passed Jean Baptiste's brigade. Suddenly frantic with worry, La Vérendrye sent out searchers. They soon found what had happened. The party had chosen to spend its first night out from the fort on an island. There they had been surprised by Sioux Indians who somehow had learned that La Vérendrye, purchaser of Sioux slaves, had danced with the Crees the year before and that Jean Baptiste and some of his voyageurs had joined their war party. In revenge they killed and decapitated every one of the campers.

From then on the way was downhill. After a period of lethargy, La Vérendrye built additional advanced posts south of Lake Winnipeg. By means of an arduous foot trip during the winter of 1738–39, he reached the southern river. In every sense it was a disappointment. The "underground" villages proved to be big dome-shaped huts built of driftwood logs and covered with earth. The inhabitants, a few of whom showed a kind of albinism in their hair and eyes, were not Tartars, but Mandan Indians. The river did not run west, as La Vérendrye had once hoped, but south and southeast. It was the Missouri, and, although he did not know it then, the whites at its mouth were the French of Illinois.

Well, perhaps one could ascend the Missouri to a height of land beyond which the Sea of the West must surely lie. (Eventually Lewis and Clark acted on just that premise.) On returning north, La Vérendrye left voyageurs among the Mandans to see what they could learn. Though meager, the data led two of the old man's sons, François and Louis-Joseph to undertake a remarkable journey on foot and by horseback (1742–43) as far west, perhaps, as the Big Horn Mountains of present Wyoming. But of the Sea they saw nothing. Sarcastically Maurepas asked whether the La Vérendryes were interested in real water or just in a sea of beaver.

While his sons were prowling the Great Plains, the father shifted his attention back to the Saskatchewan. If ever he had supposed the stream flowed west from Lake Winnipeg, which is doubtful, he knew better now. It came from the west, and, as he analyzed the new knowledge he had acquired, he grew sure that it would provide a better highway to the distant height of land than the Missouri. Furs in the north were better. Birchbark for canoes grew along at least the lower reaches of the Saskatchewan, but not along the Missouri. More important, numerous Indians from regions beyond even the reach of hearsay gathered along the Saskatchewan to trade with each other and with the middlemen who served as their commercial link to Fort York. Posts placed strategically on the lower Saskatchewan and its principal tributaries should be able to absorb the prime furs from passing flotillas and leave only discards for the English.

The theory was sound, but for La Vérendrye it came late. In 1740 his wife died. The expense of building the new posts in the north, work undertaken primarily by Pierre, Jr., increased his debts in Montreal. The Comte de Maurepas, wearied of what seemed to him twelve years of folly, grew increasingly difficult. In 1743 the exhausted trail blazer at last resigned. In what he thought would be his last testament, he wrote bitterly that his goal had not been money, as Maurepas had suspected, but an honest desire "to carry the name and arms of His Majesty into vast stretches of countries hitherto unknown, to enlarge the colony and increase its revenues."

Unbelievably, command of the Posts of the West, as La Vérendrye's creations were now called, devolved on Nicolas-Joseph, Sieur de La Noyelles, husband of one of La Vérendrye's nieces. Ill luck plagued him, too. Unable to obtain adequate supplies because of King George's War, 1744–48, Noyelles resigned in his turn. Meanwhile Maurepas had lost favor, and in an extraordinary aboutface, the new Minister of Marine showered the aging La Vérendrye with honors and in 1748, when he was sixty-three, reappointed him commander of the Posts of the West.

Joyfully his sons and he prepared for a last major push. Knowing they would need money for the effort, François and Louis-Joseph rebuilt the trading posts south of Lake Winnipeg that the Indians had burned during the war. Pierre, Jr., who had served in the east during the conflict, returned to the Saskatchewan. From his *coureurs* he learned the shape of the river as far as the junction of its north and south forks, a point that he believed must be very close to the final divide. On departing in the summer of 1749 for Montreal with a cargo of pelts, he told the men who remained in the interior to build at The Pas, where the Carrot River flows out of teeming swamps into the turbid Saskatchewan, a key staging point to be known as Fort Paskoyac.

The father never saw what his sons accomplished. In Montreal, in December, 1749, he sickened and died.

A new governor denied the appeal of the sons that they be allowed to complete the work. Command passed into the hands of Repentigny Lagardeur de St. Pierre. His second in command, the

Sieur de Niverville, occupied Paskoyac and sent ten *coureurs* an unknown distance up the South Fork of the Saskatchewan, perhaps within sight of the Rockies. But St. Pierre alienated the Indians and in 1753 his command passed on to Louis Chapt, Chevalier de La Corne. At Fort St. Louis, a small post that La Corne built on the South Saskatchewan, New France's drive toward the Western Sea reached its ultimate point.

Although the enormous empire was held together by nothing stronger than birchbark, it caused great harm to the traders of the Hudson's Bay Company. The interior reaches of every stream draining out of the west toward their posts was occupied for at least part of every year by *coureurs* versed in the way of the Indians and offering an alluring assortment of trade muskets, good gunpowder, bright vermillion, and fiery brandy.

How resist? Unable because of lack of birch to carry significant amounts of merchandise to the Indians, the manager of York Factory fell back on a method pioneered by Henry Kelsey half a century earlier. He recruited from among his laborers a former smuggler and versatile netmaker named Anthony Henday, found a place for him in one of the Indian flotillas that visited the post, and sent him out on a selling expedition. Of necessity Henday had to rely almost entirely on glibness—on sweet talk about the low prices and warm welcomes awaiting customers at the Bay.

During the single year 1754–55 he covered a thousand miles by canoe, dogsled, foot, and, for a little ways, horseback. Some of his pitches ended in failure. The Blackfeet, whom he met in the vicinity of present-day Calgary, refused to follow him to the Bay. Their reason: they did not know how to handle canoes and would have to live on fish, which sickened them. Other prospects proved more amenable, and in 1755 a huge concourse of canoes accompanied Henday down the Saskatchewan to the Nelson—yielding, at The Pas, some of their best furs in exchange for French brandy. He duplicated the triumph during subsequent years, as did Joseph Smith and Joseph Waggoner, who on three different trips that began in 1756 pushed far south among the Assiniboines.

They were flailing a dying enemy. In 1754 the last of the wars for the control of North America broke out in the colonies. Two years later it spread to Europe. As far as New France was concerned, the end began during the fall of 1759 when James Wolfe sailed up the St. Lawrence to attack Quebec. After days of nervous maneuvering, his scouts found an unguarded trail in the cliffs some two miles upstream from the city. By night the English crept up the dark path to the Plains of Abraham. The French commander, Montcalm, bungled the counterattack. After a fifteen-minute battle, during which both commanding generals died, the city fell. A year later Montreal surrendered to Lord Jeffrey Amherst, and France was finished as an American power.

The issues of fur trade competition were solved less neatly. As enterprising young men among the ranks of the victors realized the potentials of the wilderness commerce, many of them plunged recklessly ahead along the trails developed by the French. Inevitably they too clashed with the traders beside Hudson Bay. By that time the stakes were higher, the opportunities for direct confrontation greater, and the need for outlets on the Western Sea essential. The result was an internecine struggle for ascendancy far more desperate than the one that had prevailed when the contestants had been a handful of wanderers owing allegiance to different empires.

PART THREE

Pedlars Extraordinary

XV

Collision Courses

*I*n the summer of 1760 Alexander Henry, a native of New Jersey, was twenty years old, exuberant, and daring. But there was a steadiness in him, too, and even as a youth he was able to obtain almost unlimited credit from the merchants of Albany, New York.

He used his credit in 1760 to fill three large wooden bateaux with goods and attached himself as a civilian sutler to Jeffrey Amherst's army as it moved from Lake Ontario down the St. Lawrence River against Montreal. When the awkward fleet plowed into the Rapides des Cédres, forty-six of the soldiers' oversized rowboats swamped, as did Henry's three craft. Eighty-four men drowned. The young sutler stayed alive by clinging to an overturned bateau until one of Amherst's staff officers "kindly"—the word is Henry's —fished him from the turbulent water.

Undeterred by the experience, he obtained more goods on credit in Albany and recouped his losses by selling the merchandise to the English garrison at Fort Lévis, midway between Lake Ontario and Montreal. Footloose again, he moved on by snowshoe and, where the black, swift St. Lawrence was open, by canoe to Montreal. There he made contact with a Canadian who had once trafficked at Michilimackinac Island. The tales the man spun solidified Alexander Henry's hitherto nebulous dream of going inland as an Indian trader.

Although the war in Europe was not over and no treaty about

sovereignty had been signed, his merchant friends in Albany were once again willing to back him, this time with approximately eleven tons of cloth, ironware, ornaments, guns, ammunition, and rum. Henry took the cargo by bateaux through Lake Champlain to Montreal, where he arrived June 15, 1761. There he belatedly sought means for carrying out his program. He must have had a silver tongue. First he persuaded a French trader, Etienne Campion, to provide canoes, voyageurs, and experience in exchange for a share in the enterprise. Next he won from Thomas Gage, the English general in command at Montreal, a license for dealing with the Indians of the upper Great Lakes, even though the tribes there still maintained their loyalty to France.

Permission granted, Campion and he swiftly set about loading their four French-style *canots du maître*. By that time constant experimentation by both the army and the fur trades had shown that birchbark vessels could be no more than thirty-six to forty feet long and still retain maneuverability. Even then the forty-foot size was rare and used mostly on the lakes. For big rivers like the Ottawa the traders preferred a canoe five and a half fathoms (thirty-six feet) overall length, or slightly more than thirty-two feet on the bottom. Width varied from four and a half to five and a half feet. Depth was two and a half feet, with the stems, gaudily emblazoned, rising another two and a half feet above the gunwales.

Unless extra men were needed to speed goods across the portages, eight men were ample for handling a *canot du maître*. If no surplus passengers were along, a single vessel could hold sixty ninety-pound *pièces,* or packages. Add to that a thousand pounds of lyed corn, peas, grease, and hardtack, the weight of the crew, and the forty-pound sacks of personal possessions each man was entitled to take along, and the lading came to four tons or more, though the canoe itself weighed only 600 pounds. When launched at Lachine, the craft sank almost to the gunwales, a factor that added considerably to the apprehension of whatever neophyte happened to be seated inside.

Because of the English blockade Henry's trip was the first opportunity that his men had had in two years to ply their trade. Their voices rang as they picked up their paddles:

> *En roulant ma boule roulant*
> *En roulant ma boule.*

Happily they halted at the stone chapel of Ste. Anne for the traditional confession and blessing and at the entrance to the Ottawa for the nightlong regale. After that the labor came.

A century and a half of trial and error had made it habitual to the Canadians. To Henry and the Scotch and English traders who followed him, the doggedness of the men and the wild commingling of water, rock, and forest were cause for endless wonder. Some years later another user of the route, Alexander Mackenzie, was so impressed by the trail's demands that he methodically paced off and recorded, in his "A General History of the Fur Trade from Canada to the Northwest," the dimensions of scores upon scores of portages and *décharges,* the latter being spots where the bales only were carried while the canoes were dragged upward with cordelles.

On the brawling thirty-four mile Mattawa River alone, Mackenzie reported, there were eight taxing carrying places. At one, the Mauvais de Musique, "many men have been crushed to death by the canoes, and others have received irrecoverable injuries." During the years a custom grew up of placing wooden crosses at the sites of fatalities, most of them from drownings that occurred when voyageurs traveling downstream sought to avoid the portages by running the rapids. By 1800, according to trader Daniel Harmon, a single treacherous rapid had brought a cluster of thirty crosses to the bordering riverbank.

Henry soon experienced other worries than just water and rock. The Indians along the rugged north shore of Lake Huron recognized him as an Englishman and warned him to go back; otherwise the tribes at Mackinac would kill him. Instead he told Campion to pretend to be the sole owner of the cargo. He then donned the loose shirt, capote, and stocking cap of a voyageur and paddled with the men to Fort Michilimackinac, which since 1712 had stood on the south side of the strait.

The Chippewas he passed were not fooled. Sixty of them demanded a conference with him and marched into the meeting place naked from the waist up, strikingly painted, each carrying a tomahawk in one hand, a scalping knife in the other. After a time of silent smoking "while I inwardly endured the tortures of suspense," the tall chief of the delegation told Henry in a speech that has become a frontier classic, "Englishman, although you have conquered the French, you have not conquered us. We are not your slaves. These lakes, these woods and mountains were left to us by our ancestors. They are our inheritance, and we will part with them to none."

That preamble ended, he startled Henry by shifting tone and adding, "You do not come armed, with an intention to make war; you come in peace, to trade with us, and supply us with necessaries, of which we are in much want. We shall regard you, therefore, as a brother."

The Ottawas arrived next. As Henry and two other traders who had followed him from Montreal were provisioning their canoes with fresh supplies of Indian corn for visits to distant hunting grounds, a group of those Indians demanded tribute for passageway. The whites refused. Only the timely arrival of 300 soldiers of the Royal American Regiment, dispatched from Detroit to take over the French fort at Mackinac, prevented a fatal confrontation. Thus rescued, the canoes, manned by Canadians living at the post, were able to fan out toward their destinations: Lake Michigan, the upper Mississippi, the south shore of Lake Superior, and, most significant for this account, "to the Grand Portage, for the north-west." Henry, in short, was already contemplating—prematurely, it developed— using the route that the La Vérendrye family had opened to Lake Winnipeg and beyond.

Henry did not go with the canoes he outfitted. He does not say why. Perhaps (as a matter of guesswork) he was deterred by rumors of unrest among the tribes caused by the anti-English fulminations of the great chief of the Ottawas, Pontiac. In any event, his memoirs never again mention either the canoes or Campion, a lapse that leaves us knowing next to nothing about this first English effort to capitalize on the withdrawal of the French. Instead we are told only of Henry's life with the Michilimackinac Indians, among whom he made a true friend named Wamatam. Still other months he passed at Sault Ste. Marie with Jean Baptiste Cadotte, whose forebears had lived in the area ever since St. Lusson's fruitless pageant of possession in 1671.

Meanwhile Pontiac's war plans were gathering strength. Warnings reached Mackinac from time to time but went unheeded. The explosion at the fort came June 4, 1763. A large concourse of Ottawas and Chippewas gathered on a field near the stockade to indulge, so they said, in an intertribal game of *baggataway*, or, as the French called it, *le jeu de la crosse*. Although the whites were invited to attend, Henry fortunately stayed working at his desk in the house he occupied inside the palisade.

During the game the ball sailed over the stockade, apparently by accident. The gate was opened so that the players could recover it. Indians swarmed through. Their sudden war cry brought Henry to the window. From that vantage point he saw several soldiers cut down and scalped. But, he noticed, none of the establishment's Canadians were bothered.

Taking hope, he leaped across the low fence that separated his house from that of a M. Langlade. An Indian servant spirited him up into a garret. Peeking through a crack, he beheld "the ferocious triumphs of barbarian conquerors. The dead were scalped and mangled; the dying were writhing and shrieking, under the unsatiated knife and tomahawk; and, from the bodies of some ripped open, their butchers were drinking the blood, scooped up in the hollow of joined hands, and quaffed amid sounds of rage and victory."

The hider's respite was short—but long enough to save his life. By the time he was discovered and dragged from the garret, most of the madness had passed. He was put under guard with some twenty civilian and military prisoners, all English. Another seventy soldiers and one trader had been killed. Triumphantly the Indians proclaimed that Pontiac's uprising had been as successful throughout the West as at Mackinac, an exaggeration that was not corrected in Henry's mind for months.

He survived those months because of his friend Wamatam, who claimed the white as an adopted brother. Henry spent the next year wandering through the forest with Wamatam's band, his head shaved, his clothing altered, and his face painted so that he would not be recognized as white. When summer came he made his way to Cadotte's home at Sault Ste. Marie. There he learned that an English army under Sir William Johnson was advancing into the Indian country to break Pontiac's siege of Detroit. Runners from Johnson ordered delegates from the western tribes to attend a peace conference at Fort Niagara—or be destroyed. The nervous Indians of Sault Ste. Marie invited Alexander Henry to accompany them on the portentous journey, where uneasy truces were established and Pontiac's dream of expelling all whites from interior North America turned to dust.

And yet Great Britain did try to placate the distraught Indians. One great cause of their resentment was the unbridled thrust of land-hungry frontiersmen across the Allegheny Mountains into the Ohio country. Turning that migration northward into Canada, where only 65,000 people lived as compared to 1.5 million in the English colonies, would, it was hoped, not only calm the Ohio Indians but benefit the Canadian economy.

In pursuit of that goal the English ministry drew new boundaries for what was named the colony of Quebec. Its extent was limited roughly to the watershed of the St. Lawrence River from a little above Montreal to the sea. Its inhabitants were promised a degree of self-government, and growth was to be stimulated by the Proclamation of October, 1763, which temporarily closed the trans-Allegheny lands to settlement. Having no place else to go, the Anglo-American frontiersmen farther south would bend northward, or so the savants reasoned.

The interdicted territories, "not having been ceded or purchased by us, are reserved to [the Indians] as their hunting grounds." Trade within this huge reservation was limited by later decrees to fortified posts, under prices set by the government. Credit could not be advanced to the Indians; *coureurs* could not visit their villages. To insure obedience, traders were required to take out licenses and post bond for twice the value of the goods declared on their invoices.

None of this worked as it was supposed to. Would-be settlers on the Anglo-American frontier were outraged by the Proclamation; would-be traders in Quebec and Montreal, most of them opportunistic migrants from the colonies farther south, were stunned. English-speaking settlers did not turn to Canada in the numbers envisioned in London. As late as 1770 there were only 360 transplanted Englishmen in the entire St. Lawrence Valley.

But although the migrants were few, their voices were strong. Most were sutlers who had followed the army into Canada or were merchants who had hurried north from Albany, New York, in the hope of exploiting a trade that had eluded them while the French held sway. They were already in touch with powerful supply houses in London. They could command ample financing, shipping, and broad market outlets for furs—resources that war-strangled Canada badly needed.

Forming commercial alliances with French residents who knew the voyageurs, the Indians, and the trail, these newcomers grudgingly obtained the licenses required by the government and started their laden canoes toward the interior. At the same time they launched a strident campaign in England for the repeal of the obnoxious regulations. Indians, they argued, had grown used to traders visiting them and would not undertake long trips through enemy lands in order to trade at such distant posts as Michilimackinac. Unless the whites were allowed to resume old patterns of barter, the tribes of the West would turn for relief to *coureurs* pressing up the Mississippi from New Orleans and St. Louis—Spanish towns now—and the commerce so vital to Canada would be lost.

They soon had their way. Commanders at Michilimackinac, more interested in graft than in the law, were easily persuaded to issue special licenses that allowed holders to enter the interdicted Indian country. Favored thus by Captain William Howard, Alexander Henry formed a trading partnership with J. B. Cadotte of Sault Ste. Marie, spent the winter of 1765–66 between the old French rendezvous points of Chequamegon and Fond du Lac (modern Duluth), and returned to Mackinac with 15,000 pounds of beaver and twenty-five packs of otter and marten pelts.

Howard's successor at Mackinac, the famed ranger of the French and Indian wars, Robert Rogers, was even more blatant. He not only continued Henry's special privileges but also sent his own men, Jonathan Carver and James Tute, through present-day Wisconsin to the Mississippi. Ostensibly they were looking for a route to the Pacific; actually they were more interested in building up fur-trade connections for their employer.

For various reasons most of the men operating out of Mackinac turned south toward Illinois or the Mississippi rather than northwest. Indians were more numerous in the southern regions; winters were less rigorous. The northern Indians, moreover, were proving unpredictable. Because little merchandise had reached them during the war years, they were desperate for trade, but when the whites who leapfrogged past Henry to Rainy Lake in 1766 and again in 1768 sought to take advantage of the situation by overcharging them, they retaliated by plundering the canoes.

These factors—war, restrictions on the trade, and the preference of the Montreal and Albany merchants for the southwest—all played into the hands of the Hudson's Bay Company. As was noted in the preceding chapter, the appearance of the La Vérendryes and their successors in the areas around Lake Winnipeg and along the lower Saskatchewan River had prompted the men in charge of York Fort to send drummers—Anthony Henday, Joseph Waggoner, Joseph Smith—deep into the interior to prevail on the Indians to ignore the French and continue their long trips to the trading posts beside the Bay.

A remarkable system evolved, its procedures set by the habits of the Indians who lived in the broad belt of country along the Saskatchewan where the forests of the Canadian Shield ravel out onto the plains. First, there was the problem of transportation. The canoes used by the Indians, mostly Crees and Assiniboines, were small. The trip was difficult and food uncertain. Accordingly women, children, old men, and enough warriors to provide protection were left at fishing camps along the lower Saskatchewan, while the most active young males ran the rivers that led to York Fort.

As the flotilla neared its destination, the scattered vessels drew together. The occupants discharged their guns; the English replied with a salute of cannon. In the Indian view what followed was not a confrontation between buyer and seller but a reaffirmation of friendship and traditional alliances. The calumet was passed around and gifts were exchanged—beaver skins and wampum on the part of the Indians; food, clothing, liquor, and ornaments on the part of the whites.

The English sought to stabilize routines by helping the leaders, or chiefs, in the flotillas hold their positions year after year. A man of great influence could bring new customers to the fort and make sure that old ones paid for credit extended to them at previous meetings. Influence came in part from prestige. To enhance it the traders bedecked the principal men in red or blue coats modeled after regimental uniforms, in knee breeches and gay stockings, each of a different color, and in hats plumed with dyed ostrich feathers.

After the Indians had indulged in a mammoth drunk, there were more ceremonial pipe smokings and then speeches by the leaders, who begged, not for lower prices, but for tobacco and guns of good quality and for full measures of cloth and powder. The Indians had little notion of fluctuating prices. Although the cost of merchandise might change in Europe or the price of furs rise or fall, the variations were seldom reflected at the trading posts. Once a standard had been set the Indians wanted no change.

The value of all furs—fox, otter, marten, bear, moose and buffalo hides, even swan skins—was stated in units called "made beaver," or MB. Even the price of immature beaver or of extra large and glossy beaver pelts was translated into this symbolic standard, MB, the traditional value of a single pelt of average size and quality. The cost of hatchets, ice chisels, or whatever else the Indians wanted was also expressed in terms of made beaver. Thus a gun might cost fourteen made beaver; a pound of glass beads, two made beaver; and so on.

Change brought resistance. One mystery to uninitiated Europeans was the failure of price cuts—we would call them bargains—to stimulate trade. But possession beyond need was relatively meaningless to the Indians. Besides, the small size of their canoes and afterward their foot journeys onto the plains limited what could be carried. As a result a lowering of prices simply let an Indian slack off in his hunting, for at cut rates he could meet his needs with fewer pelts. About the only variations they accepted in the so-called standard of trade were shortages in measurement to cover the cost of gift giving.

To get more furs the Company had to entice more Indians to its bayside posts. This became the function of the firm's traveling salesmen even after the war had ended French competition. It was an arduous pursuit. No trees suited to the making of canoes grew near York Fort. Accordingly the Company drummers—two of the most notable after Henday were William Pink and Matthew Cocking—had to crowd into the small canoes used by the Indians. Because of space limitations personal equipment was sacrificed to bits of merchandise that could be used in ritual gift giving at the villages or as samples of what was available to Indians courageous enough to make the trip to the Bay.

Trading completed, the Indians were in a hurry to rejoin their families. Thanks to the maze of waterways that laced the region, they were able to travel from York to the lower Saskatchewan by a greater variety of routes than needs be detailed here. The reunions completed, they moved in chattering groups up the huge river, putty-colored with detritus washed down from the distant Rockies. Then, as the nights began to lengthen, the flotilla fragmented. Small bands of relatives abandoned their canoes and began to drift south on foot, accompanied by hordes of dogs.

For a while they hunted moose and beaver in the intermingled grasslands and groves. Winter drove them onto the prairies, where they lived off buffalo (more properly, bison) while gathering fox and wolf skins. Enterprising young men augmented the band's supply of pelts by traveling with dogsleds to distant tribes, notably Blackfeet, and bartering secondhand goods obtained during earlier years of trade at York Fort.

In February the bands began moving slowly back toward pre-arranged rendezvous points beside the Saskatchewan. Along the way some hunted beaver, whose pelts were now prime; others collected birchbark from nearby groves and made canoes. As they waited for the river to open, they lived on fish caught through holes cut in the ice and, as the sun edged farther north, on the clamorous waterfowl that began appearing in clouds from the south.

As soon as Canada fell into English hands, the London directorate of the Hudson's Bay Company shrewdly ordered its far-traveling salesmen to stay alert for competitors from the St. Lawrence. Because of the restrictions placed on the trade by the Proclamation of 1763, however, none appeared for five years. Then, in 1768, the merchants of Montreal succeeded in having the restraints removed. A stampede of traders poured into the lands south of the Great Lakes and along the upper Mississippi. Simultaneously, a handful of bolder souls defied distance and plundering Indians to seek the prairies beside the Saskatchewan.

The first to arrive were twelve voyageurs led by a holdover from the French regime, François le Blanc, whom the English called Franceways. Next James Finlay pushed west as far as Nipawi Rapids, twenty river miles below the junction of the North and South Forks of the swift, pale river. When Company servants chided Finlay for invading land granted to the Hudson's Bay Company by royal charter in 1670, he retorted that the governments' relaxing of trade restrictions meant that he could do business wherever he chose. Because the political climate in England was bitterly opposed to monopoly, the London committee swallowed the affront rather than risk unfriendly hearings in court. All in all, it was not a heartening prospect for launching the firm's second centennial of business in its hitherto untrammeled lands.

Matters continued to deteriorate as more and more Pedlars from Montreal—so the Company men called them—raced each other inland. William Pink and his fellows were shocked at how easily their sales efforts were turned to naught. And yet they shouldn't have been. The Pedlars freed the Indians from the long trip to Hudson Bay and won their hearts with alcohol. For a single example, Thomas Corry, ensconced in a "log Tent" at Cedar Lake (Bourbon Lake to the La Vérendryes) intercepted two Company men shepherding 160 Indian canoes toward York Factory and siphoned off as many pelts as he had merchandise to pay for—pelts that in large part were pledged on credit to the bayside firm. That year the returns at York Fort fell to 21,577 made beaver, a decline of more than 30 percent. After two years, Corry retired from the trade, a rich man.

These were not casual adventures. The Pedlars were financed by potent Montreal merchants leagued with London suppliers of first-class goods, and they were supported by the most adept wilderness men in the New World. They traveled enormous distances in craft that completely outclassed anything available to their rivals at the Bay. True, the traders in charge of each little fleet fought each other as relentlessly as they fought the Hudson's Bay Company. They debased the Indians, seduced each other's men, swaggered, resorted to intimidation, and damaged a rival's equipment whenever they thought they could get away with it. But the pangs they caused one another were scant comfort to men reading the balance sheets at York Fort.

The obvious retort was for the Hudson's Bay people to establish a big trading post in the area where competition was keenest. To this end, they turned to one of their ablest employees, Samuel Hearne.

Orphaned early in life and restive in school, Hearne had joined the Royal Navy at the age of eleven. In 1765, when he was twenty, he accepted employment as mate of a Hudson's Bay Company sloop engaged in whaling. His station was Fort Prince of Wales, the ponderous stone post at the mouth of the Churchill River, far north of York Fort. (Fort Prince of Wales was generally called simply

Churchill.) While Hearne was there, the man in charge of the post, Moses Norton, grew excited over lumps of copper brought him by a small band of Chipewyan Indians led by a chief named Matonabbee. The metal, they said, came from the mouth of a river that flowed into the Arctic Ocean far to the northwest of Churchill—a river subsequently named Coppermine.

Norton directed Hearne, a strong, affable young man with a liking for what we would call backpacking, to investigate the distant area. Logically enough, the explorer aimed directly at his goal. The effort—it filled a full year, November, 1769, to November, 1770—took him into barren tundra country where game was scarce, wood nonexistent, and the Indians undependable. Then his luck changed. While returning from his fruitless efforts, he fell in with Matonabbee, one of the original producers of the copper. Matonabbee not only agreed to guide Hearne to the "mines" by a roundabout but practical route but also to use some of his many wives as porters.

Women, the chief told Hearne, were made to work, and Matonabbee's spouses looked it. Most of them, Hearne wrote, "would for size have made good grenadiers." Supported by these red Amazons and their friends, the prospector reached the Arctic Ocean in the summer of 1761. Results disappointed him. There was less copper in sight than the Indians had indicated, and the short, ice-free summers would preclude using ships for taking out whatever ore was produced.

In spite of his negative report, the Company's London Committee were so impressed by his journey that they ordered him to challenge the swarming Pedlars by building the firm's first considerable inland post somewhere below the forks of the Saskatchewan.

Again transportation proved to be the primary difficulty. Although messengers went inland in 1773 to persuade the Indians to build and bring to York Fort several Pedlar-style freight canoes, none appeared. Hearne therefore had to divide his twelve reluctant employees and his merchandise into five groups. Each group of two or three men was allotted five small canoes and enough supporting Indians to move men and merchandise to whatever spot Hearne selected. The counterattack came none too soon. That spring, 1774, only 8,137 made beaver reached York Fort.

Hearne, accompanied by a skilled carpenter named Robert Garret and a first-class jack-of-all trades, Robert Longmoor, set out first with their five canoes and Indian helpers on July 23. Their load consisted mostly of woodworking tools, a modicum of provisions, and, as currency for paying Indian hunters during the winter, 180 pounds of good tobacco and several kegs of brandy. The last the Indian paddlers surreptitiously tapped along the way, creating payment problems for the bitter months that lay ahead.

After careful exploration, Hearne chose Pine Island as the site for his new post, already named Cumberland House by his superiors. The location seemed, at first, dreadfully desolate—a thinly forested flat plain laid down over the ages by the meandering, silt-laden Saskatchewan. Pine Island was nothing more than a long sliver of land between two channels of the braided river. At one point the northern channel touched the lower curve of a large lake whose crescent-shaped tips pointed northeast and northwest. Beside an undistinguished-looking bay that formed a part of the lake's southern shore was a hummock high enough to escape the gray sheets of water that each spring oozed across the surrounding territory. On this hummock Hearne deposited his gear.

There were advantages to the spot that escaped his unhappy men. The hillock supported ample wood for building and for fires. There were huge fish in the lake—for a time it would be called Sturgeon Lake—and in autumn and spring a myriad waterfowl would provide additional food. Of more importance, the region was a crossroads. The occupants of a post there could make contact with Indians moving north out of the prairies west of Lake Winnipegosis or floating down the Saskatchewan from as far away as the Rockies. Also, as Hearne had learned during his Coppermine expedition, Indians paddling down the Churchill River often left that brawling stream to follow the Sturgeon-Weir River to Sturgeon Lake, soon renamed Cumberland after the post. These latter Indians, many from the fabled Athabasca country that no white had yet seen, brought with them the finest beaver pelts obtainable in North America. Hearne, in short, had known what he was doing when he picked that miserable but strategic site.

Aided by the men of another five-canoe brigade that arrived shortly behind him, he erected two moss-chinked, contiguous log buildings, one a dwelling place, the other a storeroom. Actually there was little to store. Indians brazenly plundered another of his five-canoe brigades. The remaining two were forced south by tribes who wanted the prestige of having traders at their village. The kidnapping so discouraged one employee, Isaac Batt, that he deserted to some Pedlars who happened by. In the end Hearne had only eight men for outfacing at least 160 Montrealers.

In spite of his apparent weakness, the more thoughtful of those Montrealers did not give way to overconfidence. They knew the Bay Company's financial power; after all, it had been in the north for more than a century. They were aware that they were 2,500 miles or more from their supply base at Montreal, whereas Cumberland House was only 730 miles from the saltwater docks at Fort York. Nor, despite the plunderings and kidnappings, did they underestimate the hold over the Indians that ten decades of reasonably fair dealings had brought their rivals. Thus, no matter how difficult its beginnings, Cumberland House was likely to survive.

Under the circumstances the Montrealers would be well advised to reconcile their own internecine rivalries and work out new strategies of competition for dealing with their entrenched rival—a consideration that swings us back to that pioneer Anglo-American trader from Lake Superior, Alexander Henry.

XVI

The First Nor'Westers

By the end of 1774, Alexander Henry had all but bankrupted himself trying to develop copper, lead, and even silver and gold mines at various points on the islands and around the shores of Lake Superior. To recoup his fortunes and, he says, to collect debts certain Indians owed him, he decided to embark on a last major trading effort in the West.

He knew what he was up against. For a decade his partner, J. B. Cadotte, and he had maintained their post at Chequamegon. They had added another at gloomy Michipicoten, where Superior's north-trending eastern shore bends sharply west. Canoemen traveling to and from Grand Portage often stopped at the latter place to gossip about the difficulties and profits of the remote wilderness.

Take the three Frobisher brothers, Benjamin, Thomas, and Joseph, tough immigrants from Yorkshire. For a time they had worked out of Michilimackinac into the country bordering Lake Michigan. After the liberalizing of the trade in 1768 their ambitions expanded. Obtaining merchandise on credit from Isaac Todd and James McGill of Montreal (the latter some years afterward founded McGill University), they started early in 1769 for Lake Winnipeg.

Indians plundered them at Rainy Lake. Philosophically accepting the loss as a normal hazard of the business, Todd and McGill re-outfitted the brothers in 1770. That year they reached Red River, south of Lake Winnipeg, and did so well that Benjamin Frobisher, the eldest of the trio, was invited to join the firm of Todd and McGill. His job was to oversee the movement of merchandise, foodstuffs, and furs between Montreal and the staging points of Grand Portage, Sault Ste. Marie, and Michilimackinac. Much of what he handled went to his younger brothers, Thomas and Joseph.

When the Red River area grew crowded, relatively speaking, the restless pair shifted to the Saskatchewan. By subverting one of the Hudson's Bay Company's erstwhile traveling agents, Louis Primeau, Joseph Frobisher found his way through Cumberland Lake a year before Hearne built a post there. From Cumberland he paddled up the Sturgeon-Weir River to a four-hundred-yard portage that leads to the Churchill River. Joe called it the English River because it emptied into Hudson Bay; the Indians' name for it was Michinipi, or Big Water, a term remarkably like that of the distant Mississippi.

The portage between the Sturgeon-Weir and the Churchill was one of the key transportation links of the north, traveled regularly by Indians moving to and from the legendary Athabasca country. Its name was almost as long as it was—Athiquisipichigon Ouingam, or the Portage of the Stretched Frog Skin: Frog Portage for short.

Years before, Primeau explained, wandering Crees had encountered at the portage Indians so primitive that they had not known how to hunt beaver, much less how to stretch and dry skins. To illustrate the latter process, the Crees killed a big frog, stretched out its hide on a willow hoop, and hung it to a tree branch while they mocked the ignorant watchers.

Frog Portage, Primeau added, was a good place to intercept Indians bound with their furs for Hudson's Bay, because here was the fork in the routes. Those headed for Prince of Wales Fort continued down the Churchill River; those who preferred to trade at York Fort crossed to the Sturgeon-Weir. Both groups would have, as part of their bundles, some of the best stretched beaver skins in the land—Athabasca beaver. Grinning in anticipation, Joe Frobisher and his men settled down, in the spring of 1774, to wait for richness to fall on them.

It so chanced that the year before, Moses Norton, the factor in charge of Fort Churchill, or Fort Prince of Wales, had emulated York Factory by sending out his first traveling salesman, Joseph Hansom. Hansom was instructed to escort to Fort Churchill whatever Indians he met, especially those indebted to the company. He worked well and had a large convoy with him when he bumped head on into Joe Frobisher.

By any commercial definition, Hansom's companions were Hudson's Bay Company Indians. They dwelt in lands to which the company had been granted exclusive trading privileges by the royal charter of 1670. Most of them had pledged their furs to the company. But none of this made any difference to Frobisher. While his men made a show of fiddling with their arms, he blustered, passed out rum, and delivered his pitch: why should the Indians go all the way to Churchill or York when he had what they needed right here?

At first the Indians were reluctant. But when it became evident that Hansom was letting himself be outbluffed, they succumbed. Frobisher disposed of every pound of merchandise in his canoes in exchange for the choicest pelts the Indians had. When his vessels could hold no more, he contemptuously let the rest of the pelts, the coarsest ones, go on down the river. Ever afterward the nearby island-filled lake where most of the bargaining had taken place was called Lac du Traite (Trade Lake), and the name Portage du Traite was used interchangeably with Frog Portage to identify the carrying place.

Henry and Cadotte heard the tale as soon as the Frobishers' laden canoes reached Lake Superior. So did several other people. Inevitably and in spite of the distant land's reputation for intense cold, short food supplies, and bitter rivalries, a small stampede developed. Henry and Cadotte were in the middle of it, departing from the Sault for Grand Portage in June, 1775, with £3,000 worth of goods and provisions.

At Grand Portage Bay they found a handful of other traders camped in ramshackle huts as they prepared to attack the nine-mile carry and the lacework of streams that lay ahead. One would think that the formidable obstacles would invite cooperation. Instead, Henry wrote, "I found the traders in a state of extreme reciprocal hostility, each pursuing his interests in such a manner as might most injure his neighbors."

Working entirely on their own, Henry and Cadotte's voyageurs spent seven days of "severe and dangerous exertion" reaching navigable water at the head of the carrying place. Part of their burden was eight North canoes—*canots du nord*—for use in the tight, shallow waters near the divides they would have to cross. Twenty-five feet long and from four to four and a half feet of beam, a North canoe could carry twenty-five to thirty ninety-pound *pièces* and four to six men, depending on the speed desired and the manpower needed in the interior.

Like the bigger *canots du maître,* the smaller vessels were handled carefully. The voyageurs jumped overboard before the bottoms scraped and sloshed ashore with the packages through knee-deep water. Owners and their clerks were carried pick-a-back to dry land. When reloading, the men placed the *pièces* on poles laid along the canoe's fragile bottom to distribute the weight. No sharp corner was allowed to touch the bark sheathing, and after the cargo was secured it was covered with sheets of dull red oilcloth. When winds dashed spray or thunderstorms boomed, the travelers sought shelter for themselves and their merchandise under overhanging rocks or in clumps of evergreens.

In spite of their precautions and of desperate bailing with huge sponges, loads were sometimes soaked. Everything had to be unpacked then and spread out to dry. And always, after every bout with rough water, broken places in the sheathing had to be repaired from the spare rolls of bark and spruce-root thread each canoe carried with it. Then torches were lighted, gum melted, and seams fortified for the next day's run.

Finding enough high-energy food to fuel the work without sacrificing space needed for merchandise created constant dilemmas. Whenever the Henry-Cadotte flotilla encountered an Indian village along the way, the leaders tried to find out where the next mobile town might be located and then bartered for the minimum of wild rice and dried meat necessary for reaching it. The voyageurs meanwhile went so hungrily after the complaisant women that, in Henry's words, "the danger of misunderstanding was increased," and he had to take to the water again before anyone was quite ready.

Because of the interruptions, even the best crews, working up to eighteen hours each day, could not average more than 1,000 miles a month. Ever-present in the proprietors' consciousness was the grim possibility of being taken by ice before reaching their destination.

As they neared the Height of Land separating the St. Lawrence drainage from that of the Winnipeg River, the coiling streams and lakes grew so shallow that the men had to lighten the canoes by climbing out and pushing. They worked their way beside cliffs seven hundred feet tall, nosed through profusions of yellow water lilies, and clambered across one granite trail that, Alexander Mackenzie wrote later, "requires the utmost exertions of the men and frequently lames them." Not everything was rock, however. One landing place was so boggy that the crews had to drive piles into the mud and create a dock by laying down logs and evergreen boughs. Rainy River provided a blessed respite—like all other travelers there, Henry was "greatly struck with the beauty of the scene"— and after threading the maze of islands in Lake of the Woods, they carried their canoes across Rat Portage to the thunderous Winnipeg.

That river, declares modern canoeist Eric Morse, "was unquestionably the grandest and most beautiful the Montreal Northmen saw." Its waters, split frequently into multiple channels, slid in hissing rumples past ice-smoothed granite streaked with black veins and painted with lichen. At the base of each cascade it shattered into backward-curling foam and then fell placid while it twined through long, serpentine lakes bordered by thick evergreens and dancing birch. The voyageurs were not entranced. Cascades meant portages, seven of them, Mackenzie wrote, "in so short a space that the whole of them are discernible at the same moment." And mosquitos! During Henry's trip the pests descended in such clouds that is was impossible for the hungry men to aim their guns at the teeming ducks, "of which we might else have shot many."

To put such places behind as quickly as possible, the voyageurs loaded themselves prodigiously wherever the nature of the ground allowed. "There have been examples," says that most precise of observers, Alexander Mackenzie, "of men taking seven packages of ninety pounds each, at one end of the Portage [du Bonnet] and putting them down at the other without stopping."

Slowly the land flattened and the river poured into turbid, shallow Lake Winnipeg, 280 miles long. The eastern shore was bordered in most places with low cliffs, but the west was wide open to winds roaring off the prairies. Sometimes the voyageurs could hoist sails and let the canoes scud. More often they were confronted with choppy, white-toothed waves or bucking-horse swells. To be on the safe side they stayed close to the shore, although this meant long paddles around exasperating promontories. Then when the rain-freighted winds grew really fierce, they could beach the canoes, generally amid tangles of down timber, huddle under whatever shelter they could patch together, and wait the storm out.

In order to obtain enough wild rice for carrying their crew through such delays, Henry and Cadotte halted at a village of Cristenaux (Cree) Indians near the mouth of the Winnipeg River. The men made more personal arrangements. Most Cristenaux males had two or more wives and were willing to loan them out until the borrowers returned the next year. They were colorful women. Like the men, they painted their faces with red ocher and ran tattoo lines from lower lip to chin or from the corners of their mouth to their ears. They put up their long black hair in rolls that looked like horns and bound it with beaded rawhide. They wore bone ornaments in their pierced ears and bracelets made out of the metal of discarded brass kettles. Their single-piece leather dresses, given shape by decorated shoulder straps and a belt, reached to their knees. They openly hoped that their adventure away from home would produce children. Sons born of white fathers, one husband assured Henry, made bolder warriors and better hunters than full-blooded Indians. Just how bold those *métis*, or halfbreeds, could be we shall see later on.

Henry, Cadotte, and their new auxiliaries started north from the mouth of the Winnipeg River, commonly called Bas de la Rivière, on August 18, 1775. Their course led along the east shore as far as the lake's narrow waist. There they would cross to the marshy, deeply scalloped west bank by dodging from island to island. Afterward they would have to traverse the mouths of several deep bays and circle a hated promontory twenty-five miles long that they called Le Détour.

It was not an easy journey, yet for Henry's party to have spent six weeks on it is next to unbelievable. Thirty-three years later, by contrast, his nephew Alexander Henry the Younger, buffeted by daily storms, traveled from the Red River at the lake's southern extremity to the mouth of the Saskatchewan in a single week. Even more tantalizing, the older Henry nowhere explains the delay. A presumption that there were some powerful powwows and more than a little roistering along the way is inescapable, especially when one recalls Alexander Mackenzie's later sneer at the fecklessness of his predecessors. Anyway, let's look at such facts as can be exhumed.

The Henry-Cadotte group had barely left the Winnipeg River when they fell in with two canoes under Peter Pond of Connecticut, one of the stormiest and at the same time one of the most farsighted figures of the North American fur trade. Born in Milford in 1740, he had joined the army at the age of sixteen and had fought four years against the French in Canada. After being mustered out as a commissioned officer at the age of twenty, he tried a trading trip to the West Indies, then married and settled down as a shoemaker in his native town. Three years of that left him discontent and he switched to the fur trade, working southwest out of both Detroit and Michilimackinac. In 1772 he chose to visit the West Indies again, perhaps because of a hullabaloo that followed his slaying of a rival during a duel. On returning, he sought out the upper Mississippi and achieved quick profits in spite of heavy competition from both Mackinac and St. Louis.

He feared the future, however. The Quebec Act of 1774, which extended that province's jurisdiction over the Ohio and upper Mississippi regions was bringing roars of protest from the thirteen colonies farther south. Because of that and other grievances, war with England seemed possible. But if a revolution came, Quebec would, in Pond's opinion, stay loyal. If so, merchandise and pelts would flow more freely in the north than in the south. Besides the furs he saw coming out of the newly opened lands beyond Lake Winnipeg were more lustrous than anything he had handled along the Mississippi. Reasoning thus, he invested his Mississippi gains in two canoeloads of trade goods and headed out of Grand Portage for a region about which he had only hearsay information.

So far as geography was concerned, neither Henry nor Cadotte knew much more. But Henry was a fellow Anglo-American and, thanks to Cadotte's tutoring, just as tough and canny in his dealings with voyageurs and Indians as Pond was. They joined forces. Immediately thereafter a storm raged out of the west, swamped one of the Henry-Cadotte canoes, and drowned four men.*

---

* The casualty figure is Henry's. Matthew Cocking, who heard the story of the accident after the Pedlars had arrived at Cumberland House, reported that only one man was lost.

Having done what they could to salvage corpses and soggy goods, the flotilla crossed the narrows on August 21. The wreck considered, this was fair progress, but afterward the delays mounted inexplicably. Henry says that on reaching the west shore they spent a long time fishing, to the annoyance of the pelicans with whom they competed. After sixteen days they were overtaken by the Frobisher brothers, Tom and Joe, by Charles Patterson, and by unnamed others. The additions meant that the flotilla now contained thirty North canoes, at least 130 voyageurs, an unknown number of borrowed Indian women, and, almost surely, some male Indian hangers-on.

Thirty canoe loads of merchandise beside Lake Winnipeg must have been worth well over 60,000 Revolutionary era dollars. Time was precious, too—time for building huts and stockpiling food after they had reached their wintering grounds. Yet they dawdled. Fishing.

Fishing for what? All we can do is guess, our speculations helped by a few facts that Henry failed to mention in his own account. Other records show that among the proprietors he did not name in his reminiscences were two Canadians and two Frenchmen. Actually, one of the "Frenchmen" was a Swiss, Jean-Etienne Wadin, or Wadden, whom we will meet again. Like other fur traders, Wadin had a white wife and family in Montreal, a red one in the wilderness. That very summer, 1775, he acquired a halfbreed daughter whom he named Marguerite; in due time Marguerite Wadin would marry, in succession, two of the giants of the later trade, Alexander McKay and John McLoughlin. As for the Canadians, one was Peter Pangman, as abrasive in his dealings as Peter Pond. James Finlay, a pioneer of the Saskatchewan, was probably present as well.

It added up to a lot of competition, potentially ferocious because the canoes carried enough "high wine" to produce, when diluted with water, several gallons of intoxicant. On top of that the Montrealers knew by then that the Hudson's Bay Company had established Cumberland House during the preceding winter and was prepared to meet them on the Indians' own ground. Instead of continuing to fight among themselves, would it not be better to join forces against the common rival?

An added reason for combination was the ever-pressing problem of food. Henry, Cadotte, Charles Patterson, and Joe and Tom Frobisher all wanted to go to the Churchill River in the vicinity of Frog Portage. That land, however, was in the boreal forest and was almost devoid of game during the winter. With luck the men would be able to catch in nets laid under the ice enough white fish, trout, and sturgeon to exist until spring, but in warm weather the fish would quickly spoil and leave them without food for the rush back to Lake Superior. Somehow a store of more stable provisions had to be laid by for the journey.

The prairies south of the Saskatchewan offered such a food—pemmican. Indians made it by pounding thin strips of sun-dried buffalo meat into a powder, filling leather parfleches with the granulated jerky, and sealing the mass by pouring in melted buffalo tallow that hardened as it cooled. Often the cooks added berries. Always they let slip in, inadvertently, bits of leaves, sticks, sand, and drops of sweat. Pemmican could be eaten raw or boiled into a mush called rubaboo. Voyageurs liked either form better than lyed corn and performed well on it, for pemmican is one of the most nutritious foods ever developed.

If the proprietors of the 1775 flotilla combined forces, some could trade for pemmican on the prairies while the rest ventured into the forest. Afterward profits would be divided evenly.

Evenly? Furs were surely more valuable per pound than pemmican. Yet without pemmican those glossy Athabasca pelts could never be brought to market. So why not put aside jealousies, suspicions, and struggles for dubious advantage while working for the common good?

Old envies proved hard to down. The surly independents sat by the lakeside fishing, bickering, and drawing up agreements that some fancied slight led them to tear into shreds almost the next moment—or so the long delay suggests. Two weeks dragged by. Then, on September 21, snow began to fall. That touch of cold reality ended part of the recalcitrance. Peter Pangman, the Frobishers, Charles Patterson, Alexander Henry, and James Baptiste Cadotte agreed to pool resources and effort. The others held back. Wadin and his French companion decided to try their luck at Swan Lake, one of the many huge, platterlike bodies of water south of the lower Saskatchewan—an unfortunate decision, as matters developed, for Indians plundered them. Pond, a loner by nature, chose to go still farther south to Lake Dauphin. James Finlay, who possibly had some unrecorded arrangement with the main pool, apparently returned to his familiar station just below the forks of the river.

By September 25 two feet of snow lay on the ground; thin lenses of ice rimmed the lake. Galvanized into action, the paddlers raced for the mouth of the Saskatchewan, which they entered on October 1. Two miles upstream they encountered the frigid Grand Rapids, where the river, a mile wide at that point, drops forty-three feet in less than three miles. Harnessing themselves like horses to their *cordelle* ropes, the men took to the icy bank and dragged the canoes two miles against the torrent. Then they had to yield to the water and portage goods and canoes the rest of the way.

Drabness followed—a yellow, sprawling stream that entered Cedar Lake (Lac Bourbon of the La Vérendryes) through multiple channels whose banks were so low and swampy that dry camping places were hard to find. At Cumberland Lake the proprietors who had not already turned south on their own divided according to prior arrangement. Cadotte, Patterson, and James Finlay pushed up the Saskatchewan. Joe and Tom Frobisher and Alexander Henry turned north up the Sturgeon-Weir with forty-three men traveling in ten canoes. Offended by something or other, grumpy Peter Pangman withdrew from the pool and spent the winter near Cumberland House, which was then in charge of Matthew Cocking.

After the Saskatchewan the Sturgeon-Weir should have been a delight, sprightly and sparkling like crystal. But it was so full of rapids that the weary voyageurs called it the Maligne, the Evil One —"the most dangerous, crossgrained piece of navigation in the Indian country," traveler Ross Cox declared several years later. Fortunately the new partners did not have far to go. Their goal was Beaver Lake, a handsome hill-girt body of water some sixty-five miles north of Cumberland House. They arrived the night of November 1. The next day the lake froze—a close call.

Normally they would have buried the canoes to keep the intense cold from splitting a bark, but they could not chip away the frozen earth and ended up sheltering the craft on scaffolds. They arranged five log houses in the form of a quadrangle. The three proprietors occupied one. Each of the remaining four sheltered ten voyageurs.

Cutting enough wood to heat the buildings occupied the full time of four men.

To get food they chopped a row of holes through the ice and with long poles stretched out a long, weighted net in the black water beneath. Fish trying to pass through the net were caught by the gills. The device was standard throughout the north, but at Beaver Lake it failed to produce enough fish for forty-three men. Accordingly the partners supplemented the catch by angling for trout with deep-set lines, an onerous procedure where the temperature sank to thirty below zero, as it frequently did.

There were few Indians in the vicinity and, except for fishing, little to do. Bored and worried about whether the prairie section of the pool was holding together, Henry on January 1, 1776, set out to check. He took two men with him, each hauling a sled of thin boards curled upward in front and loaded with food, beaver blankets, and buffalo robes. Joe Frobisher and a single voyageur accompanied them as far as Cumberland House, just for a respite from the stagnation at Beaver Lake.

The long snowshoe journey from Cumberland House onto the plains almost finished Henry. The cold was intense and fuel hard to find. During one four-day period the wayfarers survived by melting snow and dissolving in the warm liquid just enough chocolate "to alter the colour of the water." Some four weeks out of Beaver Lake they reached Fort des Prairies just below the forks of the river, where Charles Patterson was stationed. After Henry had regained his strength, Patterson took him south to visit a village of Plains Assiniboins. A high time—wolves at their heels, a buffalo stampede, blizzards, feasting, dancing, and comely girls. Best of all, he learned that the agreement was holding and that there would be pemmican enough for the trip back to Grand Portage.

By April 7 Henry was once again at Beaver Lake. Late in May the ice began to break, and the party, traveling slowly because of the need to fish along the way, moved northward to a trading post that Joseph Frobisher had built earlier in the season near Frog Portage, the scene of his trading triumph of the preceding year. Though Henry does not mention the matter, a comparable conflict took place again.

This time the victim of the Montrealers was Robert Longmoor.

Longmoor was a tough, enduring man. During the building of Cumberland House he had frozen both big toes to the bone, then had sat quietly while Hearne cut them open and applied to the flesh "the inner Rind of the Larch Tree Root which is generally used among the natives to stop or prevent Mortification." Within six weeks Longmoor was back at work.

In 1776 Cocking sent him up the Churchill ahead of the Montrealers with orders to bring every Indian he encountered to Cumberland House. The plan fell apart on high wine. The Pedlars got the passing Indians dead drunk and at night sent their voyageurs into the red men's camp to steal their furs. When Longmoor personally tried to carry bundles of pelts past the Henry-Frobisher post, Henry accused him of thievery, arguing that the Indians' acceptance of Montreal liquor committed the drinkers to trading with the Canadians. Longmoor hooted the idea aside and tried to go on. At that Henry and his men wrenched the packages from the Bay Company trader by force.

Evidently the tactics did not yield enough furs to fill the Pedlars' canoes, and so Henry and a few men guided by an Indian woman made a run up the Churchill River in search of more. It was a successful move. They encountered a flotilla of Chipewyan Indians laden not only with beaver, otter, and marten, but also with information. Beyond the Churchill drainage, the Indians said, was a whole new river system that drained north out of the Athabasca country. A main feeder of this prodigious outflow, the Peace River, headed in the Rocky Mountains. From the feeder's source, the Indians said, "the distance to the *salt lake*"—meaning the Pacific Ocean—"was not great."

In proof of the statement the Chipewyans produced some prisoners taken in battle with a tribe that lived beyond the Rockies. Henry's party purchased, for a gun each, two of the captives, a young woman and a boy of twelve. Presumably, though Henry in his memoirs never mentioned the prisoners again, the motive behind the acquisition was a need for information.

Twice the Frobishers had won wealth by tampering with Indians attached to the Hudson's Bay Company. Such piracy was not likely to succeed a third time. A surer way would be to carry the trade into distant Athabasca ahead of everyone else. From there . . . who could say? But suggestions might be pried from the captives.

A push into the unknown would also help dispose of several bales of merchandise that the partnership had not been able to sell either on the Saskatchewan or along the Churchill. So a new bargain was struck: Thomas Frobisher and Louis Primeau would move the material into Athabasca for the winter trade of 1776–77, provided that their friends met them with provisions at a specified point along the return route.

Agreed. Doggedly then Tom, Primeau, and a handful of voyageurs (and the captives?) turned up the crystal Churchill. Exuberantly his brother Joe, Alexander Henry, Peter Pond, Jean Baptiste Cadotte, and various others rushed for the outside. Thanks to favoring winds and their own eagerness, they coursed Winnipeg Lake's storm-wracked length in days, not weeks.

It was Henry's last trip into the wilderness. His fortunes repaired, he moved to Montreal to become a supplier rather than trader of Indian goods. Partly because he wrote a book about his early experiences while those with whom he had been associated did not, his fame overshadowed theirs. Still, he was a forerunner. He had been among the first traders to reach Montreal after the conquest of Canada, and for a time Lake Superior had been his and J. B. Cadotte's private preserve. More important, he had helped establish the first cooperative organization designed to overcome, through a division of labor, the problems inherent in advancing the trade 2,500 miles from its base of supplies. He and those with him had picked up the first firm information, as distinct from rumor and hope, of a possible water link with the Pacific. Thereafter he would do what he could from Montreal to promote the development of a usable trail entirely across the continent, even to the point, eventually, of conveying his theories to a citizen of the young United States of America, John Jacob Astor.

Meanwhile, actual travel had to go on. At Grand Portage Joe Frobisher and Peter Pond, among others, picked up fresh supplies and after a carousal hurried west again. For reasons unrecorded, Pond had had enough of Lake Dauphin. This year, 1777, he went with Frobisher back to one of the series of "settlements" that the Montreal Pedlars, some working in loose union and others in bitter rivalry, were dotting across the central part of what is now the province of Saskatchewan. It was at one of those clusters of log tents that Joe learned from a messenger who snowshoed overland

from the Churchill that brother Tom had chosen to winter at Lac
Ile-à-la-Crosse, well short of Athabasca.

Perhaps Tom's voyageurs had refused to go farther either out of
fear of starvation or of a portage reputedly thirteen miles long that
lay ahead. Perhaps Primeau, who had been to Ile-à-la-Crosse, a
long V-shaped lake named for the game the Indians played on its
bordering meadows, had convinced him that no rival would ever
get that far. So why not sit tight and let the Indians come to them?
Anyway, after letting Joe know where the party was, the Pedlars
did sit tight until the spring of 1777. Leisurely then they began
trading with the Indians, who, as Primeau had predicted, showed
up on the heels of the breaking ice. Though some of the natives
slipped by them to trade with a Bay Company man named Robert
Davey, pickings were nonetheless rich enough on both the Churchill
and the Saskatchewan that the brothers were able to start for Grand
Portage with upwards of seven tons of choice fur—choice because
at those distances it did not pay to bother with anything else.

The Frobishers used the capital they had accumulated to set up
the powerful supply company of Benjamin and Joseph Frobisher.
The move did not mean abandonment of their dreams of the far
Northwest. If anything, Athabasca came closer, figuratively speaking. For only tight concentrations of capital could solve the enormous credit problems associated with the four-year time span
involved in moving merchandise from London to the far end of the
trail and then bringing back the furs to pay for the goods. Yet even
that was based on assumption. For what merchant-banker in London or Montreal could be sure that the logistics of handling canoe
freight across five thousand miles—twenty-five hundred in and as
many back—would not break down somewhere on the wind-swept
lakes or the hundreds of carrying places?

Tom Frobisher said the job was possible. But Tom was guessing;
he had not reached Athabasca. The real test, which came the next
year, 1778, was made by that cantankerous genius of the wild
lands, Peter Pond.

XVII

Broadening Vistas

For Pond the winter of 1777–78 was more crowded than he
liked. He spent it at a fort on the North Saskatchewan near the
mouth of the Sturgeon (a confusing name, since the Sturgeon has
no connection with the Sturgeon-Weir several miles farther east),
and he did a poor business. Competitors were everywhere around
him, from the Sturgeon on up the Saskatchewan another two hundred miles to the so-called "Upper Settlement" near the Eagle
Hills.

The concentration resulted from a hard winter truth: no matter
how the voyageurs strained, goods picked up during the summer at
Mackinac, still the chief outfitting center of the trade, could not be
taken farther inland than this stretch of mingled prairie and forest.
As soon as ice threatened, each trader settled down at the cluster of
huts that best suited his purposes and prepared to do commercial
battle with other Canadians and with persistent Robert Longmoor
of the Hudson's Bay Company.

Alcohol continued to be the trade's principal weapon. When it
failed, some of the Pedlars took to bullying the Indians physically
to keep them from rivals. There were repercussions. Three whites
that the Montreal men sent onto the prairies to trade at a native
village were slain by Indians brooding over treatment received
earlier at Sturgeon River.

When the chaotic season of 1777–78 ended, the loose partner-

225

ship of which Pond was a member found itself with four or five canoeloads of goods still on hand. The merchandise may have represented an unintended surplus, or it may have been held back deliberately in order to give some member of the group a head start on the long trail to Athabasca. In any event, opportunity was beckoning, and Pond was selected to answer.

He and his voyageurs accompanied the returning flotilla as far as Cumberland Lake. From there they fought their way, cursing heartily, up the boiling Sturgeon-Weir to the Churchill. Their tempers smoothed out then, for the Churchill proved to be a classic canoe stream. Strings of sparkling cascades bound together granite-cupped lakes fringed by evergreens. True, there were whirlpools and submerged snags to guard against, flinty portages to cross, and occasional rains to endure. But most summer days were idyllic— soft breezes, thin streaks of clouds. Querulous terns and sandpipers whirled up like bursts of sun-brightened spray. Flocks of pelicans were like restless snow on the sandspits.

Good camping spots abounded. At dusk, which that far north lingered past ten o'clock, the flotilla landed. After unloading the canoes, the voyageurs lifted them carefully onto the beach, overturned them, and repaired the day's damage. Meanwhile the cook hung a huge black kettle over a fire of driftwood and boiled pemmican into rubaboo. Stomachs filled, the men collapsed under the shelter of oilcloth and canoe into a sound sleep that seldom was allowed to last until dawn. Often enough when the shout *"Levez! Levez!"* brought them up, rubbing their eyes, the corruscations of the aurora still filled the northern sky.

As the flotilla advanced, the granites and gneisses of the Shield, whose edges the Churchill skirted for much of its length, fell away and the scenery became more placid, but, in the eyes of Alexander Mackenzie, no less beautiful. He rhapsodized in his "General History" over Lake Ile-à-la-Crosse, the abundance of fish, fowl, moose, and deer, "the richness of its surrounding banks and forests." For years the meadows beside the lake furnished a spring rendezvous site for Cree Indians bound downriver with the fruits of their winter hunts. They played tumultuous games of lacrosse, often against the Chipewyans who came out of the tundra country to the north, then feasted, danced, and sang before the best of their young men and women launched the trading trips to Hudson Bay—trips which, if the Pedlars had their way, soon would be things of the past.

The existence of that rendezvous had lulled Thomas Frobisher into stopping at Ile-à-la-Crosse. Pond's ambitions were less easily assuaged. On he went into a string of increasingly shallow lakes (one would be named Peter Pond Lake after him), through swamps, and along shrinking streams whose rocky bottoms posed a constant threat to the laden canoes.

The dwindling of the last stream forced him onto a carrying place sometimes called Portage La Loche and sometimes Methye Portage. A sandy trail led north for eight miles through spindly jack pines. Straining under their tumplines, the voyageurs brought a portion of the bales to the first *posé*, dumped the loads in a pile, then returned for more, ending finally with the canoes. Then on to the next *posé* and the next, until they reached white sand beaches bordering a lake a mile long. Back into the canoes the *pièces* went for the short traverse to the lake's opposite side. Then out again to a four-mile trail that climbed through rolling hills.

The slight gradient ended at the brink of a precipitous hillside that Alexander Mackenzie later estimated was eight hundred feet high. The forty-mile view of the narrow valley bordering the long ridge on which he stood was, in his estimation, "romantic, and ravishing." After reading such hyperbole, modern sportsmen have been disappointed. What the voyageurs who had to negotiate the drop thought of it is not a matter of record. The way was so steep that canoes and some packages had to be cradled on sleds for the lowering. As the men working the ropes struggled to keep their bare or moccasined feet from sliding out from under them, there was not one who did not visualize with dread the outward climb the following spring.

A stream they named Clearwater rushed them west some eighty miles to the northward surge of the Athabasca. Pond followed the latter stream another 160 miles or so to a spot that struck him as suitable for a fort. Inasmuch as huge Lake Athabasca was only thirty or forty miles away, the question arises as to why he did not seek it out.

One can hazard two guesses. Just beyond the point where he halted, the Athabasca River debouches into a delta that brackets the southwest corner of Lake Athabasca with a maze of streams, lakelets, and soggy muskeg. The Peace River, pouring in from the southwest, encloses the northwest of the lake with a similar delta. The Indians threaded the commingling labyrinths by a variety of routes. Near the point where Pond halted, the many trails came together, a natural rendezvous site. That was one gain.

Until reaching the delta, the Athabasca flowed with a hard current. Winter's ice was swept out of it nearly a month before it disappeared from the lower delta and the lake. This circumstance would allow Pond to start east with his furs sooner than if he had camped beside the lake. Where summers were short, each extra day of travel time was another gain.

The appearance of a white trader spared the Indians their long annual journey for trade goods. Overjoyed, they flocked to the log post with furs and information. With the aid of gestures and an untutored translator, Pond tried to orient himself. After the Peace and Athabasca had mingled in Lake Athabasca, where did the waters go?

North, the Indians said, to a larger body of water. Some thought it might be the sea. But in time Pond found others who declared that it was truly a lake, later named Great Slave Lake, and that its outlet river flowed west.

West! If that were so, then the river probably was not the Coppermine, which Hearne had followed to the Arctic Ocean six years before. And if it was not the Coppermine, where did it end? In the Arctic? Or in the Pacific?

Where did those two oceans join—if they did?

Unbearably tantalized, Pond shifted his questions to the east-flowing Peace, the breach it made in the Rockies, and the lands that lay beyond. The answers came much as they had to Alexander Henry: skyscraping mountains that the snow never completely left, canyons more tremendous than any on the route to Montreal, and then, not far away, the salt lake.

How far? The Indians were vague, or else the translations made them seem so. But, Pond gathered, the distance could perhaps be covered in a month.

A month! To anyone who had toiled up the Ottawa from Montreal (which itself was nearly a thousand miles from the sea), over Grand Portage, through Lake Winnipeg, and along the Churchill, the implications were heart-stopping. For if Athabasca could be reached in a month by either the Peace or the river that flowed out of Great Slave Lake, then the logical method of exploiting this grand new fur preserve would be from a station on the West Coast. Moreover, the area lay outside Rupert Land, the drainage system claimed by the Hudson's Bay Company. That meant a new monopoly could be established there, if the antagonistic traders of Montreal reconciled their differences and if the government granted the necessary sanctions.

That year Pond had neither time, equipment, canoes, nor men for exploration. By the time the trading season ended in the spring, he had acquired more pelts than he could carry in a single trip back to his waiting partners. This ironic richness raised the familiar dilemma: how much space should he sacrifice to pemmican—pemmican made from the meat of the woods buffalo that ranged through the brushlands along the Peace River—and how much should he retain for those glossy skins?

He made his calculations and stored the furs that could not be crowded into the canoes in one of the huts where the party had wintered. He cut the margin of safety thin, and when he passed Cumberland House, the journal keeper there noted that the men were suffering from hunger. Presumably, however, the partners who had sent him to Athabasca met him shortly thereafter at some prearranged spot and saved him with fresh provisions.

Their strength restored, he and his men turned straight back without continuing to Grand Portage. Back through those twisting lakes across the infamous twelve-mile Methye Portage. Back to the cold of nights twenty hours long, to the questions, the speculations —and to the stored furs that the Athabasca Indians, untarnished as yet by the trade wars that were corrupting their fellows along the Saskatchewan, had not pilfered. But because the impact of those wars, and others, would soon bring marked changes to Pond's career and eventually to the Athabascans, it is well to pause here for a glance at what was happening farther south.

In the fall of 1778, at about the time Pond's men were struggling northward across Methye Portage, a drunken Indian was making such a nuisance of himself at a post in the Eagle Hills near the Saskatchewan that a trader there sought to quiet him by adding laudanum to his next gulp of whiskey. By coincidence the same idea occurred to another white. The Indian died of the inadvertent double slug.

There were other grievances. The Pedlars would meet prospective customers on the prairies and pass out free alcohol. They claimed, as Alexander Henry had, that this obligated the Indians to bring their furs and pemmican to the donors' post. If the Indians objected, they were menaced with drawn swords or their horses were impounded in the post's courtyard. Sometimes the Indians themselves were incarcerated, and on one occasion a bullyboy named Charles McCormick ripped up a hide tipi with his hunting knife to show his displeasure over its owner's attempt to trade elsewhere.

The Indians brooded over these episodes throughout the winter. On returning to the post in the spring of 1779, they precipitated a fight. After outbursts of gunfire had killed two whites and an unknown number of Indians, the traders lost heart and fled with a few furs under cover of darkness. At sunrise the victors swarmed through the abandoned post, looting it of its remaining furs and merchandise before setting the buildings afire.

The pessimism engendered by this defiance was intensified by the discovery that Robert Longmoor planned to build—and in the fall of 1779 did build—a solid, well-appointed Hudson's Bay Company Fort, named Hudson House, at a spot on the North Saskatchewan from which he could challenge each of the Pedlars' "settlements." Clearly the Montreal men were going to have to respond with some firmer organization than the loose partnerships that had contented them so far. For one thing, the members of such associations took out their profits in direct proportion to the merchandise and labor each contributed. Since the profits might not be enough to cover their debts to their suppliers, each member also conducted on the side whatever additional business suited him, by whatever methods he chose. As a general thing these extracurricular activities aggravated rather than relieved tensions.

Simultaneously, the American Revolution was increasing the problems of the men who supplied the traders. British blockades choked off traffic that had once moved through New York to Albany and thence to Michilimackinac. This strangulation led several merchants who had once operated out of Albany to join the Loyalists streaming north to Montreal. (Some 10,000 Loyalists entered Canada during the war.) Led by doughty Simon McTavish, these one-time New Yorkers did much to revolutionize the handling of goods destined for the upper Great Lakes.

The canoe route along the Ottawa, Mattawa, and French rivers to the north shore of Lake Huron could be traveled swiftly enough to make it practical for transporting laborers and lightweight merchandise. For downward-bound furs that had to catch the autumn's last ships to London, it was indispensible. It was, however, one of the most expensive routes per ton mile in the world, because every night and at every carrying place the ninety-pound bales had to be lifted out of the canoes and afterward put back in again.

A combination of bateaux on the St. Lawrence, sailing ships that were often hobbled by contrary winds on the lakes, and wagons creaking slowly over the Niagara portage provided a cheaper way for moving goods in bulk. Sailing vessels were especially useful for carrying, from the growing areas near Detroit to the distribution points of Michilimackinac and Sault Ste. Marie, the tons of corn consumed each year by the voyageurs. By carefully integrating canoe travel with a network of freighting craft on the lakes, Simon McTavish and his peers made significant additions both to the volume of the fur trade and the distances it covered.*

In 1778 the government banned private vessels from the lakes. Thereafter fur-trade goods had to share space with military cargoes in vessels run by the army. The reason for the order was a not ill-founded fear that private merchants might, if unrestrained, conduct contraband dealings with the revolutionists and their Indian allies in the western country. (Rebel George Rogers Clark, for instance, was raiding successfully in Indiana and Illinois that year.) But moving freight at the whim of the military produced such crippling delays that, according to the long-faced merchants, their voyageurs were in danger of starving for want of corn.

Additional delays were occasioned by laggard licensing. Although the trade had been "free" since 1768, men could not enter the Indian country without permits signed by the governor—a reminder that disruptive behavior in the interior could result in a

---

* It should be remembered that in terms of volume more than half of Canada's fur trade still funneled through Mackinac into what is now upper Michigan, Wisconsin, Minnesota, and northern Iowa.

person's being barred from the trade. Burdened with war work, Governor Haldimand's office did not issue the licenses for 1779 as promptly as the merchants wished, and their incomes suffered.

Protests by an individual or even by a firm availed little. But, the sufferers reasoned, a consortium of several firms might prove more effective. With that in mind Simon McTavish and Benjamin and Joseph Frobisher put together a partnership of nine of the fur trade's most potent companies. In addition to merchants operating out of both Montreal and Michilimackinac, it embraced some of the traders in the field—traders who, naturally enough, were connected by chains of debt to the participating supply houses. Because the agreement was an *ad hoc* affair aimed primarily at placing pressure on the government, it was to last for one year only. Results proved so salutary, however, that in 1780 the contracts were extended for three more years. Two years later the flimsy edifice collapsed, largely because of the violences of Peter Pond.

In the summer of 1780 Pond came down from his second trip to Athabasca brimming with plans for a new approach to the far Northwest. Having had no rest since 1775, he chose to winter at his ease at Michilimackinac. There, either by letter or through personal contact, he infected Alexander Henry with his excitement. It was a natural development because Henry, too, it will be recalled, had glimpsed, in the tales told by the Indians, the possibility of a water link to the Pacific.

Henry relayed the potentials inherent in that link by letter to Sir Joseph Banks, one of England's great naturalists and geographers. Skilled voyageurs, Henry said, could reach the northwest coast from newly opened Athabasca within thirty days. There, at some convenient port, they could build a small vessel for exploring the Pacific littoral and making contact with Asia. The way found, goods could start moving between England and China across the American continent "& a Valuable New Commerce [would] be opened and Secured to his Majesty's subjects."

In writing Banks, Henry was pitching none too subtly for government support in developing the new trade route. Nothing happened. The government was beset with a global war arising out of the American Revolution, and the Montreal merchants with a run of disasters in the interior.

The first of the troubles was an upsurge of Indian hostility. In 1781, the year Pond returned to the *pays d'en haut,* three whites among a group building a post on the Assiniboine River south of Lake Winnipeg were killed and the rest driven out of the area. A Saskatchewan band tried to break into Robert Longmoor's Hudson House. Remembering the atmosphere of dread that these and other incidents instilled in them that summer and fall, some traders later declared, on the basis of little firm evidence, that the Indians had been plotting a general uprising like Pontiac's and were forestalled only by the advent of a hideous epidemic.

Far to the south Dakota Sioux in 1780 picked up smallpox from white traders on the Mississippi. From there the disease swept like a prairie fire west and then north. It reached the forks of the Saskatchewan in November, 1781, and Cumberland House the following month. It completely terrified the Indians. Anyone who caught the plague was considered doomed and straightway abandoned, although ordinary care might have saved many lives. More unnecessary deaths were caused by sufferers jumping into icy water to relieve their raging fevers.

The dead were left to wolves and to the Indian dogs that swarmed in every village. Traders protected many corpses (after helping themselves to the beaver robes in which the dying had wrapped themselves) by covering the bodies with logs. At Cumberland House and perhaps at some of the Pedlars' forts, goods were fumigated with burning sulfur (no indication appears as to how sulfur happened to be on hand), and ailing Indians who sought food and medicine were freely given what there was. Strangely, only a sprinkling of whites contracted the disease and not one died. But there were so few hunters in the field that year that fur returns in the spring of 1782 were negligible.

Pond started for Athabasca just ahead of the outbreak. Ice caught him on the Churchill River a hundred miles or so west of Frog Portage. Seeking a wintering ground rich enough to compensate him for lost Athabasca, he swung south to Lac La Ronge.

That area was already covered, and had been for the past few years by the Swiss trader, Jean Etienne Wadin, snugly ensconced in a stockaded log fort with his wife and at least one child, seven-year-old Marguerite. Relationships between the men are not clear. Some sources say that both were still members of the Northwest

Company; others, that Wadin had been blackballed when the agreement was extended in 1780. Be that as it may, they were inflexible individualists with their own notions about how trading should be carried on. To these differences can be added the strains of cabin fever, worries over the declines in trade caused by smallpox, and Pond's explosive temper.

In March, 1782, Wadin invited Pond and his clerk, Toussaint Le Sieur, to dinner. During the festivities, at which Wadin may well have imbibed too much, Pond and Le Sieur fell by prearrangement into a sham scuffle. While Wadin's wife and child watched in horror, Wadin lurched out to separate the fighters, who by then had drawn their guns. Two shots were fired. Both "accidentally" struck the peace-maker. As he dropped to the floor, bleeding profusely from a severed artery in his thigh, his guests fled. Although his wife and a voyageur or two who ran in at the sound of the shot did what they could to revive him, he expired in agony without describing the facts of the conflict.

One of Wadin's outraged employees carried affidavits concerning the affray to Governor Haldimand in Quebec. Warrants were issued, but there is no indication that a trial was held, perhaps because the courts decided they lacked jurisdiction over the Indian country.

Other men, notably Peter Pangman on the Saskatchewan, also proved disruptive, and the agreement among the Pedlars fell apart. For the dogged traders of the Hudson's Bay Company the demoralization should have been a golden opportunity—except that they, too, suffered catastrophe. In the summer of 1782 French warships captured both Churchill and York. Deprived of supplies, the men in the interior survived by the thinnest of margins. Chief Matonabbee, who had taken Hearne to the Coppermine River, was so dismayed that he committed suicide (Hearne was taken prisoner at Churchill), and for three years the century-old firm paid no dividends.

None of these upheavals interfered with Pond's passionate desire to learn the geography of the continent's northwestern corner. In 1783, supported by backers untroubled by his murder of Wadin (if it was murder), he set out once again from Grand Portage for Athabasca. Until that year he had traveled incredible distances by simply following rivers and lakes, guessing at direction by the slant of the sun, the position of the north star, and the way moss grew on the trees. Distance was calculated loosely by the number of times the guide of the brigade allowed the canoemen to pause for a smoke. Thus, though he could get to Athabasca, he did not know where it was in the sense a geographer knows—a truth brought home by the Hudson's Bay's Company's recent hiring of a surveyor, Philip Turnor, whose sole duty was to pinpoint on an accurate map the exact location of each company establishment.

Pond was no surveyor; in fact, as a journal he had kept years earlier on the Mississippi shows, he was next to illiterate. But he decided to do what he could. At Grand Portage, whose latitude and longitude were known, he obtained a compass. Every time his canoes changed course during the next 2,500 miles, he jotted the fact in a notebook. He accepted the judgment of experienced canoemen about distances and translated their leagues into miles by multiplying by three, a considerable exaggeration as time would prove. During the long winter nights that followed he produced the first map, albeit a rough one, of the Canadian Northwest.

On returning to Grand Portage in the summer of 1784 he was confronted with radical changes. Most devastating to fur men was the boundary between Canada and the United States as established by the peace treaty ending the revolution. Everything south of the Great Lakes, including Lake Michigan, went to the Americans. West of Lake Superior the line was the Pigeon River and the canoe route to Lake of the Woods. This meant that every center of the fur trade—Niagara, Detroit, Michilimackinac, the south shore of Sault Ste. Marie, Grand Portage, and the great carrying trail to the upper Pigeon—all were lost.

The dismay occasioned by the treaty allowed Joseph and Benjamin Frobisher and Simon McTavish to agitate for a renewed union of the major fur-trading interests. Some of the stormy petrels of the old union were dead or retired; others like Peter Pangman, it was thought, could be ignored. Meanwhile fresh efforts were badly needed to coordinate shipping on the Great Lakes with the canoe runs on the rivers, for delineating trading areas, and for providing the voyageur's three essential foods—corn, wild rice, and pemmican. In addition a powerful union could bring pressure to bear on the government to relax continuing restrictions against private vessels on the lakes and not least, to seek boundary rectifications with the Americans.

By the time Pond reached Grand Portage the new union, again

called the North West Company, was in operation. One share out of sixteen was reserved for him. Because it would be his job to organize the trade's richest and most difficult district, Athabasca, he felt he should have had two shares, as the other leaders in the company had. After shouting out his objections, he swept up his maps in a temper and started via Montreal for his first visit to his home in the United States in more than ten years.

Traveling with him were Peter Pangman and John Ross, both outraged because they had received no shares at all. In Montreal the disgruntled trio called on representatives of the firm of Gregory, McLeod & Company. Until 1783 this efficiently run organization had conducted its principal business through Detroit, but because of the new boundary they were contemplating switching to the northwest. The offer of three winterers of the stature of Pond, Pangman, and Ross to join them clinched the decision.

Talks were hardly underway when an agent of the new North West Company—one suspects Joseph Frobisher—pulled Pond aside with an irresistible siren song. The North West Company was applying to the government for a ten-year fur-trade monopoly covering all Canadian lands not reserved to the Hudson's Bay Company. In return the new monopoly would explore the western half of the continent at its own expense. Pond's maps and his availability for future examinations of the wilderness would have considerable weight with the government. And, of course, if the monopoly were granted, that would be the end of Gregory, McLeod, Pangman, and the rest. Why not come back to the winning side?

Tied in with this was electrifying information about Captain James Cook's explorations of the Pacific Coast in 1778. As preliminary accounts had made clear—accounts confirmed by the Admiralty's publication in 1784 of the expedition's official records—two discoveries of note for the fur trade had emerged. One revealed the dazzling number of sea otter pelts that could be taken on the rugged coast for sale in the rich markets of China. The other concerned a deep inlet in southern Alaska, since named Cook's Inlet. This fjordlike bay, Cook had believed, was the estuary of a great river.

The theory galvanized Pond's imagination. His river—the one that flowed west out of Great Slave Lake—did not continue to the Arctic Ocean as he had hitherto halfway believed. Instead, so he reasoned, it curved around the northern tip of the Rockies and debouched into Cook's Inlet. When he compared his erroneous estimate of distances with Cook's figures concerning the inlet's latitude and longitude, his excitement soared. Athabasca was even closer to the Pacific than he had thought—perhaps no more than six days' travel from Great Slave Lake!

Nor was that all. In Connecticut he encountered a book recently published by a fellow Yankee, John Ledyard, who had sailed with Cook as a marine. In that book Ledyard expatiated enthusiastically on the possibility of using the Northwest Coast as the base for an American fur trade with China. Rumors afloat in Connecticut added that potent shipping interests in Philadelphia were considering picking up the idea. It may even be that Pond himself contributed bits of information to the flurry of talk during a visit he made, its exact nature unrecorded, to a session of the Continental Congress in March, 1785.

By April he was back in Montreal, content now with a single share in the new North West Company. As a representative of the company he composed for the government a summary of the data he had gleaned. He added that an Indian returning from the West Coast had told him of a Russian fort there.* Accordingly he begged the government to grant the North West Company the ten-year monopoly it sought so that the firm could place trading posts "all over the Country, even to the Sea Coast; by which means so firm a footing will be established as will preserve the Valuable trade from falling into the hands of other powers."

Meanwhile there was work to be done. After handing his synopsis to Governor Haldimand, who forwarded it to the Colonial Office, Pond hurried by the Ottawa route to Grand Portage. There he found that the opposition he had helped create and then had deserted—the Gregory-Pangman combination—was still very much alive. It had recruited in Pond's place a physically powerful young Scot named Alexander Mackenzie and was unloading at its docks goods and alcohol enough to cause serious trouble for the Nor'-Westers.

---

* A curious statement. Pond had left Athabasca in 1783 and the first permanent Russian post in Alaska was not built on Kodiak Island until the following year. The Indian, however, may have been talking of fugitive Russian sea-otter traders working along the Aleutian chain well out from the mainland.

Pond's assignment was to organize the new Athabasca Department—to establish posts as far north as Great Slave Lake, to arrange with the Indians for ample food, to make sure furs were properly baled and canoes ready to move the instant the ice broke. As soon as those routines had been established, then perhaps he could yield to his obsession and try to reach the Pacific—perhaps even continue across Siberia to England, for had he not prepared a map that he intended to submit to Empress Catherine the Great?

As he went about his chores, opponent John Ross and Ross's clerk, Laurent Leroux, dogged every step he made. The result, early in 1787, was a flareup remarkably like that involving Etienne Waden. Some of Pond's men fell into a scuffle with John Ross. Perhaps the fight was over some fish nets. Perhaps the Nor'Westers were using force to keep certain Indians from going to Ross's post to trade. Anyway, the attack seems to have been instigated by Pond and during the course of it Ross was slain.

The rival brigades carried the news along with the season's catch of pelts as far as Lake Ile-à-la-Crosse. There it was picked up by Roderick McKenzie (he was a cousin of Alexander Mackenzie's but spelled his name differently) and by Nor'Wester William McGillivray, nephew of Simon McTavish. Unlike other members of the opposing companies, the two young men were firm friends and had traded side by side without rancor. On hearing of the murder, they assembled a picked crew of paddlers and sped ahead of the brigades on a record-breaking trip to Grand Portage, where the executives of both firms were gathering to arrange the coming year's business.

Their arrival created consternation. Reports of excessive use of alcohol and of indefensible strongarm tactics were already stirring questions among government officials. Now murder again. Licenses might be denied to the worst offenders; certainly requests for special consideration would receive scant attention. Wisdom dictated that the traders put their houses in order before Governor Haldimand or the Colonial Office cracked down.

Backed by Joseph Frobisher (Benjamin had just died), Simon McTavish summoned a meeting of all the principal merchants and traders then present at Grand Portage. Out of it emerged still another North West Company. The number of shares was increased to twenty. One share went to each surviving partner of the erstwhile opposition—John Gregory, Norman McLeod, Peter Pangman, Alexander Mackenzie. The last named, whose birthdate is uncertain, was by far the youngest of the new firm's partners, being either twenty-five or, more probably, twenty-four years of age that summer.

McTavish also used the occasion to place himself in command of the combination. Offhand, he seems an unlikely choice. He lived extravagantly, drank heavily, gossiped maliciously, and fornicated lustily with red women and white—he once said of himself that he "was like a fish out of water when not in love." But his dissipations did not reduce his capacity for hard work, and he had one of the shrewdest business heads in Canada. Having brought the North West Company together, Joseph Frobisher and he, who together controlled seven shares of North West Company stock, formed the firm of McTavish, Frobisher & Company. Four more complaisant shares followed wherever they led. Thus they had no trouble naming themselves exclusive import agents and bankers for the North West Company. They charged for these services commissions of five percent and six percent respectively, in addition to the profits their seven shares produced. The business would soon make McTavish the richest man in Canada and bring him the nickname, "The Marquis."

It was McTavish, probably, who decreed that Alexander Mackenzie, just in from the Churchill River, should turn straight around and push back to Athabasca that same season. Pond was to spend the winter of 1787–88 teaching the young man the routines of the district and then in the spring come out with the returns of the district. After facing the music in connection with Ross's death—the Nor'Westers had no fear of his being convicted—he was to make himself useful as a lobbyist for the company. Or, if he preferred (he was nearly fifty years old), he could sell his stock and retire. As for his hope of finding the way west about which he had speculated so long, that was now as dead as both Etienne Waden and John Ross. His heir apparent, by McTavish's order, was that relentless perfectionist Alexander Mackenzie.

PART FOUR

Beyond the Mountains

XVIII

Salt Water at Last

*I*n some ways Alexander Mackenzie loomed bigger than life. His portrait in the National Gallery of Canada at Ottawa shows a dark-eyed Byronesque figure presumably capable of conquering either hearts or raging torrents. His physical resilience was notable even in a land of powerful males; according to William McGillivray, the two of them occasionally snowshoed 700 miles just to have Christmas dinner with a friend.

Though not addicted to alcohol, Mackenzie was able to drink all the other roisterers at Montreal's famed Beaver Club under the table. Like most fur traders, he took Indian women into his post as bedmates. He fathered at least one halfblood son. A white woman in Montreal, her identity now unknown, presented him with an illegitimate daughter, and some biographers suggest there were more. He did not seek the quiets of domesticity until he was forty-eight years old and a knight of the British realm. His bride is said to have been thirteen years old.

Ambition gave him a strong sense of his own worth. With Indians he was marvelously patient. With whites he could be by turn ill-tempered and then so aloof that in the estimation of historian Bernard De Voto he suffered from a "paralysis of personal emotion." Yet it is impossible to read his letters and his account of his explorations, ghost-written though it was, without sensing the infec-

243

tious quality of leadership that again and again roused his men into achieving more than they believed possible.

He was a native of the storm-battered Outer Hebrides Island of Lewis, as far north in its part of the United Kingdom as Lake Athabasca was in the New World. His mother died when he was ten, and his father thereupon emigrated to New York state with the three children still remaining at home. On the outbreak of the Revolution, the elder Mackenzie joined a Loyalist regiment. Alexander was sent for safety's sake to Canada.

At the age of fifteen he went to work in the Montreal office of what became the fur trading firm of Gregory, McLeod & Company. As we have seen, that company decided, following the close of the War of American Independence, to challenge the Nor'Westers for the trade beyond Lake Winnipeg. Although Alexander Mackenzie was only twenty at the time and had never passed a full trading season in the Indian country, his employers thought highly enough of his potentials that they offered him a partnership if he would winter on the remote Churchill River.

When Gregory, McLeod & Company was absorbed by the North West Company, Mackenzie retained his partnership and became Pond's understudy in Athabasca. He did not care for Pond personally, but he absorbed like a fever his mentor's passion for finding a canoe route to the Pacific—a discovery that might well help the company win its hoped-for monopoly from the government.

Meanwhile, the struggle between the competing firms had led their traders to risk the onset of ice while pushing deeper and deeper into Athabasca—west up the Peace River and north down the Slave, the name for the mingled Peace and Athabasca rivers beyond Lake Athabasca. Recklessness made the efforts costly. In 1786, for instance, Pond's clerk, Cuthbert Grant, lost two canoeloads of goods and five men to a not-very-severe rapid while trying to reach Great Slave Lake ahead of winter.

As a solution to the difficulty, the expanded North West Company in 1787 located an advance depot near the misty waterfall that marked the outlet of Rainy Lake. The site was some 350 canoe miles west of Grand Portage. Not the least of its advantages was one the La Vérendryes had discovered half a century before: almost unlimited quantities of wild rice for nourishing the canoemen.

As soon as merchandise arrived at Grand Portage, clerks and

voyageurs spread it out on long tables in the warehouses, sorted it according to the requests of the different inland posts, and bundled it into new canvas-wrapped, ninety-pound *pièces*. Handpicked crews labored with these bales up the nine-mile carrying place, loaded them into *canots du nord,* and hurried them through the winding streams and over the granite portages to Rainy Lake. There about August 1 they met the weather-blackened voyageurs who had left Athabasca late in May. The parties exchanged goods for furs, howled through a regale, and then started back toward their respective destinations.

The exchange at Rainy Lake saved the Athabascans 700 miles— a month—of arduous travel. The gain led Pond and Mackenzie, working together in Athabasca during the winter of 1787–88, to reorganize their own department. Always in their minds was the dream that, if all worked out as they hoped, the district would become not just a collection point for furs but a grand staging depot on the way to the Pacific.

The first step was to move Pond's "Old Establishment" from its site beside the Athabasca River to a more central location beside Lake Athabasca itself. The next was to find a man capable of supervising the work while Mackenzie pressed ahead of the furs to Grand Portage and won from the partners permission to make a dash for the ocean during the summer of 1789.

Their choice as supervisor fell on Alexander's cousin, Roderick McKenzie. Rory, as Alexander called him, was a studious, sweet-tempered, intelligent misfit in the fur trade. He hated its brutalities and isolation, and planned to leave at the end of the current trading season. He was a thoroughly reliable employee, however, and Alexander was determined to have him. In January, 1788, he traveled by snowshoe to Ile-à-la-Crosse, where Rory was stationed, turned on his charm, and won his way.

During Alexander's absence that summer (1788), Roderick searched the southwest shore of Lake Athabasca for a suitable location on which to build Fort Chipewyan. His choice fell on a conspicuous promontory six miles east of the complex delta of the Athabasca River. A post at the tip of the peninsula could be easily defended from hostile Indians. Fish congregated in the deep water off the point in enormous numbers, and access to the Peace River through the intertwining deltas was relatively easy—an important consideration for brigades bound either up the Peace toward the Rocky Mountains or down the Slave to the barely known north-lands.*

The fort was habitable when Alexander returned in the fall, eager to launch his crucial expedition. As spring neared, his men collected special bark, watape, and gum. With those materials they built, under Mackenzie's supervision, a canoe thirty-two feet long—large for the area. They prepared twenty-five *pièces* of goods for use primarily in winning the good will of Indians along the way. Several bales of pemmican and corn provided rations, but, since these would not be enough, extra powder and ball for hunting were added in waterproof kegs.

The voyageurs were carefully chosen. There were four French-Canadians and a wandering German, John Steinbruck, who some-how had found employment as a North West Company canoeman. Two of the French Canadians were allowed to take their Indian wives with them as camptenders. Five Indians went along in two small canoes to help hunt and convince suspicious strangers that the party came in peace. The leader of the five traveled in one canoe with his two wives. Two males paddled the second small craft. The fleet was to be accompanied as far as the north shore of Great Slave Lake by Laurent Leroux and a crew assigned to reopen a post that had been abandoned during the Pre-Rainy Lake era.

The trip began at 1 A.M., June 3, 1789. The first leg was known. In spite of disagreeable weather and occasional rough water, the wayfarers spent only a week reaching the central part of Great Slave Lake's southern shore. There they were halted by terrifying sheets of ice. Seeking refuge, they turned eastward through chan-nels protected by a chain of islands. This was not the direction they wanted to go, but it did bring them to a small trading post that sheltered them from the downpours of rain that day after day swept the lake's 300-mile expanse.

---

* In making his choice Roderick reckoned without the ice and the Indians. Wind heaped up such jagged floes against the point that canoes were delayed in leaving for Rainy Lake in the spring. The Chipewyans from the north disliked crossing to the south shore to trade. About ten years later, consequently, the post was shifted to the northwest shore.

After nearly two weeks of the miseries of waiting, Mackenzie decided that the lake was open enough so that the party could risk crossing to Leroux's destination on the north shore. By scooting from one big island to another, they gained that goal on June 23. Leaving Leroux to his trading, the explorers edged west, wary of ice floes camouflaged by rippling water and gauzelike patches of mist. Though they picked up a local Indian to serve as guide, he knew little more about this section of the lake than they did, and they kept blundering into and then having to leave one deceptive bay after another. A week of hard paddling under clouds of mosquitoes went by before they felt the pull of a mighty current.

With sails hoisted the canoes surged down the stream so fast that the cloven water hissed around the bows with a sound like boiling water. For more than 200 miles the river thrust mainly west. Then, as the serrated white peaks of the Rockies came into view, it bent northwest, parallel to the range. Day after day it held that direction.

Mackenzie had a sextant with him. He was no surveyor, but he had learned to take the sun's altitude and, by using prepared nautical tables, to make fairly accurate estimates of his latitude. As his figures kept rising toward 65° and then above, his heart sank. They had gone far past the latitude ascribed by James Cook to the Alaskan inlet that bore his name; there was no break visible in the mountains and thus no hope that the river would reach the Pacific.

The land flattened, the stream split into multiple channels. Mackenzie chose the middle course and presently reached a wide expanse of water. Although it was July 11, icebergs were visible. In spite of the water's brackish taste, he thought he had encountered another of the north's vast lakes. But that night the rising tide wet the baggage the men had left close to the shoreline, and a little later, as they prowled among the islands, they saw whales. So his fears were confirmed; he had come to an ocean, but not the one he wanted.

Physically, it had been a stupendous achievement—1,075 miles from Great Slave Lake in fourteen days, an average of 75 miles a day. And now, with no exultation to buoy them, the men had to go back, fighting the same current that had made their swift descent possible. Mile after mile they bucked it by harnessing themselves like mules into the *cordelle* ropes and stumbling ahead through mud, in hip-deep water, or over debris left piled on the banks by the receding spring runoff.

Whenever they met Indians who could be enticed into conversation, Mackenzie plied them with questions through his interpreters. Snatches of what he learned led him to believe that beyond the mountains there was another huge river. (Probably he was hearing of the Yukon.) Still farther west was a lake of undrinkable water that bearded white men (Russians perhaps) visited in big canoes, trading iron and other fine things for sea-otter pelts.

The thought of what he was missing put Mackenzie beside himself. As the mountains drew nearer, he determined to hike to the crest of the closest peak for a view that might reveal an opening. The wild quest led through dense underbrush to a swamp too large to circle. Obsessed, Mackenzie plunged ahead regardless, wading through muck to his waist until exhaustion forced him to give up and return to the riverside camp.

On September 12, after an absence of 102 days, the party regained Fort Chipewyan. This was early enough so that, when Rory returned from Rainy Lake with the winter's consignment of merchandise, Alexander was well refreshed. Meticulously, as was his custom, he pressed ahead with what he knew most of his partners would value more than exploration—namely, the streamlining of the firm's most productive district.

For the latter work he received his reward when he went out with the furs in the early summer of 1790. As the convoy neared Rainy Lake, he and other partners from the northwest climbed into express canoes manned by veteran voyageurs and raced ahead to Grand Portage to attend the annual meeting of winterers and Montreal agents.

Already the post was assuming the proportions that visitors of a later date would remember so vividly. A tight stockade, its pickets tipped with vermillion paint, ran from an oval, island-screen bay of crystal water back to the foot of a tall hill whose forests were scarred by old burns. Inside the enclosure were sixteen structures, most of them built of sawn planks brought by sloop across Lake Superior. There were dwelling houses for permanent employees, offices, warehouses, a stone powder magazine roofed with tin. Off to one side was a *cantine* where voyageurs, generally with Indian prostitutes hanging to their arms, turned their wages back to the company in exchange for large headaches and small trifles. The Montreal agents found more sumptuous accommodations in bedrooms opening off the company meeting hall.

Dominating these buildings was a messhall ninety-five feet long and thirty deep, its front shaded by a verandah. Inside, as many as a hundred men were seated at a time and fed according to their rank in the company hierarchy. Canoemen ate lyed corn. Partners, clerks, guides, and interpreters dined, Mackenzie reported, on "bread, salt pork, beef, hams, fish and venison, butter, peas, Indian corn, potatoes, tea, spirits, wine etc., and plenty of milk, for which purpose several milch cows are constantly kept." Mechanics, who occupied a middle spot on the social ladder, got lyed corn brightened with tastes of the upper-class diet. In the evenings the tables were cleared out so that the gentry could dance to the music of bagpipes, violins, flutes and fifes. Their Indian wives and mistresses, visitors from the outside were surprised to learn, "could behave themselves well, and . . . danced not amiss."

A thousand or more white males assembled at each rendezvous. (No one counted the Indians, women, and incredible swarms of dogs.) About 350 of the whites were canoemen who brought in merchandise and food from Montreal and Milchilimackinac. There were sailors as well, for by 1790 the company had two small sloops plying Lake Superior and in 1793 would add the seventy-five ton schooner *Otter*. The northmen, hundreds of them, generally slept in tents outside the stockade. The humbler "porkeaters" from Montreal crawled, as was their custom on the trail, under the shelter of their overturned *canots du maître*.

Self-pity was not one of Alexander Mackenzie's flaws, but this year it touched his pen when he wrote Roderick that little attention was paid during the meetings to his epic journey. Yet what was there to say? He had proved that Pond's surmise about a connection with Cook's Inlet was wrong. His glimpse of the icy ocean confirmed Hearne's and Cook's belief that the sailing ships of the time could not negotiate a Northwest Passage through the Arctic Sea. Negative triumphs, however, did not further the company's quest for special government consideration. Unimpressed, the partners did not even offer to name the river, the second longest in North America, after its explorer. That was done years later by the famed Arctic traveler, Sir John Franklin.

This does not mean that his other accomplishments were under-valued. Under Roderick's and his management the Athabasca Department was turning out 20,000 made beaver a year. Potentials for more abounded, as his examination of the fur fields around and beyond Great Slave Lake made clear. In recognition of services rendered and as a stimulation for the future he was granted, at the 1790 meeting, another share in the company, so that at the age of twenty-six he became the most potent of the wintering partners. It seems likely, too, from the way affairs developed during succeeding years, that he was also given permission to try again to reach the Pacific, this time by ascending the Peace.

In addition he received that summer a stark reminder of his inadequacies as an explorer. Both on his way to Grand Portage and on his return, he met at Cumberland House the surveyor Philip Turnor, employed by the Hudson's Bay Company to map its routes and trading posts. With Turnor were two first-class traders, Malcolm Ross and Peter Fidler, whom the surveyor was training in the use of sextants, chronometers, telescopes, and theodolites. Whenever that trio arrived anywhere, they knew exactly where they were. This was more than Mackenzie did. After talking to Turnor he realized that he could not say where on the globe his river ran or where it reached the sea. As a consequence he could not relate it usefully to any other spot in Canada. The deficiency was one he vowed then and there to remedy.

On dispatching his men from Fort Chipewyan to their wintering grounds that fall (1790), Mackenzie ordered them to ask every Indian they saw about streams beyond the mountains. They returned in the spring with garbled accounts of what seemed to be two rivers. One, in the north, was evidently the same stream (the Yukon?) of which he had heard during his return from the Arctic. The other, about which nothing was clear, ran farther south. Reports of it awoke old echoes—the Great River of the West. As a theoretical concept it had tantalized Champlain and had been a magnet for La Vérendrye. As the mythical River Ourigan, from whence the name Oregon derives, it had played during the late 1760s an ambiguous role in Robert Rogers' fuzzy plans for creating, with the aid of Jonathan Carver and James Tute, a private fur preserve somewhere beyond Minnesota. Now here it was again, apparently a reality at last but still shrouded in such vapors that Mackenzie gave up trying to make sense out of the reports.

In 1791 he journeyed east once more with the furs. From Grand Portage he continued to England, whether at his own expense or at the company's is unknown. He spent the winter studying surveying. He read trader John Meares' new book about the sea-otter trade with the Orient that was being developed from a central base at Nootka Sound on the west coast of what became Vancouver Island, and he followed closely the quarrel over control of the area that came within inches of bringing England and Spain to war. Clearly the opportunities inherent in linking beaver and otter to the markets of both China and London were greater than even Peter Pond had surmised.

Mackenzie was committed to forging those links. By the time he had finished his studies, so he vowed, every foot of the way to the western sea would be known. Beginning at Montreal on his return in 1792, he took notes on each stretch of the river and paced off the distance of every portage. Others were at work, too. On reaching Fort Chipewyan he found that, in addition to keeping affairs there in apple-pie order, Roderick had sent two men far up the Peace River to hew timbers for building a post that could serve in the spring as Alexander's jumping-off place for the Pacific.

Rory had other interesting items to impart. Philip Turnor, Peter Fidler, Malcolm Ross, Ross's Indian wife and children, and four employees had arrived in Athabasca in two canoes during the fall of 1791, while Alexander had been on his way to England, and had spent the winter looking over the area as far as Great Slave Lake. Because of their shortages of food and the crankiness of their canoes, Fort Chipewyan had shone brightly in their eyes. They had admired their rivals' method of gathering pemmican from the Peace River, so that there would always be food on hand for winterers setting out to trade and for the spring brigades departing for Rainy Lake. They saw, almost with incredulity, that the post's warehouses contained a two-year supply of goods, so that work could continue even though early ice or accidents on the long trail prevented a supply flotilla from arriving on schedule. They had nodded approval over the efficiency with which great nets were regularly spread under ice sometimes five feet thick, so that every man at the post could have an allowance of eight pounds of fish a day.

They browsed through the little library that Rory and Alexander had put together. They sipped vintage wine during long evenings of good talk by a roaring fire. With some reason, their own circumstances considered, they had declared that Fort Chipewyan deserved to be known as the Athens of the North.

Why had they been there? In conjunction with a ship captain named Charles Duncan they were looking for a shorter way from Hudson Bay to Athabasca than the one that dipped far south to the Saskatchewan. The hope was that, by nosing a sloop along the northwestern shore of the bay, Duncan could find some hitherto overlooked inland passage. Concurrently Turnor's group was searching the watery inland for a chain of lakes or intertwining streams that would connect Athabasca to whatever opening Duncan found.

Their luck? None, Rory said. After their long winter treks and laborious interrogations of the Indians had failed to reveal a practical route, Turnor and his followers had returned to York by the regular route down the Churchill and Saskatchewan Rivers.

All this amused the Northwest Company clerks at Fort Chipewyan. In their opinion the Hudson Bay Company simply did not have the canoes, canoemen, or food-gathering organization necessary for the penetration of Athabasca by any route, new or old. The bayside people, moreover, were quarreling among themselves over the districts to which they should devote such resources as they had. So it was jumping at shadows to suppose that Turnor's appearance presaged an invasion.

Mackenzie did not share the mirth. The north was vast and little known. If Turnor should find a direct way west from Fort Churchill, ocean-borne goods could be landed closer to Athabasca than Rainy Lake was, an advantage instantly apparent to anyone who had just traveled, as he had, the whole costly canoe trail from Montreal. Even the roundabout way from York Factory by the Saskatchewan was shorter than the route from Grand Portage. Sooner or later the company would master the techniques needed to capitalize on its geographic advantage. No, this was not the time for complacency. For, if Mackenzie failed to find a direct supply trail to the Pacific and if the Bay people did locate one from their inland sea, then the richest region the Nor'Wester's possessed would be hard to hold.

Thanks to Rory's preparations, Alexander was able to start up the Peace River with three trading canoes for his winter quarters on October 10, 1792. Because of dread of ice the voyageurs worked with a will. They went west first and then south for more than 200 miles. On November 1, 1792, they passed the site of today's village of Peace River, Alberta, and shortly thereafter were welcomed to their stopping place by bursts of musket fire from two whites and seventy or so Indians.

The whites had worked well in anticipation of their arrival. They had cut and stacked enough pickets eighteen feet tall and seven inches in diameter to enclose a square 120 feet to the side. They had dug a trench three feet deep for receiving the posts and had squared enough logs for building living quarters and storerooms. None of the structures had been erected, however, and Mackenzie's men, all of whom had just toiled to Rainy Lake and back, had to pitch tents as their only defense against the deepening frost.

The crews spent the first several days equipping the Indians for their winter hunt. When building began, the cold was so intense that ax blades were as brittle as glass. Progress was slow. Mackenzie did not move out of his tent into his log house until two days before Christmas. Almost immediately thereafter Chinook winds and warm rains from the Pacific washed the snow from the ground and gave the river ice the appearance that it had when breaking up in the spring. The mildness lasted until February. Then the wind shifted and cold returned so bitterly that Mackenzie's watch would not run.

Late in April spring arrived with a burst. After sending six canoes stuffed with furs to Fort Chipewyan, Mackenzie put his own specially made craft into the water. Smaller than the one he had taken to the Arctic, it measured twenty-five feet inside. Its beam was four feet nine inches, yet it was light enough that two men walking on a good trail could carry it three to four miles without resting—which may reveal as much about the voyageurs as about the canoe.

The fragile craft was heavily laden: ten men, one large dog to act as sentry and to help hunt, and 3,000 pounds of food, arms, trade goods, and, because Mackenzie knew his people, extra quantities of rum. Six French-Canadians, two of whom had been on the trip to the Arctic, manned the paddles. Two Indians went along as hunters and interpreters. Mackenzie's second in command was clerk Alexander McKay. This time there were no women; Mackenzie does not indicate why.

Launching occurred without ceremony on May 9, 1793. Except for chill nights and the unending, high-pitched whine of swarms of mosquitos by day, the first part of the trip was a delight. Flowers gleamed; newborn buffalo calves frisked through the rippling grass. Friendly Indians trotted along the banks, conversing with the occupants of the canoe and occasionally begging to be ferried across the spring-swollen river. Now and then Mackenzie complied, for he was anxious to locate a certain aged man who, during a winter visit to the fort, had described to him the splitting of the Peace far inside the mountains. Under no condition, the man had warned, should the explorers swing up the north fork, for it frayed out into small streamlets plunging down the sides of gigantic peaks. But the south fork, he said, would lead to a divide beyond which a mighty river rolled to the sea.

The directions ran contrary to Mackenzie's expectations. He still believed (wrongly) that the northern river of which he kept hearing emptied into Cook's Inlet. By contrast, the reports that he picked up of a river to the south were fuzzy and contradictory. No coastal explorer, and he had read all their accounts, mentioned a major river in the south. Besides, if he went much farther south, he would add unwelcome miles to his proposed supply line. Yet the old Indian had been insistent: don't go north. If the fellow were with them when they reached the forks—but they did not find him.

At 2 P.M. on May 17, at a point a bit west of present-day Fort St. John, British Columbia, the snow-whitened peaks of the Rockies appeared ahead. Hearts leaped. Only nine days to gain this sight— perhaps the way was not going to be so bad after all.

They reckoned without a stony ridge that some miles further on cut directly across their route. The river had hewn a V-shaped trench a thousand feet deep through the barrier. Later surveyors would find that the canyon was twenty-five miles long and that in that distance the water dropped 270 feet, a monstrous torrent when spring melt filled the chasm from bank to bank.

For two days the voyageurs fought the flood, mostly by towing. Occasionally they had to unload and portage across protruding ledges. When the bank they were following grew too sheer for footholds, they found quiet pools and paddled to the opposite shore.

Rolling rocks endangered both the workers and the canoe. Stops for repairs were dismayingly frequent. As resentment increased and the rapids showed no sign of diminishing, Mackenzie sent scouts ahead. Their reports led him to decide on a back-breaking expedient: they would climb out of the precipitous canyon and portage to the far tip of the V, a prospect made gloomier still by persistent rain.

They had to chop out a trail to the top of the hillside, cautiously lift the canoe stage by stage with ropes snubbed around tree trunks, and then, slipping and stumbling, hoist up the ninety-pound bales. The land on top was cluttered with down timber and roughened by gullies and rocky ridges. Gaining the canyon's upper end consumed three days.

After that ordeal the cold that flowed down from the towering peaks on either side, the slashing rain, and the constant labor with setting poles seemed almost ordinary. Regularly Mackenzie rewarded hard work with praise and lifted spirits with extra rations of rum. His own zest was fired by signs of an almost infinite treasure in beaver.

On the last day of May they reached the point where the river split. The Indians, the voyageurs, and Alexander McKay wanted to turn north. The river looked easier and the distance to the Pacific, to judge from Mackenzie's observations and his memory of Cook's surveys, was shorter. But the old Indian at the post had been insistent: don't go north. Against the stunned protests of his men, Mackenzie ordered the canoe south up what became known as the Parsnip. (The northern branch was later named the Finlay, after the first man to explore it. It proved as hopeless for transportation as reported.)

The Parsnip had overflowed its banks. Mosquitos were a torment, camping places hard to find. At times the explorers could move forward only by seizing overhead branches and pulling. They had to patch and repatch the canoe. Finally, as the stream grew shallow and hope sank, they found Indians and after interminable talk prevailed on one to lead them to a portage 817 steps long that took them to Pacific drainage.

The way stayed hard. They had to clear away fallen trees and once, when the current sent the canoe caroming from bank to boulder and back, they were able to save it only by leaping over-board and hanging onto the gunwales until their feet found pur-chase enough so that they could drag the craft ashore. By the time they had put it together again, mostly with oilcloth and hope, it weighed almost twice as much as when they had started.

In time they reached a swift brown flood whose Indian name was Tacoutche-Tesse. (Today it is the Fraser.) It swept them past wooden houses, temporarily abandoned, that were larger than any-thing Mackenzie had seen since leaving the forested East. The first Indians they met proved hostile, but Mackenzie coolly faced them down and began groping for information. Meanwhile, he had to fight the growing panic of his men with exhortations and judicious applications of rum.

In the end the Indians convinced him that the Tacoutche-Tesse would not serve. It ran far, far south through frantic canyons and past warlike tribes before reaching the sea. He should turn back to today's Blackwater, ascend it as far as possible, and then strike west along foot trails used by Indian traders moving back and forth between the coast and the mountains.

All that wasted effort! Dispiritedly the wayfarers turned back against the thundering rapids. Their canoe collapsed and they had to build a new one of laboriously gathered bark, watape, and cedar slats. On leaving the water they hid the new craft, of which they were very proud, under a pile of boughs and buried whatever pem-mican and ammunition they could not carry for use on their return journey.

Their loads were heavy—ninety pounds each for the voyageurs, seventy pounds plus scientific instruments for both Mackenzie and McKay, and forty-five pounds each for the two Indians. The guides they had hired struck off at a faster pace than the burdened men could match, yet the procedure turned out to be proper, for it fore-warned the villagers ahead that the approaching strangers were harmless.

They crossed the stony uplands of the Coast Range and started down the plunging Bella Coola. The people of the numerous vil-lages were friendly. They feasted the whites on salmon and occa-sionally gave them exhilarating rides in big canoes made of cedar wood. But as the party neared the fjords that thrust far inland from the Pacific, their receptions grew chillier. Finally only a single

Indian could be persuaded to continue with them in the leaky vessel they were able to borrow for threading a way through the mountain-girt channels.

The glimpse of the open ocean they gained near the mouth of Dean Channel was satisfaction enough for the voyageurs, but Mackenzie made them wait in chill fog for the skies to clear so that he could bring his telescope to bear on Jupiter's moons and determine, as he had been unable to do at the mouth of the Mackenzie River, exactly where they were. During this period, while they subsisted on scanty rations and rainwater caught in rock pools, they were harassed by local Indians, one of whom claimed to have been shot at by white men on a sailing vessel. The ship, Mackenzie eventually learned, belonged to George Vancouver's exploring expedition and had visited this very spot only weeks before—a favorable omen, perhaps, for the land-ocean linkage he was seeking.

His observations completed, he mixed vermillion in melted grease and printed in large letters on the face of the seashore rock beside which they had camped one of the famous declarations of North American exploration: "Alexander Mackenzie, from Canada, by land, the twenty-second of July, one thousand seven hundred and ninety-three." Of the weary men watching the performance there was not one word.

The return trip was less arduous, in part because the way was known, fear was allayed, and, mostly, because the rivers had shrunk back within their banks. On August 24, they passed the fort from which they had departed in May and by early September they were back at Fort Chipewyan.

For Mackenzie the letdown was terrible. Rory had been transferred to another post and, once the winterers had been dispatched, little work remained to distract him. Glumly he wrote his cousin, "What a pretty situation I am in this winter—starving and alone—without the power of doing myself or anyone else any service." Overwhelmed by lethargy, he could not even bring himself to work up his field notes into a coherent journal. Night after night he was plagued by nightmares: dead faces staring and staring at him.

By day doubts came. He had reached his goal, he had seen the limitless water. But the route he had followed would not justify building a supply depot on the coast so that Athabasca and the upper Churchill could be served from the west. The backbreaking old route from Montreal, vulnerable to attack from Hudson Bay, would still have to serve, unless . . . and his imagination roamed like a hunting dog across the full sweep of the continent, searching for a solution.

By spring he thought he had found it.

XIX

Cross Purposes

*D*uring the company's 1794 general meeting at Grand Portage, Mackenzie increased his proprietorship in the firm from two shares to six, an extraordinary expansion. In all likelihood he contracted to buy the additional shares from men who were retiring, but the purchases had to be confirmed by the other partners. Their approval came with a roar, not so much because he had made history's first transcontinental crossing of America north of Mexico but because the journey had revealed beaver grounds that would increase the value of everyone's holdings.

Potentially wealthy because of the transactions, Mackenzie started for Montreal, never again to return to the far Northwest or to the mother of his halfblood son. His thoughts were very much on the area, nevertheless. As a result he did not go to Montreal by the direct Ottawa River route, but took a ship through the Great Lakes. This enabled him to call at Niagara on the Lieutenant Governor of Upper Canada, John Graves Simcoe, and present him with a plan for restructuring the fur trade.

On paper the proposal was alluringly simple. The government of Great Britain should charter a monopoly into which the interests of all fur partnerships could be "reconciled and blended." That done, merchandise could be brought through Hudson Strait either to James Bay or to the western shore of the main bay in the heart of the continent, and the long, perilous carriage from Montreal would thus be eliminated. Moving the goods from the new bayside depots to the Indian country would still be done in canoes by Canadians, for they were a people "infinitely more capable of the hardships of Indian life, and all the vicissitudes and dangers incident to the Trade, than Europeans." In this way the interior could be supplied with heavy goods without recourse to the backbreaking trail he had pioneered to the Pacific.

Furs, by contrast, were compact. *They* could be carried across the Continental Divide to, Mackenzie said, the great "River of the West." (By this time he had heard of the discovery in May, 1792, of the Columbia River estuary by the American, Robert Gray. Naturally he jumped to the conclusion that his Tacoutche-Tesse and Gray's river were the same.) Meanwhile, permanent depots manned by experienced Indian traders would be established at selected spots along the coast for the collection of sea-otter pelts, a pursuit for which the wandering ocean vessels currently conducting the commerce were ill-suited. These sea-otter pelts and beaver brought westward from the interior would then be marketed in the Orient through arrangement with the East India Company, "who possess the Privilege of the Chinese market."

Like most original designs, this one was synthesized from familiar elements. Members of James Cook's exploring expedition and the Asia traders who followed their lead had described the new Pacific commerce in purse-tingling detail. On hearing, beside the Churchill River, of streams leading to the Pacific, Alexander Henry had re-awakened, in a letter of 1781 to Sir Joseph Banks, the ancient hope of reaching the Orient by crossing North America. During the winter of 1790–91, Simon McTavish had sought to gain ingress into Hudson Bay by asking Prime Minister William Pitt to quash the transit monopoly held by the Hudson's Bay Company—a request Pitt had denied with the statement that changes in a royal charter could be wrought only by voluntary action on the part of the company or by a special act of Parliament.

Mackenzie's contribution was to stitch the many threads—a single fur-trading company with transit rights through Hudson Bay, travel across the rest of the continent by canoe, the linking of beaver and sea-otter into a single commerce, and special marketing privileges in China—all into a coherent whole. At least it was coherent to him. The thought that the various organizations involved might not wish to relinquish individual rights in exchange for a share in the new enterprise seems not to have rippled his serenity. All he needed to bring everyone hurrying into line, he believed, was government approval.

Simcoe was impressed. Declaring that Mackenzie "seems as intelligent as he is adventurous," he sent a resume of the plan to the heads of the Committee of the Privy Council for Trade and Foreign Plantations. Obviously this is what Mackenzie wanted—a trial balloon to test official reaction. Less obviously—evidence on the point just doesn't exist—he may also have hoped that the interview would force some sort of response from testy old Simon McTavish, who had a tendency to turn deaf when confronted with plans that might in any way diminish his powers, as a blending with the Hudson's Bay Company would.

Nothing happened. The government was engrossed by the Napoleonic wars then wracking the continent. The same wars were dislocating the North West Company's fur markets abroad, and its operations at home were being unsettled by a rising host of troubles. For the time being at least, Mackenzie's revolutionary project would have to wait.

The most severe of the company's internal problems was disaffection among its own employees. Several clerks, Roderick McKenzie among them, felt that their efforts in the *pays d'en haut* entitled them to greater participation in company affairs and profits—that is, to more shares—than they were receiving. Others felt that the company's agents, McTavish, Frobisher & Company in Montreal and McTavish, Fraser & Company in London, were not paying sufficient heed to their specifications about the goods they ordered.

Their disgruntlement was brought to a head by the sudden elevation of Simon McTavish's nephew, William McGillivray, to a commanding position in McTavish, Frobisher & Company. No one questioned McGillivray's abilities—just his associations. He had been born dirt poor near Loch Ness in 1764, but fortunately for his future his mother's brother was Simon McTavish. First, Simon had provided his nephews, Will and Duncan McGillivray, with good educations. Then, during Will's twentieth year, Uncle Simon had brought him across the ocean to work in the fur country as an apprentice clerk for a term of five to seven years. His salary was standard: £100 a year plus shelter when it was available, food, and a limited amount of clothing.

He filled the job well. He was redheaded, tall, handsome, and articulate. By nature he was amiable. During the struggles between the North West Company and Gregory, McLeod & Company, he and his principal opponent, Roderick McKenzie, had traded side by side without rancor. After John Ross had been killed in Athabasca by Peter Pond's men, they traveled together in a special canoe to Grand Portage to spread the news. Out of that, as we have seen, had come a union of the companies, followed by Pond's retirement. The withdrawal left room for one more wintering partner. Using £800 almost certainly provided by Simon McTavish, McGillivray snapped up Pond's share. With Simon glowering out across the meetinghall, the rest of the winterers obediently voted to confirm the purchase, as required by the by-laws.

As a wintering partner, McGillivray continued to perform well —for three years. At the end of that short period, during which older men advanced not a jot, he was tapped by his uncle for a full partnership in the agency firm of McTavish, Frobisher & Company. No more mosquitos, gray pemmican breakfasts, or fetid Indian lodges for William McGillivray. His special job now, after a trip to London to see how affairs were managed there, was to shepherd each year's shipment of goods from Montreal to Grand Portage and answer on the spot the winterers' complaints about the selection of material, the sale of furs, and the handling of promotions.

The questions were sharp. Some of the edge came from envy, but more from insecurity. There was a natural split in the company between the agency men who provided capital that was translated into merchandise and the winterers who turned the merchandise into fur. Because the money people—McTavish, Frobisher & Company in Montreal; McTavish, Fraser & Company in London—held the largest block of shares in the North West Company, they could dominate decisions unless the individualistic winterers presented a united front. This seldom happened. It would happen less often, some of the disgruntled winterers now felt, if silver-tongued William McGillivray were used to lobbying for whatever the slippered gentlemen from Montreal wanted. In other words, the winterers were not true partners and would not be unless they increased their voting power. Or so the rebellious ones, Roderick McKenzie among them, grumbled whenever policy decisions went against their hopes.

Searching for a spokesman, the disaffected turned during the summer of 1795 to Alexander Mackenzie. After analyzing the crises besetting the trade in general, he decided to help, for, while serving the suppliants, he could also advance his own ambitions.

At a meeting in Montreal with Simon McTavish he faced the dictatorial old Marquis with certain disagreeable circumstances Simon knew about but preferred to ignore. First was the hostility of the plains Indians. Because buffalo provided those tribes with nearly everything they needed in the way of food, clothing, and shelter, they were not as subservient to the traders as were the Indians who lived in the less fruitful forest belts. They consented to deal with the whites, wrote Duncan McGillivray, only because of three desires. The first was rum. "They undergo every hardship and fatigue to procure a Skinfull of this delicious beverage, and when a Nation becomes addicted to drinking, it affords a strong presumption that they will soon become excellent hunters. Tobacco is another article of as great demand, . . . as it constitutes a principal part of their feasts & Superstitious ceremonies. . . . As for ammunition, it is rendered valuable by the great advantage it gives them over their enemies."

Drunken revels at the trading posts, tolerated for the sake of profit, were a familiar threat to life and limb. Danger arising from commerce in guns was newer. Tribes short of firearms often blamed the traders for their defeats—if the whites had not passed out weapons, the attacks would have failed—and during the summers of 1793 and 1794 several revengeful bands sought balm for their humiliations by launching attacks against both North West and Hudson's Bay Company forts. Several men died, and at one Hudson's Bay Company establishment on the Saskatchewan even women and children were massacred. The result was a widespread abandonment of vulnerable locations in favor of more defensible sites.

Men who had suffered from or were likely to suffer from such experiences, Mackenzie argued, naturally felt that their services deserved more recognition than they received at Grand Portage.

Another threat to morale had just been raised by the final settlement of the boundary dispute with the United States. Although the peace of 1783 had granted the new American nation all territory south of the Great Lakes and south of the canoe route between Grand Portage and Lake of the Woods, Britain had refused to evacuate the area. For more than a decade British soldiers occupied the forts at Niagara, Detroit, and Michilimackinac. British civilians controlled every crucial communications center within the ceded area. The government's stated reason: it was keeping the posts as security for debts allegedly owed by the United States to dispossessed Loyalists.

Canadian fur traders applauded the stand. As long as their country held the forts, an Indian buffer state could be maintained in the Ohio-Upper Mississippi regions, and the southwest commerce in beaver pelts could continue as before. During the early 1790s, however, American forces soundly defeated the Ohio Indians, and would-be settlers of the region thereupon vociferously demanded the surrender of the forts. Overburdened by the Napoleonic wars, the British government chose not to press the issue, and under the terms of Jay's Treaty (1794) agreed to evacuate the posts on or before June 1, 1796.

The border area evacuated, what would happen to the company's great depot at Grand Portage, which stood on American soil? To be sure, the 1783 treaty had granted traders of both countries the right to operate on either side of the boundary, but in effect Canadians so completely dominated the commerce that few Americans had risked challenging them. Now, however, American military and customs officials might seek to aid their countrymen by harassing the base at Grand Portage and the border canoe routes in a dozen petty ways. Rather than risk that the Nor'Westers decided to build a new depot on Canadian soil.

The step took time. First a new route had to be found. Aided by Indians, Roderick McKenzie "rediscovered" in 1797 the longer, more difficult way the early French traders had followed out of Thunder Bay up the Kaministiquia River and over the Great Dog Portage. In 1799 his cousin Alexander helped obtain from the Indians a grant of land on which to build the new post; it lay on the north bank of the northernmost of the three channels through which the Kaministiquia River debouched into the bay. He also obtained, in 1798, land on the Canadian side of Sault Ste. Marie, so that a small canal could be built to speed the passage of canoes free of possible American obstructionism.

These were expensive projects and called for careful preparation: work on the new fort at Kaministiquia did not begin until 1801. Meanwhile the shift of circumstances south of the border was causing another dilemma to traders accustomed to working in the evacuated area. Should they stay in the land they knew or seek other fields?

Some who had married below the border or who had otherwise built up strong tribal connections decided to remain. Others, correctly foreseeing harassment at the hands of American officials, decided to shift north, even at the risk of fighting the Nor'Westers. Fortunately for their determination, the strong Montreal supply houses that had financed them in the south proved willing to abet them in their new endeavors.

On the face of things, the change appeared reckless. In 1795 the North West Company controlled an estimated seventy-nine percent of the fur trade north of the border. The Hudson's Bay Company absorbed fourteen percent. A meager seven percent went to independents.

The situation was not static, however. The Hudson's Bay Company was working, in its thorough, dogged way, to increase its share of the business. Its traders had recently invaded that part of Rupert Land that arched around the lower end of Lake Winnipeg, the seventy-million-acre basin drained by the Red and Assiniboine rivers, an area rich in both pemmican for food and beaver for export. A handful of independents thrust into the same region, so that by the mid-1790s there were twenty-one posts in the area. That meant more work and fewer returns for the Nor'Westers who once had had the region almost entirely to themselves. Naturally they wanted the gathering at Grand Portage to recognize the difficulty.

Simultaneously the Hudson's Bay people were developing a new kind of plank boat, sharp at both ends, for use on the lower Hayes River, which led to York Factory, on Lake Winnipeg, and on the broad Saskatchewan. The craft, called York boats, were bigger and heavier than canoes. They had no grace in swift water and, indeed, in many places had to be supplemented by canoes. But York boats could be towed up rapids by *cordelle* ropes and hauled across the portages on greased skid timbers, if enough patient Orkneymen were put to the task. York boats were far more stable and hence faster under sail than canoes. They held more cargo, needed fewer repairs en route, could be run up onto a beach without damage. Thus they did not have to be unloaded and reloaded at every stopping place. Their life span was far greater than that of canoes. Hulking things, yes, like the company that developed them. But the more thoughtful Nor'West partners who watched them moving heavy ladings farther and farther up both forks of the Saskatchewan were not inclined to join in the derisive laughter of the canoemen.

Growing competition from the Bay people and the invading southerners put the dissatisfied winterers of the North West Company in a strong bargaining position. Unless their complaints were heeded, they might well carry their skills to the opposition. Accordingly, Mackenzie told McTavish, the company would be well advised to give the most active protesters the increased voice in affairs they wanted and offer guarantees to other promising young men that when the current partnership agreement expired in 1799, the firm would open its gates enough to take care of their aspirations as well. Nor was that all. Consideration should be given to the possibility of bringing other Montreal supply houses into the business. This would water down the influence of McTavish, Frobisher & Company, but it would also deprive would-be independents of sources of capital.

As an earnest of his sincerity, Mackenzie offered to help the new expansion along its way by surrendering, for issue to new wintering partners, the six shares he held.

There was a price. In return he would expect to be made a full partner in McTavish, Frobisher & Company. Such eminence, he probably reasoned, would help him implement the continental trading monopoly that was becoming his obsession.

He won his partnership. The number of shares available to field men was increased, and in that way defections were forestalled. Little else he had recommended came to pass, however. After flirting briefly with McTavish's offers of union, the Montreal supply firms that once had operated primarily south of the border decided not to risk falling into his orbit but to try the north on their own.

At first these invaders worked independently, supporting winterers whose capabilities they knew. Soon, however, distance forced cooperation and amalgamation. Led by the well-financed Montreal house of Forsyth, Richardson & Company, five major outfitters and their field men in 1800 signed partnership papers bringing into being an organization officially named the New North West Company. The members of the old establishment, once scorned as Pedlars by the Hudson's Bay Company, promptly nicknamed the upstarts the "Potties," from the French term *poté*, a small pot and hence, by extension, a trivial quantity. In time both names were supplanted by the informal designation "XY Company," from the letters "XY" painted on the new company's bundles as identification marks.

The first prominent Nor'Wester to defect to the Potties was that battler against commercial infidelity—Alexander Mackenzie! For a short time he had enjoyed his new job as agent. Each winter he shared bachelor quarters in Montreal with William McGillivray. Both were in their early thirties, handsome and robust, and their highjinks raised the eyebrows of even that tolerant city. Each summer the two of them escorted the coming year's stock of trade goods to the rendezvous at Grand Portage and basked in the wild welcome that greeted the appearance of ships and canoes. Old friendships to renew, fresh adventures to hear of. And certainly the work that accompanied the celebrations was demanding enough. But for Mackenzie, a discoverer by nature, the routine soon became stifling.

Realizing finally that his partners in the agency firm of McTavish, Frobisher & Company did not really wish to participate in a continentwide trading monopoly, he took to haranguing the winterers. Again he was frustrated. Disliking Mackenzie's hold on the young men, and especially on Duncan McGillivray, McTavish eased Alex into other fields. Much of his time was spent in New York, arranging for John Jacob Astor and other American shippers to act as fronts for the marketing of Canadian fur in China. (The restrictions of the East India Company did not extend to non-Britons.) The work disgusted Mackenzie. Details were dull, and he disliked the subterfuges—subterfuges that would be unnecessary if his proposed monopoly took shape.

Hope of escape came in 1798 when Joseph Frobisher announced his retirement. Immediately Mackenzie sought to use the opening as a ladder for climbing to the top of the company. The showdown came at Grand Portage the following year. The scene, its details unknown, shook the rendezvous. McTavish struck back furiously. The winterers supported Mackenzie. William McGillivray sought to act as peacemaker, even though, in his words, Mackenzie's "pretensions were unreasonable & inadmissable." To no avail. Ill-tempered and vindictive, Mackenzie stalked out of the meetinghall. The true root of the problem was probably summed up best by gossipy old Alexander Henry, who wrote a friend in Detroit, "The cause as far as I can learn was who should be first—McTavish or McK. and as there could not be two Ceasars [*sic*] in Rome one must remove."

After a winter of shilly-shallying, Mackenzie joined the Potties, receiving in return for his support and money four of the New North West Company's nineteen shares of stock. In connection with his duties he traveled to London. There he employed a facile writer, William Combe, to help him put into shape a two-volume book wherein his adventures could serve as dramatic background for his ideas about a "common concern" for carrying on the Canadian fur trade. Resoundingly entitled *Voyages from Montreal on the River St. Laurence through the Continent of North America to the Frozen and Pacific Oceans in the Years 1789 and 1793 with a Preliminary Account of the Rise, Progress, and Present State of the Fur Trade in That Country*, the massive effort, published in 1801, was a greater success than even Alexander Mackenzie, growing vainer by the year, could have imagined. The public was entranced; foreign-language editions were rushed to press. Napoleon ordered copies, and King George dubbed the author Sir Alexander. Even across the years one can all but hear the grinding of Simon McTavish's teeth.

As the social lion of the moment, Mackenzie could gain at will audiences with England's most influential men. He used the advantage at once, calling on Lord Hobart, Principal Secretary of State for War and the Colonies, and presenting him with an oral outline of the government-supported trade monopoly that had engrossed his thinking for nearly a decade.

There were refinements now. The "common concern" had grown to embrace whale fisheries as well as trade in land and sea furs. Moreover, Mackenzie by then had absorbed the official account of George Vancouver's explorations in the North Pacific, including a description of Lieutenant William Broughton's trip up the Columbia River almost to the foot of Mt. Hood. There Broughton had laid claim to the surrounding countryside on the grounds that the American, Robert Gray, had never penetrated beyond the river's estuary. Bemused by Broughton's declaration that the area would furnish a fine site for a colony and convinced still that the Columbia and Tacoutche-Tesse were the same stream, Mackenzie recommended that Britain cinch its claim by placing a settlement and supply depot at the river's mouth. If another establishment were formed at Nootka; if the Hudson's Bay Company yielded "unlimited" transit rights from the Atlantic; if the Montreal companies were allowed the share in the trade of the interior that they had inherited from the French; and if the South Seas and East Indian companies were persuaded to grant the common concern unfettered access to China, then a commerce of great value to the empire would result. In the process of developing it, Britain's imperialists would sweep from the North Pacific the American sea adventurers who were absorbing more and more of the otter trade.

Lord Hobart was not bowled over by the presentation. Dryly he said that the current struggle between Canada's two North West companies made talk of a single continent-spanning monopoly premature. Let the antagonists reconcile their differences before contemplating global strategies.

Controlling his exasperation as best he could, Mackenzie accepted the remark as a prerequisite. He reduced his oral proposal to a memorandum entitled "Preliminaries to the Establishment of a Permanent Fishery & trade in Furs &c in the Interior and on the West Coast of North America," mailed it to the Secretary's office on January 7, 1802, and next, Sir Alexander now, returned to Lake Superior to face McTavish once more in the hope of bringing about peace.

He could not have arrived at a more inopportune time. The old North West Company was pouring thousands upon thousands of pounds into its construction projects. The Ojibwa Indians who built canoes for the company on St. Joseph's Island at the northwestern tip of Lake Huron were overwhelmed by demands for additional craft with which to outrace competition to every fur-producing section of the north. New docks for schooners stood at the lower and upper ends of the cascades of Sault Ste. Marie. A wagon road had been built between those docks and draft animals had been imported to speed the movement of corn, flour, and heavy merchandise from ship to ship. A sawmill turning out endless planks for the new establishment at Kaministiquia added to the traffic. Canoes carrying valuable bales of colored beads, silver armbands, twist tobacco, and high wine, plus wide-eyed new recruits for the *pays d'en haut* avoided the jams by sliding easily through the locks of the little canal.

Four hundred miles away at the far side of the lake were the rising buildings at Kaministiquia. The swamps beside the delta's north channel had been drained, and the deep, sluggish stream was lined with stone embankments against which the North West Company's lake schooners, the *Invincible* and the *Otter,* could be berthed. When finished, the huge stockade, built of pickets fifteen feet tall, would enclose more than thirty buildings, including a two-story main hall fronted, like the one at Grand Portage, with a long porch approached by a broad staircase. A sight to see—and what did the Potties have to match it? Kennels only. No canals, docks, lake schooners, or sawmills. How, McTavish sneered, did Mackenzie intend to weigh those differences when setting up his marvelous concern?

Beneath the sarcastic question lurked a bitter worry. Despite shortages of equipment and manpower, the XY Company (now sometimes called Sir Alexander Mackenzie and Company) was managing by sheer determination to follow their rivals throughout the Northwest, even into Athabasca, and were matching them post for post. Floods of alcohol did not serve to turn back their stubborn opposition. In 1802 the North West Company sent approximately 15,000 gallons of spirits into the Indian country; the XY group, 5,000 gallons. The debaucheries that followed shocked even the veterans of earlier trade wars, but brought no lasting advantage to anyone. Just what recompense did Mackenzie propose for having launched the competition that unleashed such deviltries?

The deviltries, the XY people retorted, were primarily the creatures of the other side. Writing angrily to government officials in Quebec from his meager depot at Grand Portage, Mackenzie's partner, John Richardson of Forsyth, Richardson & Company declared, "the Indians have been stimulated to commit actual pillage, and to fire upon the Canoes of the New Company. Attempts have been made to debauch and entice away their servants. . . . Their Property has also been destroyed by underhanded Acts." To keep force from prevailing over justice, he concluded, the government should locate both a military installation and a civilian magistrate at Kaministiquia.

To this outburst Alexander Mackenzie added his amen. Without actually naming the North West Company in his letter, he too urged the creation in the Indian country of a law enforcement agency capable of preventing the contending fur companies "from abusing any Power which Superiority of Numbers or Strength may accidentally confer and which shall secure to each, the fruits of fair honest and industrious exertion."

Prophetic words. On August 2, 1802, in an Indian village near the North Fork of the Saskatchewan, an XY clerk named Joseph Lamothe, acting in self-defense, killed a North West bullyboy, James King. The cause was a quarrel over the division of furs both claimed as being due their companies for goods advanced on credit earlier in the year.

Unlike earlier killings arising from the stress of competition, this one brought neither remorse nor reconciliation—nor even, because of lack of jurisdiction, a trial.*

Thoroughly discouraged, Mackenzie wrote Lord Hobart's Undersecretary of State for War and the Colonies that prospects for a voluntary union of the two companies seemed remote. But, he added stubbornly, if his company were granted transit rights through Hudson Bay, then the overextended Nor'Westers would have to come around. With this declaration went a private determination: if the government declined to intervene, then he would use private means for acquiring the vital rights, even if it meant purchasing the Hudson's Bay Company outright. Then let the Nor'Westers beware.

Unhappily for his resolve, the North West Company could use the same strategy for squeezing the XY group. McTavish, moreover, unlike Mackenzie, would have no squeamishness about applying physical pressure in order to force the Governor and Committee of the Hudson's Bay Company to move the way he wanted. Then let the Potties beware.

---

* The episode did lead to a Parliamentary act that empowered the governor of Lower Canada to appoint justices of the peace for the Indian country with authority to hear evidence and remand guilty persons to Lower Canada for punishment. Oddly, the first justices were members of the warring companies: Duncan and William McGillivray of the Nor'Westers and Alexander Mackenzie and John Ogilvy of the XY Company.

XX

One More Thrust

$\mathcal{D}$uring the early years of the nineteenth century, the Hudson's Bay Company seemed ill-prepared to meet the attacks of its confident rivals. Wartime naval blockades halted the marketing of pelts on the continent. As profits dwindled and the costs of merchandise soared, stock dividends shrank from eight percent in 1794 to four percent in 1801. During the same period shares that had been worth £100 each dropped to £60.

To the agents of the XY Company, the dismal record suggested the possibility of picking up the London company at a bargain price. Almost as if conferring a favor, they offered £103,000 for the firm's assets and chartered privileges.

The North West Company tried a blunter, cheaper approach. In defiance of the Hudson's Bay Company's royal charter, McTavish sent a 150-ton ship through Hudson Strait into James Bay—the Bottom of the Bay, as the English called it—occupied Charlton Island, and erected forts at the mouths of some of the rivers that drained into the shallow inland sea. Unctuously then, Duncan McGillivray, one of McTavish's many nephews, called on the Governor and Committee at Beaver House in London. To those stony-faced gentlemen he announced that his firm would end its invasion in exchange for transit rights through Hudson Strait to the Hayes River, first step on the way to Lake Winnipeg, the Saskatchewan—and the Pacific.

The Governor and Committee's first impulse was to seek relief through the courts. But how valid, really, was the charter that Charles II had granted the firm 164 years before? Once again (this was not the first time the question had arisen) they called on top-flight chancery lawyers for opinions, and again they were confronted with ambiguities. King Charles, the barristers reported, most probably had been acting within his rights when conveying to the original stockholders of the company clear title to all lands that drain into Hudson Bay, enormous though the area had turned out to be. But commercial monopoly did not necessarily accompany land monopoly, for the granting of trade privileges was a prerogative of Parliament.

There was another cloud. French traders had worked out of the Great Lakes area into the heart of Rupert's Land, as the company's grant was called, long before the English had ventured away from their bayside posts. Those early trips, the French had insisted, had given them an easement, as it were, to the commerce of the country, no matter who held title to the land. Now the Canadians from Montreal were saying that they had succeeded to the same rights by virtue of England's conquest of Canada. The courts might agree.

Faced with that possibility, the company decided not to sue over the invasion of James Bay, but to stall. Circumstances favored a strategy of delay. Unlike the partners of the XY and North West companies, whose income was derived from an annual division of profits, the stockholders of the Hudson's Bay Company had other resources and could afford to wait. Why not let the negotiations drag while its antagonistic suitors fought each other to exhaustion?

The Canadian firms were not as strong as they boasted. To keep their steadily lengthening lines of trade from breaking down, they needed the services of more and more supervisors, both partners and clerks who hoped to be partners. In 1787, for instance, the total number of shares in the North West Company had been sixteen. In 1792 the number rose to twenty; in 1799, to forty-six; in 1802 to ninety-two. Assuming that the costs of merchandise and the selling price of fur remained roughly constant (which in actuality they did not do), a partner in 1802 could not match the income of his predecessors of fifteen years earlier unless the number of furs acquired from the Indians rose by a staggering 575 percent.

So insatiable a demand could not have been met without the aid of technological improvements. First, the manufacturers of felt learned to manufacture good beaver hats from fur taken at almost any season. Prime "coat beaver" lost much of its superior attractiveness, and traders grew more indifferent to quality than before. Second, the catching of beaver became easier. Originally the Indians had run them down with dogs, had shot them with guns or bows and arrows, or, after breaking into their frozen lodges with pointed sticks, hatchets, and iron chisels, had netted them as the animals tried to flee. During the 1790s, however, steel traps came into use, their effectiveness immeasurably increased by baiting them with castoreum, a scent made from glands cut from the beaver's own groin.

Surveyor-trader David Thompson, of whom we will hear more later on, gives a graphic picture in his *Narrative* of the harms brought to the Indians by trapping. After the Ojibwa had first learned to use the device, he wrote, they "were rich, the Women and Children, as well as the men were covered with silver brooches, Ear Rings, Wampum, beads and other trinkets. Their mantles were of fine scarlet cloth, and all was finery and dress. Every intelligent Man saw the poverty that would follow the destruction of the Beaver but there were no Chiefs to control it. . . . Four years afterwards [1797] almost the whole of these extensive countries were denuded of Beaver, the Natives became poor, and with difficulty procured the first necessaries of life, and in this state they remain, and probably for ever."

The process, it is worth noting, was speeded by a small but steadily increasing number of "freemen." Some were former *engagés* of the companies who did not wish to leave the wilderness; others were *métis*, or halfbreeds. More were eastern Indians, Iroquois, Abnakis, and Nipissings, who roamed farther and farther afield with their families and their traps, doing business at whatever trading post was handiest. Occasionally the fur companies themselves took some of the nomads west to instruct untutored tribes in the art of trapping.

Ravenous demands for beaver; unlimited alcohol for providing Indian hunters with incentive; devastating new means for capturing the quarry—these led to a quick depletion of areas that in the days of limited desires and primitive technology had long maintained satisfactory rates of productivity. The result was inevitable. As soon as the returns from a region declined appreciably, the whites raced each other into new areas, searching for streams still unspoiled and Indians still naïve enough to be lucrative customers.

As the rate of expansion accelerated, increasingly onerous burdens fell on the freight system. Soon almost as many men were engaged in bartering for food and then transporting it to the points where it was needed as were employed in procuring and moving trade goods and fur. The great forts of the interior were warehouses for provisions first and trading posts only secondarily. Kaministiquia gathered corn, flour, and salt pork. Rainy Lake collected wild rice. Pemmican from the Red River and its tributaries was stored at Bas-de-la-Rivière, where the Winnipeg River flows into Lake Winnipeg. An annual 500 or so bales of Saskatchewan pemmican were gathered for the cluster of rival posts beside Cumberland Lake. The buffalo of the Peace River country fed the brigades moving into and out of Fort Chipweyan. In all cases the depots were located so that provisions reached them by traveling downstream or across lakes, a strategy in placement that reduced both the amount of time and the number of paddlers required for completing the work during the short season of open water.

The men sustained by this tightly coordinated effort were the greatest resource that the Montreal-based companies possessed. (Men—and, it seems, sometimes women. At least this entry appears in Alexander Henry the Younger's journal for Setpember 13, 1809: "At 4 P.M. I arrived at Fort Vermillion [on the upper Saskatchewan] . . . with a brigade of 11 canoes, loaded with 28 pieces each, and manned by five men and one woman," which apparently means one woman per canoe. Were women equal to the demands of the trade? One was. In 1806 a Mary Fubbester of the Orkney Islands disguised herself as a man in order to follow her lover into the Hudson's Bay Company. She worked well enough so that her sex was not discovered until the birth of her child far up the Red River on December 29, 1807.)

Most would-be voyageurs were young on entering the *pays d'en haut*. Each carried his own paddle, its blade painted according to his fancy, his own camp utensils, and generally a character reference from his village curé. Each signed a contract binding him to his employer for a specified number of years. The ending of the contract period seldom meant freedom, however. The men, extravagant by nature and ill-paid in merchandise whose value was exaggerated by high markups, generally ended each year deeply in debt to the company, so that they had to continue working to pay their bills. As part of their job they passed on both their skills and their amazing *esprit de corps* to the constant influx of newcomers who were used as *milieux* (middlemen) in the canoes of nearly every brigade.

To modern readers one of the mysteries of the trade was the willingness of these French-Canadians to take desperate risks and perform prodigious labors for very little in return. But they did not want much in today's terms. At the top of their list were occasional stupefying drinking bouts with fellow voyageurs and easy fornication with uninhibited Indian girls. David Thompson says that he easily lined up recruits for a difficult winter trip south to the Missouri River because the men wished to experience for themselves the famed sexual acrobatics of the Mandan women.

Vanity was another motive. A voyageur carried 180-pound loads across foot-tangling portages and paddled as many as twenty hours a day simply because he needed to prove his masculinity to his companions. Duncan McGillivray tells of a race between two brigades on Lake Winnipeg that was so intense as to be almost murderous. In the darkness a man fell overboard. As he was "almost sinking under the weight of his cloathes, [he] cried out to 2 canoes that happened to pass within a few yards of him to save his life *pour l'amour de dieu;* but neither the love of God or of the blessed Virgin . . . had the least influence on his hardhearted countrymen who paddled along with the greatest unconcern, and he must have certainly perished if his own canoe had not returned." This contest, waged only for its own sake, lasted until the exhausted paddlers called it off by mutual consent after forty-eight hours of continuous strain.

They had this recompense. Those who had crossed the Height of Land that hemmed in Lake Superior were acknowledged as members of a select brotherhood by being baptized with water sprinkled from an evergreen bough. From then on they had the right to don gay sashes at Grand Portage or Kaministiquia, put feathers in their caps, and strut down to the camp of the porkeaters from Montreal, stand spraddle-legged in front of them and invite a fight with the boast, "*Je suis un homme du nord.*"

Another bond came from the way they traveled together month after month, each proud of his canoe, his fellows, his brigade. On the trail they were under the charge not of one of the "gentlemen," but of one of their own class who had risen, because of superior ability, to be a guide. It was he who chose each camping place, announced the rest pauses when the men could fire up their clay pipes, and decided how each rapid should be met. The guide was also responsible for the property in the canoes under his supervision. His was the almost impossible task of making sure that liquor kegs were not surreptitiously tapped during the march (all travel was called a march) and that goods were not harmed by rough handling.

A brigade was made up of a group of canoes bound for the same destination. David Thompson states that the number of craft in a brigade ranged from four to eight; Alexander Henry in the quotation recently given speaks of eleven canoes in his unit. Whatever the number, a guide was seldom given charge of more than four, so that a brigade might contain two or three guides.

Brigades having the greatest distance to cover left the rendezvous first. A space of two days was left between the units to prevent overcrowding on the carrying places. Under sail the canoes could sometimes reach a speed of eight miles per hour. Paddling, its rhythms maintained and its boredom assuaged by the choral singing of simple melodies, attained an average of six miles an hour on calm water. (Actually distances were measured not in miles or leagues, but in the number of pipes smoked during the day.) Landings were made toward dusk. While the cook hung up his kettle (unless the pemmican were to be eaten raw, as it often was), the men overturned the canoes, patched the torn places in the ruddy sheathing, and, lighting torches, applied melted spruce gum to all the seams.

Warm breakfasts were prepared by boiling corn, rice, or pemmican throughout the night. At departure time, dawn or even earlier, the pot was lifted from the fire and placed, still boiling, in one of the canoes. It remained hot until a pause was made for breakfast some two hours later.

It is easy to idealize those skilled, cheerful, volatile, chance-taking, long-enduring children of the wilderness. Though most were illiterate, they were by no means unintelligent. They readily learned the languages and ceremonies of the Indians among whom they spent much of their time. But they could be troublesome. They

were not dependable unless watched. Though most of them duti-
fully asked for God's blessings at the chapel of Ste. Anne near the
mouth of the Ottawa River, they seldom kept their religion in
working order once they had passed the first Indian encampment.
They were uncontrollable when intoxicated. Trader Daniel Harmon
wrote that he would rather have fifty drunken Indians around his
post than five drunken Canadians. No matter how long the trail or
how tedious the winter nights all they found to talk about, again
according to Harmon, was "Horses, Dogs, Canoes, and Women,
and strong Men who can fight a good battle."

In spite of the profane orders of their guides, they were incor-
rigibly careless. At the portages and when landing to camp, they
worked with furious dispatch but also with great confusion. They
ripped the stout canvas covers of the bundles they were carrying
by banging them indifferently against protruding limbs; they piled
pièces helter-skelter at the *posés;* they grinned with insouciant
shrugs at the sound of breakage.

As the trails lengthened and the number of partners who had to
be provided with profits increased, the accountants of the North
West Company sought for means whereby these unnecessary expenses could be reduced. Very soon their jaundiced eyes fastened
on the "light" canoe, a term that described the craft's lading and
not its weight.

After a winter at the remote posts, partners and clerks on the
verge of becoming partners were eager to reach the rendezvous at
Grand Portage or Kaministiquia, and loath to leave it afterward.
And why not enjoy as many carefree days as possible? The furs—
or merchandise, as the case might be—were moving ahead under
charge of the guides. By selecting a special crew and burdened only
with personal baggage, a man could gain many extra days of merriment beside Lake Superior. Along the way, moreover, to borrow
the half-envious, half-sarcastic words of Philip Turnor of the Hudson's Bay Company, he could expect that "his Feather Bed [would
be] carried in the Canoe, his Tent, which is exceeding good, pitched
for him, his Bed made and he and his girl carried in and out of the
Canoe and when in the Canoe he never touches a Paddle unless for
his own pleasure."

At the general meeting at Kaministiquia in 1804 the North West
company cracked down on the practice. Light canoes were banned.

Henceforth partners and clerks had to stay with their brigades, supporting the guides with the authority of their presence. They were allowed one companion, either wife or servant, and space enough to hold eight packs of personal possessions for the two of them. The rest of the canoe was filled with normal freight.

One privilege remained, however. When canoes ascending the North Saskatchewan reached the buffalo plains, they were met by men from nearby forts leading saddled horses and carrying hunting rifles. Freed from their cramped quarters in the toiling birchbark canoes, the gentlemen raced joyously across the flat land, slaying buffalo that were butchered by workers from the post. For obvious reasons the area was called La Montée, and everyone enjoyed the stretch—exhilaration for the riders and a change of diet for the voyageurs.

The banning of so revered and ingrained a privilege as the light canoe is indicative of the uneasiness that afflicted the North West Company as the number of days required to reach fresh beaver grounds steadily increased. Soon it would not be possible, even with a relay point at Rainy Lake, for goods to travel from Montreal to the Mackenzie River below Great Slave Lake or to the upper reaches of the Peace, deep within the Rockies, during the twenty-three or twenty-four weeks when the rivers were free of ice. Shortening the journeys by acquiring transit rights through Hudson Bay thus became not a means toward reaching Mackenzie's dream of a trans-global commerce, but an end in itself. Yet, by fighting each other while dickering for those rights, the XY and North-West companies were increasing the capacity of the Hudson's Bay Company to resist. Would it not be better to present a united front by coming to terms? Winterers on each side urged just that. But unforgiving Simon McTavish, his judgment clouded by the vindictiveness and pride that characterized so many Highland Scots, refused to listen while Alexander Mackenzie led the opposition.

Human frailty provided a solution. Late in June, 1804, McTavish fell ill. On July 6, aged fifty-four, he died. The aftermath would have appalled him. On November 5, negotiators freed of his influence signed a contract amalgamating the rivals into a single, hundred-share firm called the North West Company. Significantly Alexander Mackenzie, who owned several shares, was barred from active participation in management because of his own stormy nature.

Pressure on natural resources was lightened only slightly by the unification. Enough beaver still had to be found so that the company could meet the expectations of its many partners and clerks and pay the wages of the voyageurs and *engagés* who were carrying supplies across all Canada east of the Rocky Mountains. Inevitably a systematic penetration of those mountains had to follow. But could the effort be sustained from Montreal? Reaching the upper Saskatchewan, the Athabasca country, and the Mackenzie River below Great Slave Lake was already straining the canoe brigade to the utmost.

Meanwhile, the ever-troublesome Americans had raised new threats by purchasing Louisiana Territory. According to reports just received from North West Company traders on the Missouri River, an official exploring expedition led by Captains Meriwether Lewis and William Clark was already moving across the newly acquired region toward the Columbia. If the party reached the Pacific and if its findings encouraged private traders to follow, there would be unexpected rivalry in the Far West.

Sobered by these reflections, the Nor'Westers quietly ended their profitless invasion of James Bay (profitless because the Indians there had remained loyal to the Hudson's Bay Company) and in 1805 offered the English firm an annual rent of £2,000 for transit rights through Hudson Strait to the Hayes River. Simultaneously the partners attending the 1805 meeting at Kaministiquia directed Simon Fraser, then twenty-nine years old, to establish posts inside the Rocky Mountains from which he could explore "The Great River of the West" in the hope of tying the Pacific littoral firmly to Canada by means of a true transcontinental system. Both strategies, it should be noted, were based on wishful thinking: first, that the Hudson's Bay Company would prove cooperative, and, second, that Fraser would find the River of the West to be less formidable than Alexander Mackenzie had reported it to be. (More wishfulness: Mackenzie, it was believed, might have been diverted from the Tacoutche-Tesse by Indians who did not want white traders to reach the tribes farther south.)

Fraser was used to difficulties. He had been born in 1776 in what is now Bennington, Vermont, to Scottish immigrants. When he was scarcely a year old, his father had joined General Burgoyne's army on its ill-fated drive south from Canada into the rebellious

American colonies. Captured, the elder Fraser had died in prison. His widow, tormented by unfriendly neighbors, had been hard put to maintain the family until they were able, at war's end, to migrate north. There, aged sixteen, young Fraser had found employment as a clerk in a Montreal supply house. He soon moved into the fur country as a Nor'Wester and performed so well during the struggle with the XY Company that in 1802 he had been elevated to a full partnership.

He was squat, roundheaded, and powerfully muscled. By nature he was dour, envious, ambitious, and unremittingly energetic. The first part of his new assignment required him to build a supply base for his projected mountain posts at the lower end of the Peace River Canyon, the dogleg gorge that had given Mackenzie's crew so much trouble in 1793. Fortunately he had as assistants two very able clerks, James McDougall and John Stuart.

The accomplishments of these three men and their *engagés* during the years of preparation almost defy credibility. They reached the eastern end of the Peace River Gorge in the fall of 1805. While Stuart halted there with part of the voyageurs to build a rough post called Rocky Mountain Portage House, Fraser and McDougall labored with the rest of the party across the long, harsh carrying trail to the gorge's upper end. Taking to the water again, they retraced Mackenzie's route part way up the Parsnip and then, following Indian leads, veered up a sidestream to what they called Trout Lake. (Eventually it would be renamed McLeod Lake.) The friendliness of the neighboring Sekani tribe led them to erect on the lake's shore a crude log habitation that later grew to be Fort McLeod. Leaving three men to winter at that awesomely remote spot, the others returned on snowshoes to Rocky Mountain Portage House.

Shortly after Christmas a furious quarrel split the trio at Trout Lake, two against one. They abandoned the post and in the bitterest sort of weather made their separate ways back to the Portage House. Alarmed for the goods and furs at the deserted post, McDougall and a few companions, whites and Indians, hurried there with dogsleds.

All was well, and because McDougall disliked being idle he took a three-and-a-half day trip through the snow-shrouded forests to what the Indians called Nakazleh. (Later it would become Stuart

Lake.) It was a fantastic place, studded with islands and fringed by innumerable bays. "I do not know," a later trader wrote, "that I have seen anything to compare with this charming prospect in any other part of the country." Moreover, its outlet stream, a tributary of the Nechako, drained into the Tacoutche-Tesse. Thus a post built there, in a country crammed with beaver, could be supplied from the Pacific—if the waterways proved navigable.

Elated by the prospects, McDougall dispatched a small party under a voyageur named Dallaire to Fraser: here was a place for a major post! The word almost did not get through. The rivers were just opening, and a cornice of ice crashed into Dallaire's canoe, damaging it so that the men had to flounder the rest of the way on foot.

Meanwhile, Rocky Mountain Portage House was earning its name. For as long as the snow stayed firm in the spring, Fraser kept a string of workers toiling overland to the upper end of the gorge, bearing merchandise either on their own backs or dragging it on sledges. Working with the skimpy bark provided by the region, Stuart in the meantime supervised the building of new canoes.

The men were ready before the ice-clogged river was. Launching did not come until May 20, 1806. Peppering his journals with slurs about Mackenzie's observations, Fraser led his fort-builders up the Parsnip. They wrecked one canoe, but Stuart was able to improvise another. After supplying the post at Trout Lake, they returned to the Parsnip and followed Mackenzie's trail across the divide to the turbulent waters of the Tacoutche-Tesse. It was a roundabout way to travel to Stuart Lake, but Fraser wanted to test the navigability of all the headwater streams of the main river.

After reaching the Nechako, the party turned north, still hammered by spring floods. A she-bear attacked two voyageurs who were trying to run down her cubs and mauled one, says Fraser, "in a shocking manner. Had not the dogs passed there at that critical moment [how often the fur men took dogs in their crowded canoes!], he would have been torn to pieces." A mere incident. The portages were what really taxed them, but finally, after swinging out of the Nechako into the Stuart River, they reached their goal—an arduous triumph that told them nothing about the Tacoutche-Tesse itself.

Unfortunately they reached Stuart Lake ahead of the annual salmon run and nearly starved while building what became one of the richest posts in the Northwest, Fort St. James. From there they moved south to Natleh Lake (later Fraser Lake) and built the precursor of Fort Fraser. The next winter all the posts did a brisk trade in the richest, blackest beaver Fraser had ever seen.

Reinforcements did not appear until late in 1807—two canoes in charge of clerks Hugh Faries and Jules Quesnel. The newcomers brought interesting bits of information picked up during the summer rendezvous. The great post at Kaministiquia had just been renamed Fort William, after William McGillivray, new head of the North West Company. The Hudson's Bay people had rejected all offers for transit rights and, rumor said, the Nor'Westers were going to hit hard at the Londoners' inland trade in an effort to change their minds. Meanwhile hopes for finding a supply route to the Pacific had brightened. According to reports drifting in to Fort William from the Missouri, the Americans under Lewis and Clark had returned east during the summer of 1806 after a successful trip to the western ocean. Now more than ever it was necessary for the Nor'Westers to emulate the feat. Perhaps Fraser would be the one to triumph—or perhaps success would go to the company's great mapmaker, David Thompson, who had been ordered to spend the summer of 1807 opening new beaver grounds beyond the headwaters of the Saskatchewan.

Fraser wanted the victory. During the winter his augmented crew built, as its base camp, Fort George at the junction of the Tacoutche-Tesse and Nechako rivers. During a moment of reverie as he contemplated the wild and beautiful lands, their leader remembered his mother's tales of the Scottish Highlands. Homesick for what he had never seen, he decided to call the area New Caledonia. In time the name would be changed to British Columbia, but for years New Caledonia glowed in men's minds as one of the brightest spots of the fur trade.

On May 28, 1808, he and his explorers started toward the sea. There were nineteen voyageurs, two Indians, clerks John Stuart and Jules Quesnel, and Simon Fraser—twenty-four men in four canoes. For food they carried dozens of bales of dried salmon, many of which they cached along the way to nourish their return journey.

They soon learned that the Indians had not been resorting to trickery when turning Mackenzie back. Scrambling ahead on foot from the point where their predecessor had halted, Stuart, Fraser, and six men saw a flooded river crowded to madness in a canyon botton scarcely fifty yards wide. Yet the bordering slopes seemed too high and precipitous to permit the portaging of the canoes. Accordingly the voyageurs, confident of their skills—weren't they men of the north?—decided to risk the whirlpools and heaving cascades if the canoes were partly unloaded.

The first craft to try the run was instantly spun out of the control of her five paddlers. Only luck enabled them, after wild gyrations, to find lodgment on a protruding ledge of flat rock. Realizing that any effort to continue would result in their death, the rest of the party inched down the hillside to help them, plunging daggers into the ground to serve as handholds.

With ropes and precarious boosting, the teetering workers managed to lift the precious canoe out of the canyon bottom to the top of the hill. During the next two days they were able, with the help of the Indians, to carry two more canoes and much of the baggage to the same point. The fourth canoe and several expendable bales they left behind. Assisted by four pack horses produced by their red friends, they portaged through dense timber and rocky gullies to the lower end of a long sequence of rapids—a journey not without incident, for one horse fell over a cliff, smashing their medicine chest and the kit in which Stuart carried his account books and personal papers.

So it went, a constant choice between agonizing carrying places and sickening rapids. Fortunately Indians were everywhere and generally helpful. From them they heard of white men on the headwaters of an eastern tributary that flowed into the Tacoutche-Tesse some distance farther south. The strangers, Fraser reasoned, had to be either Americans detached from the Lewis and Clark expedition or David Thompson's Nor'Westers from the Saskatchewan. On the strength of the latter hope, he named the broad, blue-green stream the Thompson.

Even before Fraser's group reached the roaring entrance of the Thompson, the Tacoutche-Tesse had become utterly unnavigable. On June 11, the men abandoned their canoes and, being assured that the sea was only ten days distant, took to walking. The trip used up the rest of the month. Different bands of Indians accompanied them from village to village, providing guidance and food and occasional wooden canoes for ferrying them across gentler

stretches of the river to easier hiking. It was a wild trail, nevertheless, endangered by falling boulders and so narrow in some places
that the burdened men had to turn face in to the rock in order to
worm along the cliff sides. Indians hauled them up one set of ledges
with a swaying pole, and they had to creep over bridges that had
not been designed for such weights as they were carrying. As Fraser
dryly put it, "We had to pass where no human should venture."

As the mountains began to dwindle, the stream left its persistent
southern course and bent sharply west. From the Indians, whose
possessions indicated frequent contact with coastal trading vessels,
they procured, one by one, small wooden dugouts. In these they
passed beside stunning groves of cedar trees whose trunks were
thirty feet in circumference, cursed the black clouds of mosquitos,
and marveled at one Indian community that occupied a house 640
feet long and sixty broad, fronted by strange totem poles and filled
with more chambers than they had an opportunity to count.

In spite of such sights their overwhelming reaction was of disappointment. They were beginning to feel the reach of the tide up the
river, and Stuart's observations—he was the astronomer of the
party—clearly showed that they were well north of the known latitude where the Columbia flowed into the Pacific. This was a different river. And under no circumstances could it be used as a
supply route. Unless David Thompson was having better luck in his
explorations, the Americans might well win the first lodgment beside the western ocean.

Yet, even though the effort would be fruitless, they wanted to see
the ocean they had struggled so hard to reach, and they pushed on.
Unlike the Indians upstream, those near the delta proved hostile
and sought to bar their way in big wooden boats, "singing a war
song, beating time with their paddles on the sides of their canoes,
and making signs and gestures inimicable." The whites, however,
had firearms. "Confident of our superiority, at least on the water,
we continued."

A little farther on they caught a glimpse of what today is the
Strait of Georgia, and beyond its blue waters the snow-capped
peaks of Vancouver Island. Landing, they sought to look over a
huge Indian "fort," but animosity was so intense that they retreated
to their canoes and, aided by the tide, moved back upstream to
friendlier regions.

The snow melt was passing and the waters in the river were falling. Largely because of that—and because of familiarity with the route—the men were able to make the 500-mile return journey in thirty-five days, one less than the downward trip had taken.

Fraser's own feelings about the journey have not survived. Perhaps they resembled those of his clerk Jules Quesnel, who wrote a Montreal friend, *"Se Voyage n'a pas tourne au soins de la Société. . . . This voyage did not meet the needs of the company and will never be of any advantage to them, this river not being navigable, but we have nothing to reproach ourselves with, having done what we set out to do."*

No reproach—but regrets surely. Like Mackenzie, Fraser never gave a name to the stream that led him only to disappointment. That was done for him in 1813, when David Thompson labeled it "Fraser River" on the huge map he was preparing for the company. Fair enough. After all, the mapmaker had not seen the river Fraser called Thompson. For, contrary to Indian rumor, Thompson had been farther south all that while, seeking to unravel some of the most complex geography on the North American continent.

XXI

Many a Slip

*D*avid Thompson has been exalted by his admirers as a model of what fur traders should have been. He understood the Indians among whom he worked better than did most of his fellows. He possessed phenomenal physical endurance. While mapping the principal landmarks of the huge territory lying between Hudson Bay and the Pacific, the Missouri River and Lake Athabasca, he covered at least 55,000 miles by canoe, dogsled, on horseback, and afoot, often under the most adverse circumstances. His personal life, these admirers continue, was equally praiseworthy. He was pious, sober, and faithful. When finally he retired from the trade, he took his halfbreed wife and children with him to Montreal, rather than abandon them in some Indian camp as many traders did.

Detractors see a different man—one who was disloyal to his employers, bore grudges, and shaved the truth in the narrative he wrote of his adventures. A coward, he was unable to hold his men together at times of crisis, and because of his failings he cost his country the opportunity to extend its sovereignty over the entire drainage system of the Columbia River. But even those who depreciate his personal characteristics agree with his admirers in calling him the greatest North American geographer of his time.

This enigmatic trader-cartographer was born of Welsh parents in Westminster, England, on April 30, 1770. He was not quite two when his father died. Unable to support him and a baby brother, his mother placed him, aged seven, in the Grey Coat School, a charity institution of exacting standards. After receiving seven years of good basic education there, he signed on as an apprentice in the Hudson's Bay Company.

The fourteen-year-old lad arrived in the New World during the difficult years when the company was struggling to recover from the twin blows of 1782: the smallpox epidemic that had decimated the fur-producing tribes and the simultaneous destruction of its principal bayside forts by French warships. During those same years the North West Company was taking shape, and the fur men of the Hudson's Bay Company were at odds with each other over how best to meet the new opposition. Service under such circumstances was rigorous, and Thompson increased its difficulties for himself by a crippling accident. While dragging a sledload of firewood toward Manchester House on the North Saskatchewan, where he had been stationed for the winter of 1788–89, he fell and severely fractured his ankle. Amateur repair work by the master of the post left him in agony for months.

A year later he was still unable to operate effectively outdoors. Accordingly he was sent downstream to Cumberland House to help with the paperwork there. At that point misery turned into a blessing. The man in charge at Cumberland was the Hudson's Bay Company's able surveyor, Philip Turnor. Turnor taught the limping youth how to take observations and make charts. From then on practical astronomy was David Thompson's passion.

His apprenticeship completed and his leg healed at last, he became associated with Malcolm Ross in an endeavor to work out a direct route from Hudson Bay to Lake Athabasca. The endeavor, which stretched across years, was a failure. There were many reasons—a dearth of competent guides at critical points, swampy streams ill-suited to travel by big canoes, the need to trade as well as explore, and obstacles raised by colleagues who wanted men and supplies used elsewhere. When finally the two explorers were able to launch a concerted effort, Thompson bungled matters and landed the party in a cul-de-sac where they spent a starving winter.

The error came at an inopportune time. Thompson had just been chosen to replace Ross, who was retiring, as "Master to the Northward." The promotion should have been exciting to an ambitious charity-school "graduate" of twenty-seven. Instead he threw up his job and without having given his employers the least notice went on foot in May, 1797, to a nearby post run by Alexander Fraser of the North West Company. There he signed on with his former company's most ruthless rival.

The simple explanation is that the Nor'Westers needed a surveyor to map their posts and trade routes in reference to the United States boundary and that Fraser offered Thompson better pay for the job than he was currently receiving. Professor Richard Glover of the University of Manitoba finds subtler reasons. He believes that Thompson feared responsibility, especially in view of his recent blundering. Rather than face the scorn of the men over whom he had just been placed, he switched to a company where mockery was not so likely to follow him the rest of his days.

Be that as it may, he performed well in his new position. Despite temperatures that reached 40° below zero, he traveled south to the Missouri River and placed that stream in proper geographic relationship to the rivers of the Canadian Midwest. He found a lake that he believed was the source of the Mississippi. Though later surveyors chose a different lake a few miles farther south, he made an important point: the boundary as laid down in international treaties—a boundary drawn on the assumption that the Mississippi headed farther north—would have to be redefined. He topped this by making the first survey of the south shore on Lake Superior and well deserved the praise given him by no less a person than Alexander Mackenzie when they chanced to meet at Sault Ste. Marie in May, 1798.

His boundary work completed, Thompson shifted north to the Churchill River and by dogsled and on horseback worked out a route between one of its upper tributaries, the Beaver, and the North Saskatchewan. He also traded in his spare time, a duty that in 1799 required him to make the arduous summer trip to Grand Portage to attend the company's annual rendezvous. (Kaministiquia had not yet been built.) Still, there were compensations. On June 10, during a brief pause at the company's post at Ile-à-la-Crosse, he married, *au façon du nord,* Charlotte Small, the halfblood daughter of Patrick Small, a founder of the Northwest Company, who on retiring had left his family behind.

Thompson was twenty-nine, Charlotte fourteen. Where and when they first met is not a matter of record. Their honeymoon presumably consisted of the thousand-mile canoe trip to Lake Superior, climaxed by a few days at the uproarious meeting at Grand Portage. Then back they went over the Height of Land to the Winnipeg River, across the often stormy lake of the same name, and up the Saskatchewan to Fort George, two score miles or so west of the present boundary between the provinces of Saskatchewan and Alberta. A few years earlier Fort George had been a powerful place housing eighty workers and an equal number of women and children, but Indian troubles and the company's constant westward push had led to its temporary abandonment. It had quickly gone to ruin, and the newlyweds and the rest of the party had to patch together fresh quarters for the coming winter.

In the spring of 1800, as grinding ice floes piled up in jagged ridges along the bank of the river, Thompson and a few men saddled some of the fort's horses and followed the stream across prairies and through forests toward the mountains. They passed the spot where the Nor'Westers' Fort Augustus and the Hudson's Bay Company's Fort Edmonton stood cheek by jowl on a high bluff for mutual protection against those scourges of the prairies, the Blackfeet. Then, still following the broad trough of the river, they swung southwest past the site of today's Edmonton and at length reached the company's new (1799) Rocky Mountain House, named for the superlative view it commanded of glacier-streaked peaks now embraced within Banff and Jasper National Parks.

Indians insisted that trails crossed that formidable uplift. Being the man he was (and unaware still of plans already formulated in Montreal), Thompson must have itched to test the way. But he had completed his survey well enough so that he could lay down with fair accuracy the upper river's southwesterly course, and now it was time to leave again for Grand Portage. Switching to canoes, the party sped with the Rocky Mountain House brigade back down the floodwaters of the North Saskatchewan to Fort George, where more canoes were waiting with furs baled and parfleches crammed with pemmican for the long journey.

Inasmuch as Charlotte was not yet hampered by children, she may have traveled with the gathering fleet. The journals do not say; women are seldom mentioned in fur trade accounts. Except in rare instances little more is said about the nature of the wayfaring itself. Still, something of the wonder of the trips through that almost untouched wilderness can be gleamed from reminiscences left by partner Duncan McGillivray, who made a similar run down the Saskatchewan from Fort George in 1793.

"It was a Grand Sight to me," McGillivray recalled in his old age, "to see such a Grand River, the innumerable herds of Buffaloes & Deers & many grizle Bears on its Banks feeding & crossing in such numbers that we often got our canoes amongst them & shot hundreds without need. There lay sometimes upwards of a thousand dead on some low points drowned when crossing in the Spring on the ice & washed ashore. Amongst them were to be seen often the Bears feeding upon the carcases."

In 1800 more than memories were on McGillivray's mind. For years his imagination had been fired by Alexander Mackenzie's proposals for a continentwide trade, and he continued to urge the expansion after Mackenzie's angry resignation from the Nor'Westers' supply agency of McTavish, Frobisher & Company. Moreover, Duncan spoke with authority, for he had taken Mackenzie's place as a partner in the supply house and thus, along with his brother William, had access to the ear of his autocratic uncle, Simon McTavish, the terrible-tempered "Marquis" of the fur trade. He was so intent on reaching the Pacific, indeed, that he offered to leave his comfortable new office in Montreal and spend another winter in the interior in order to lead the venture in person.

McTavish agreed. At the Grand Portage rendezvous of 1800 the wintering partners added their rubber stamp. To clerk David Thompson's delight, he was chosen as Duncan McGillivray's assistant.

What followed is not wholly clear. Thompson's party apparently left Grand Portage ahead of McGillivray's and reached Rocky Mountain House late in September. On October 5, he and seven men, two of them Indians, saddled riding horses, loaded three pack animals with merchandise, and started south up the Clearwater River. (That stream, incidentally, has no connection with the Clearwater that flows into the Athabasca.)

Conceivably this southward cast had been authorized at Grand Portage as a preliminary scouting expedition. More probably, Thompson was taking advantage of an unexpected opportunity. Somehow word had reached Rocky Mountain House that a timorous group of Kutenai Indians—twenty-six men and seven women

—had crossed from the western side of the mountains and were hiding in the eastern foothills in hope of establishing contact with white traders.* The Indians had with them 110 beaver pelts and a few other furs, but right then fur was not Thompson's main interest. He needed the geographic information the Kutenais could provide. Obtaining it, however, meant incurring the displeasure of the potent Blackfoot confederacy.

There had been a time when the high plains areas of southwestern Alberta and the adjacent regions of Montana had been controlled by Flathead (Salish), Shoshoni (Snake), and Kutenai Indians. They had considered themselves invincible, especially after obtaining horses from tribes in contact with the Spanish settlements of New Mexico. The Blackfeet had offset that advantage, however, by acquiring firearms from the westward-pushing French and had fallen so ferociously on the horse Indians that the latter had fled for refuge across the craggy defiles of the Rockies.

Thompson was familiar with these tribal displacements. As a seventeen-year-old lad he had traveled from the lower Saskatchewan to the high plains with a party of Hudson's Bay Company prairie salesmen and had spent the winter of 1887–88 in a Piegan village near the site of modern Calgary. (This was the year before he had broken his leg at Manchester House.)

During his sojourn he had learned that the Blackfoot confederacy consisted of three bands, the Pikuni or Piegans, the Kainah or Bloods, and the Siksika, or true Blackfeet. Of these three groups the Piegans lived nearest the mountains. They had borne the brunt of the fighting when the confederacy had displaced the region's original occupants, and they were the most alert to prevent the vanquished from reaching white traders and obtaining guns and powder for redressing the scales. Indeed, Thompson's knowledge of the Piegans, his acquaintanceship with influential chiefs, and his ability to speak a little of their language may account, along with his geographic abilities, for his appointment as Duncan McGillivray's second in command.

From the Clearwater his group of Nor'Westers crossed, still in October, 1800, to the Red Deer River. On its banks they encoun-

---

* There are many ways to spell the tribal name. Ethnologists use "Kutenai" for the Indians. American geographers use "Kootenai" for the boundary-crossing river of their homeland; Canadians prefer "Kootenay."

tered a large camp of Piegans whose war chief was named Kootanne Appe, or Kootanne Man. The name suggests that the chief, born a Kutenai, had been seized by Piegans during a raid on his people, and adopted into the victorious tribe, a method of compensating for population losses that was common among most North American Indians. Kootanne Appe had grown up to be a remarkable warrior. He stood six feet six inches tall. In 1787, the year that Thompson had first visited his village, he had led 250 Piegans more than 1,500 miles south to New Mexico and in a daring raid had seized the horses and mules of a Spanish pack train loaded (Thompson says) with silver, a commodity of no value to the Indians. Equally active at home, he had fathered twenty-two sons and four daughters by five wives.

Ceremoniously Thompson and he renewed their old friendship. The white chief then passed out presents, traded a little, and rode on with his men, hoping that he had disguised his true intent. By unrecorded means the party found the lurking Kutenais and persuaded them to visit Rocky Mountain House. It was a nerve-wracking trip. The Piegans, who had not been fooled, harassed the group throughout its journey but did not quite dare attack, out of fear that bloodshed might prompt the whites to cut off their supplies of ammunition and alcohol.

After being royally entertained at Rocky Mountain House—the opening wedge, the whites hoped, of a lucrative transmontane trade —the visitors avoided their old enemies by slipping away to the north. Thompson sent two French-Canadians, La Gassi and Le Blanc, across the mountains with them to learn the trails and cement the alliance.

Duncan McGillivray had meanwhile been exploring on his own. On arriving at Rocky Mountain House and learning that Thompson had gone south, he decided to scout the foothills to the north, also on horseback. The venture, which took him as far as the upper reaches of streams that flow into the Athabasca River, revealed no promising passes through the mountains. As a consequence Thompson and he decided that their best bet was to retrace if possible the route followed by the Kutenai party on its way east.

They began the trip with four *engagés* on November 17. This time they traveled on past the Red Deer to the Bow River, placated the Piegans they met, and then turned westward up the last-named stream. The days were short, the weather bitter. Terrified by whooping blizzards and by the steep cliffs bordering the icy river near the present town of Exshaw, the *engagés* (to judge from an ambiguous remark in one of Alexander Mackenzie's letters) mutinied and refused to go farther.

By December 3 they were back at Rocky Mountain House—a short trip but a harsh one. McGillivray was so crippled by rheumatism brought on by exposure that he spent the rest of the winter and spring on crutches. Unable to resume the adventure when the weather opened in June 1801, he ordered James Hughes, resident manager, so to speak, of Rocky Mountain House, to lead another attempt, this time by way of the Sheep River, which enters the North Saskatchewan some miles above Rocky Mountain House.

Because of poor guidance, water too turbulent for canoes, and land too rough for horses, the effort collapsed. Thompson may have been just as glad. On June 10, their second wedding anniversary, Charlotte bore a daughter they named Fanny, the first of twelve children. Instead of being on the far side of the mountains, wondering about his wife's well-being, Thompson could now spend the rest of the summer and the following winter with her.

It was his last period of relative quiet. The growing intensities of the struggle with the XY Company turned the Nor'Westers' attention from the mountains back to the regions being invaded by the challengers. Thompson's part in the strife, constantly interrupted by the need to trade on the side, was the completion of his survey of the interior so that journeys between posts, whether by winter or summer, could be shortened if possible or, that failing, could at least be facilitated by the spread of exact information—the sort of data sought by a motorist today whenever he unfolds a highway map.

The amalgamation of the warring firms in November, 1804, necessitated a search for new beaver grounds so that the ambitions of the increased number of partners in the reorganized North West Company could be satisfied. As was noted in the preceding chapter, Simon Fraser was sent up the Peace River with orders to found new trading posts and *then* search for a supply route to the sea. Simultaneously preparations were launched for a parallel movement farther south.

By this time (1805) La Gassi and Le Blanc had returned from

the Kutenai country with information about a practical route across the Rockies. Travelers should push up the North Saskatchewan past the Kootenay Plains, a broad valley cupped between the rugged lower ranges. They should then swing up the south fork of the dwindling river to a gap between massive, glaciated peaks whose elevations, it would be learned years later, approached 11,000 feet. This gap opened onto a westward plunging torrent eventually named Blaeberry Creek. Since pack horses would be needed for the traverse, a trail would have to be cut for them through the western slope's dense evergreen forests.

And, by the way, there was this curious fact: the big river on the western side of the mountains ran north, not south. Thus it could not be Alexander Mackenzie's south-flowing Tacoutche-Tesse. Presumably, then, it was a tributary—big enough, according to the two *engagés,* to be used as a supply route from the Pacific, once the company had learned whether the Indians at its headwaters could produce enough beaver to justify opening the way.

In hindsight the first step that followed this report seems very humble, as practical measures generally do. In 1805, the year Simon Fraser received his initial instructions, the council at Kaministiquia directed John McDonald of Garth, the partner currently in charge of Rocky Mountain House, to open a trail from the North Saskatchewan to the big, north-flowing river beyond the pass. Next he should build canoes and cache them at the mouth of Blaeberry Creek, so that whoever crossed the mountains could ascend the river and investigate the potentials of the homeland claimed by the Kutenais. Once that had been determined (it was the same sort of procedure being followed by Fraser) the traders could *then* start wondering about the path the river followed on its way to the sea.

McDonald delegated the construction work to a halfbreed clerk, Jacques Finlay, nicknamed Jaco. Jaco cut out the trail and built the canoes with a small crew during the summer of 1806. That same year David Thompson, who had been elevated to a full partnership in the company in 1804, learned that he had been designated to conduct the preliminary investigations. This meant that the furlough he had been scheduled to take in 1808—his first vacation in a quarter of a century—might have to be delayed by at least one and possibly two years.

Apparently he obeyed without complaint. As solace he took his family—by then it numbered three children—with him to Rocky Mountain House in the fall of 1806. Active preparations began in the spring of 1807. He worked covertly, for he did not want the traders of a nearby Hudson's Bay post to guess his intentions and follow him. As for the Piegans, praise be he did not have to worry about them that year. American trappers were pushing up the Missouri River on the trail of Lewis and Clark, and, rumor said, the tribe's principal warriors had gone south to attack them and thus avenge the death of two braves whom Meriwether Lewis had shot near the Marias River the preceding summer.

On May 10, the whites left Rocky Mountain House in two segments. Thompson, his family, and three *engagés* rode along the river bank with the horses that would be needed for portaging the party's baggage across the divide. Five other men paddled a canoe laden with trade goods and 300 pounds of pemmican. Their leader was clerk Finan McDonald, six feet four inches tall, fiery red of hair and beard, with courage to match.

Snow blocked both groups a little short of the divide. Because grass had not yet appeared at that altitude (and, as a result, neither had game), Thompson sent McDonald and some of the men back to the Kootenay Plains with the horses. Chilled by winds blowing across what is now called the Mt. Freshfield glacier, the rest huddled in wretched shelters to wait for the pass to clear. Nineteen days of terror followed. Wind raged; avalanches roared, "sweeping Mountain Forests, whole Acres at a Time from the very Roots, leaving not a Vestige behind; scarcely an Hour passed, without [our] hearing one or more of those threatening noises."

Finally, on June 25, they were able to struggle with the horses across the pass to Jaco's trail. About forty miles long, it proved so steep and narrow they could scarcely negotiate it. Furiously Thompson wrote, "It is the opinion of every Man with me, as well as mine that Jaco Finlay ought to lose at least half of his wages for having so much neglected the Duty for which he was so expressly engaged at 150 pounds pr. year, besides a Piece of Tobacco & Sugar, & a Clerk's Equipment." On top of that they discovered that, because Jaco had not properly sheltered the canoes he had built, the whole job had to be done over.

A difficult and suspenseful summer followed. In their new canoes the party pushed southward up the forested trough of the river to a lovely, mountain-girt lake. Near its outlet they built stout log quarters surrounded on three sides by a heavy stockade. The fourth side was protected by a bank that dropped precipitously to the swirling river. During this period they lived on the meat of wild horses that abounded in the vicinity and on salmon that were just arriving from the sea, their flesh turning flabby and tasteless as spawning time neared.

In mid-August two Kutenai Indians arrived with startling information. News of the Nor'Westers' arrival, the visitors said, had spread swiftly throughout the adjacent countryside, and a large party of Flathead and Nez Percé Indians camped in what is now the northwestern part of Montana had promptly set out to trade with them. A war party of Blackfeet and Piegans intercepted the travelers and forbade the journey, whereupon the frustrated Indians had veered southward to trade at "a military post" recently built by forty-two Americans, two of whom had reputedly been members of the Lewis and Clark expedition.

As proof that such a post existed, the Kutenais handed Thompson a letter addressed to "Foreigners who may at present be carrying on a Traffic with Indians within our Territories." The missive was dated July 10, 1807, Fort Lewis, Yellow River, Columbia, and was signed by a Lieutenant James Roseman and a Captain Zachary Perch. Enclosed was a list of restrictions placed on foreign trade by a General Braithwaite.

Thompson doubted very much that a boundary between American and British claims west of the mountains had been drawn since his departure from Fort William the previous summer. If his surmise was correct, then he had as much right to be where he was as the Americans had. Consequently he disdained replying to the letter, even though the realization that rival Americans were in the vicinity was unsettling.

Far more worrisome was harassment by Piegan Indians. Three parties of them confronted him between August 26 and October 30. Some simply sneaked around spying. Others yelled threats and, according to one of his later tales, even kept the whites besieged within the log fort for several days. Thompson retorted with adroit mixtures of bluff and diplomacy. He showed the less truculent of the visitors around the fort in order to impress them with its strength, warned them that by venturing onto Kutenai territory they were inviting attack, and sent rich presents to his old friend, war chief Kootanne Appe, who, he correctly suspected, was lurking nearby with a large force. Because of these counters and because of the Indians' reluctance to lose men in a direct confrontation, no serious attack materialized. But the constant pressure was unnerving, a dread given acute dimensions on his learning through the wilderness grapevine that members of the Blackfoot confederacy had recently seized and looted Fort Augustus on the Saskatchewan.

The mysterious Americans kept up their pressures, too. On December 24, Indians brought him another letter, this one signed by "Jeremy Pinch, Lieut." It chided him for not answering the first communication and accused him of arming allies of the Blackfeet to the injury of the Americans. Such antics could not be permitted in "these Countries, certainly the property of the United States both by discovery and Cession."

Who were the Americans? Army records of the time list no General Braithwaite, no Captain Perch, no Lieutenants Roseman or Perch, no Fort Lewis on the Columbia. In other words, they were private trappers, their identities still a matter of conjecture, who were using military pseudonyms in an effort to run the Canadians out of the country.

Thompson, of course, had no way of detecting the falsehood. But he had no intention of running, either. Stiffly he replied to "Perch" that although he was not in a position to settle territorial disputes, it was his opinion that the explorations of the lower Columbia by Lieutenant Broughton of George Vancouver's expedition had given Britain a sounder claim to the region than anything the United States could offer.

He next sent copies of the correspondence by dogsled across the mountains to the Saskatchewan, perhaps in time to catch the winter express that each year carried reports of recent activities from the interior to Sault Ste. Marie. There the data was collated for the use of the Montreal agents as they journeyed to Fort William to complete plans for the coming year. Obviously everyone at the rendezvous would be deeply concerned by this information about the rapid advance of the Americans.

The episode also lent urgency to his own assignment of winning the allegiance of the mountain tribes. Late in April, traveling sometimes by canoe and sometimes by horse, he thrust south with a small party into what is now northern Idaho and the northwestern corner of Montana. Hunger—once the men had nothing to eat but the rotting carcass of a deer they found—flooded lowlands, and hair-raising portages high on the sides of precipitous canyon walls turned the trip into a desperate ordeal. By the time he returned to Kootenai House on June 5 he should have been worn out, but with unflagging resilience he gathered up the furs at the post and started with his family back toward the Saskatchewan.

By then Charlotte was seven months pregnant with their fourth child. Possibly that is the reason that Thompson dropped her and the rest of the family at Boggy Hall, a trading station some miles downstream from Rocky Mountain House, though as a general thing the women of the fur country were not deemed to need delicate treatment. Freed of encumberances, the father then sped on toward Lake Superior.

At this point Thompson's critics raise sharp questions. Why didn't he send the furs out with an underling and devote his own energies to learning where the river beyond the mountains entered the sea, especially since he knew that Americans were already pressing westward?

The only way to answer the question is by conjecture. He did not reach Rocky Mountain House until after the regular brigade had started east. Utmost speed and hence utmost discipline would be needed if his furs were to reach Rainy Lake House in time to be turned over to the voyageurs who would take them to Montreal. He may not have had a subordinate on hand to whom he was willing to entrust the task. (Finan McDonald had remained in the mountains with most of the engagés.) The need for speed may also explain his leaving Charlotte and the children, the oldest barely seven, at Boggy Hall.

Or he may have wanted to discuss with his partners the implications of the American threat, a suggestion that assumes he learned at Rocky Mountain House that his letters had indeed gone out on the winter express. Or his reasons may have been personal—a hope that as a reward for what he had accomplished he would be allowed to take his furlough after all, ensconce himself in quiet quarters in Montreal, and work without interruption on the map for which he had been collecting data during more than two decades.

If such was his hope, it was doomed. By driving his men hard he reached Rainy Lake on August 2—and then, after two days' rest, turned around and headed west again.

It is difficult to believe that he was not acting under emergency orders. But what orders?

To found a depot beside the sea? The explanation seems inadequate. That very summer Simon Fraser was exploring the Tacoutche-Tesse, still presumed to be the Columbia, and there was no need yet to supplement his efforts. Meanwhile Americans were already in the mountains, and it was essential that they be kept from taking over beaver grounds the Nor'Westers badly needed for maintaining profits. Checking them by holding the loyalty of the mountain Indians was to be Thompson's job. It is not a thesis that can be documented, but at least it explains why one of the era's most active explorers made no immediate attempt to reach the Pacific even after crossing the Continental Divide.

He did work diligently to develop a prosperous trade, however. He had good help—brawny Finan McDonald and sharp-witted James McMillan as clerks, plus a steadily increasing number of French-Canadian voyageurs and eastern Indians, the latter sent west to trap and to teach trapping to the mountain tribes. Fortified thus, he spent all of 1809 and the first half of 1810 scouring the principal streams of southeastern British Columbia, northwestern Montana, northern Idaho, and northeastern Washington. Either in person or through clerks acting under his direction he built posts in each of the areas named.

By listening to the Indians, by taking constant observations, and by heeding the kind of intuitive hunch that comes to persons immersed in their calling, he solved the erratic geography of the rivers. The stream into which Blaeberry Creek emptied was the true Columbia! After flowing north for several score miles, it made a hairpin bend around what became known as the Selkirk Mountains and began the tumultuous drop that would take it to the Pacific.

It was a powerful magnet, drawing huge tributaries into its embrace. The Kootenay River, which provided Thompson with his main highway into what is now American territory, started south but then described its own hairpin curve in northwestern Montana and flowed north through long, drowned valleys to join the Columbia near modern Castlegar. The Clark's Fork (which becomes the Pend Oreille after passing through the lake of the same name in Idaho) rose farther south in Montana and raced northwest, a fine, cold stream but dangerous for canoes. The Tacoutche-Tesse? If it did not leave its southern course and swing into the sea farther north than was supposed (as Simon Fraser learned that it did), then it too was another tributary of one of the grandest river systems known. All this Thompson divined without following any of those tributaries to the parent stream or even the Columbia itself below Blaeberry Creek—an extraordinary feat of geographical deduction.

Meanwhile, early in 1810, he caught up with some of the Americans he was laboring to outdo. A group of them, accompanied by Flathead Indians, had ventured into one of Montana's broad central valleys to hunt bison and trap beaver. Blackfeet surprised them and killed two men, a Flathead and the leader of the whites, Charles Courtin, or, as Thompson spelled the name, Charles Courter. When a squabble developed over the disposition of the dead man's property, the whites sent a message to Thompson, asking him to act as referee. He complied and so learned at first hand of the discouragement of his rivals. Their casualties since 1807 had been high and because they were afraid to venture onto the plains, the furs they had obtained either rotted in cache or were pillaged by the Piegans. Thompson's opposition had deepened their dejection, and, for the time being at least, most were ready to withdraw.

By contrast Thompson's men had collected so many pelts during the winter of 1809–10 that the bales overflowed the warehouse at the Montana post. Thompson was obliged to put the surplus into his own room and move outside into a tent. Yet he, too, lived in constant dread of the Piegans. When the time came to move the pelts east in the spring, he considered avoiding the regular trail by descending the Clark's Fork and Pend Oreille to the Columbia and then ascending the latter stream to Blaeberry Creek. The ruse did not work. The tributary was too rough for canoes, and he had to turn back to the customary route when he was only thirty miles from the main stream. It was an agonizing trip—floods and melting snowbanks, lost horses, shortages of proper bark for repairing the canoes, hunger, and always the dread of ambush. Signs he saw along the way convinced him that he had missed a Piegan war party only by the luck of timing.*

No more. His postponed furlough was due at last. In mid-June he started with a heavily laden packtrain up Blaeberry Creek toward the pass. Snow four feet deep blocked the burdened horses, but Thompson was determined to press ahead. In company with a small group of hand-picked men he floundered over the divide and at the Kootenay Plains found canoes that had been cached for him. Leaving McMillan to wait for the pack train, he sped downstream, picked up his wife and children at the fort where they had lived during the past year, and joined the main brigade.

On July 13 the chanting men swung into the North West Company post at the mouth of the Winnipeg River. There "I left my little family with her sister-in-law to the care of a good Providence." The map! Freedom at last for the map!

On July 22 he was at Rainy Lake. There he was halted by a message from Fort William. Developments in connection with the American thrust toward the Pacific made it necessary for him to turn back once more to defend the company's western interests.

---

* He was not alone in his fears. Joseph Howse of the Hudson's Bay Company twice followed him across the mountains to present-day Montana, but refused to try a third time because of the Blackfoot threat. Ironically, those two belated crossings to Blaeberry Creek resulted in the pass's being named Howse Pass, not Thompson Pass.

XXII

Substitute Gateway

*I*n order to understand this second postponement of Thompson's furlough, it is necessary to review the snares laid for the North West Company by the richest man in the United States, John Jacob Astor. Astor had begun his career by carrying sacks of trinkets on his back to Indian camps in upper New York State. Finding that he could sell more fur than he obtained as a pedlar, he began going to Montreal to buy what he needed. Because he was a good customer with a pleasing personality, he was soon on close terms with the leading merchants of the Canadian city, especially old Alexander Henry, who had started his career at Michilimackinac beside the strait between lakes Huron and Michigan.

Even after the American occupation of the border forts in 1796, Michilimackinac had remained the center of what Canadians called the southwestern trade. Astor may have visited the area himself in quest of pelts. He certainly sent agents there. They had scant success. Although Canadian traders took out American citizenship papers for convenience in dealing with customs officials, they continued to buy their goods from and send their pelts to the St. Lawrence. Astor still had to visit Montreal in order to obtain skins that had originated within the United States.

While brooding about this he came across Meriwether Lewis's report to President Jefferson concerning fur-trade possibilities in the Far West—stringing posts from the Missouri River to the

Columbia, using Indian horses for connecting the navigable waters of the two streams, and sending supply ships around Cape Horn to a depot at the mouth of the western river. To this proposal Astor's imagination added other ingredients—sea-otter pelts acquired by coastal vessels plying the rugged inlets as far north as Russian Alaska and an agreement with the Russians whereby he would send foodstuffs and trade goods to Sitka in exchange for still more furs. The best of the pelts would be swapped in China for tea, silk, and other Oriental exotics that could be sold in the cities of the eastern United States. Pelts rejected by the Chinese would be disposed of in London or Germany. Since Astor's ships already traded with China and his European agents already marketed surplus pelts there, he would have no trouble establishing outlets.

Still bolder was his hope of linking the trade south of the Great Lakes to his proposed invasion of the Rocky Mountains and the Pacific Coast. He could do that by gaining control of the Michilimackinac Company, through which the principal supply firms of Montreal conducted their business inside the United States. (The same firms also supplied the Nor'Westers.) A heady vision! As soon as the pieces had been stitched together, John Jacob Astor would hold the bulk of the American wilderness within the cup of his hands.

The scheme, as he himself would have admitted, was not wholly original. Through Alexander Henry and other acquaintances in Montreal, Astor was familiar with Alexander Mackenzie's proposal that the Nor'Westers build a depot at the mouth of the Columbia in order to ease their freight problems while linking land and marine fur trading activities. Astor knew, furthermore, that Simon Fraser and David Thompson were already in the Rockies, and he surmised that, as soon as they had established posts there, they would search for a way to the Pacific.

But, although the Nor'Westers had moved first, Astor was not without resources. His ships could trade furs in the Orient; theirs were barred by the monopoly of the East India Company. As an American citizen, he could import goods through Michilimackinac for the southwestern trade. The Montrealers no longer could. The increasing deadliness of the Napoleonic Wars had led both France and England to interfere with American shipping bound for blockaded European ports. In retaliation Jefferson and later Madison, intermittently, imposed a series of nonintercourse decrees that were making the Montreal merchants squirm.

Hoping to lead from strength, Astor in 1808 won from the legislature of New York State a charter for what he called the American Fur Company. He told Jefferson by mail that he planned to drive the Michilimackinac Company out of business. Jefferson wrote back extending his blessings. Astor showed charter and letter to the Montreal supply men on his next visit and said that the American Fur Company would purchase the Michilimackinac Company for half a million dollars. He added casually that he would throw in another $50,000 for a free hand on the still-unoccupied Columbia.

The offer was rejected.

Astor nevertheless decided to press ahead to the Pacific. He incorporated the Pacific Fur Company, laid plans for sea and land expeditions to the Columbia, and sent agents to Montreal to recruit experienced Canadian traders and voyageurs with whom to strengthen his force of American frontiersmen. In spite of his show of boldness, however, he was uneasy about the prospect of unrestrained competition beyond the Rockies in lands where national sovereignty had not been determined and government help could hardly be expected.

At that point the off-again, on-again presidential embargoes against British importations came to his rescue (at least for a while) by depriving British traders operating inside the United States of essential merchandise. Deciding that they would have to accept an American partner in order to send goods to those unhappy men, the Montrealers approached Astor. This time the American offered to buy half the Michilimackinac Company provided that the North West Company took a third interest in his Pacific Fur Company. His object was to preclude competition in the West by making the Canadians his partners there.

Reluctantly the Montrealers consented—with a proviso of their own. Their wintering partners were looking forward to increased profits from new beaver grounds between the Rocky Mountains and the Coast, and the Montreal agents could not cut this hope by a third without the winterers' permission.

Details of the proposal were rushed to Fort William. After long bickering the winterers agreed, largely because someone realized that no one had yet delineated what was meant by "Columbia." If the partnership with Astor were confined to regions adjacent to the Coast, thus enabling the Nor'Westers to operate without restriction in the Rockies, the loss of a third of their Western income might not hurt so badly.

Again a messenger was rushed to Rainy Lake to intercept Thompson. The letters the man carried have not survived, but a partial reconstruction can be made from other documents in the Coe Collection at Yale University.* First Thompson was given the background of the negotiations. He was told what he probably already knew: Simon Fraser had learned that the Tacoutche-Tesse was not the Columbia—and was not navigable, a development that intensified the need to obtain a foothold on the Columbia. He was informed of Astor's recruiting drives for sea and land expeditions to the far coast. Finally, he was informed that, although the new partnership agreement with the American would prevent competition on the coast, he should secure to the exclusive use of the North West Company the posts he had located on the western side of the Rockies.

With feelings he never described, Thompson turned around, taking with him four canoeloads of merchandise for the Rocky Mountain forts.

Meanwhile the United States government had again relaxed its embargo on British imports. Deciding that they no longer needed Astor south of the Lakes, the Montrealers let the agreement lapse. Conceivably they could have rushed information about this radical change to Thompson, but why? The 6,000 pounds of goods in his canoes would be more necessary than ever for strengthening his mountain posts against Astor's incursions. If he then continued to the Pacific as scheduled, he would pick up data about the American competitors that might be advantageous later on. Consequently he was allowed to continue up the long streams thinking he was on his way to meet new partners.

From the beginning he was disturbed by the prospect of Indian troubles en route. The tribes of the high plains, always less amen-

---

* These documents, which have been generally overlooked by historians, were published by Dorothy Wildes Bridgwater, editor, "John Jacob Astor Relative to his Settlement on the Columbia River," *The Yale University Library Gazette*, XXIV, 2, October, 1949.

able to manipulation by white traders than were the more dependent red people of the forests, had grown progressively belligerent. The Assiniboines created constant trouble with their horse-stealing. The Crees were angry at all whites because the Hudson's Bay Company had stopped buying wolf skins. As Thompson had learned on his way east that summer, the arrogance of the Blackfoot Confederacy had led the company traders to replace various of their beleagured posts in present-day Alberta with a single strong bastion called Terre Blanche, or White Earth, located a few miles downstream from the site of today's Edmonton. Rival traders of the Hudson's Bay Company had joined the move, and now the plains were presented with the unusual spectacle of competing posts sheltered inside the same stockade at Terre Blanche.

Thompson was aware that he had contributed his bit to the unrest. During the preceding year he had traded to the Flatheads by his own account "upwards of twenty guns . . . with several hundreds of iron arrowheads, with which they thought themselves a fair match for the Peeagan Indians, in battle on the Plains." That battle had taken place during July, and during his ascent of the river he learned the results—seven dead Piegans and thirteen wounded. Worse yet, some of the casualties had been inflicted by Finan McDonald and other whites traveling with the Flatheads. Moodily Thompson summed up the episode: "This was the first time the Peeagans were in a manner defeated, and they determined to wreck their vengeance on the white men who furnished arms and ammunition to their enemies." Already, in his estimation, he was a marked man.

In the fall the North Saskatchewan was a difficult stream to ascend. The current in the broad-bottomed, steep-sided valley was swift, the water shallow. The voyageurs either thrust the canoes forward with iron-tipped poles or climbed wearily out on the bank and harnessed themselves in the tow lines. Bored by the slow progress and constricted views, Thompson shifted to horseback at Terre Blanche for the rest of the journey to the Kootenay Plains, where a pack train waited to lift the goods over Howse Pass. He planned to avoid lurking Indians by keeping in the woods well back from the curving stream.

Such a procedure was contrary to company policy. Partners

were supposed to stay close to their canoes. The decree was widely ignored, however, and so Thompson's request at Terre Blanche for saddle animals raised no eyebrows. To make sure that his brigade was progressing satisfactorily, he promised to contact it every few days.

The canoes departed at 4 P.M. Saturday, September 8, 1810. Thompson felt no need to follow until the morning of the eleventh. A strangely assorted party went with him—his clerk, William Henry, an unidentified man named Kenville, two *engagés,* a young Ojibwa Indian who may have been Thompson's personal servant, and three women. Some curiosity attaches to the women. Was Charlotte Thompson, who often accompanied her husband on his journeys, among them? If so, what of the four children, including a baby born a few months earlier? Or was the family waiting at some unnamed post for the father's return from his long and dangerous journey?

Thompson's clerk, William Henry, it should be added, was the twenty-seven-year-old son of Alexander Henry the Elder. By coincidence another Alexander Henry, the elder's nephew and William Henry's cousin, was the trader in charge of the Nor'Westers' section of the conjoined White Earth posts. To distinguish him from his uncle he was called Alexander Henry the Younger, and it is from the restrained entries in his journal that most of our knowledge of the next days is deprived.

On September 15 Thompson's party made contact on schedule with the four canoes and then withdrew again into the woods. Down at Terre Blanche, meanwhile, Alexander Henry the Younger was making preparations to reopen Rocky Mountain House, which had been temporarily closed, as soon as supplies reached him from below. The craft—eleven of them—did not appear until September 21. Sourly Henry grumbled in his journal, "The Indians, like ravenous wolves on the scent of a carcass, came hotly after the canoes, attracted by the smell of liquor." That insatiable thirst would play its role, too, in the succeeding mixups.

As quickly as he could manage, Henry dispatched four canoes upstream to Rocky Mountain House; one of them carried his family and personal baggage. On the twenty-sixth, Henry himself, two clerks, two *engagés,* and some hunters followed on horseback. Like Thompson, they contacted their canoes at a post upstream.

Then, unlike Thompson, they crossed to more open land on the south side of the river. They did not see the winding stream again until they neared Rocky Mountain House on October 5. They had supposed that the post was empty and were surprised to see smoke curling from the chimneys.

After splashing across the river, they learned that the place had been occupied for nearly two weeks by the men of Thompson's canoe brigade. Of Thompson himself there had been no sign since September 15. No one could guess whether he was above or below the post—or, for that matter, whether he was alive.

The men's story was short. They had first paused at Rocky Mountain House on September 21. When Thompson's horseback party did not arrive on time they had decided, for fear of ice, to push ahead anyway. About forty miles above Rocky Mountain House they had been stopped by Piegan Indians who told them that because of the killing of their friends by Flatheads using guns purchased from the North West Company, no more whites were to enter the mountains. The Indians who delivered the order had not been offensive, but they had been firm. After waiting two days for Thompson, who did not appear, the brigade dropped back to the shelter of Rocky Mountain House.

Alexander Henry, a conscientious man, decided that somehow or other the canoes had to be delivered to the men waiting in the mountains. While his clerk and he were sparring over who should undertake the dangerous task, events were given a new twist by the appearance of the very Indians who had blocked the brigade in the first place. This patrol had with it a horse from Thompson's cavalcade and articles of clothing that Alexander Henry recognized as belonging to his cousin William. The Indians said they had found the objects near an abandoned camp not far from where the canoes had been stopped.

The report led Henry to suppose that Thompson and his cousin had avoided the Piegans and had hurried on to the Kootenay Plains—what else but excessive haste would account for the lost horse and clothing?—and were waiting for the canoes at the foot of the trail leading to the pass. If so, the need to move the canoes upstream ahead of winter was more urgent than ever.

The clerk agreed to go with the brigade. For his part Henry with no great difficulty managed to get the Indians in the vicinity dead drunk. At 2 A.M. October 12, while the red guards snored peacefully, the four canoes started off through the dim starlight.

At 6 P.M. that same day William Henry arrived from below in one of the four canoes that Alexander had dispatched earlier from Terre Blanche to Rocky Mountain House. David Thompson, William reported, was downstream, camped in a dense copse of evergreens where he would not be spotted by the Piegans.

As nearly as can be determined from the perfunctory account of the episode that Thompson penned for his autobiography many years later and from the terse entries in Alexander Henry's journal, this is what had happened. Thompson, one of the best geographers on the continent, riding through an area with which he was famil-iar, had managed to strike the Saskatchewan several miles farther upstream than he intended. Luckily he had spotted signs of lurking Piegans before they had detected his party. Going into hiding him-self, he sent some of his group off to locate the canoes, which he surmised were somewhere downstream, between his present loca-tion and Rocky Mountain House. Thompson says, though no other record does, that the searchers discovered signs of a battle between the canoemen and the Indians. In spite of that, the searchers fired their guns in the hope of drawing an answering salvo from the canoes.

At that Thompson went into a blue funk, fearful that the shoot-ing would attract Piegans rather than voyageurs. But he did not lose his head as completely as his critics charge. Convinced now that he could not cross the Rockies by the normal route, he decided to open another. To that end he ordered his *engagés* to slip up to the Kootenay Plains and bring the pack horses to an appointed rendezvous near the Brazeau River, a big northern tributary that entered the North Saskatchewan some sixty miles below Rocky Mountain House. The horse herders were to avoid detection by using an "interior" trail, and, anyway, the Piegans would not be particularly concerned about traders *leaving* the mountains.

Strangely, he made no effort to learn whether his canoemen had retreated to the closest logical shelter, Rocky Mountain House. Fearing perhaps that the place would be surrounded by Indians, he gave it wide berth as he rode swiftly—fled, if you like—to his evergreen hiding place high above the Brazeau, the point from which he planned to start his new crossing.

Who was with him other than Henry and the young Ojibwa is unknown. The three women who had left Terre Blanche with the party vanish like smoke from the record. In any event, the hiders had little food and Thompson would not permit hunting lest Indians discover them. They were starving when William Henry saw his cousin's canoes working upstream toward Rocky Mountain House and joined them in order to bring help. For Thompson would not budge. He was still afraid—and still determined to work out a new northern trail.

In some dismay Alexander recalled the canoes he had dispatched upstream during the dead of night. He then paid Thompson a hurried visit in his copse but failed to change the geographer's mind. There *was* another pass at the head of the Athabasca River. Iroquois and Nipissing trappers had found it a few years earlier, and Thompson was convinced that by using dogsleds he could cross it. A new route. Never again, he vowed, would Rocky Mountain or Columbia canoes be subjected to the murderous whims of the Blackfoot Confederacy.

Again the Indians were deceived with drink; again the canoes slipped by them in the darkness. Thompson says that his herders brought twenty-four horses down from the Kootenay Plains. Alexander Henry wrote that animals for the trip were purchased from the Indians. Both accounts may be partly correct. In any event, on October 28, 1810, twenty-four men, including Thompson, Willian Henry, and an Iroquois guide named Thomas, began the northwesterly march toward the Athabasca River. With them they led twenty-four heavily laden horses and several dogs.

It was a hellish trip. They spent more than a month fighting the cantankerous animals through thick, runty growth, some of it burned and toppled by old forest fires. Hungry from short rations, the men reached the Athabasca River on December 3. After ascending it a short distance, they halted to prepare for the shift from horse to dogsled travel. It took them the rest of the year to build a house (William Henry would stay there with the horses and such supplies as they could not carry) and make snowshoes and dogsleds.

Although little snow had fallen, temperatures dropped to $-32°$. The men grumbled openly. At intervals Thompson sent ten of them back to Rocky Mountain House, ostensibly for supplies but more probably because he realized that his recent timorousness had cost him their respect and he would not be able to control them as difficulties mounted.

On December 30 the best of those who remained bade William Henry farewell and started up the Athabasca River among the towering peaks now embraced within Jasper National Park. They had ten sleds and four horses, the latter piled with meat. The improvident French-Canadians attacked the food as if there was enough to last forever. "Upon my reproaching them for their gluttony," Thompson wrote later, "the reply I got was, 'What pleasure have we in Life but eating.' "

Soon it became evident that the sleds were loaded too heavily and that part of the cargo would have to be cached. Every dog was vital now, but the men flogged them furiously nevertheless. It was a sport, Thompson wrote. They crippled some, killed one. By January 5, 1811, when Thompson's thermometer registered −26°, they had discarded two sleds for lack of animals. The next day they abandoned the horses on a frozen marsh where brittle grass showed above the snow. Later Thompson learned to his astonishment that the animals had survived the winter.

Their Iroquois guide led them from the main river up a tributary now known as the Whirlpool. On January 10 they came in full view of the pass, squeezed between ice-sheathed peaks. Legend says that a voyageur traveling the route half a dozen years later spat and declared with a mixture of awe and disgust, "I take my oath that God Almighty never made such a place." But at least Thompson's people were blessed with clear weather. Following their guide's advice, they loaded their sleds with firewood and that night camped on a snow-filled flat at the foot of an enormous glacier "of a fine green color."

The descent to the Wood River on the western side was so steep that dogs and sleds came down in dismaying tangles. The change in climate was astounding—mild temperatures and such soft wet snow that after the dogs had reached the bottom of the slope they could scarcely move. After five days of fruitless wallowing Thompson went into camp where the Wood and Canoe rivers mingle before joining the Columbia as it curls around the northern tip of the Selkirk Mountains. His intent was to wait until April, the season for raising bark, then build a canoe and return to a voy-aguer's native habitat, the open river.

The trees were enormous—as much as forty-two feet in girth—and the gloom oppressive. "We were pygmies," Thompson wrote. The prospect of a long wait in a crude hut in that sunless forest so discouraged four of the men that they deserted and climbed back over the pass. Thompson sent three others to William Henry with a desperate appeal for supplies. With no foreknowledge of how loyal the trio might be he settled down with a single companion to wait out the gray days.

On February 17 the messengers, aided by an Indian, returned with two sledloads of pemmican. In April they began their search for bark, only to discover that the birch on the western side of the mountains produced a sheathing too thin for canoes. Forced into ingenuity, they tried cedar wood. They split it into long, thin strips, drilled holes, overlapped the edges, sewed the boards together with split pine roots, and gummed the joints in the usual fashion. The result was a usable craft sharp at both ends, twenty-five feet long and three and a half wide.

Conceivably they could have descended the Columbia in their improvised canoe, but the men refused to risk the journey with so small a party. Because Thompson was in no great hurry—he as-sumed he was on his way to meet his new partners—and because he wished to urge his Rocky Mountain traders to resist any incur-sions by the Astorians, he did not press matters. Up the river they went, their canoe loaded with 235 pounds of provisions and three pieces of goods (270 pounds), all that remained of the three tons with which he had left Rainy Lake.

Even with this light weight the trip was exhausting. Often the men could move the canoe only by snowshoeing along the bank and towing it. When that failed, they jumped into the water and pushed. Once they had to build a toboggan on which to slide the improvised craft across a frozen lake. Early in May they were able to enlist the help of passing Iroquois and Nipissing Indians, but even so they spent twenty-eight days covering the 200 miles to his old post near the headwaters of the river. They might have been better off carrying their meager possessions on their backs.

That was not the end of the stubbornness. Convinced in spite of his labors that he had found the best way across the mountains, Thompson sent orders east that supplies for the following winter be delivered to him at the western foot of Athabasca Pass, near the Canoe River.

As the weather opened and the usual floods inundated the land, he visited each of his Rocky Mountain posts, finishing with one constructed during the winter by Finan McDonald and Jaco Finlay beside the Spokane River some ten miles northwest of the present city of the same name. Not until then did he feel any pressure to visit the mouth of the Columbia. He began the trip by riding horseback with two Iroquois Indians and five French-Canadians to Kettle Falls (Thompson used the Indian name Ilthkoyape Falls), buried now under water impounded by Grand Coulee Dam. At the falls the travelers built another cedar canoe and on July 3, 1811, started through rough, largely treeless country toward the Pacific.

He showed little panic now. On meeting strange Indians he landed and, with his men inconspicuously covering him from behind, approached them in defiance of whatever signs of hostility they showed. Handing out British flags, he made his pitch on behalf of the North West Company. A more formal effort came at 6 A.M., July 9, at the confluence of the broad Snake with the main river. Ordering his men to erect a stout post, he attached to it a sign declaring:

"Know hereby this country is claimed by Great Britain as part of its territories, and that the N.W. Company of Merchants from Canada do hereby intend to erect a factory at this place for the commerce of the country around. D. Thompson." What more he could do to keep the company's unwelcome American partners pinned to the coast he did not know.

Soon the river bent sharply west. The bordering hills were corrugated with bold columnar rocks. Ahead rose tall, forested mountains dominated by the majestic snow cone of Mt. Hood. Thunderous rapids appeared, compressed between jutting promontories of basalt. Portaging was necessary there and at other frightening rapids, the Cascades, farther downstream. Then the hills flattened out, the river broadened between dense evergreens. Islands were frequent. They felt the tug of the tide. With seals sporting around the canoe, they paddled swiftly with the ebb, eager for a glimpse of the ocean that relatively few of their countrymen had yet seen.

High waves encountered on July 14 forced them to portage across Tongue Point, a long, narrow peninsula that protruded from the south bank. On the far side, the river's full estuary sprang into view. Some nine miles away were two misty headlands guarding the entrance. Nearer at hand, in a small clearing among gigantic trees, were four log huts built by Astor's seafarers, who, Thompson learned shortly, had arrived only three months before.

As his cedar canoe glided up to the dock, the residents welcomed him in astonishment. They were a heterogeneous mixture— peak-headed Chinook Indians, Kanakas imported from the Hawaiian Islands, French-Canadian voyageurs hired in Montreal, American backwoodsmen. And Canadian bourgeois, most of them one-time clerks in the North West Company.

The Canadians were incredulous when Thompson told them that the winterers of the North West Company had agreed to buy a third of Astor's Pacific enterprise. They had left New York on their ship *Tonquin* months after the meeting at Fort William and had heard of no such arrangement. But after Thompson had showed them the orders he had received at Rainy Lake, they agreed to protect themselves against future criticism by a curious exchange of letters.

Being careful not to state that an amalgamation had actually occurred, Thompson wrote the ranking officers at Astoria— Duncan McDougall, David Stuart, and Robert Stuart—as follows: "With Pleasure I acquaint you that the Wintering Partners have acceded to the offer of Mr. Astor, accepting one third of the business you are engaged in. . . . I have only to hope that the respective parties at Montreal may finally settle the arrangements between the two companies. . . ." To which the others replied that they thanked him for "the pleasant intelligence . . . and with you sincerely wish that final arrangements may take place to the mutual satisfaction of both parties." So all was well. Thompson had lost no race to the sea, as his critics have long contended, because there was no race. He had simply paid a visit to potential partners —whose activities he secretly hoped to constrict as best he could.

The next day he and his men crossed the choppy waves of the

estuary to Cape Disappointment for an unrestricted look at the ocean. Thompson was deeply moved. Two Nor'Westers, Mackenzie and Fraser, had reached saltwater ahead of him, but he was the first to descend a stream that would be useful for freight canoes. But until his partners learned what he had done and sent ships to the Columbia, cargoes for his mountain posts would still have to follow the long trail across the plains and the Rockies. The thought stirred him. It was time to return for the consignment he had directed be sent him at the mouth of the Canoe River, a thousand miles away.

He started upstream on July 22. He learned he had not dissuaded the Astorians from entering the upper country when David Stuart decided to accompany him with eight men traveling in three clumsy dugouts. Though Thompson was annoyed, the reinforcements proved welcome. Tight times ensued before the combined parties succeeded in outfacing the upstream Indians, who demanded exorbitant tribute for helping haul Stuart's awkward craft over the rocky carrying places.

After the worst danger was past, Thompson pulled ahead in his more maneuverable canoe. Even so, strong currents buffeted him sorely; and so he chose, as only an astronomer could have, a remarkable shortcut.

In passing through what is now the state of Washington, the Columbia describes a huge C, its open end facing east. Thompson decided to strike across that open end. Guided by instruments, he ascended the Snake River to the Palouse and followed the latter stream northward as far as it was navigable. He then acquired horses by trade from the Indians and rode almost due north to Spokan House. After a brief rest there he continued northwest to Kettle (Ilthkoyape) Falls, built another canoe, and resumed the journey by water. The saving in distance was almost a hundred miles; more important, he had by-passed four hundred miles of difficult river.*

At the mouth of the Canoe River Thompson found, after a short mixup, some of the goods he wanted. He forwarded the bales to

---

* David Stuart's party left the Columbia at the mouth of Okanogan River, where they built one post, and continued to Kamloops, British Columbia, where Nor'Westers soon moved in beside them—just as competing Astorians later moved in beside the Nor'Westers' Spokan House.

Finan McDonald, who was waiting for them at Ilthkoyape Falls. That done, Thompson crossed Athabasca Pass to William Henry's post and brought in the rest of the merchandise, bucking a heavy October snow along the way. Piling the pieces into cedar canoes, he returned to Ilthkoyape Falls, obtained horses, and rose east past Spokan House into western Montana, where he spent the winter.

On coming out in the spring of 1812 with 122 packs of the glossiest sort of fur, he and a fellow partner, John George Mc-Tavish, retraced the same roundabout journey via the Falls. After crossing Athabasca Pass they wormed their canoes (birch ones now that they were east of the mountains) through shallow rivers to Lake Ile-à-la-Crosse and followed the standard route down the Churchill River to the Sturgeon-Weir and Lake Winnipeg. Men clucked and wagged their heads. What a staggering way to go from Montana to Montreal! Yet, until some arrangement was made about sending ships to the mouth of the Columbia, what alternative was there? The Rocky Mountain tribes, well armed now, had rejected a Piegan proposal for peace—no one, the Saleesh said, could trust a Piegan—and the wars were still on. David Thompson would undertake journeys that frazzled the men with him, but he lived in terror of Blackfeet. No circuit that outdistanced them was too laborious.

Moreover, he was right. At first the company had objected to what he was doing. The minutes of the annual meeting of 1811 stated crisply that the Athabasca route was too expensive and difficult and "therefore the Trade should continue to be carried on by the Route of the Saskatchiwane River." The Piegans, their peace offering rebuffed, quickly changed that dictum, however, and pack trains through Athabasca Pass became the official link in the trail to the Pacific.

That was for the future, however. Meanwhile, McTavish and Thompson were pushing east as fast as possible in order to reach Fort William in time for the annual rendezvous. As they neared Rainy Lake, they began hearing rumors of startling developments. One said that a Scottish nobleman, Thomas Douglas, fifth Earl of Selkirk, had recently obtained from the Hudson's Bay Company 116,000 square miles of land reaching from the waist of Lake Winnipeg south to the headwaters of the Red River in what is now North Dakota and Minnesota. The Earl insisted that he wanted the land simply as a refuge for poor Scottish crofters who had been displaced from their farms in the Highlands by the spread of large-scale sheepraising. But did he need 74 million acres for his colonies —a kingdom called Assiniboia that was five times the size of Scotland? Above all, why had he picked an area where several North West and Hudson's Bay Company posts traded not for furs alone but also for the pemmican needed by their canoe brigades? What was to happen to those establishments?

The whole proposal was too absurd to be given credence. Besides, there were more immediate dangers to think about. War had just broken out between the United States and Great Britain. This electrifying news, the travelers learned, had been brought to Fort William only days before by a special messenger from the small British garrison stationed on St. Joseph Island near Sault Ste. Marie. The American fort on Michilimackinac Island, the messenger went on, was not yet aware of the declaration and might yield to a surprise attack. Could the North West Company send armed voyageurs to help?

Indeed it could! Here was an opportunity to aid in the recovery of the lands south of the Great Lakes that had been yielded to the Americans at the Peace of Paris in 1783—lands on which Astor was inexorably tightening his hold. Eagerly the meeting had whooped through resolutions to form a Corps of Voyageurs and send it east to join the attack.

Nor was that all. Astor could now be attacked by force beyond the mountains. To that end one of the partners was ordered to accompany the fur brigade to Montreal, take the company's 350-ton ship, the *Isaac Todd,* to London and outfit her as a privateer. Impressed by the company's patriotic activities around the Great Lakes, the government would probably grant the *Todd* a letter of marque, authorizing her to strike at American property in the Pacific—that is, at Astoria. Meanwhile, armed parties would go overland from Fort William to the posts beyond the Rockies, ready, when the time came, to descend on Astoria from the rear. If bloodshed could be averted by purchasing Astor's beleaguered possessions at bargain rates, that would be permissible. But, one way or another, the Americans must be driven from the Columbia.

At Rainy Lake the overlanders met David Thompson and John George McTavish coming east with their furs. Obedient to instructions, McTavish swung around to return to the Columbia. Thompson continued to Fort William. There he was greeted uproariously by the men who still remained at the post. After cheering him to the rafters, they voted him a hundred pounds a year so that he could go to Montreal and finish his great map.

Somewhere on the way east he had picked up his family. A little nervous over the possibility of American raids on the trail, they joined the last of the east-bound canoes. It was a confused and final exit. Except for routine boundary surveys a few years later, David Thompson would never return to the lands to which he had given so much.

PART FIVE

The Great Struggle

XXIII

The Giant-Killer

A t first the course of the war brought joy to Fort William.
British troops supported by trader-led voyageurs and Indians conquered Michilimackinac, forced the evacuation of Fort Dearborn
(present Chicago), and after a brief siege captured Detroit. The
strategic post of Prairie du Chien on the Mississippi succumbed,
and the fury of the Indians on the plains drove American traders
from the upper Missouri. Again the fur men of Canada dreamed
of a flourishing "southwest" trade in which John Jacob Astor
would have no part.

Affairs on the Columbia progressed just as smoothly. Armed
canoemen moved in beside the post the Astorians had established
in the interior. They told of the *Isaac Todd* and of the British
blockade that they said would keep Astor from sending supplies
to the Pacific. The North West Company partners were so confident of a quick victory that they even ordered John Stuart to work
out a combined horseback and river supply trail from his remote
New Caledonia district to saltwater at the mouth of the Columbia.
His arrival at Astoria with furs he planned to send outside by
British vessels drew the nerves of the Americans still tighter.

Threats of war were not their only worry. They had lost their
trading ship *Tonquin* to Indian attack off the west coast of Vancouver Island. The rigors of the overland crossing had led two of
their principal partners, Ramsay Crooks and Robert McClellan, to

withdraw from the company and return east. Although Astor had tried to send help, mishaps had stopped his ships short of their goal. Discouraged and isolated, the Astorians on October 16, 1813, offered their posts, supplies, and furs to the waiting Nor'-Westers for the bargain price of $58,000. The Canadians accepted for fear that, if Astoria fell to a naval assault, the booty would be sold at auction for the benefit of the British government. A purchase allowed everyone to salvage something.

Six weeks after the contracts had been signed, the warship *Raccoon,* a faster sailer than the *Isaac Todd,* arrived to conquer Astoria. Though the sale left nothing to attack, Captain Black decided to have his mite of glory. He raised the Union Jack over the post, which had been renamed Fort George, and went through a ceremony of possession. The peace commissioners of the United States would later argue successfully that the charade constituted an act of war, with consequences of considerable import to the Pacific Northwest. But that is getting ahead of the story.

Among the passengers on the *Raccoon* was an able North West Company partner, John McDonald of Garth, so-called to distinguish him from other McDonalds in the company. Forty years old in 1814, he was a small, waspish man with one crippled arm and unlimited energy. Knowing that the annual gathering at Fort William would want to learn of events on the Columbia, he decided to cross overland as rapidly as possible.

He began the eastward journey with a brigade toiling upstream to the various posts west of the mountains—North West Company posts now. After the danger of Indians and the labors of the most difficult portages had been passed, he and a handful of others pushed ahead of the main body in a light express canoe.

They were in a hurry, and so it is significant that, although McDonald was familiar with Howse Pass, he chose to cross Athabasca. Near the mouth of the Wood River the party abandoned its canoe, put fifty-pound packs on their backs, and undertook the spring hike that would draw groans of anguish from later decades of travelers—a steep climb through melting snow and dozens of wet crossings across the cliff-girt stream.

At Jasper House on the eastern side of the pass, they built a bark canoe. By means of intricate maneuvers in shallow streams and difficult portages from creek to creek, they worked their way to the North Saskatchewan and sped down it to Lake Winnipeg. There they learned that south of them on the Red River angry canoemen of the North West Company were squaring off against the desperate settlers of the Earl of Selkirk's new colony. Deciding that this crisis was more urgent than the message he was carrying to Fort William, McDonald swung his canoe toward Red River, to learn what he could of the trouble and, if possible, restore peace.

Although the colony of Assiniboia and its sponser can be described after a fashion, neither can be made quite credible. As a descendant of the legendary Robert the Bruce, Thomas Douglas, born in 1771, claimed one of the great names in Scotland, but as the youngest of seven sons he had scant expectation of inheriting the family title. Yet—and what must be the odds against this?—his six brothers died before their father, two in infancy, and at the age of twenty-eight Thomas became the fifth earl of the ancient line.

Intelligent, well educated, and strongly independent, he took seriously his obligations as a wealthy man. He worked for the abolition of the slave trade and was particularly touched by the plight of Highland tenants being ejected from their small farms by landlords who wanted the acreage for sheep. Thinking that a fresh start in the New World might answer the problem, he established two colonies in Canada for them, one on Prince Edward Island and the other, much less successful beside Lake St. Clair, near Detroit.

On encountering in Alexander Mackenzie's voyages a short paragraph about the fertility of the lands held by the Hudson's Bay Company south of Lake Winnipeg, he decided on a major effort there. The company scorned him: farmers in a fur-trade area a thousand miles from markets for their produce? Nonsense!

Selkirk thereupon determined to purchase control of the company, a strategy perhaps suggested by the fact that his handsome wife, whom he had married in March, 1807, happened to own a small number of shares in the firm. For a time Sir Alexander Mackenzie joined him. It was a short-lived alliance. Mackenzie had a fur-trader's antipathy toward settlement of any kind—his goal was wresting transit rights through Hudson Bay for the Nor'-Westers—and, when he discovered Selkirk's intent, the association

ended in a shower of sparks. Small matter. Two of Selkirk's relatives by marriage, Andrew Wedderburn (who later changed his
name to Andrew Wedderburn Colvile) and John Halkett, joined
him in buying slightly more than twelve percent of the company's
stock.

At the time it was not a valuable holding. The Napoleonic Wars
had disrupted fur markets so thoroughly that in 1808 the company
warehouses bulged with what normally would have been a three
years' supply of pelts. Labor was difficult to recruit, shipping costs
were high, and competition from the North West Company, which
handled two-thirds of the furs exported from Canada, seemed impossible to overcome. In 1809 the company skipped its dividends,
and the directors began to talk of withdrawing from the trade.

At that point Selkirk, Wedderburn, and Halkett manipulated
their holdings in such a way as to gain voting control. Wedderburn,
an unusually competent businessman, promptly launched a series
of organizational reforms, including profit-sharing incentives for
traders. Selkirk meanwhile applied for a grant of land embracing
most of the drainage system of the Red and Assiniboine rivers. He
stated that the colony he proposed would provide food and laborers
for the company and would offer retiring workers an attractive
place in which to spend the remainder of their lives. He promised
that the settlers would not trade in furs or produce alcohol for sale
outside the colony.

The North West Company agents in London, who held enough
shares in the rival firm to permit attendance at its stockholders'
meetings, fought the grant furiously. Perhaps Selkirk was a true
humanitarian. Nevertheless the land he wanted covered the buffalo
plains from which the firm (and the Hudson's Bay Company)
drew much of the pemmican needed by a thousand canoemen.
Moreover, the grant's southeastern boundary extended almost to
Rainy Lake, and the land could be used, if unfriendly rivals
wished, to disrupt the mainline route to Fort Williams.

From the Nor'Westers' standpoint a development of such potential danger could not be allowed. In spite of the objections of their
representatives, however, Selkirk received his principality. Glumly
one of the Nor'Westers wrote his partners, "It will require some
time and I fear much expense . . . before he is driven to abandon

the project, and *yet"*—the pen slashed strong lines under the words
—*"he must be driven to abandon it."*

To the North West Company traders in the field, the fears at
first seemed exaggerated. They were strongly established in Selkirk's would-be Assiniboia. Their powerful Fort Gibralter sat in a
tight corner formed by the junction of the Red and Assiniboine
rivers (the heart of modern Winnipeg) in such a way that it could
command passage along either stream. Subordinate posts occupied
strategic sites on the upper waters of both rivers. These posts provided livelihood for numerous Indians and halfbreeds called *métis*
by each year purchasing tons of buffalo pemmican from them. An
alliance like that could not be easily broken by alien farmers.

Most of the halfbloods were the offspring of company traders
and Indian women. They remembered the ties as they congregated
in their mobile skin villages beside the Red and at choice spots
near the Assiniboine. A dream of their leaders, some of whom had
been sent abroad by their fathers to be educated, was the formation
of an independent nation of *métis*—on land that this Earl of
Selkirk, whom none of them had ever seen, now claimed was his.

Made complacent by such allies, the Nor'Westers in the area
were inclined to pity the first destitute colonists. Their sufferings
on the trip to Hudson Bay and then southward through Lake
Winnipeg had been almost incredible. They were short of equipment. Their crops failed, and they survived two winters by moving
up the Red River to Pembina near the United States boundary.
There, housed in wretched huts and Indian tipis, they eked out a
living by hunting and trading with the *métis*.

Inadvertently their purchases prepared the way for a sudden
ending of compassion. As the nearby herds were thinned out and
prices rose during the winter of 1813–14, the pemmican traders
of both the North West and Hudson's Bay companies transferred
their activities to the central stretches of the Assiniboine River near
today's Brandon, Manitoba.

This local shift was accompanied by a widespread food crisis.
Americans cut off the flow of corn into the upper lakes by gaining
control of Lake Erie and recapturing Detroit. Simultaneously high
water destroyed the wild rice crop for scores of miles around Rainy
Lake. This meant that the brigades moving from Lake Winnipeg

to Fort William and beyond would have to draw more heavily than ever on pemmican from the buffalo plains.

The colony had its needs, too, for a hundred new arrivals were expected in the summer of 1814. Hoping to make sure that there would be enough pemmican on hand to carry them until harvest time, Selkirk's appointee as governor of Assiniboia, Miles Macdonell, and the colony's sheriff, John Spencer, jointly issued a proclamation forbidding the export of any foodstuffs whatsoever from Assiniboia during the next twelve months. Pemmican already gathered, whether by the North West Company or the Hudson's Bay Company, was to be surrendered to Spencer at the colony's new Fort Douglas, two miles upstream from the Nor'Westers' Fort Gibralter. Macdonell would release it bit by bit to the canoe brigades, on request, as their needs demanded. Whatever was appropriated for the colony would "be paid for by British bills at the customary rates."

The more violent partners among the Nor'Westers seethed with fury. Surrender *their* pemmican? Concede Selkirk's absolute title to more land than there was in England, Scotland, Wales, and Ireland combined? Admit that the officers of an upstart agricultural colony could command the destinies of the people who, as heirs of the French, had developed the area while the English had sat moribund beside their frozen bay? Never! The 479 ninety-pound bags of pemmican stored at Fort La Souris, where the river of that name ran into the Assiniboine, would stay there until they chose to distribute in their own way to their own brigades.

Macdonell thereupon issued a warrant for the food's seizure and sent Sheriff Spencer upstream with a posse. Injudiciously the governor allowed Hudson's Bay Company traders to join the party. They chopped their way into La Souris and lugged the contraband across the river to the Hudson's Bay Company post of Fort Brandon.

To firebrand Nor'Westers these actions were incontrovertible proof that Selkirk's basic intent was the disruption of their trade for the benefit of the Hudson's Bay Company. After damning the confiscations as "a system of insult and rapacity almost unparalleled in the predatory annals of the Buccaneers," a posse of their own seized and confined Spencer on charges of burglary. Both sides thereupon began to arm.

At that point John Macdonell of Garth arrived. Sensing, as did most of his partners on the scene, that their voyageurs did not want to fire on colonists whose sufferings had stirred their sympathies, and that the last thing the colonists wanted was to lose what little blood they had left, he managed to work out a compromise. Macdonell surrendered 200 bags of pemmican in exchange for the Nor'Westers' promise to divert some of their canoes to York Factory and bring back oatmeal for the colony. Macdonell promised further that the furs in the diverted canoes would be transported on Hudson's Bay Company ships free of charge to England.

It was the last effort at accommodation. When the peacemakers reached the North West Company rendezvous at Fort William, they were lined up in front of the meeting and excoriated by the firm's relentless head, William McGillivray. Their company and his, he shouted, had not grown to be the giant of the North American fur trade by compromising. The times called for determination, not flabbiness. Let no man forget.

Developments the following spring seemed to underscore his point. The first was the Peace of Ghent that concluded the war with the United States. Signed on December 24, 1814, the treaty declared that all territories captured during the war were to be returned to their original owners. Overnight the Canadian hope of regaining the fur trade south of the Great Lakes was ended. The effect was to attach more importance than ever to the trade of the northwest.

That trade was threatened on two fronts, somewhat nebulously on the Columbia and with acute directness in Athabasca. The Columbia worry arose from the failure of a joint British and American boundary commission to agree on a boundary between their countries' claims west of the Rockies. Accordingly the diplomats devised the so-called Convention of Joint Occupation, which granted citizens of both nations equal rights of commerce and settlement. One lure for the Americans was a decision that the investiture of Astoria by the *Raccoon* had been an act of war and that the fort should therefore be returned to Astor. As matters turned out, the Nor'Westers were by then so firmly established west of the Rockies that Astor decided against trying to buck them. But the end of the war started other American fur men up the Missouri. How long would it be before they spilled across the divide and took Astoria as their due?

There was still time to plan for that. The crisis in Athabasca was immediate.

It was not a new threat. The Hudson's Bay Company had attempted earlier invasions, hoping perhaps that the chill acceptance they had been accorded on the North Saskatchewan would prevail on the Arctic watershed as well. Not so. The huge, cold district beyond Methye Portage was the heart of the northwest trade, and the Montrealers were determined not to yield a pelt of it. Again and again, both in Athabasca and at the key forwarding posts at Ile-à-la-Crosse, bullyboys of the North West Company had harassed the English traders so violently—slashing their fishing nets, subverting their Indians, tightening their nerves with nighttime salvos of gunfire outside their stockades—that each time the company had withdrawn.

The new invasion, launched in the spring of 1815, promised to be more formidable. It was well equipped and big—140 men in twenty canoes. Its burly leader, cocky in a sealskin cap decorated with a golden tassle, was a former Nor'Wester named Colin Robertson, sometimes known behind his back as Mr. Lofty. A bold innovator, Robertson had not recruited his hands among the novice fishermen of Scotland, the source of most Hudson's Bay Company labor, but among the experienced voyageurs of Montreal. As he took them past Fort William over the Height of Land that the Montreal company considered its private preserve, the partners sought to stop him, so Robertson believed, by setting forest fires and prevailing on the Indians not to sell him food.

Like John McDonald of Garth before him, he was diverted by events at the Red River colony. During the winter a master underminer of faiths, Duncan Cameron, had quietly won the confidence of some of Selkirk's discouraged settlers. He listened to their tales of woe, suggested to them that they had been sent into the desolate region as cat's-paws of the Hudson's Bay Company, slyly described the *métis* as more savage than the Indians, and then whispered that the North West Company would find better, safer lands in Upper Canada (Ontario) for all those who wished to go.

One hundred and forty followed him. Sixty remained. To discourage that persistent minority, the *métis* drove herds of horses back and forth across the sprouting crops and set fire to the vacated houses. As smoke clotted the sky, all but four of the remaining group fled past the north end of Lake Winnipeg to a new post, Norway House, that had just been built to facilitate transportation between the Bay and the plains.*

On reaching Lake Winnipeg and learning what had transpired, Colin Robertson decided that the colony needed his attention more than Athabasca did. He sent his brigade to its destination under an overconfident, ill-prepared lieutenant named John Clarke, then pursued the colonists to Norway House, rallied their spirits, and brought them back. They were soon followed by several boatloads of fresh Scottish recruits under a new governor, Robert Semple. Red River appeared to be back in business.

Both moves—Clarke's advance into Athabasca, where he built several posts, and Robertson's reestablishment of Red River—led to horror. The Nor'Westers deep in the interior persuaded the Indians not to trade food to Clarke's invaders; the result, combined with Clarke's own rashness, was the death of sixteen persons from starvation. A winter of friction at Red River was climaxed on June 19, 1816, by the *métis* slaying of twenty-one colonists, Governor Semple among them.

By coincidence, the Earl of Selkirk had decided at that very time to pay his first visit to the colony. Emulating Robertson's boldness, he followed the regular trail from Montreal to the interior with twenty-seven canoes filled with new settlers recruited from a regiment of mercenary Swiss and German soldiers just disbanded after service in the war against the United States. He had intended by-passing Fort William by pushing through Fond du Lac at the western tip of Lake Superior, but when terrified messengers told him of the massacre he swung furiously into Thunder Bay and battered down the gates of the hostile post. There he arrested three of the company's principal men—William McGillivray, Kenneth McKenzie, and towering John McLoughlin—on charges of complicity in murder and dispatched them in heavily guarded *canots du maître* to Canada to stand trial.

Near the eastern end of Lake Superior a squall swamped one of the overloaded craft. Kenneth McKenzie and eight other men per-

---

* The builders of the new post had been recruited in Norway; hence the name.

ished. McLoughlin, later revered as "the Father of Oregon," was dragged unconscious from the water and revived only after a long period of frantically administered artificial respiration. Family legend insists that the experience turned the gigantic trader's heavy head of hair snow white.

Reports of the violence at last persuaded the Governor-General of Canada to send investigators to Red River. Fighting there stopped, to be replaced by lawsuits that dragged a costly way through the courts in Canada. Although most of the Nor'Westers whom Selkirk had arrested during the summer and following winter were acquitted, the experience left abiding scars. Nor were hurts assuaged by a drop in company profits from £192,222 in 1816 to £70,658 in 1818—a two-thirds slash in each partner's annual income.

There was little hope of improvement, for war still smoldered in the far Northwest. Traders incarcerated their rivals; Colin Robertson spent eights months locked inside his own fort. Indians were corrupted, canoe brigades raided. Every so often reports of new deaths trickled down to the lower country, and at Fort William an angry reaction set in against the Montreal agents' continued insistence that the way to win the conflict was not to yield.

That strategy, McLoughlin and Angus Bethune retorted in open meeting, had brought only bloodshed and near bankruptcy. For the sake of their futures, to say nothing of lives still unspent, they wanted a settlement with the Hudson's Bay Company.

When William McGillivray scorned the suggestion, eighteen disaffected winterers gave powers of attorney to McLoughlin and Bethune and sent the pair to London to see what they could do. The defiance galvanized the company's Montreal and London agents into a parallel move. Far more sophisticated in the ways of finance and commercial politics than the winterers were, the agents elbowed McLoughlin and Bethune aside and entered into negotiations that quite possibly resulted in better terms than the two men from the forests could have gained.

Be that as it may, in March, 1821, the companies united under terms too complex to be outlined here. Ostensibly the union was a coalition of equals; actually victory belonged to the firm that until recently had been by far the smaller of the two, the Hudson's Bay Company. Supreme command stayed in London, and the deputy

governors in North America were appointees of the London committee. Because unrestrained competition had produced chaos, the
government granted the new organization a total monopoly of the
fur trade from coast to coast, subject only to the right of Americans
to trade in the Oregon country under the privileges given them by
the Convention of Joint Occupation.

Order after centuries of disorder: Alexander Mackenzie would
have liked that. He would have been glad to know that a thousand
miles of laborious and costly trail from Montreal to the heart of
the continent had been eliminated by transit through the Bay. He
would have approved of the energy with which George Simpson,
the deputy governor in whose department the Columbia lay, began
plans for the Pacific bastion Mackenzie had recommended years
before, a massive complex later named Fort Vancouver. But, ice-
blooded and unforgiving though he was, he might have been appalled at what his dream had cost.

XXIV

Sea to Shining Sea

*T*hat part of Canada tributary to the St. Lawrence was sorely hurt by the victory of the Hudson's Bay Company. Merchandise intended for the interior no longer came to Montreal but was landed at York Factory. The canoe manufactory that the French had opened at Trois Rivières closed down. The once-bustling depot at Rainy Lake turned into an ordinary trading post. After 1821 the annual trade rendezvous was held either at York Factory or Norway House, and the great council hall at Fort William no longer rang with the songs of the winterers and their agents.

Travel styles changed. Boats replaced canoes as the workhorses of the rivers. What Nor'Wester of the early days would have believed such a revolution?

This does not mean that canoes vanished. They were too versatile. They could be built wherever suitable birch trees grew. They could thread small streams and nose into isolated lakes that lay beyond the reach of boats. For decades after the amalgamation they provided the only practical means of traversing the water-laced granite masses between Lake Superior and Lake Winnipeg—a labyrinthine stretch that long baffled surveyors looking for an all-Canadian railroad route between the St. Lawrence and the growing Midwest.

Canoes gripped men's imaginations. George Simpson, who after 1825 became the sole director of all Hudson's Bay Company operations in North America, loved them passionately. They suited his penchant for dash and style. He boasted of the speed records he set in them. Panache! He traveled with hand-picked voyageurs, a bagpiper to strike up tunes as he neared a post, a personal servant to slice him a bit of cold meat and pour him a sip of wine at each brief lunch stop. Whenever a Simpson brigade swirled up to a landing, men gawked and admired. Just the same, *they* traveled the main rivers in boats. Simpson, hardheaded and practical beneath his showy romanticism, saw to that. Boats saved money by turning liabilities into gain.

As was noted earlier, birch trees adequate for canoes did not grow within a hundred miles of either York Factory or Churchill, and the Hudson's Bay Company traders did not learn to make the craft until competition had forced them inland. But canoes needed skilled crews, and there was no tradition of canoe handling in the Orkney Islands of Scotland, source of most of the company's servants. Worse, the Orkneymen did not seem able to acquire the knack during their relatively short terms of service inland.

But those tough Orkney fishermen could handle boats, and plenty of fine white spruce for constructing them grew along the banks of the Saskatchewan. And so by 1800 a new craft had evolved—the York boat, as famous in its way as the *canot du maître*.

The keel of a York boat averaged thirty feet in length. Its overall length was forty-two feet. This meant considerable shear—protruding beaks—at both bow and stern. Such a craft could carry seventy-five or so bales of merchandise and drew about two feet of water. On difficult rivers it was propelled by eight oarsmen (not paddlers) and a steersman who stood in the stern manipulating a long sweep. In a canoe, the bowsman, or *avant,* bawled out orders concerning each movement of the vessel. In a York boat the commander was the steersman, for he was the only one facing forward.

York boats could carry more sail than canoes (under sail they were steered with a rudder) and, being more stable, could risk longer traverses in cutting across indentations in a lake's shore. They could survive blows against rocks that would stave in a canoe, and, as has been remarked, they did not have to be unloaded and reloaded at each camping spot. But to Simpson their great advantage was economy: the pound/man ratio of a York boat was higher than that of a North canoe. That was enough for Simpson, in spite of the miseries involved in moving a brigade of boats from York Factory to Lake Winnipeg and on beyond.

Tangled threads of rivers drain from Winnipeg and its environs into Hudson Bay. The main stream, the Nelson, carries such a tremendous volume of water through the jagged rocks of the Canadian Shield and then falls off into such a frustrating series of wide, gravelly shoals that travelers seldom tackled it. Instead they chose the Hayes, its different sections known during fur-trade days by a series of different names unnecessary to reconstruct in this short summary.

Between the lower Nelson and the lower Hayes was Point of Marsh, a flat, narrow, swampy peninsula covered with scrub willow and saw grass. York Factory was located on this semi-liquid tongue a little above the mouth of the Hayes. Ships from abroad had to anchor far out in the shallow bay; at low tide the dwellers at the factory were confronted with three miles of mud flats. Plank walks led across the soggy ground to the docks. When spring melt filled the rivers, most of the cellars of the post's twenty-nine buildings filled with water. But goose hunting was fine.

Here merchandise from England was sorted, packed, and loaded into York boats. As soon as winds and tide favored, sails went up and the long-nosed craft scudded easily ahead until the current grew too strong for the breeze. Then out came the tracking lines, and half the crew took to the shore while the other half assisted with poles, oars, and sweep. The land work was hard, a straining scramble along steeply tilted, muddy banks, through briars, over fallen trees. During long June days, when work lasted from 2:30 A.M. to 9:30 P.M. the men alternated positions every hour or so.

After more than a hundred miles of this the boats entered the tortured granite of the Shield. At some rapids the workers carried the cargo and then dragged the boat up the river with the tow line. At others they had to portage both the bundles and the boat. If two boats were traveling together, as was generally the case, doubled crews could sometimes lift each craft and carry it ahead. More often part of the group boosted on the gunwales while others heaved on a tow line. In places a corduroy of logs was laid on the ground to facilitate sliding the burden ahead.

The laborers were plagued by thick, humid summer heat, insufferable clouds of mosquitos, and constantly wet clothing, for as soon as a boat was in the water it showed a perverse tendency to hang up on boulders, whereupon everyone went overboard to lift and tug. Injuries were frequent. Although a few long lakes provided relief, crews generally spent sixteen or more days covering the four hundred miles to Norway House. Only a person who had witnessed the struggle, wrote Arctic explorer Sir John Franklin, could form "an adequate idea of the exertions of the Orkney boatmen in the navigation of this river."

Norway House was similar to Fort William in being the main hub of the company's trade. The council of Chief Factors and Chief Traders (positions analogous to the North West Company's wintering partners and clerks) often met there in June to discuss policies laid down in London and presented to the meeting by George Simpson. Furs were delivered there from Red River, the prairie posts west of Lake Winnipeg, the Saskatchewan, the Churchill, Athabasca, and beyond. Beaten free of dust and moths, the pelts were then rebaled and sent to York Factory. The families who came to the rendezvous with the traders enjoyed a few days of conviviality, and then the boats in which they had arrived were reloaded and pointed back toward the scattered posts.

Except for occasional miscellaneous items intended for the northernmost posts of New Caledonia, no freight crossed the Rocky Mountains. On that side of the continent Fort Vancouver filled the part played in the east by both York Factory and Norway House. Ships that had circled Cape Horn tacked a hundred miles up the broad western river to the sprawling bastion that for twenty years was the province of regal John McLoughlin. There furs were gathered from Spanish California, from coastal vessels plying as far north as Russian Alaska, from New Caledonia, and from all the tributaries of the Willamette and Snake rivers. Similarly merchandise and some food supplies went from Fort Vancouver back to each of the many posts, to the ships, and to the mobile trapping brigades.

Because birch suitable for canoes did not grow west of the Continental Divide, boats were also the principal vessels on the Columbia. They differed markedly from the York boats of the east. Some, like the one David Thompson had built for his descent of the

Columbia, were made of strips of cedar, imitated a canoe's shape, and were called canoes. More common were bateaux. According to artist Paul Kane, who traveled through the Columbia area in the late 1840s, the western boats were clinker-built and, unlike most bateaux, had bottoms that were slightly rounded rather than flat. Like York boats they were about thirty feet long and tapered at both ends, but with less shear.

The Columbia bateaux were paddled, not rowed. Probably this was the result of custom. Not many Orkneymen crossed the mountains, and labor in the West was performed mostly by French Canadians, Iroquois Indians and halfbreeds. They did not understand oars, but were experts with paddles.

A Columbia brigade, Simpson once wrote, presented "a curious mixture of races and languages. Our crew of ten men contained Iroquois who spoke their own tongue; a Cree halfbreed of French origin, who appeared to have borrowed his dialect from both his parents; a North Briton who understood only the Gaellic of his native hills; Canadians who, of course, knew French; and Sandwich [Hawaiian] Islanders, who jabbered a medley of Chinook [a West Coast Indian tribe] and their own vernacular jargon. Add to all this that the passengers were natives of England, Scotland, Russia, Canada, and the Hudson Bay territories; and you have the prettiest congregation of nations, the nicest confusion of tongues that has ever taken place since the tower of Babel."

But if freight did not cross the Rockies annual dispatches did, by means of an amazing operation known as the York Express. Every spring McLoughlin and his army of clerks at Fort Vancouver compiled for the use of the council meeting at York Factory or Norway House a record of the principal happenings in the district. They rendered a meticulous accounting of how the goods that had reached Fort Vancouver by ship the previous winter had been distributed, and made preliminary estimates of the quantity of furs the merchandise would produce. The sheaves of foolscap covered by these figures were put with private mail into waterproof dispatch cases and turned over to a brigade charged with reaching York Factory in the shortest possible time. Copies of the documents were also sent by ship to London.

Each cross-country brigade was accompanied by people who were retiring or leaving on furlough. Families frequently went along, as did occasional distinguished visitors like botanist David Douglas, for whom the Douglas fir is named. Thus there were often enough people to fill two or more bateaux, a convenience at the portages where two crews—or else local Indians hired for the job —were needed to carry a single boat.

From the Cascade Mountains to the Rockies, the Columbia was a powerful, rapid-torn stream. Over the years the roaring waters of the most notorious *dalles* caused as high a proportion of casualties as did the Ottawa in the East. Riverside posts providing relief and supplemental provisions were fewer than on the Saskatchewan. In eastern Washington wind-blown sand and the glare of sun on water and naked stone were constant torments. In the upper reaches, where the stream poured its springtime flood between steep, heavily timbered ridges, poles had to be brought into play, the grueling labor relieved by occasional back eddies. Another problem was what Simpson called "Chinook love Fever"—the syphilis and gonorrhea the voyageurs had picked up from coastal Indians who had been infected by the sailors of trading vessels. Their sufferings reduced their efficiency, and, according to Simpson, treatment, based generally on folklore, was the responsibility of whatever commissioned officer was in charge of the brigade.

The 900-mile ascent from Vancouver to the Canoe River consumed from five to six weeks of sixteen-hour days. About a mile above the mouth of the Canoe River was an uninhabited transfer point called Boat Encampment. There the bateaux were cached for the use of the westbound express. Snowshoes were taken from their storage places and food, equipment, and personal possessions were arranged in sixty-pound bundles for backpacking across the pass.

It was a terrible slog. That early in the year snow still lay deep under the massive trees. Nights were cold. Each day's hike began before sunup and involved repeated fordings of the Wood River, a tributary of the Canoe. Men emerged from the water, Simpson said of his crossing in April, 1825, "so benumbed with Cold . . . they actually could not stand."

As altitude increased, snow deepened. By midday heat was a problem. Snowshoes sank in the softened drifts; clothes grew soaked with perspiration. Near the top prodigious avalanches roared, "sending forth Clouds of drift resembling immense volumes of Smoke." At the summit there was a brief celebration with rum and water—water dipped from two adjoining ponds that Simpson had named the "Committee's Punch Bowl" in honor of the Hudson's Bay Company's London directorate. One pond drained northeast into the Arctic Ocean, the other west into the Pacific.

Towering on either side were peaks that David Douglas in 1827 named Mounts Hooker and Brown after two noted English botanists. He assumed that their tops were 16,000 or 17,000 feet above sea level and that they were the highest peaks in North America. The estimates aroused considerable scientific curiosity, and when John McLoughlin was returning from a furlough in 1839 the Royal Geographic Society equipped him with instruments for making rough calculations. He found Athabasca Pass to be about 6,000 feet above sea level—its exact elevation is 5,724 feet—and guessed that the peaks were about 4,000 feet higher. Accurate surveys seventy years later placed Mt. Brown's elevation at 9,156 feet and Mt. Hooker's at 10,782, a sharp deflation of Douglas's estimate. But before we smile it is well to remember the excruciating toil that led travelers to believe they had attained such exalted elevations.

Another day was generally enough to bring the expressmen down to open ground where horses sent from Jasper House awaited them. Grumbling at the unaccustomed galling of the saddles, they rode until the descending stream was big enough for canoes, which also were waiting in readiness. Joyfully they ran the Athabasca River two hundred miles to Fort Assiniboine. There they returned sullenly to horses.

If they had been Nor'Westers, they would have continued in canoes along the Athabasca for a few more miles. After turning up a side stream, they would have crossed a height of land to the Beaver River. That difficult stream would have led them to Lake Ile-à-la-Crosse, where they would have joined the traditional route of the Northwest—the Churchill River, the Sturgeon-Weir, the Saskatchewan, and Lake Winnipeg.

Simpson, despite his love for canoes, had abruptly closed that route to and from Athabasca Pass. During his 1824 journey west, much of it in the company of John McLoughlin, he had discovered that boats could travel from Norway House to Edmonton on the

North Saskatchewan in fewer days than his canoes could follow the Churchill-Beaver River route to Fort Assiniboine. Yet Fort Assiniboine was only seventy miles northwest of Edmonton House.

Calculating carefully, he decided it would be cheaper for the men of the York Express to ascend the North Saskatchewan in company with the brigade of boats bound for Edmonton House and transfer there to horses for the ride to Fort Assiniboine, where the water journey would continue by canoe up the Athabasca to the limit of navigation. In pursuit of this objective he ordered a small party under a freeman named Jacques Cardinal to cut a path through the intervening forests. The "road" Cardinal created closely paralleled the route David Thompson had followed to the Athabasca River during his flight from the Piegans in the late fall of 1810.

George Simpson considered Cardinal's horse trail to be "tolerably good." His cousin, Aemelius Simpson, traveling west in 1826, disagreed. Horses sank to their bellies in numerous swamps. In forested sections the way was so narrow that they banged their loads distressingly against tree trunks. Burned areas were not well cleared, and the cavalcade was lucky to average fifteen miles a day. The revised route nevertheless remained the standard way west. During the late 1850s an official government exploring expedition under Captain John Palliser discovered that knowledge of all other passes, including Howse Pass, had faded from men's memories.

The boat run from Edmonton down the North Saskatchewan to Norway House was, in comparison to what had gone before, almost a lark. Although the current was strong, the river lay south of the Shield and was little troubled by rapids. A holiday mood encompassed the assembling brigades. Most of the commissioned gentlemen of the area were escaping from their posts to attend the annual council meetings and regain contact with wider horizons. Their families generally went with them. If the gathering was held at York Factory, women and children waited at Norway House. Sometimes as many as 300 people congregated there, living in tents and subsisting largely by fishing for themselves or buying fish from others.

Traveling scientists and traders on furlough often continued from Norway House to Montreal or Quebec by the old canoe route developed by the French, so that summer crossings of the continent from west to east were by no means uncommon. Neither were journeys in the opposite direction. Last-minute dispatches could be sent from London to Montreal after the annual supply ship had left England for Hudson Bay. Transferred to specially manned, lightly burdened express canoes at Montreal, these messages could be sped to Norway House ahead of dispatches carried by sailing ship through the storm-wracked bay.

At Norway House letters for the Columbia were added to the normal bundle carried west by the returning York Express—the minutes of the just-completed council meeting, directives concerning the handling of troublesome conditions (American expansionism, for instance), the invoices of goods that had been sent around Cape Horn, and so on. When all was in readiness, generally in mid-July, passengers for the West climbed into the express boats and the 2,500-mile journey began—a journey that would fill every daylight hour for the next three and a half to four months.

Of those annual trips, that of 1838 was one of the most unusual and certainly the most tragic. Among the passengers who came from Montreal to Norway House to catch the express were Fathers Norbert Blanchet and Modeste Demers, Catholic priests being sent to Oregon to care for the spiritual needs of the growing numbers of French Canadians employed at Fort Vancouver or retiring to farms in Oregon's Willamette Valley.

Another pair of travelers were Robert Wallace and Peter Banks, highly trained young English botanists. Their assignment was to gather specimens of West Coast trees, shrubs, and flowers for transplanting on the estate of the Duke of Devonshire at Chatsworth, England. The special equipment needed for the work was forwarded around Cape Horn. The scientists, like the priests, traveled by canoe from Montreal to Norway House.

Because the council was held at Norway House that year, the gathering was large. John McLoughlin was there, bound via Montreal for a vacation in England. Almost surely he talked at length with both the priests and the botanists. His son, dark, moody John Jr., who had crossed the mountains from Fort Vancouver with him, was waiting to return with the westbound boats. Also in attendance was Robert Miles, the chief accountant at York

Factory. Miles was accompanied by the teen-age girl who passed as his daughter.

Actually Maria "Miles" was the illegitimate offspring of George Simpson, himself an illegitimate son, and of Betsy Sinclair of the Red River colony. A lusty dallier as well as an impetuous canoe-man, Simpson, to borrow his own words, liked "to deposit a little of my Spawn" wherever convenient. Often he sent word ahead to posts he was approaching, requesting that bedmates be made ready for him. His attachment to Betsy Sinclair was not like those casual liaisons, however. Real affection flowed between them, but Betsy's humble circumstances and Simpson's overweening social ambitions precluded matrimony. Accordingly he prevailed on his close friend and employee, Robert Miles, and Miles's wife to adopt Betsy's Maria.

At Norway House botanist Robert Wallace and Maria fell in love. Intimates who knew Maria's identity tried to break up the match, fearful of the way Simpson, who was in London that summer, might react, for the girl was very young. They failed. Within two weeks of their meeting, the lovers were married by one of the priests and almost immediately embarked with the York Express.

Troubles were no more than routine until the party reached Athabasca Pass. There the seventy-two ill-broken horses the express used for the crossing kept throwing riders and loads and dashing off among the trees and swamps. At Boat Encampment, only two bateaux were waiting. They would not hold the large party, and so a third of the group, the newlyweds among them, were delegated to stay behind until an additional boat could be sent back. Both priests and young John McLoughlin were with the advance party.

The wait at Boat Encampment lasted from October 14 to 22. During that period stories of the river passed back and forth over the campfires, and it seems probable that everyone there heard of the Dalles des Morte, "the Rapids of Death," named for eight men who had perished there twenty years before. It was less than a day away.

When a bateau at last appeared, twenty-six people, including the crew crowded aboard—far too many. Among them were three women and six children. At the rapids of Death all disembarked and half the baggage was portaged to the lower end of the rapids. The voyageurs who took the lightened craft through the churning water came within an inch of swamping. When the passengers reboarded, many were terrified by the near disaster they had just witnessed.

At the next rapids waves crashed over the gunwales and the sluggish craft began to spin. As it careened toward the shore, young Wallace swooped up his bride, apparently intending to jump overboard and claw his way with her to the bank. But the push of his foot on the gunwale came just as a giant reflex wave boiled up on the far side. The combined thrusts flipped the boat upside down.

Fourteen people gained the shore, and the voyageurs were able to retrieve the battered bateau from the eddy where it lodged. But twelve people had vanished—both botanists, Maria, five children, and four male company employees. The survivors halted at a new post just then being constructed many miles downstream and waited seventeen days while new boats were readied and searchers combed the river banks in the hope that some of the missing might have crawled ashore and still be alive. They found the bodies of three children and buried them at the new post. That was all.

There was no other trail like it in North America, perhaps in the world. From Montreal to Fort George (Astoria) it was close to 4,000 miles long. Less than five percent of that distance involved traverses by land. After the delineation of the "Oregon" boundary in 1846, its course was modified so that travel could stay entirely within British territory. The changes resulted in very little shortening in miles and none in difficulties. During the three centuries of its development—the trail's use tapered off only with the completion of the first Canadian transcontinental railroad—it took more lives than did any other of the famed trails of the continent's westering.

Unlike the major trails of North America it was not a public thoroughfare. Although the Hudson's Bay Company was generous about providing passage for persons traveling on important errands, generally religious or scientific, the trail's use during periods of both monopoly and competition was almost entirely commercial. Except for the Red River colonists, who used only a short part of it, settlers as such never traveled the trail, and, because of its nature, could not have done so. And yet if the history of Canada is, as the late Professor Harold Innis has stated, in large part the history of the fur trade, then the story of this hard, bitterly contested highway that made the trade possible is also an essential part of that proud public heritage.

BIBLIOGRAPHY

Several of the books in the following bibliography have been reprinted one or more times. I have cited the date of the edition I used. I have made no effort to distinguish between hardcover editions, paperback editions, and photocopy facsimilies. Dots at the end of a title indicate that I saw no point in repeating the lines of descriptive material that some authors saw fit to tack onto their book's names.

GENERAL ACCOUNTS

Adney, Edwin T., and Howard I. Chapelle. *The Bank Canoes and Skin Boats of North America.* Washington, D.C. 1964.

Blair, Emma (ed.). *The Indian Tribes of the Upper Mississippi and the Great Lakes.* 2 vols. Cleveland, Ohio, 1911–12.

Brebner, John Bartlet. *Canada.* Ann Arbor, Mich., 1960.

———. *The Explorers of North America, 1492–1806.* London, 1933.

Burpee, Lawrence J. *The Search for the Western Sea.* 2 vols. Toronto, 1935.

Creighton, Donald. *Dominion of the North.* Toronto, 1962

———. *The Empire of the St. Lawrence.* Boston, 1958.

De Voto, Bernard. *The Course of Empire.* Boston, 1952.

Dictionary of Canadian Biography.

Glazebrook, G. P. de T. *A History of Transportation in Canada.* New York, 1969.

Hodges, Frederick W. *Handbook of American Indians.* 2 vols. Patterson, New Jersey, 1959.

Innis, Harold A. *The Fur Trade in Canada.* Toronto, 1956.

Josephy, Alvin. *The Indian Heritage of America.* New York, 1968.

Knauth, Percy. *The North Woods.* New York, 1972.

Landon, Fred. *Lake Huron.* Indianapolis and New York, 1944.

McInnis, Edgar. *Canada: A Political and Social History.* New York, 1959.

McPhee, John. "The Survival of the Bark Canoe." *The New Yorker,* Feb. 24 and March 4, 1975.

Morse, Eric. *Fur Trade Routes of Canada, Then and Now.* N.p., 1968.

Morton, Arthur S. *A History of the Canadian West to 1870–71.* Toronto, 1973.

Morton, W. L. *The Kingdom of Canada.* Indianapolis and New York, 1963.

———. *Manitoba, A History.* Toronto, 1967.

Nute, Grace Lee. *Lake Superior.* Indianapolis and New York, 1944.

———. *The Voyageurs.* St. Paul, Minn., 1955.

———. *The Voyageurs' Highway.* St. Paul, Minn., 1965.

Olson, Sigurd. *The Lonely Land.* New York, 1961.

Oliver, E. H. (ed.) *The Canadian North-West . . .* 2 vols. Ottawa, 1914–15.

Ray, Arthur J. *Indians in the Fur Trade.* Toronto, 1974.

Rich, E. E. *The Fur Trade and the Northwest to 1854.* Toronto, 1957.

———. *Montreal and the Fur Trade.* Montreal, 1966.

———. *The History of the Hudson's Bay Company, 1670–1870.* 2 vols., London, 1958–59.

Rotstein, Abraham. "Fur Trade and Empire: An Institutional Analysis." Ph.D. dissertation, University of Toronto, 1967.

Russell, Carl P. *Firearms, Traps & Tools of the Mountain Men.* New York, 1967.

Saum, Lewis O. *The Fur Trader and the Indian.* Seattle, Wash., 1965.

Warren, William W. *History of the Ojibway Nation.* Minneapolis, 1957.

THE FRENCH PERIOD

Primary Sources

Adams, Arthur T. (ed.) *The Explorations of Pierre Esprit Radisson.* Minneapolis, 1961.

Biggar, H. P., *et al.* (ed.). *The Works of Samuel de Champlain.* 6 vols. Toronto, 1922–36.

Burpee, Lawrence J. *Journals and Letters of Pierre Gaultier de Varennes de la Vérendrye and His Sons* . . . Toronto, 1927.

Kellogg, Louise P. (ed.) *Early Narratives of the Northwest, 1634–1699.*

Kenton, Edna (compiler). *The Jesuit Relations and Allied Documents.* New York, 1954.

Lahontan, Louis Armand de Lom D'Arce, Baron de. *New Voyages to North America* (edited by Reuben G. Thwaites). Chicago, 1905.

Thwaites, Reuben G. (ed.). *The Jesuit Relations.* 73 vols. Cleveland, 1896–1901. (Material useful to this book was drawn from Volumes 19, 33, 34, 40, 42, 43, 52.)

Zoltvany, Yves. (ed.) *The French Tradition in America.* Columbia, S.C., 1969.

Secondary Accounts

Bishop, Morris. *Champlain: The Life of Fortitude.* New York, 1948.

Crouse, Nellis M. *La Vérendrye, Fur Trader and Explorer.* Ithaca, N.Y., 1956.

Eccles, W. J. *The Canadian Frontier, 1534–1760.* New York, 1965.

———. *France in America.* New York, 1972.

Hunt, George T. *The Wars of the Iroquois.* Madison, Wis., 1940.

Kellogg, Louise P. *The French Regime in Wisconsin and the Old Northwest.* Madison, Wis., 1925.

Kenyon, W. A., and J. R. Turnbull. *The Battle for James Bay, 1686.* Toronto, 1971.

Lamb, Harold. *New Found World.* Garden City, N.Y. 1955.

Morison, Samuel Eliot. *The European Discovery of America: The Northern Voyages.* New York, 1971.

———. *Samuel De Champlain, Father of New France.* Boston, 1972.

Nute, Grace Lee. *Caesars of the Wilderness: Médard Chouart, Sieur des Groseilliers, and Pierre Esprit Radisson, 1618–1710.* New York, 1943.

Parkman, Francis. *La Salle and the Discovery of the Great West.* Boston, 1918.

———. *The Old Regime in Canada.* London, 1918.

Pendergast, James F., and Bruce Trigger. *Cartier's Hochelaga and the Dawson Site.* London, 1972.

Sprague, Marshall. *So Vast, So Beautiful a Land.* Boston, 1974.

Steck, Francis Borgia. *The Jolliett-Marquette Expedition, 1673.* Quincy, Illinois, 1928.

Trigger, Bruce G. *The Impact of Europeans on Huronia.* Vancouver, Toronto, Montreal, 1969.

Articles

Eccles, W. J. "The Social, Economic, and Political Significance of the Military Establishment in New France." *Canadian Historical Review,* 52 : 1. March, 1971.

Flandrau, Grace. (ed.). "Vérendrye Expeditions in Quest of the Pacific." *Oregon Historical Quarterly,* 26 : 2. June, 1925.

MacDonald, L. R. "France and New France: The Internal Contradictions." *Canadian Historical Review,* 52 : 2. June, 1971.

Wilson, Clifford. "La Vérendrye Reaches the Saskatchewan." *Canadian Historical Review,* 33 : 1. March, 1952.

Zoltvany, Yves. "New France and the West." *Canadian Historical Review,* 46 : 4. December, 1965.

THE BRITISH PERIOD

Primary Sources

Ballantyne, Robert M. *Hudson Bay.* Edmonton, 1972.

Barker, Burt B. *Letters of Dr. John McLoughlin . . . 1829–32.* Portland, Ore., 1948.

Coues, Elliott, *New Light on the Early History of the Northwest: The Manuscript Journals of Alexander Henry* [the younger] *and David Thompson.* 2 vols. Minneapolis, 1965.

Cox, Ross. *The Columbia River* (edited by E. I. and Jane R. Stewart). Norman, Okla., 1957.

Douglas, David. *Journal . . .* New York, 1959.

Gates, Charles M. (ed.). *Five Fur Traders of the Northwest.* Minneapolis, 1965.

Franchère, Gabriel. *Journal of a Voyage . . .* (edited and with an introduction by W. Kaye Lamb). Toronto, 1969.

Henry, Alexander (the elder). *Travels and Adventures in Canada and the Indian Territories . . .* Edmonton, 1972.

Lamb, W. Kaye (ed). *The Journals and Letters of Sir Alexander Mackenzie.* London, 1970.

———— (ed.). *The Letters and Journals of Simon Fraser, 1806–08.* Toronto, 1960.

———— (ed.). *Sixteen Years in the Indian Country: The Journal of Daniel Williams Harmon, 1800–1816.* Toronto, 1957.

Masson, L. R. *Les Bourgeois de la Compagnie du Nord-Ouest* . . . 2 vols. New York, 1960.

Merk, Frederick (ed.). *Fur Trade and Empire: George Simpson's Journal, 1824–1825.* Cambridge, Mass., 1931.

Morton, A. S. (ed.). *The Journal of Duncan M'Gillivray . . . on the Saskatchewan, 1794–95.* Toronto, 1929.

Rich, E. E. (ed.). *Colin Robertson's Correspondence Book, September 1817 to September 1822.* Toronto, 1939.

———— (ed.). *The Letters of John McLoughlin . . . 1825–1846.* 3 vols. Toronto, 1941, 1943, 1944.

Spry, Irene (ed.). *The Papers of the Palliser Expedition, 1857–1860.* Toronto, 1968.

Thompson, David. *Narrative . . . 1784–1812* (edited by John B. Tryell). Toronto, 1916.

————. *Narrative . . . 1784–1812* (edited by Richard Glover). Toronto, 1962.

Tyrell, J. B. (ed.). *Journals of Samuel Hearne and Philip Turnor.* Toronto, 1934.

Umfreville, Edward. *The Present State of Hudson's Bay . . .* (edited by W. Stewart Wallace). Toronto, 1954.

Wallace, W. Stewart (ed.). *Documents Relating to the North West Company.* Toronto, 1934.

———— (ed.). *The Pedlars from Quebec, and Other Papers on the Nor'Westers.* Toronto, 1954.

White, Catherine M. (ed.). *David Thompson's Journals Relating to Montana . . . 1808–1812.* Missoula, Mont., 1950.

Secondary Accounts

Bryce, George. *The Remarkable History of the Hudson's Bay Company . . .* London, 1900.

Campbell, Marjorie W. *The North West Company.* Toronto, 1973.

————. *McGillivray, Lord of the North West.* Toronto, 1960.

Chalmers, John W. (ed.). *On the Edge of the Shield: Fort Chipewyan and Its Hinterland.* Edmonton, 1971.

Davidson, Gordon Charles. *The North West Company.* Berkeley, Calif., 1918.

Gray, John Morgan. *Lord Selkirk of Red River.* London, 1963.

Howay, F. N., W. N. Sage, and H. F. Angus. *British Columbia and The United States.*

Innis, Harold A. *Peter Pond: Fur Trader and Adventurer.* Toronto, 1930.

Johanson, Dorothy O., and Charles M. Gates. *Empire of the Columbia.* New York, 1957.

Kane, Paul. *Wanderings of an Artist* . . . Toronto, 1925.

Kellogg, Louise P. *The British Regime in Wisconsin and the Northwest.* Madison, Wis. 1935.

Landerholm, Carl (compiler). *Notices and Voyages of the Famed Quebec Mission to the Pacific Northwest* . . . Portland, Ore., 1956.

Lavender, David. *The Fist in the Wilderness.* Garden City, N.Y., 1964.

Mackay, Douglas. *The Honourable Company: A History of the Hudson's Bay Company.* Toronto, 1949.

Martin, Chester. *Lord Selkirk's Work in Canada.* Oxford, 1916.

Morton, A. S. *Sir George Simpson, Overseas Governor of the Hudson's Bay Company* . . . Portland, Ore. 1944.

Porter, Kenneth W. *John Jacob Astor.* 2 vols. Cambridge, Mass. 1931.

Pritchett, John P. *The Red River Valley, 1811–1849.* New Haven, Conn. 1942.

Ross, Alexander. *The Red River Settlement* . . . Minneapolis, 1957.

Ross, Eric. *Beyond the River and the Bay.* Toronto, 1970.

Smith, James K. *Alexander Mackenzie, the Hero Who Failed.* Toronto, 1973.

Wagner, Henry R. *Peter Pond: Fur Trader and Explorer.* New Haven, Conn., 1955.

Articles

Bridgwater, Dorothy (ed.). "John Jacob Astor Relative to His Settlement on the Columbia River." The Yale University Library *Gazette,* 24 :2. October, 1949.

Creech, E. P. "Brigade Trails of British Columbia." *The Beaver,* March, 1953.

Davies, K. G. "From Competition to Union," in *Aspects of the Fur Trade.* St. Paul, Minn., 1967.

"Edward Ermatinger's York Factory Express Journal . . . 1827–1828." Royal Society of Canada, *Proceedings and Transactions,* 1912.

Elliott, T. C. (ed.). "The Discovery of the Source of the Columbia River." *Oregon Historical Quarterly,* 26 : 1, March, 1925.

———. "The Strange Case of David Thompson and Jeremy Pinch." *Oregon Historical Quarterly,* 40 : 2, June, 1939.

Gerry, Nicholas. "Diary . . . 1821." Royal Society of Canada, *Proceedings and Transactions,* 1900.

Mitchell, Elaine A. "New Evidence in the Mackenzie-McTavish Break." *Canadian Historical Review,* 41 : 1. March, 1960.

Morton, A. S. "The North West Company's Columbia Enterprise and David Thompson." *Canadian Historical Review,* 17 : 3. Sept., 1936.

Morton, W. L. "The North West Company: Pedlars Extraordinary," in *Aspects of the Fur Trade.* St. Paul, 1967.

Ruggles, Richard I. "The West of Canada in 1763: Imagination and Reality." *The Canadian Geographer* 15 : 4. Winter, 1971.

Smiley, H. B. "The Dalliance of David Thompson." *The Beaver.* Winter, 1970.

Stevenson, J. A. "Disaster at the Dalles." *The Beaver.* Sept., 1942.

Tessendorf, K. C. "George Simpson." *The Beaver.* Summer, 1970.

INDEX